SOUTHERN BOOTS AND SADDLES

The Fifteenth Confederate Cavalry C.S.A.
First Regiment Alabama and Florida Cavalry

1863-1865

Arthur E. Green

HERITAGE BOOKS
2007

HERITAGE BOOKS
AN IMPRINT OF HERITAGE BOOKS, INC.

Books, CDs, and more—Worldwide

For our listing of thousands of titles see our website
at
www.HeritageBooks.com

Published 2007 by
HERITAGE BOOKS, INC.
Publishing Division
65 East Main Street
Westminster, Maryland 21157-5026

Copyright © 2005 Arthur E. Green

Other books by the author:

*Too Little Too Late: Compiled Military Service Records of the 63rd Alabama Infantry C.S.A.
with Rosters of Some Companies of the 89th, 94th and 95th Alabama Militia C.S.A.*

All rights reserved. No part of this book may be reproduced or transmitted in any form or by any means, electronic or mechanical, including photocopying, recording or by any information storage and retrieval system without written permission from the author, except for the inclusion of brief quotations in a review.

International Standard Book Number: 978-0-7884-3813-1

In memory of my mother and father
Jacob Rhoads Green
Pauline F. Smoke Green

TAKE A STROLL IN THE MIST

Linger awhile, and walk with
me into the shadowy mist that
was yesterday. Stroll across
the faded pages of history
and learn from our hardships,
Learn the ways of a better life.

Pass me not, for I am the spirit of your
ancestors
In your veins flow my blood
and the blood of my fathers.
Linger awhile, if only for a moment,
and through your thoughts
I will know that I am remembered.

Unknown

The young cavalryman whose photograph appears on the cover is Pvt. William D. Rodgers. He is wearing a hat with the insignia of the Simpson Mounted Rangers which became Co. E of the 15th Confederate Cavalry. Courtesy of Florida State Archives, Tallahassee, FL.

My thanks to Mr. Joseph Ringhoffer for providing the rolls of microfilm from which the transcription of the service records was taken.

Thanks, also, to Callie for her support.

CONTENTS

Abbreviations 4
Introduction 5
History 9
Captions and Record of Events 16
Roster Notes 20
Roster 21
Illustrations
    Pvt. William D. Rogers- Simpson Mounted Rangers . . . . Cover and 161
    Pvt. Red Berry Bryars. 40
    Pvt. Stephen B. Richerson 156
Appendix 213
    Organization of the 15th Confederate Cavalry 213
    On the Free State of Jones 214
    Mount Pleasant 215
    References 215
    Miscellaneous documents pertaining to the 15th Confederate Cavalry 217-226

ABBREVIATIONS

A. A. G.	Assistant Adjutant General
A. C.	Army Corps
A. and I. G.	Adjutant and Inspector General
A. S.	Assistant Surgeon
C. S. A.	Confederate States of America
F. & S.	Field and Staff
Gen.	General
G. H.	General Hospital
G. O.	General Order
Lt.	Lieutenant
M. S.	Master Sergeant
O. R.	Official Register of the War of the Rebellion
P. A. C. S.	Provisional Army Confederate States
P. M.	Provost Marshal
POW	Prisoner of War
Pvt.	Private
Q. M.	Quarter Master
qout.	Quotidian - occurring daily
R. O.	Recruiting Officer
Sgt.	Sergeant
S. O.	Special Order
tert.	Tertian - occurring ever third day
U. S.	United States of America
Vols.	Volunteers

15TH CONFEDERATE CAVALRY

INTRODUCTION

By all means read the chapter called History. It should, however, be labeled Significant Dates, Places and Events. The real history lies in the chapter entitled Roster. The issues, events, dates and places are of a time gone by. The Confederate cause no longer exists. After more than 140, years much discussion and disagreement still exists as to the reasons the war occurred. The men who were a part of this group are still a part of us, and their blood courses in many of our veins. No one is left alive that remembers any individual person, but we can learn much from their written record. There is no doubt that they were, for the most part, brave men who lived and fought for the Southland and, in their minds, for a very just cause. Their wives and families would say that they also contributed much to the Confederacy because these men were absent from their homes for the duration of the war or perhaps forever as was the case in many instances. This book is an effort to tell their story and make them live again on paper at least.

The history of the 15th Confederate Regiment given here draws heavily on the *Official Record of the War of the Rebellion* as few other sources that document their actions were found. Colonel Henry, or Harry as he was called, Maury was in command of the 2nd Alabama Infantry until the spring of 1862. He was a cousin of Major General Dabney Maury and Commodore Matthew Maury. The 2nd Alabama Infantry formed the Confederate garrison of the captured U.S. Fort Morgan at the eastern approach to Mobile Bay. Besides serving as infantry, it was trained in heavy artillery and it manned the guns of the fort. The 2nd Alabama Infantry also served for a time at Fort Pillow, Tennessee, under General J. M. Withers of Mobile.

The organization of the15th Confederate Cavalry (1st Regiment Alabama and Florida Cavalry) was completed in September 1863 by the consolidation of Murphy's Battalion Alabama Cavalry, the 3d Battalion Florida Cavalry, Captain Arrington's and Barlow's Companies Alabama Cavalry and Captain Smith's Company Florida Cavalry.
Company A was formerly Company A, 3rd Battalion Florida Cavalry.
Company B was formerly Captain Richard Smith's Company of Florida Cavalry. (Marianna Dragoons)
Company C was formerly Captain Barlow's Company Alabama Cavalry.
Company D was formerly Company B, 3rd Battalion Florida Cavalry.
Company E was formerly Company C, 3rd Battalion Florida Cavalry Simpson Mounted Rangers
Company F was formerly Captain Arrington's Company A, City Troop, Mobile, Alabama.
Company G was formerly Company B, Murphy's Battalion Alabama Cavalry.
Company H was formerly Company C, Murphy's Battalion Alabama Cavalry.
Company I was formerly Company D, 3rd Battalion Florida Cavalry.
Company K was formerly Company D, Murphy's Battalion Alabama Cavalry.

Company A was from Jefferson and Leon Counties, Florida. - Magnolia Rangers
Company B was from Butler County, Alabama, and Jackson County, Florida. - Marianna Dragoons
Company C was from Baldwin County, Alabama, - Baldwin Rangers
Company D was from Butler County, Alabama and Escambia County, Florida. - Bragg Mounted Rangers.
Company E was from Butler County, Alabama, and Santa Rosa County, Florida.- Simpson Mounted Rangers
Company F was from Mobile County, Alabama - Mobile City Troop
Company G was from Mobile County, Alabama- Mobile Dragoons
Company H was from Mobile County, Alabama - Dorrance Rangers
Company I was from Santa Rosa and Walton Counties, Florida
Company K was from Choctaw County, Alabama

The Simpson Mounted Rangers that became Company E of the 15th Confederate Cavalry was organized at Milton, Santa Rosa County, Florida. It was named for E. E. Simpson of Bagdad and Milton, Florida. About July or August of 1862, it was united with two other companies, as follows Company A - Captain Roth H. Partridge, Company B - Captain J. B. Vaughn and Captain Norvell R. Leigh, Company C to form the 3rd Battalion Florida, Cavalry. The 3rd Battalion of Florida did service from Choctahachee River to Perdido Bay. In August of 1862, it was ordered to Mobile and joined with two additional companies of Florida troops, Company I - W. B. Amos and Captain Richard L. Smith's Marianna Dragoons. Soon after arriving in Mobile, the Florida troops were combined with Alabama Companies as follows: Murphy's Battalion three companies of Alabama Cavalry, Thomas C. Barlow's Company of Alabama Cavalry and Captain Edward T. Arrington's Mobile City Troop.

The particular reason for combining these small regiments of independents is not found but must have occurred for the obvious. A single cohesive body of mounted soldiers under a central command and commander would be a much more effective force to be dealt with by opposing forces and much easier to be dealt with by the Confederate Army Command. The first muster roll for the 15th Confederate Cavalry was at the Dragoon Camp at Halls Mills, Alabama, on September 12, 1863. Camp Halls Mill is about ten miles west of downtown Mobile. It was an ideal site for a large garrison with a sizable creek (Halls Mill Creek) and a large flat open area suitable for drilling the men and horses. It lay near major roadways of the time, Andrew Jackson's Military Road, Three Notch Road and Pascagoula Road (or the Old Spanish Trail of olden times) and present day U.S. Highway 90.

The cavalry thought of themselves as a hot-shot military group and made the most of it. They would be the forerunners of our modern top gun fighter pilots of today. They moved fast and were noted for hit and run tactics with special weapons. The men furnished their own horses and drew compensation for the use of the animal equal to their pay. The infantry and some civilians called the cavalry "Chicken Thieves"as a matter of course. You will see while reading the individual service records that lenient time was provided to those men who were without a horse so that they could search out a replacement. Muster rolls indicated when a man was dismounted so that his pay, which he probably would never draw, could be adjusted accordingly. It is said that some of the sabers were made by a skilled metalsmith in northwest Florida at Bagdad of saw blades. Most mounted men carried a weapon with a shortened barrel and a side arm.

A number of the men are shown as having served on extra duty and or detached service. You will find men assigned to "work on the gunboats." The *Baltic* is one gunboat mentioned. This must have been an assignment such as working on the space shuttle today. Notations refer to gunboat work going on at Mobile and Montgomery, Alabama. Other interesting assignments were to "work at the government fisheries." Colonel Maury may have used this as a punishment as some of these cavalry men were seen to desert after receiving the government fisheries as their assignment.

Most deserters seemed to make for the Navy Yard at Pensacola, Florida, or home, and Federal Communications in the Official Record mentions much of their intelligence coming from CSA deserters. There is one notation of two "colored cooks" that came in to the Navy Yard from the 15th Cavalry giving numbers and placement of Confederate troops.

The organization of the regiment would only exist from the September 12, 1863, date until April 1865, or nineteen months. But not so for some of the men who served in their preceding regiments. Some of them had served the Confederacy from early in 1861. Many of the vanquished POW's were not released until May or June 1865, so they were occupied with war longer than those who were surrendered in the field. It is interesting to note the higher rate of desertion among these mounted cavalrymen than regular infantry regiments. It could be explained by their mobility or simply the cocky attitude of the mounted soldiers. Many times men appeared on the muster rolls after the notation of "absent without leave" with no noted stigma attached to their record. The cavalry was considered a desirable assignment, and you will note several members that were sent back to their "proper" commands when they were irregularly mustered or for other infractions.

We see men enlisted as early as April 15, 1862, in Captain T. C. Barlow's Alabama Cavalry. Captain E. S. Amos was enlisting men in his Company D of the 3rd Battalion of Florida Cavalry at Milton, Florida, as early as September 17, 1861. This may have been a significant date as the 15th Regiment was formed two years later on September 12, 1863.

The author has adopted the modern term of POW to represent those men taken prisoner. There was not such a designation used in the period of the War between the States. .

15TH CONFEDERATE CAVALRY

HISTORY

The reader will find additional stations of the various companies shown in the section called *Captions and Records of Events* contained in the next chapter. The notations by commanders contained with company muster rolls will have slight variations from the overall regimental history and will note the location of some short-term assignments.

In one of the earliest reports of the regiment Colonel Harry Maury on November 15, 1863, reports to the Chief of Staff at the Confederate Department of the Gulf that he has returned to his camp today with his whole army and Federal prisoners. Maury reports that the *Lafayette*, a very heavy ironclad, constantly lies about Bayou Sara [Louisiana]. Plundering parties of Federals are transported a few miles from the river by wagon train under convoy to gather supplies. These parties were reported to number from 50 to 500 men. He states that he learned at Whitestown, the Sunday before, that a foraging party was near Tunica, Louisiana. This was a 40-mile ride from Whitestown, and he advanced to that point with six companies of cavalry. Two companies were left to follow with the artillery as quickly as possible. About four o'clock in the afternoon they found the Federal party, about 300 of them, at a plantation and under the cover of a floating ironclad vessel. The Southern troopers immediately charged and drove the Federal soldiers in confusion to their transports. Fifty or 60 bluecoats were killed and 25 prisoners were captured. After the action, the CSA Cavalry reported three slightly wounded men and camped for the night on a creek near the river.

Next morning Captain Arrington and Company F, along with Major Floweree and Lieutenant Mason, were sent to select a position where the artillery might attack the transports. No suitable spot was found, but a Federal party was located ashore killing beef and protected by two pieces of artillery. The company was ordered to dismount and they attacked on foot with carbines and killed four of the enemy with first fire. The raiding party of Yankees withdrew with their artillery and departed down the river after returning a harmless but furious shelling in the direction of the Southerners.

Maury reports that his regiment, the 15th Confederate Cavalry, is much improved in discipline and efficiency and has had no sickness. He is not pleased with the imperfect equipment, specific equipment he does not name, and the "miserable" saddles which he says, "On a forced march would ruin the back of every horse I have." With two days to rest the horses of the artillery, Maury starts for home base at Camp Halls Mill, near Mobile, taking his prisoners along.
[OR, Series 1, Vol. 53, p. 911-912.]

Field and Staff Muster Roll of the 15th Confederate Cavalry gives this account of the Tunica, Louisiana, expedition. Note the differences between this report and Colonel Maury's above, in dates and details. "On the 22 day of October left Halls Mills, Ala. with the regiment. Marched in a northerly direction crossed the Pascagoula River at Farley's Ferry on the 25 of Oct. Pearl River on the 2 of November passing through Holmesville and Liberty, Miss. on the ? Came on a foraging party of the enemy two hundred strong at Tunica Landing, West Feliciana Parish, La. on the Mississippi River. Completely routed them capturing between 20 & 30 and killing between 40 & 50. One man from Co. B, Private L. Myrick, wounded in the arm. Took up the line of march on the next day and returned by mostly the same route to the camp at Halls Mill, Ala., reaching there the 23d of November. The distance traveled from the 22 of Oct. to the 23 of November was reported to be 600 miles."

November and December 1863, were spent perfecting their cavalry drills at Camp Halls Mill, Alabama.

The regiment left Mobile for Citronelle, Alabama, on February 1, 1864, and remained there until the 14th and returned. Then they again left Mobile for Jones County, Mississippi, by railroad on March 2, for the purpose of breaking up a large body of deserters led by Newt Knight who were organizing into companies, battalions, etc., and were committing numerous depredations upon the citizens. Four men who were found were hung, and a number of others were sent to their commands. Some were brought back to Mobile as prisoners for trade or exchange. The regiment returned to Mobile and was ordered to Citronelle on March 27. The orders were countermanded on the 29th. This was not the first or last action against the Jones County group by the Confederate government. Several groups of CSA Cavalry were called in over a period of time to try to control this unruly and dangerous group. In some instances, the Cavalry became somewhat unruly as well becoming part of the problem instead of a solution.

The regiment left Mobile on the March 31, [1864] for Pollard, Ala., a distance of 75 miles and arrived at Pollard on April 2.

On April 16, 1864, a nervous and watchful U. S. Brigadier General Alexander Asboth at Pensacola, Florida, advised his headquarters at the Department of the Gulf that Colonel Maury and Lieutenant-Colonel Myers had arrived with a full regiment, the 15th Confederate Cavalry, well mounted and well armed at the Seven-Mile Station [on the railroad seven miles north of Pensacola] and at Turners Mill four miles west of Pensacola and five miles north of Bayou Grand with an advance post at Jackson's Bridge over Bayou Chico Creek 1 3/4 miles from the mouth of Bayou Grand. General Asboth was of the opinion that the Confederates with heavy forces at Pollard and a half circle of troops from the head of the Choctawhatchee Bay to the camps at McDade's Pond, Pollard, Fifteen- Mile Station on the Pensacola Railroad and the mouth of the Perdido and on alert at Camps Withers and Powell are planning an attack. He was convinced enough that the U.S. Navy Yard was put on alert and the hospital was removed to Navy ships. General Asboth had every reason for concern as he was deep in Confederate territory with his back to the Gulf of Mexico and dependant only on the U.S. Navy for support. [O R, Series I, Vol 35, part II, page 56-57]

May 25, 1864, General Asboth reported that Colonel Maury's command was attacked at Jackson Bridge, Florida, and has returned to Fifteen-Mile Station.

June 3, 1864, Brigadier General Asboth had revised his assessment to only five companies of the Second Alabama Infantry at Pollard. He reported Colonel Maury to be at Fifteen-Mile Station, Seven-Mile Station and Turners Mill about 500 of the 15th Confederate Cavalry with three pieces of artillery at Fifteen-Mile Station. Three additional companies of the 15th were located (according to General Asboth) at and near Milton [Florida] with the remainder of the regiment on the Perdido. [O R, Series 1, Vol. 35, part II, page 111]

A Naval Operation by the Cavalry? On June 25, 1864, there was a very interesting and unusual operation for a Cavalry regiment off Yellow River, Florida. It concerned Company I of the 15th Confederate Cavalry and the capture of two schooners and 15 men below the mouth of Yellow River and another in East Bay. Captain W. B. Amos and his men left Milton, Florida, with two small boats downbound, for whatever unstated reason, and discovered a small schooner lying two miles below the mouth of Yellow River with her sails down. He landed his men and made his way to the schooner and captured her. Soon he discovered another sail coming up the bay. He secreted his men until she came near and captured her and her crew as well. Captain Amos then sent his two boats back up to camp with the prisoners, took the small schooner and some of his men and sailed down to East Bay. Here he heard that there was a schooner by the name of Osceola anchored out about four miles from shore and that five men and some small arms were aboard. He waited until dark, boarded her and ordered the crew to surrender. Three of the boat's crewmen made for their guns and were quickly killed, and the other men surrendered. The Cavalry/Naval operation then proceeded to split the little group up and sail both schooners back to camp. This may be a one and only for a cavalry regiment. [O R, Series 1, Vol. 35, pt. 1, page 404-405]

July 11, 1864, Maury stated that they have been ordered to protect the M & O. Railroad [at Mobile] and Pascagoula.

July 21-25, 1865, U. S. Forces under Brigadier General Alexander Asboth marched 30 miles north from Fort Barrancas and attacked the three companies of 7th Alabama Regiment [G, E and I] of Confederate Cavalry at Camp Gonzales. Here they captured, after a half-hours fighting, a newly built Fort Hodgson and eight prisoners and commissary stores along with livestock. General Asboth then advanced toward Pollard and encountered cavalry resistance at the junction of the Pollard and Perdido Railroad Station Road. Another three butternut-clad southerners were captured in this engagement. From the captured men, the general learned that the Confederates had destroyed the telegraph station and burned the Pine Barren Bridge to delay the advance of the bluecoats along the Pollard Road. Asboth ordered Captain Schmidt of the 14th New York Cavalry to demonstrate his company on the Pollard Road while General Asboth took his troops along the Perdido Station Road with the purpose in mind to cut the telegraph line and destroy the 30-yard-long trestle below Perdido Station. His plans were to go south between the Perdido River and Mobile Bay and capture Confederate Camps Withers and Powell and break up the Bon Secour Saltworks before returning to Fort Barrancas. General Asboth learned from reliable sources, before executing his plan, that considerable countermeasures (troops) had been sent from Mobile and that Colonel Maury and the 15th Cavalry had already arrived with additional support to number 1300 men and a light battery of six guns. General Asboth deemed it wise to divert his small force and return by way of Swan's Place to Gunboat Point at the mouth of Bayou Grand and thence back to camps at Barrancas, Florida.

July 24, 1864, Asboth reports that Maury has returned to Mobile to protect the city but has returned to vicinity of Pensacola on August 3.

On August 5, 1864, Mobile Bay fell to U.S. Naval Fleet lead by Admiral David G. Farragut.

August 7, 1864, Confederate Cavalry appeared at the mouth of Bayou Grand at Gonzales' house. They were shelled by U. S. artillery and U. S. Navy guard ships. Brigadier General Asboth credits the "rebels" with setting fire to their ally's buildings, destroying them. It was well known that Gonzales had southern sympathies so it is a little suspect as to who really fired the buildings. Brigadier General Asboth now reports that he believes three companies of the 15th Confederate Cavalry are at Pine Barren Bridge with four pieces of artillery and three companies of the Seventh Alabama Cavalry near Gonzales' house on the Pensacola Railroad. [O R, Series 1, Vol. 35, part 1, page 424-425]

Aug. 24, 1864, the regiment was ordered to Tensas River [on the eastern side of Mobile Bay].

Still relying on Confederate deserters and refugees, Brigadier General Asboth on September 14, 1864, reports that Colonel Harry Maury with the 15th Confederate Cavalry was concentrating a force between the Perdido and Mobile Bay. The camps were at Greenwood Plantation [just north of Loxley] and H. Sibley's [Sibley's Mill was just east of present day Spanish Fort, Alabama]. He estimates the Confederate numbers to be 2000 to 3000 infantry, 700 cavalry and 4 pieces of artillery. He has information on a small force at Pine Barren Bridge Headquarters at Pollard and an advance post at Gonzales just north of Pensacola. [ditto]

On November 17, 1864, Lt. Colonel A. B. Spurling of the 2nd Maine Cavalry with his Maine troops and the 1st Florida Cavalry, a force of 450 mounted men, left Camp Barrancas at noon. They proceeded north to ford the bayou [Bayou Grand] at Gunboat Point and bivouacked for the night at a point on the Pensacola to Montgomery Railroad that lay about four miles from Fifteen-Mile House and 11 miles north of Pensacola. The Yanks arose and started out at 3 a.m. the following morning. They met three Confederate pickets about dawn. A bit further four more grey-clad men were captured from their picket post, and again in a mile six more men were captured along with their reserves. Proceeding to Pine Barren Creek Bridge, the party determined that the bridge was in bad shape from water action due to recent rains which carried a portion of the bridge away. Pickets were quietly captured without alarming the camp while the U.S. Cavalry force crossed unseen. A sudden dash upon the unsuspecting Confederates resulted in nearly every man being captured at their post along with equipment and horses. In all, 38 men with 47 horses, three mules and 47 rifles were captured all without loss or injury to any U.S. Cavalrymen. The majority of the Southern cavalry men captured were members of Captain Leigh's Co. E and a sprinkling of Captain Vaughn's Co. D. The captured group was lead by Lt. William Townsend of Co. E. Lt. Colonel Spurling then had his men set about burning the barracks, stables and commissary stores at the camp. After crossing the remainder of the bridge it was burned, and the Federal troops returned to Barrancas. The Prisoners were carried along and were sent on to New Orleans by November 21 and transferred to Ship Island, Mississippi, May 10, 1865, and eventually to Vicksburg. [OR., Series 1, Vol 44, pages 418 - 419]

On November 20, 1864, the Confederate Department of Alabama, Mississippi and East Louisiana with Lt. General Richard Taylor in command included the District of the Gulf under the command of Major General Dabney H. Maury. In Maury's command was Brigadier General Alpheus Baker's Brigade with the 37th Alabama Infantry, 40th Alabama Infantry, 42nd Alabama Infantry, 54th Alabama Infantry and 22nd Louisiana. General Maury's command also included Brigadier Bryan M. Thomas's Brigade of 1st Alabama Reserves under Colonel D. E. Huger, McCulloch's Brigade of 774 effective including **15th Confederate Cavalry**, 7th Mississippi Cavalry, 8th Mississippi Cavalry, 18th Mississippi Battalion Cavalry, and the 2nd Missouri Cavalry. The Post of Mobile Alabama was also under General Maury and included 4th Alabama Reserves, 21st Alabama (detachment), Alabama Cadets and [Mobile] City Battalion along with two detached units, the 3rd Battalion Alabama Reserves and 4th Battalion Alabama Reserves. Maury's total personnel amounted to 13,225. Lt. General Richard Taylor's command further included the District of North Alabama and District of Central Alabama (Posts at Demopolis, Montgomery, Selma, Cahaba, Opelika, Talladega, and Tuscaloosa). The grand total of Taylor's command was 32,583 men.
[O R, Series 1, Vol. 45, pt. 1, pages 1232-1233.]

By December 1. 1864, returns show that Major General Dabney Maury now lists a separate artillery department under the command of Colonel Isaac W. Patton, the Culpepper (South Carolina) Battery, Owens' (Arkansas) Battery and the Water Batteries under Colonel Marshall J. Smith, and he has reorganized the department. He is now shown in command of the Department of the Alabama, Mississippi, and East Louisiana. The organization now included Burnett's Command and McCulloch's Brigade of 1942 men (with the 15th Confederate Cavalry) had been transferred from General Liddell's command to the west side of the bay and was reported in motion in Florida at the time of filing. [O R, Series 1, Vol 45, pt II, pages 632-634]

On December 8, 1864, McCulloch's Brigade and Maury's Calvary were sent north toward Leaksville and Buckatunna, Mississippi, to protect telegraph lines and the Mobile and Ohio Railroad threatened by Federal troops. [O R, Series 1, Vol. 45, pt. II, page 668]

On December 15th, Major General Maury reports that a column of enemy cavalry of 4000 men and eight guns marched from Baton Rouge, Louisiana, through east Louisiana and Mississippi to a point just east of the Pascagoula River with their object being to destroy the Mobile and Ohio Railroad and surprise Mobile. Indeed U.S. Brigadier General J. W. Davidson and Chief of Cavalry reported from West Pascagoula on December 13, that he had encountered terrible weather, bad roads,

15TH CONFEDERATE CAVALRY

crossed several rivers and finally on December 9 encountered Confederate troops from McCulloch's (Second Missouri) Brigade of Forrest's Command and the 15th Confederate Cavalry and 8th Mississippi. He estimated the Confederate forces at 2500 cavalry and artillery and could call upon several thousand infantry from Meridian where General Richard Taylor had his headquarters. General Davidson proposes to sit tight at East Pascagoula for the time being.[O R, Series 1, Vol. 45, pt. 1, pages 786-787]

The 15th Confederate Cavalry was sent to Blakeley on March 22, 1865.

Battle of Blakeley, April 3- 9, 1865. On April 9, after the fall of Spanish Fort, which was only about five miles south, Major General E. R. S. Canby's Federal bluecoats moved in force against the Confederate fortifications at Blakeley. Blakeley was defended largely by General Bryan Thomas's reserves and a few soldiers who escaped from the works at Spanish Fort. The battle-experienced 21st Alabama Infantry did add some heft to his command. Brigadier General Francis Cockrell's Missouri Infantry and Sears's Brigade of Mississippi Infantry under Colonel Thomas Adaire were in the rifle pits as well. U.S. Brigadier General James I. Gilbert describes the Confederate scene before the Blakeley's earthen fortifications as covered with felled timber in every direction, torpedoes planted before the works, wire stretched from stump to stump, a double line of abatis and a very strong line of fortifications. The total of southern defenders were about 3500 men. There were nearly 26,000 well-fortified Federal troops in the area.

When in the late afternoon of April 9, at about 5:30 p.m. the Bluecoats rushed the works at Blakeley, they completely overpowered the outnumbered defenders and pushed them from their works. Some escaped west to the CSA gunboats standing off shore and other were drowned trying to escape. Many Confederates were captured but there were a few inexcusable instances where men who had surrendered were killed by the Federal forces. The escape of the 15th Cavalry was not recorded or was lost in the final days of the war but escape they did and took their mounts and men north toward Clairborne and Greenville. The regiment may have split into more than one force at this point. Companies A and B had been left in Florida guarding strategic locations. A group of the 15th soon encountered Federal Cavalry at Mount Pleasant near the Baldwin County Line.

After a short fight the 15th lost two commissioned officers and 72 enlisted men captured by Brigadier General T. J. Lucas commanding Cavalry forces at Mount Pleasant, Alabama, ten miles south of Claiborne, Alabama, on April 11, 1865. They were turned over to the Provost Marshal of the U.S. 2nd Division, 13th Corps A.C. on April 17, 1865. The 15th also lost small arms, horses and two battle flags in the encounter. Lucas had been posted to Claiborne with his cavalry which numbered 1554 men and a battery of rifled guns to block the Alabama River and any retreat from Mobile in that direction. [O R, Series 1, Vol. 49, pt. I, page 98]

April 11, 1865,
Special to the Mobile Register, Bay Minette, Ala. January 27, ?

Mr. C. H. Driesbach of Blackshear, Baldwin County, Alabama, was a survivor of the Civil War and before his death gave the following interview:
Mr. Driesbach says little is said of some of the closing combats that proved vital to the South and where many Alabama heros "went west" whose names are cherished by those who have survived but whose identity has long been lost in the cataclysm that followed.
It was April 11 during 1865 according to Mr. Driesbeck that one of the last battles was fought near here and, although outnumbered by the federal troops, a strong resistance was put up. It was in this battle he recalls that Harry Davis, the

flagbearer of the Confederate soldiers although mortally wounded, propped himself up against a tree and held the flag aloft and vainly tried to give the "Rebel yell."

The battle occurred in Monroe County when what was estimated 3000 federal troops, under the command of General Lucas, clashed with the 15th cavalry commanded by Lieutenant Colonel [Thomas J.] Myers and a company of mounted infantry commanded by Captain T. C. English. Captain English was a brother of General McClelland of which company Mr. Driesbach was a member and was one of the few survivors after the engagement.

"Our company was guarding a bridge on Little River between Baldwin and Monroe Counties," Mr. Driesbach says, "while the 15th Alabama cavalry or rather part of it was at Clairborne, Monroe County. On the morning of April 11, 1865, General Lucas and his men were coming up the highway from Stockton. The Confederate troops came together at or near what is now know as Eliska. The federal troops numbered about 3000 while our side had something like 200. Arrangements had been made between Captain [T. C.] Barlow and Colonel Myers that Captain Barlow's company should make a detour and reach the rear of the enemy and then advance in echelon formation. The strength of the enemy was not known at that time. Colonel Myers decided to wait and attack the enemy in front."

"Shortly after Barlow left on his mission, [Captain Edward T.] Arrington's company of the 15th cavalry used as advanced guard met the enemy and it plainly saw they were outnumbered. Colonel Myers then gave the command to charge, and at the same time the "Rebel yell" went up. We drove the advance guard back to about one-fourth mile when we came in full contact with the enemy consisting of about 3000 men. The fighting which was fierce continued for about 20 minutes when we were forced to retire. Harry Davis, the flag bearer, was shot in about 20 feet of where I was at, and getting off his horse, sat down by a pine tree and when last seen was holding the Confederate flag aloft.

Besides several being killed, 50 of our men were captured by the enemy. In the retreat William H. H. Greenwood and myself accompanied the few of the regiment which was left to a rendezvous near Clairborne, Alabama. About April 20 all troops in south Alabama were ordered to Gainesville to be payrolled. Davis, the flag bearer, died from his wounds and was buried in what is now known as the home of Captain C. A. Marriott."

April 13, 1865, Assistant Adjutant General Lt. Colonel E. Surget passed General Dick Taylor's order through Choctaw Bluff command to keep Maury's Cavalry west of the Alabama River so that they could keep the garrison at Choctaw Bluff advised on the whereabouts of the enemy and prevent them from crossing the river.

On April 14, 1865, the badly used up 15th with Lt. Colonel Myers in command blew up the magazine of Choctaw Bluff and evacuated the site, afterward they rode to Oven Bluff and some of the group went on up river.

On April 15, 1865, Colonel Maury was in Mobile wounded due to being thrown from his horse.

April 18, 1865, **John Randall** of Co. G, Mobile Dragoons, 15th Confederate Cavalry was shot and wounded at Eight-Mile Creek Bridge in Whistler, Alabama. This is just northwest of Mobile. He died the same day. It was reported that he was part of a scouting party. The Mobile Register reported that he may have been the last man to die in the conflict. (The Register article may have meant East of the Mississippi.)

15TH CONFEDERATE CAVALRY

When the regiment was ordered to the eastern shore of Mobile Bay by the Federal threat, Companies A and B were left behind in Florida to guard posts there and were captured in a separate body from the main unit in Gainesville, Alabama. These prisoners are noted as being surrendered in Tallahassee.

Some of the 15th were surrendered at Tallahassee, Florida, by Major General Sam Cook CSA in command of Confederate Forces in Florida to Brigadier General E. M. McCook USV commanding U.S. forces in Tallahassee, Florida and the vicinity on May 22, 1865. Some of these surrendered men were paroled in Madison, Quincy, and others at Tallahassee, Florida, in May 1865. Those shown in Quincy and Madison were not likely in Tallahassee at the time of surrender. This surrender was in compliance with the terms of a Military Convention made on April 26, 1865, at Bennett's House near Durham's Station, North Carolina, between General J. E. Johnston CSA and Major General W. T. Sherman USA and approved by Lt. General U. S. Grant USA. A few individuals from the 15th Confederate Cavalry were paroled at the headquarters of the 16th U.S. Army Corps at Montgomery, Alabama, in June of 1865, while others shown as stragglers were paroled at Selma in May and June 1865.

The bulk of the men were surrendered by Lieutenant General Richard Taylor on May 14, 1865, at Citronelle, Alabama, to U.S. Major General E. R. S. Camby. The men themselves were not present but were located and paroled in Gainesville, and Mobile, Alabama, at the time of surrender.

CAPTIONS AND RECORD OF EVENTS

15 CONFEDERATE CAVALRY
(1st Regiment Alabama and Florida Cavalry)

The following information is transcribed from the filed note cards with the Military Service Records of the 15th Confederate Cavalry. The actual Muster Rolls referred to are <u>not</u> in the Military Service Records. They are transcribed as recorded and no effort was made to correct spelling, etc. Where locations were known, additional information such as the state was added.

Field and Staff Muster Roll September and October 1863. 15th Confederate Cavalry. Dated October 31, 1863. Halls Mill, Alabama.

On the 22 day of October left Halls Mills, Ala., with the regiment. Marched in a northerly direction crossed the Pascagoula River at Farley's Ferry on the 25 of Oct., Pearl River on the 2 of November passing through Holmesville and Liberty, Miss on the ? Came on a foraging party of the enemy two hundred strong at Tunica Landing, West Feliciana Parish, La. on the Mississippi River. Completely routed them capturing between 20 & 30 and killing between 40 & 50. One man from Co. B Private L. Myrick wounded in the arm. Took up the line of march on the next day and returned by mostly the same route to the camp at Halls Mill, Ala. reaching there the 23d of November. Distance traveled from the 22 of Oct. to the 23 of November 600 miles. G. M. Rowe, Copyist

Field and Staff Muster Roll Dec. 31 to April 30, 1864. Dated April 30, 1864. Pollard, Ala.

The regt. left Mobile for Citronelle on the 1st Feb. and remained there until the 14th and returned. Left Mobile for Jones County, Miss. by R.R. on the 2nd March for the purpose of breaking up a large body of deserters who were organizing into Companies, Battalions, etc. and were committing numerous depredations upon the citizens. Four (4) who were found were hung a number of others were sent to their commands & some were brought to Mobile as Prisoners for trade. The Regt. returned to Mobile and was ordered to Citronelle on the 27th March and ordered countermanded on the 29th. Left Mobile on the 31st March for Pollard, Ala. a distance of seventy five miles (75) and arrived there on 2nd April. G. M. Rowe, Copyist

----

Company A Muster Roll for Sept. 12, 1863. Dated September 12, 1863, shows company stationed at Mobile, Ala.

Company A Muster roll for September and October 1863. Dated November 30, 1863. Halls Mills, Alabama.

We left here on the 22 Oct 1863 proceeded as far as Tunica on the Miss River. There met & repulsed the enemy with heavy loss on their side. We captured 25 prisoners & their entire forage train & returned to this place on the 23 inst. in good order & without loss having accomplished the distance of 600 miles in 31 days. John Ulmer, Capt. commanding Co. A 15 Conf. Regt Cav. G. C. West, Copyist.

Company A Muster Roll of November and December 1863. Dated January 1, 1864. Halls Mills, Ala.

The Co. has been stationed at Halls Mills for the past two months during which time it had been much improved in the Cavalry Drill. F. A. Taylor, Lt. Comdg Co. A 15 Con reg Cav. January 4, 1864

Company A Muster Roll for March & Apr. Dated Apr. 30, 1864. Pettis Bridge to St. Rosa Co. Fla.

Company A Muster Roll for May & June 1864. Dated June 30, 1864. Pollard, Ala.

Company B Muster Roll for September 12, 1863, shows the station of the company as Pascagoula, Miss.

15TH CONFEDERATE CAVALRY 17

Company B Muster Roll for September and October 1863. Dated November 30, 1864. Hall's Mills, Ala.

On the 18th of October left East Pascagoula, Miss, where the company had been stationed 2 months and arrived on the same day at Halls Mills near Mobile, Ala. Distance marched 35 miles. On the 22nd of October left Halls Mills with the regiment, marched in a westerly direction, crossed the Pascagoula River in Farleys Ferry on the 25th of Oct. Pearl River at Columbia, Miss. on the 2nd of Nov. passing through Holmesville and Liberty, Mississippi on the 3rd. Came upon a party of the enemy at Tunica Landing in West Feliciana Parrish in Louisiana on the Missississippi River. Completely routed them capturing between 20 & 30, killing about the same number. One man of Co. B. Private S. Myrick wounded in the arm. Took up the line of march on the next day and returned by nearly the same route to Halls Mill reaching Camp on the 23rd of Oct.[November] Distance marched from the 22nd of Oct. to the 23d of Nov. 600 miles.

Company B Muster Roll for November and December 1863. Dated December 31, 1863. Halls Mills

Left Halls Mills, Ala. Nov. 31, 1863 and arrived at East Pascagoula, Miss. Left East Pascagoula, Miss Dec. 31, 1863. Distance marched 37 miles.

Company B Muster Roll for January and February 1864. Dated February 29, 1864. Bayou La Battre, [Batre]Ala.

Left Halls Mill the ninth of Feby. and marched to Citronelle, Ala. a distance of 35 miles and left Citronelle the 14th Feby and marched to Bayou La Battre [Batre] a distance of 51 miles.

Company B Muster Roll for March and April 1864. Dated April 30, 1864, shows station of company at Greenwood, Ala.

Company B Muster Roll for May and June 1864. Dated June 30, 1864, shows station of Company at Gonzalia, Fla.

Company C Muster Roll for September 12, 1863, shows the station of the company at Camp Hall's Mills.

Company C Muster Roll for September and October 1863. Dated Oct. 31, 1863, shows the station of the company at Hall's Mills.

This regiment, the 15th Confederate Cavalry Col. H. Maury Commanding, left Halls Mill Ala. Mobile Co. on the 22nd of October 1863, marched to the Mississippi river and returned to this place (Halls Mills) a distance of 300 miles on the 23rd of November 1863.

Company C Muster Roll for November and December 1863. Dated December 30, 1863, shows the station of the company at Halls Mill.

Company C Muster Roll for December 31, 1863 to June 30, 1864, shows company stationed at Camp Powell.

The Co. left Mobile with balance of the Regiment for Pollard, Ala. on the 1st day of April, 1864, and was then ordered near Pensacola Navy Yard. Remained in that vicinity until April 26th on which day it was ordered to Camp Powell near Perdido Bay 50 miles east of Fort Morgan on detached duty where it still remains.

Company D Muster Roll for September 12, 1863, shows the station of the company at Hall's Mills.

Company D Muster Roll for September and October 1863. Dated October 31, 1863. Since last muster the company has been on scout thirty days at Pascagoula, Miss. [Signed] W. P. Rice, Lt. Com. Co.

Company D Muster Roll for November and December 1863. Dated December 31, 1863, shows station of the company at Halls Mills, Ala.

Company D Muster Roll for January and February 1864. Dated February 24, 1864, shows station of the company at Halls Mills, Ala.

Since the Company was last mustered it has been on scout in the State of Mississippi for twenty two days. [Signed] W. P. Rice, 1st Lt. Comdg. Company.

Company D Muster Roll for March and April. Dated April 30, 1864. Shows station of the company near Milton, Fla.

Company D Muster Roll for May and June. Dated June 30, 1864. Shows station of the company at Milton, Fla.

Company E Muster Roll for September 12, 1863, shows station of the company at Hall's Mills, Ala.

Company E Muster Roll for September and October 1863. Dated October 31, 1863, shows station of the company at Halls Mills, Ala.

We left Halls Mills near Mobile, Ala. on the 22nd Oct. order commanded of our Col. (H. Maury) and marched in the direction of the Mississippi river passing through Columbia, Holmesville, Liberty and Enteria [enter La.?] and then to Tunica on the Miss river where we attacked the enemy in a few hundred yard of his gunboats completely routed him and driving him to his gunboats with considerable slaughter, capturing a number of prisoners, wagons, mules, horses and without the loss of a man. The distance marched there and back six hundred miles. Time required for the march thirty one days.

Company E Muster Roll for November and December. Dated December 31, 1863. Show station of the company at Camp Halls Mills, Ala.

Company E Muster Roll for March and April 1864. Dated April 30, 1864, shows the station of the company at Camp Pitts Bridge, Fla.

Company E Muster Roll for May and June 1864. Dated June 30, 1864, shows the station of the company at Camp Pitts Bridge, Fla.

Company F Muster Roll for September 12, 1863, shows the station of the company at Hall's Mills.

Company F Muster Roll for September and October 1863. Dated October 31, 1863, shows the station of the company at Halls Mills.

This regiment (the 15th Confederate Cavalry) Col. H. Maury, Commanding left this place on October 22, 1863 & marched to the Miss. river and returned to this place (Halls Mills) on the 23d of November 1863, a distance of 300 miles. During that time this company was twice engaged with the enemy and on the morning of the second engagement proceeded in driving them to their gunboats. Lieut. W. T. Holland had his horse killed during the final days engagement Nov. 8, 1863.

Company F Muster Roll for November and December 1863. Dated December 31, 1863, shows the station of the company at Halls Mills.

Company F Muster Roll for March and April 1864. Dated May 1, 1864, shows the station of the company at Gonzalia, Fla.

Company F Muster Roll for May and June 1864. Shows no date or station.

Company G Muster roll for Sept. 12, 1863, shows the station of the company at Hall's Mill.

Left East Pascagoula July 7, 1863, for Halls Mill, 31 miles. Left Halls Mill July 12, 1863, for Camp Murphy, 7 miles. Left Camp Murphy August 6, 1863, for Halls Mills, 7 miles. Have had Scouts at West Pascagoula & Biloxi on the coast & as far West as Pearl River.

Company G Muster Roll for September and October 1863. Dated October 31, 1863, shows the station of the company at Hall's Mills.

Captain John H. Marshall with a detachment of sixteen men had a skirmish with the enemy at Shieldsboro, Miss. on the 20 Oct. 1863, in which Capt. Marshall was severely wounded. On November 8, 1863. Col. Harry Maury Com'd the 15 Confederate Rgt. Cavalry with a portion of his command and including Co. G met a marauding party of the enemy at Winbush Plantation about two miles from Tunica, on the Mississippi River. The reported loss of the enemy including prisoners was forty five. No casualties in Co. G. One Corp. and one private reported without leave have been satisfactorily accounted for.

Company G Muster Roll for November and December 1863. Dated December 31, 1863, shows the station of the company as Halls Mill.

Company G Muster Roll for December 31, 1863 to April 30, 1864. Dated April 30, 1864, shows the station of the company at Canal Station, Alabama.

Company H Muster Roll for September 12, 1863, shows the station of the company at Hall's Mills.

Company H Muster Roll for September and October 1863. Dated November 30, 1863, shows the station of the company at Halls Mill. This company marched from Camp at Halls Mill on the 22 October 1863 on a scout - proceeded to Tunica in Feliciana Parish, La. & returned on the 24th November 1863, - being about 31 days in which it marched about (600) six hundred miles.

Company H Muster Roll for November and December 1863. Dated December 31, 1863, shows the station of the company at Hall's Mills.

Company H Muster Roll for December 31, 1863 to April 30, 1864. Dated April 30, 1864, shows the station of the company at Camp Gonzalia, Fla.

Company H Muster Roll for December 31, 1863 to June 30, 1864. Dated June 30, 1864, shows the station of the company at Perdido Mills, Fla.

Company I Muster Roll September 12, 1863, shows station of the company at Hall's Mills.

Company I Muster Roll for September and October 1863. Dated October 31, 1863, shows the station of the company at Hall's Mills, Ala.

This company has been doing duty on the Coast for forty five days.

Company I Muster Roll for November and December 1863. Dated December 31, 1863, shows the station of the company at Hall's Mills.

Company I Muster Roll for December 31, 1863 to April 30, 1864. Dated April 30, 1864, shows the station of the company at Milton, Fla.

Company I Muster Roll for May and June 1864. Dated June 30, 1864, shows the station of the company at Milton, Fla.

Company K Muster Roll for September 12, 1863, shows the station of the company as Hall's Mills.

The ? is absent at the present time on detached service one Captain is at Pascagoula, one Lieutenant at Mobile with 20 men enrolling conscripts also some privates at various points to numerous to mention.

Company K Muster Roll for September and October 1863. Dated October 31, 1863, shows the station of the company at Mobile, Ala.

Company K Muster Roll for November and December 1863. Dated December 31, 1863, shows the station of the company at Mobile, Ala.

The company was detached on provost guard duty in Mobile on the 23 day of September 1863, by Major General D. H. Maury and were ordered to report to Colonel H. Maury at Hall's Mills on the 31 Day of December 1863, by order of Major L. Sayre Provost Marshal General.

Company K Muster Roll for December 31, 1863 to April 30, 1864. Dated April 30, 1864, shows the station of the company at Canoe Station, Baldwin County, Ala.

Company K Muster Roll for May and June 1864. Dated June 30, 1864, shows the station of the company at Gonzalia, Fla.

On sixth of May they marched from Canoe Station, Ala. to Gonzalia, Fla. an outpost near Pensacola a distance of thirty five miles.

ROSTER NOTES

These documents can include but are not limited to letters, orders, requisitions, signed receipts, discharge papers, medical records and parole. It is nearly impossible to capture every notation in these files and it is suggested that serious researchers obtain copies of the individual files from the U.S. National Archives or other providers. You will find these transcribed service records are not complete and are selective as recorded here. The major purpose here is to identify those men who were associated with the regiment. The compiler has attempted to include any personal information and any major or significant events that appear in the individual files. A special effort was made to note the date of the last entry for each man. Many items such as presence or absence on muster rolls or hospital admissions, furloughs and instances of pay are sometimes omitted here. * signifies that there is original paperwork contained in the microfilm file over and above the standard card files. ** signifies significant amounts of paperwork is present. My apologies in advance for any unintentional oversight.

Official 15th Confederate Cavalry First Muster Roll is dated September 12, 1863. You will note that many muster roll entries end on April 30, 1864, while others end June 30, 1864. We must assume that the company muster rolls did not survive past that date. Some notations differ from the first muster roll taken on September 12, 1863, and the next company muster roll which was for September and October 1863. The latter was dated on October 31, 1863, and reflected the current designation for the individual which may have changed from September 12. The regiment presented muster rolls for September 12, 1863; September and October 1863; November and December 1863; December 31, 1863 through April 30, 1864, and finally May and June 1864. There were none found past that date.

Lieutenant General Richard Taylor CSA surrendered the 15th Confederate Cavalry and other Confederate forces under his command to Major General E. R. S. Canby USA at Citronelle, Alabama, on May 14, 1865. A marker is present on the site at Citronelle, north of Mobile. The men were not present but were paroled in Mobile and Gainesville, Alabama.

Some of the 15th were surrendered at Tallahassee, Florida, by Major General Sam Cook CSA in command of Confederate forces in Florida to Brigadier General E. M. McCook USV commanding U.S. forces in Tallahassee, Florida, and the vicinity on May 22, 1865. Some of these surrendered men were paroled in Madison and Quincy, Florida, and others at Tallahassee in May 1865. Those shown in Quincy and Madison were not likely in Tallahassee at the time of surrender. This surrender was in compliance with the terms of a military convention made on April 26, 1865, at Bennett's House near Durham's Station, North Carolina, between General J. E. Johnston CSA and Major General W. T. Sherman USA and approved by Lt. General U. S. Grant USA. A few individuals from the 15th Confederate Cavalry were paroled at the headquarters of the 16th U.S. Army Corps at Montgomery, Alabama, in June of 1865, while others shown as stragglers were paroled at Selma in May and June 1865.

From letters in his file and authored by Lt. W. McR. Jordan, he locates Camp Lomax and Bluff Springs as being near Pollard, Alabama. The letters can be found in his file but are not contained in these transcribed records.

Camp Forney was, for a time at least, located in East Pascagoula, Mississippi. See file of Pvt. Frank Kling, Co. K. and J. F. Luther.

P & G RR that is referenced as the enlisting location of some men's enlistment was the Pensacola and Georgia Railroad.

15TH CONFEDERATE CAVALRY

ROSTER

A

Adair, William., Pvt. Co. F.
Enlisted on October 1, 1863, at Mobile, Alabama. On extra duty at Mobile, Alabama, as a courier for A.A.C. from January 21 to January 31, 1864. Drew clothing on August 29, 1864. POW surrendered at Citronelle, Alabama, on May 4, 1865, and paroled at Gainesville, Alabama, on May 14, 1865. Residence shown as Mobile, Alabama.

Adams, B. F., Pvt. Co. G.
Enlisted on October 7, 1861, at Dragoon Camp by W. Barnwell. POW captured on October 25, 1864, at Escambia County, Florida, by a detachment of the U.S. 1st Florida, Cavalry. His name appears on a return of prisoners in confinement at Fort Pickens, Florida, for the month of October 1864, joined [was confined] October 27 per order of General Gailey. Transferred to New Orleans, Louisiana, on November 19, 1864. Released at New Orleans upon taking the Oath of Allegiance to the U.S. on January 7, 1865. His Oath shows that he was a resident of Camden, Maine, light complexion, brown hair, blue eyes, 5 foot 8 inches and was a deserter that came into the Federal lines at Pensacola, Florida, on October 25, 1864. In his file is a handwritten note from headquarters of Lafourche District at Tibodaux, Louisiana, on January 18, 1865. "Captain Bigelow, I send you one Dr. B. F. Adams, who has been a surgeon in the Rebel Army and has never taken the Oath of Allegiance. You will administer to him the required Oath. By command of Brig. Genl R. A. Cameron." In a letter written on November 1, 1864, he appeals to be allowed to take the Oath and return to Maine. He attempts to explain his intentions to desert from Pollard, Alabama, but was instead captured by U.S. Cavalry near Pensacola where they confiscated his fine horse. He reports that "there is a man in this city [New Orleans] that use to belong to my company and he left us last winter in Pascagoula, Miss. a Mr. Bennett."

[US] Hd.Qts. Dist. of West Florida
Barrancas Oct. 25, 1864

Lt. Col. Cristinsen
A.A.Gen. Hd. Qts. Mid Dept. W. Miss.
Col.,
I have the honor to report that B. F. Adams purporting to be a private of Co. G, 15th Confed. Cav. & who was taken outside our lines to day, states that Col Maury left Pollard yesterday Morning for Greenwoods Plantation (about 30 miles from the Tensas River) where the Hed.. Qts. of the Regt is stationed. The different Cos. of the 15th Cav. are being relieved by Cos. of the 8th Miss. Cav. & they are all ordered to report at Greenwoods. Capt. Amos' Co. of 15th Confed was to be relieved yesterday at Milton Fla. by the Cos. of the 8th Miss. & the two Companies stationed at Pine Barren Bridge by two more Cos. of the 8th   McCollough's Brigade (consisting of 3 small Regts.) Culpepper's Battery & other 54th Ala. Inf. comprise the troops stationed at Pollard.
The 15th Confed. & Tobins Battery which is attached to the Cav. are all the troops that are at Greenwoods. The Battery has Six (6) pcs. 4 brass & two howitzers & two iron pcs.

Very Respectfully
Your obdt. Servt.
J. Baily
Bvt. Brig. Gen'l Comdg.

There are considerable original papers and letters in this file relating to B. F. Adams capture or surrender. **

Adams, W. W., Pvt. Co. K.
Enlisted on August 20, 1864, at Hall's Mills, Alabama. Born Choctaw County, Alabama, age-18, eyes-grey, hair-light, complexion-fair, 5 foot 10 inches, occupation a farmer.

Adkinson, Daniel Ingram Britton, Co. I
It is reported that there is a grave bearing this name in Old Sardis Cemetery, west of Samson, Geneva County, Alabama.

Adkinson, John, Pvt. Co. I.

Agnew, Hiram. B., Pvt. Co. K.
Enlisted on September 12, 1863, at Hall's Mills, Alabama. Age-18, eyes-dark, hair-dark, complexion-dark, 5 foot 0 inches. POW surrendered Citronelle, Alabama, on May 4, 1865, and paroled at Gainesville, Alabama, on May 14, 1865. Residence Choctaw County, Alabama. *

Agnew, L. B., 3rd Corporal Co. K.
Enlisted on March 17, 1862, at Washington County, Alabama. POW surrendered at Citronelle, Alabama, on May 4, 1865, and paroled at Gainesville, Alabama, on May 14, 1865. Residence Choctaw County, Alabama.

Agnew, S. W., Pvt. Co. K.
Enlisted on March 17, 1863, at Washington County, Alabama. POW surrendered at Citronelle, Alabama, on May 4, 1865, and paroled at Gainesville, Alabama, on May 14, 1865. Residence Choctaw County, Alabama. *

Alba, P. F., 2nd Sergeant Co. K.
Enlisted on April 25, 1862, at Mobile, Alabama. POW surrendered at Citronelle, Alabama, on May 4, 1865, and paroled at Gainesville, Alabama, on May 14, 1865. Residence Brown County, Texas.

Alderman, Benjamin F., Pvt. Co. B.
Enlisted on February 14, 1863, (Captain Richard Smiths Company Cavalry Marianna Dragoons) at Marianna, Florida. Appears on a roll of POW's captured by Brigadier General T. J. Lucas commanding Cavalry forces at Mount Pleasant, Alabama. Captured on April 11, 1865. Appears on a roll of POW's turned over the Provost Marshal of the U.S. 2d Division, 13th Corps A.C. on April 17, 1864. POW forwarded from Mobile, Alabama, to Ship Island, Mississippi.

Alexander, W., Pvt. Co. F.
Enlisted on October 1863, at Mobile, Alabama. Reported to be absent on detached service since November 21, 1862, by order of General Forney. Appears absent and detached at Commissary Dept. Mobile, on a company muster roll for September/October 1863.

Allen, A. S., Pvt. Co. H.
Enlisted on September 2, 1862, at Mobile, Alabama. [There is also a card filed here in error for Pvt. A. S. Allen, Co. C, 13th Regiment Alabama, who was admitted to Receiving and Wayside Hospital, or General Hospital No. 9, Richmond, Virginia, on August 16, 1863.]

Allen, David, Corporal Co. D.
Enlisted on May 1, 1862, at Pensacola, Florida. Deserted on December 10, 1863.

Allen, W., Pvt. Co. H.
POW surrendered at Citronelle, Alabama, on May 4, 1865, and paroled at Gainesville, Alabama, on May 14, 1865. Residence Baldwin County, Alabama.

Allen, William, Pvt. Co. D.
Enlisted on April 24, 1862, at Pensacola, Florida. A company muster roll reports him on extra duty as a teamster since last muster on scout. Signed by his mark.

Allen, W. W., Pvt. Co. E.
Enlisted on September 17, 1861, at Milton, Florida.

Allman, M. C., Pvt. Co. F.
Enlisted on October 1, 1861, at Mobile, Alabama.

Amason, Washington, Co. D.
Enlisted on March 1, 1863, at Camp Tatnall. March/April 1863, muster roll he is shown on special duty at Bluff Springs, Florida. Drew clothing on August 28, 1864. Signs by his mark.

Amos, H. C., Pvt. Co. I.
Enlisted on June 28, 186_, at Conecuh County, Alabama.

Amos, J. W., Sergeant Co. E.
Enlisted on September 17, 1861, at Milton, Florida. Promoted from 4th Sergeant to 2nd Sergeant on May 1, 1864. POW captured at Escambia County, Florida, near Pensacola on November 17, 1864. Captured by a detachment of 1st Florida Cavalry and 2nd Ma. Cavalry under the command of Lt. Colonel Spurling of the 2nd Ma. Cavalry. Appears on a register of POW's at New Orleans, Louisiana that was confined on November 21, 1864, and transferred to Ship Island, Mississippi on December 10, 1864. Reported to have been received at Ship Island on December 13, 1864, and transferred to Vicksburg, Mississippi, on May 1, 1865.

Amos, W. B., Captain Co. I.
Enlisted on October 4, 186_, at Santa Rosa, Florida. Commissioned as Captain on October 4, 1862. Appears present on a company muster roll for September 12, 1863. Paid $140 on September 30, 1863, for service as Captain for the month of September 1863. He signs muster roll as commanding the company and also certifies as Inspector and Mustering Officer. On December 30, 1863, at Halls Mill, Alabama, he requisitioned for his company; 102 jackets, 104 pair of pants, 110 shirts, 100 pair of drawers, 100 cups, 12 pair of boots. On February 10, 1864, he requisitioned 200 grain saxs and 30 lbs of rope at Halls Mill, Alabama, required for making nose bags and corn wallets for use of the company. The rope for a picket rope. On February 12, 1864, he requisitioned another 200 grain saxs and 34 lbs. of rope for the same purpose. On July 22, 1864 he requisitioned six mess pans, six camp kettles and two skillets with lids at Camp Cumming. POW surrendered at Citronelle, Alabama, on May 4, 1865, and paroled at Mobile, Alabama, on June 8, 1865. Residence Santa Rosa County, Florida. Age-45, complexion-fair, eyes-blue, hair-light, 5 foot 6 inches.
** There are numerous requisitions and pay vouchers in his file.

Amus, J. M., Pvt. Co. I.
Signed a Parole at Headquarters of the 16th U.S. Army Corps at Montgomery, Alabama, on May 31, 1865. Hair-light, eyes-grey, complexion-fair, 5 foot 8 inches.

Anderson, A. H., Pvt./Corporal Co. A.
Enlisted on March 8, 1862, at Monticello, [Florida]. Promoted to Corporal on October 10, 1863. He is also shown as having enlisted on March 8, 1862, at Station 3 P&G RR. POW surrendered at Tallahassee, Florida, on May 10, 1865. Paroled at Tallahassee on May 24, 1865.

Anderson, W., Pvt. Co. F.
Enlisted on June 1, 1863, at Camp Withers. His file notes: "W. Anderson was paid $192 by roll only paid him $72 for 3 months." Company F muster roll for March/April 1864, reports that he deserted on December 28, 1863.

Anderson, Winfield, Pvt. Co. A.
Enlisted on February 23, 1864, at Monticello, Florida. POW surrendered at Tallahassee, Florida, on May 10, 1865. Paroled at Tallahassee on May 24, 1865.

Antonio, Henry, Co. C.
Drew clothing on August 28, 1864.

Ard, Reuben, Pvt. Co. A.
Enlisted March 12, 1863, at Camp Lomax. He is shown absent without leave deserted since August 1, 1863, on a company muster roll for September 12, 1863. Appears present September 15, 1863, on a company muster roll for September/October but absent again without leave since December 30, 1863, on a November/December roll. March/April 1864, roll shows him absent in confinement charged with desertion. May/June roll shows him absent sentenced to hard labor by Provost Marshal in Mobile, Ala. Drew clothing on August 24, 1864. He appears August 31, 1864, on a Muster roll of Company C, Detachment of Troops from the Camp of Correction, ordered to duty by Major General Maury and commanded by Major R. A. Harris at the mouth of Dog River near Mobile. Admitted to Ross Hospital in Mobile with febris intermittes tert. on September 24, 1864, returned to duty on October 1, 1864, and again admitted with febris intermitttens qout. on November 2, 1864, returned to duty on November 6.

Armstead, William J., Pvt. Co. B.
Enlisted on September 17, 1863, at Camp Jackson, Florida. Appears absent detailed as a Acting Master Sergeant with Ala. & Fla. Batln. Cavalry. Appears present Acting 2nd Master Sergeant, without a horse since October 28, on a muster roll for September/October. Shown present and Acting 2nd Master Sergeant on roll for November/December. POW captured Quincy, Florida, on May 23, 1865. Surrendered on May 10, 1865, at Quincy, Fla.

Arnett, William H., Co. H.
Drew clothing on September 7, 1864. Admitted to Ross Hospital, Mobile, Alabama, on September 29, 1864, with febris remittens. Returned to duty on October 12, 1864.

Arrington, Edward T., Captain Co. F.
Entered Confederate service on May 7, 1862. Elected Captain on May 7, 1862. Paid $422.75 on July 31, 1862, at Mobile for 3676lbs. of beef at 11 1/2 cents per lb. Paid $379.10 on October 30, 1862, at Mobile, Alabama, for 3791 lbs of beef furnished to troop. Paid $140

on January 4, 1863, for service as Captain Co. F for month of December 1862. Paid $479.40 on January 31, 1863, at Mobile, for 4524 lbs fresh beef at 10 cents per lb. and 18 bushels of potatoes at $1.50 per bushel. Paid $257.50 on February 26, 1863, at Mobile for 10 bushels of potatoes at $1.50 per bushel and 2425 lbs. of beef at 10 cents per lb. On April 1, 1863, at Camp Withers, Mobile, Alabama Captain Arrington signed a requisition for 30 days supply, corn and fodder for 109 horses and 4 mules, a total of 40,680 lbs of corn and 23,730 lbs of fodder. He shows the feed is for animals of the City Troop Co. A, 3rd Brigade, Mackalls Division, CS Army. Paid $525 on March 28, 1863, at Mobile for 2625 lbs of Fresh Beef at 20 cents per lb. Appears absent with leave on a company muster roll for September 12, 1863. On October 1, 1863, at Halls Mill he requisitioned feed for 76 horses. Here he shows the Company as Company F, 15th Confederate Cavalry, by November 1st the number of horses were down to 50 in Company F at Halls Mill. Muster roll for September/October reports him absent with leave. November/December he is reported absent without leave. On December 1, 1863, at Halls Mill he requisitioned for Company F the following; 108 jackets, 108 pants, 153 shirts, 153 pair drawers, 153 caps, 108 pair boots, 30 blankets. On January 14, 1864, on a requisition for fuel he reports the personnel of Company F as 2 Captains, 6 subalterns, 100 non-commissioned officers, musicians and privates. Rolls for March, April, May and June 1864, he is reported present. He appears on a company Roster for May 12, 1864, at Pollard, Alabama. On animal feed requisition for March 1, 1864, the count of horses has risen to 90 animals. On March 25, 1864, at Halls Mill he requisitioned for Company F the following; 40 pair pants, 40 jackets, 40 pair shoes, 37 shirts, 7 blankets. He appears on a company roster for July 12, 1864, at Camp Cumming. He signed for clothing for Company F on August 29, 1864. His name appears on a company roster for January 1, 1865, at Spring Hill. ** There are numerous requisitions and pay vouchers in his file over and above those referred to here.

Askew, Charles H., Pvt. Co. Co. B.
Enlisted on March 14, 1862, at Marianna, Florida. POW captured at Greenville, Alabama, on April 26, 1864, by 3d Brigade U.S. Cavalry commanded by Brigadier General Lucas operating out of Pensacola, Florida Paroled at Greenville.

Atchinson, B. T., Pvt. Co. K.
POW surrendered at Citronelle, Alabama, on May 4, 1865, and paroled at Gainesville, Alabama, on May 14, 1865. Residence Washington County, Alabama.

Atkinson, D. J., Corporal Co. I.
Enlisted as 4th corporal on January 12, 1863, at Conecuh County, Alabama.

Atkinson, John, Pvt. Co. I.
POW captured at Andalusia, Alabama, on March 23, 1865, by U.S. Cavalry forces under Brigadier General Lucas operating out of Pensacola, Florida. Appears on a roll of POW's in front of Blakeley, Alabama, on April 8, 1865. Received at Ship Island, Mississippi, and transferred to Vicksburg, Mississippi, on May 1, 1865.

Avery, C. B., Pvt. Co. C.
Enlisted on April 15, 186_, at Stockton, Alabama. POW surrendered Citronelle, Alabama, on May 4, 1865, and paroled at Gainesville, Alabama, on May 14, 1865. Residence Baldwin County, Alabama.

B

Baggett, W. S., Pvt. Co. D.
Enlisted on March 1, 1863, at Mobile, Alabama. March/April muster roll reports him present on special duty near Bluff Springs, Florida, and [previously] absent 90 days without leave. May/June muster reports him present but absent without leave for 90 days since last paid and dismounted for 80 days.

Bailey, G. L. J., Pvt./Corp. Co. G.
Enlisted on March 22, 1862, at Dragoon Camp. POW surrendered at Citronelle, Alabama, on May 4, 1865, and paroled at Gainesville, Alabama, on May 14, 1865. Residence Washington County, Alabama.

Baird, (Beard) J. W., Pvt. Co. K.
Enlisted at Halls Mill, Alabama, on September 21, 1863. Appears on a descriptive list dated October 9, 1863, at Mobile, Alabama. Here he is shown as age-18, eyes-dark, hair-dark, complexion-dark, 5 foot 6 inches, born in Mobile City, Alabama, occupation-clerk, paid-$50 bounty. He is shown on daily duty as a courier for Colonel H. Maury after December 31, 1863. J. W. Baird was paid $96.80, at Mobile, Alabama, on January 18, 1864, for four months pay at $12 per month plus 40 cents per day for his horse, 122 days. J. W. Beard, was paid $360 at $3 per day at Mobile, Alabama, on February 15, 1864, for pay on detached services with Major Davis, Provost Marshal from October 13, 1863, to February 13, 1864. POW paroled at Mobile, Alabama, on April 21, 1865. His parole is in his file.* Also see file of Lt. **R. A. Powe**.

Baker, Beverly, Sergeant Co. B.
Enlisted on April 20, 1862, at Marianna, Florida. POW captured April 11, 1865, at Claibrone, Alabama, (Mount Pleasant, Alabama) by General T. J. Lucas' Cavalry command. Forwarded as prisoner from Mobile, Alabama, to Ship Island, Mississippi.

Baker, E., Pvt. Co. F.
Enlisted on August 27, 1862, at Camp Withers.

Baker, George, Corporal/Pvt. Co. I.
Enlisted on October 12, 1863, at Santa Rosa, Florida. POW captured at Marianna, Florida on September 27, 1864. Appears on a roll of POW's received at Ship Island, Mississippi, on October 21, 1864. Sent to New York on November 3, 1864, by order of Captain M. R. Marston. Received at Fort Columbus, New York Harbor on November 16, 1864, and transferred from Fort Columbus to Elmira, New York on November 19, 1864. Received at Elmira, New York, on November 20, 1864, and transferred for exchange on February 13, 1865. Paroled at Elmira on February 9, 1865, and forwarded via Point Lookout, Maryland, to James River for Exchange. Appears on a list of Confederate POW's received at Bolwares & Cox Wharf, James River on February 20, 1865, among 3038 paroled CSA prisoners. Admitted to General Hospital, Richmond, Virginia, on February 22, 1865, with geltes. Furloughed at General Hospital Richmond on March 2, 1865, for 30 days. Admitted to Receiving and Wayside Hospital or General Hospital No. 9, Richmond, Virginia, on February 21, 1865. Sent to Chimbroazo Hospital [Richmond, Virginia]. Signed a petition for an Oath of Amnesty at Milton, Florida, on June 16, 1865. He states: "I am 23 years of age my home is in Walton County, Fla. I volunteered in Co. I ,15th Confed Cav. Oct. 4th, 1862 and served until Sept. 22, 1864 at which time I was captured at Shoal River and exchanged Feb. 15th 1865. I have taken no further part in the existing Rebellion." Signed June 16, 1865, George Baker. Pvt. Baker then signed an Oath of Allegiance, No. 521, on

15TH CONFEDERATE CAVALRY

June 16, 1865, at Milton, and received at Certificate of Amnesty. There is a copy of his petition, Certificate of Amnesty and Oath in his file.

Baker, James Dukes, Pvt. Co. C.
Enlisted on December 27, 1863, at Santa Rosa, Florida.

Baker, John, Pvt. Co. B.
Enlisted on May 3, 1863, at Marianna, Florida. POW captured at Mount Pleasant, Alabama, by General Lucas Cavalry Command on April 11, 1865. Appears on a list of POW's that were forwarded from Mobile, Alabama, to Sand Island, Mississippi.

Baker, Lawrence, Pvt. Co. B.
Enlisted on March 14, 1862, at Marianna, Florida. POW surrendered at Tallahassee, Florida, on May 11, 1865, and paroled at Quincy, Florida, on May 22, 1865.

Baker, Murdock, Pvt. Co. I.
Enlisted on October 4, 1862, at Santa Rosa, County, Florida.

Ball, H. C., Pvt. Co. C.
Appears on a roll of POW's of Co. F, 2nd Regiment Mississippi, Cavalry Reserves CSA commanded by Colonel E. A. Case that were surrendered at Meridian, Mississippi, by Lt. General Richard Taylor to Major General E. R. S. Canby, on May 4, 1865, and paroled at Mobile, Alabama, on May 22, 1865. His residence is show as Green County, Mississippi.

Ball, Henry, Co. A.
Drew clothing on September 7, 1864.

Bancroft, J. C., Sergeant Co. F.
Enlisted on August 4, 1862, at Camp Withers.

Ballard, J. H., Pvt. Co. E.
Enlisted on May 12, 1862, at Greenville, Alabama. A company muster roll for March/April 1864, reports that he "Deserted while on furlough to Butler County, Alabama, about 1st Jany 1, 1864, and is now probably lying in the woods in Butler County."

Baltzell, George A., Trumpeter/Pvt. Co. B.
Enlisted as 2nd Trumpeter on March 14, 1862, at Marianna, Florida. POW surrendered at Tallahassee, Florida, on May 11, 1865, and paroled at Quincy, Florida, on May 20, 1865.

Bancroft, S. C., Pvt. Co. K.
Appears on a roll of POW's commanded by Captain D. McKellar that were surrendered on May 4, 1865, and paroled at Gainesville, Alabama, on May 14, 1865. Residence Mobile County, Alabama.

Bainister, Jr., M., Clerk 15th Confederate Cavalry
Appears on a file marked Detailed L. R. - A. M. & E. La. [Alabama, Mississippi and East Louisiana] May 31, 1864. This note filed in error with Pvt. **Bankester. H.**

Bankester G. W., Pvt. Co. C.
Enlisted on October 27, 1863, at Camp Powell, Alabama.

Bankester, H., Pvt. Co. C.
Enlisted on June 7, 1864, at Camp Powell, Alabama. Appears on a roll of POW's of divers companies and commands commanded by Lt. Colonel R. H. Lindsay that were surrendered at Citronelle, Alabama, on May 4, 1865, and paroled at Meridian, Mississippi, on May 13, 1865. Residence Baldwin, County, Alabama.

Bankister, Louis, Pvt. Co. C.
Enlisted in April 15,1863, at Stockton, Alabama.

Banta, H., Pvt. Co. F.
Enlisted on October 1, 1861, at Mobile, Alabama.

Baptiste, Vincent, Pvt. Co. G.
Enlisted on June 14, 1863, at Camp Taylor.

Barber, N. M., Pvt. Co. K.
Enlisted on July 28, 1863, at Camp Halls Mill, Alabama.

Barclay, C. A., Pvt. Co. A.
Enlisted on October 1, 1862, at Camp Lomax, Florida. Detailed as nurse at General Hospital, Greenville, Alabama, on February 15, 1864, by order of General Maury. May/June company muster roll reports that he was discharged on May 7, 1864, by Medical Examining Board at General Hospital, Greenville. His name appears on a record of the U.S. 16th Army Corps at Montgomery as having been paroled at their headquarters on May 13, 1865. His parole reports him 5 foot 8 inches, hair-light, eyes-blue, hair-sandy. A copy is in his file. His Certificate of Disability for discharge is also in his file and reports the following: enlisted at Monticello, Florida, born-Twiggs County, Georgia, age-28, hair-red, a farmer by occupation. His disability is reported to be due to phthisis .[tuberculosis]

Barclay, W. D., Pvt. Co. A.
Enlisted on March 7, 1863, at Station 3 P&G RR. POW surrendered at Tallahassee, Florida, on May 11, 1865, and paroled at Tallahassee, Florida, on May 15, 1865. He is described as hair-red, eyes-blue, complexion-fair, 5 foot 9 inches. His parole and Oath of Allegiance is in his file.

Barkley, Albert, L. (Bartley, A. L.), Sergeant Co. B.
Enlisted on May 12, 1863, at Marianna, Florida. POW surrendered at Quincy, Florida, on May 11, 1865, and paroled on May 24, 1865.

Barlow, James, Pvt. Co. A.
Enlisted on October 8, 1862, at Camp Tatnall, Florida, November/December 1863 company muster roll reports that he deserted from Camp Ward, Alabama, on August 15, 1863.

Barlow, L. (Luther), Pvt. Co. C.
Enlisted on May 10, 186_, at Camp Powell, Alabama. He appears on a roll of POW stragglers of CSA Army that were surrendered at Meridian, Mississippi, on May 4, 1865, and paroled at Mobile, Alabama, on May 19, 1865. Residence Mobile, Alabama.

Barlow, T. C., Captain Co. C.
Received his commission as Captain on April 18, 1862. Requisitioned 1/2 Doz. bottles of Airbian Liniment and 1/2 Doz. bottles of Sprits Nitre for horses, at Mobile, Alabama, on July 26, 1862. Requisitioned and received one pair counter scales and weighs, one meat saw and

one butcher knife at Fort Morgan, Alabama, on July 20, 1862. Requisitioned 31 days feed for 95 horses and 12 mules, received at Mobile for Shell Banks near Fort Morgan on August 1, 1862: 39,804 lbs. corn and 46,438 lbs. of fodder [hay]. He signed on September 30, 1862, for 1993 lbs. rations of fresh beef at Fort Morgan, Alabama, for Company A, Coast Guard, Alabama stationed at Shell Banks. Again on October 10, 1862, at the same location for 722 lbs. of fresh beef. Requisitioned on January 10, 1864, at Camp Halls Mill, Alabama; 14 jackets, 29 shirts, 14 caps and 17 pair pants. Requisitioned 20 pair of shoes on February 28, 1864, at Bayou La Batre, Alabama. Requisitioned clothing on March 25, 1864, at Camp Halls Mill, Alabama; 41 pair pants, 41 jackets, 25 pair shoes, 41 shirts and 7 blankets. Paid $560 on August 29, 1864, for service as Captain from January 1 to April 30, 1864; four months at $140 per month. Appears present on company muster rolls from September 1863, to June 30, 1864, except November/December roll reported him absent without leave since December 28. Signed a Parole and Oath of Allegiance at Gainesville, [Alabama] on May 14, 1865. His parole is in his file. ** Captain Barlow is buried in Baldwin County, Alabama, in the Barlow Cemetery, off Alabama Highway 225.

Barnacastle, William, Pvt. Co. E.
Enlisted on November 1, 1862, at Camp Lomax, Florida.

Barr, U. G., Pvt. Co. K.
Enlisted on March 17, 1863, at Washington County [Alabama?]. Appears on a roll of POW's commanded by Captain D. McKellar that were surrendered at Citronelle, Alabama, on May 4, 1865, and paroled at Gainesville, Alabama, on May 14, 1865. Residence Choctaw County, Alabama.

Barrington, Edmond P., Pvt. Co. A.
Enlisted on April 21, 1862, at Monticello [Florida]. POW surrendered at Tallahassee, Florida, on May 10, 1865. Paroled at Tallahassee, on May 16, 1865. He is described as hair-light, eyes-gray, complexion-light, 5 foot 10 inches. He signed his parole with his mark "X". His parole is in his file.

Barrow, Charles, Pvt./Corp. Co. D.
Enlisted on May 1, 1862, at Pensacola, Florida. Promoted from the ranks to 4th Corporal on January 1, 1864.

Barrow, James V., Corp./Pvt. Co. D.
Enlisted on April 24, 1862, at Pensacola, Florida. Reduced to ranks from 4th Corporal on January 1, 1864. He is reported on extra duty as a teamster from March until June 30, 1864.

Barton, Uriah, Pvt. Co. I.
Enlisted on October 4, 1863 at Santa Rosa, Florida. November/December 1863, muster roll reports him as deserted.

Bateaste, Noel, Pvt. Co. F.
Drew clothing on August 29, 1864. Admitted to Ross Hospital, Mobile, Alabama, on October 19, 1864, with febris intermittens tert. Returned to duty on December 7, 1864.

Bates, W. J., Pvt. Co. C.
Enlisted on April 15, 1862, at Stockton, Alabama. POW paroled on April 18, 1863, at Fort Pickens, Florida. Appears on a roll of POW's, a detachment of Company C of the 15th Confederate Cavalry commanded by Captain T. C. Barlow that were surrendered at

Citronelle, Alabama, on May 4, 1865, and paroled at Gainesville, Alabama, on May 14, 1865. Residence Baldwin County, Alabama.

Battiste, John, P., Pvt. Co. H.
Enlisted on March 4, 1864, at Mobile, Alabama.

Baughman, J. A., Pvt. Co. C.
Enlisted on April 16, 1862, at Blakeley, Alabama. Company C muster roll for December 31, 1863, to June 30, 1864, reports that he died, no date given.

Beal, F. O., Pvt. Co. E.
Enlisted on June 1, 1863, at Camp Lomax, Florida. Appears present, a substitute for **Abraham Black** on June 1, 1863.

Beard, G. W., Pvt. Co. C.
Enlisted on October 30, 1862, at Camp Powell, Alabama. There is a record filed that G. W. Beard, Co. C. 9th Reg. Ala. was admitted to Receiving and Wayside Hospital or General Hospital No. 9, Richmond, Virginia, on April 2, 1865, sick. [This is likely filed in error.]

Beardslee, Joseph, Pvt. Co. G.
Enlisted on April 28, 1863, at Camp Taylor. Appears present under arrest on a company muster roll for September 12, 1864. Appears present on muster rolls from September 1863 through April 30, 1864. Appears on a roll of men on detached service in the Commissary Department, CSA that were surrendered by Lt. General Richard Taylor at Citronelle, Alabama, on May 4, 1865, and paroled at Meridian, Mississippi, on May 11, 1865. Residence Pascagoula, Mississippi. Note in the file that Joseph Beardsley, Co. G, 15 Confederate Cavalry, "his detail has requested to herd cattle". See personal papers of **W. T. Edwards**, Major & C.S. [Major Edwards papers are not with the service records of the 15th Confederate Cavalry.]

Beasley, Merida, Pvt. Co. D.
Enlisted on November 1, 1862, at Camp Tatnall, Florida. He is also reported to have enlisted at Camp Lomax, Florida.

Beck, J. J., Pvt. Co. D.
Appears on a register of Paroled POW's. Paroled on June 19, 1865, at Headquarters of 16 U.S. Army Corp, Office of Provost Marshal, Montgomery, Alabama. Hair-dark, eyes-hazel, complexion-light, 5 foot 8 inches.

Bedgood, James, Pvt. Co. A.
Enlisted on June 9, 1863, at Camp Lomax, Florida.

Bedgood, Stephen, Pvt. Co. A.
Enlisted on May 11, 1863, at Camp Lomax, Florida. Company muster roll for May/June reports that he was discharged by Medical Examining Board at General Hospital, Greenville, Alabama, with a Surgeons Certificate of Disability. [Not in his file.]

Belnce, A., Pvt. Co. C.
POW received at Ship Island, Mississippi on May 13, 1865, from Provost Marshal at Mobile, Alabama. Captured at Mount Pleasant, Alabama, on April 11, 1865. Appears on a roll of POW's that were transferred to New Orleans, from Ship Island on June 8, 1865.

15TH CONFEDERATE CAVALRY

Belch, John H., Pvt. Co. B.
    Enlisted on May 27, 1863, at Marianna, Florida.

Bell, Gamaliel, Quartermaster Sergeant/Pvt. F&S/Co. D.
    Enlisted as Q. M. Sergeant on August 22, 1863, at Camp Lomax, Florida. Reduced to ranks on December 26, 1863, by order of Colonel Maury. Appears present on January/February 1864, muster roll. Here he is reported in Co. D, enlisted on January 1, 1864, at Halls Mill, Alabama. Appears present on special duty as Quartermaster clerk on bi-monthly muster rolls from March through June 30, 1864. POW's of Company H, 15th Confederate Cavalry, CSA surrendered at Citronelle, Alabama, on May 4, 1865, and paroled at Gainesville, Alabama, on May 14, 1865. Residence Greenville, Butler County, Alabama. His payment voucher for $318.58 is in his file.

Bell, G. S., Pvt. Co. E.
    Enlisted on October 2, 1862, at Camp Lomax, Florida. Deserted about August 12, 1863, "and went to the enemy at Pensacola."

Bell, James, Pvt. Co. F.
    Enlisted on April 15, 1863, at Stockton, Alabama. POW surrendered at Citronelle, Alabama, on May 4, 1865. Paroled on June 13, 1865, at Mobile, Alabama. Age-27, complexion-dark, eyes-dark, hair-brown, 5 foot 10 inches, residence-Baldwin County, Alabama.

Bell, J. M., Pvt. Co. D.
    Enlisted on October 6, 1862, at Camp Tatnall, Florida. Company muster roll for September/October reports that he deserted on August 26, 1863.

Bell, W. R., Corporal/Sergeant Co. A.
    Enlisted on April 21, 1863, at Monticello, Florida. Promoted to 1st Sergeant on October 10, 1863. POW surrendered at Tallahassee, Florida, on May 10, 1865. Paroled on May 18, 1865, at Madison, Florida. ** There are several requisitions in his file but difficult to read.

Bellamy, Benjamin A., Corporal/Sergeant Co. B.
    Enlisted as 3rd Corporal on May 3, 1862, at Marianna, Florida. Promoted from 3rd to 2nd Corporal on November 1, 1863. POW surrendered on May 10, 1865. Paroled on May 22, 1865, at Quincy, Florida.

Bellamy, Richard, B., Pvt. Co. B.
    Enlisted on February 24, 1863, at Marianna, Florida. POW surrendered at Tallahassee, Florida, on May 11, 1865. Paroled on May 22, 1865, at Quincy, Florida.

Bennett, Joseph, Pvt. Co. E.
    Enlisted on September 5, 1862, at Camp Lomax, Florida. POW captured at Pine Barren, Escambia County, Florida on November 14, (some records correctly show November 17,) 1864, by a detachment of 1st Florida Cavalry and 2nd ME Cavalry. Appears on a record of POW's at New Orleans, Louisiana, confined on November 21, 1864, and transferred to Ship Island, Mississippi, on December 10, 1864. Transferred to Vicksburg, Mississippi, from Ship Island on May 1, 1865.

Bennett, T. B., Pvt. Co. E.
    Enlisted on September 5, 1862, at Camp Lomax, Florida. Muster roll for November/December 1863, reports him present on special duty in saddler shop. Rolls for January 1,

1865, through June 30, 1865, also report him present on special duty at saddler shop from December 1, 1864. His name appears among POW's of Company C, 15th Confederate Cavalry, CSA that were surrendered at Citronelle, Alabama, on May 4, 1865, and paroled at Gainesville, Alabama, on May 14, 1865. Residence Greenville, Butler County, Alabama.

Berry, Woodson P., Pvt. Co. B.
Enlisted on April 6, 1864, at Atlanta, Georgia.

Bethea (Betha), Hugh, Pvt. Co. I.
Enlisted on May 6, 1864, at Conecuh County, Alabama.

Bethea, John H., Pvt. Co. E.
Enlisted on March 12, 1864, at Camp Halls Mill, Alabama.

Bilbe, H. Q., Pvt. Co. K.
Appears on a roll of POW's of Company K, 15th Confederate Cavalry, CSA that were surrendered at Citronelle, Alabama, on May 4, 1865, and paroled at Gainesville, Alabama, on May 14, 1865. Residence Jackson County, Mississippi.

Bilbo, J. C., Pvt. Co. K.
Enlisted on September 1, 1862, at Camp Forney.

Bird, Martin, Pvt. Co. A/E/I.
Enlisted on June 21, 1863, at Camp Lomax, Escambia County, Florida. Muster roll for March/April 1864, reports him transferred to Company E, 15th Confederate Cavalry on January 1, 1864. He appears present on a company I muster roll for May/June 1864.

Bishop, C., Pvt. Co. C.
Enlisted on April 16, 1864, at Blakeley, Alabama. Appears on a roll of POW's of Company C, 15th Confederate Cavalry, CSA that were surrendered at Citronelle, Alabama, on May 4, 1865, and paroled at Gainesville, on May 14, 1865. Residence Baldwin County, Alabama.

Black, Abraham, Pvt. Co. E.
Enlisted on November 1, 1862, at Camp Lomax, Florida. Company muster roll for September 12, 1863, reports that he was discharged on June 1, 1863, as having furnished a substitute in the person of **F. O. Beal**. Appears present on a company muster roll for May/June 1864. Here he is shown as having enlisted on June 7, 1864, at Pitts Ridge, Florida.

Black, Herny, Pvt. Co. E.
Enlisted on September 17, 1861, at Milton, Florida.

Black, E. L., Pvt. Co. C.
Enlisted by Captain T. C. Barlow for three years. POW surrendered at Citronelle, Alabama, on May 4, 1865, and paroled at Gainesville, Alabama, on May 14, 1865. Residence Baldwin County, Alabama.

Blake, I. L., Pvt. Co. C.
POW surrendered by at Citronelle, Alabama, on May 4, 1865, and paroled at Gainesville, Alabama, on May 14, 1865. Residence Baldwin County, Alabama.

Blake, S. H., Pvt./Corporal Co. E.
Enlisted on September 17, 1861, at Milton, Florida. Promoted from ranks to 3rd Corporal

on May 1, 1864. POW captured on November 17, 1864, at Escambia County, near Pensacola, Florida, by a detachment of 1st Florida Cavalry and 2nd ME Cavalry under the command of Colonel Spauling. Appears on a register of POW's at New Orleans, Louisiana, that were confined on November 21, 1864. Transferred to Ship Island, Mississippi, on December 10, 1864. Received at Ship Island on December 13, 1864, and transferred to Vicksburg, Mississippi, on May 1, 1865.

Blocker, John D., Pvt. Co. G.
Enlisted on October 6, 1862, at Dragoon Camp.

Bludsworth, (Bloodsworth) H. D., Pvt. Co. G.
Enlisted on April 9, 1862, at Bayou La Batre, Alabama. Age-22, eyes-hazel, hair-dark, complexion-dark, 5 foot 5 inches, born-Henry County, Ala. Drew $50 bounty for enlistment.

Bludsworth, M. E., Pvt. Co. G.
Enlisted on September 16, 1863, at Dragoon Camp.

Bobe, J. V., Pvt. Co. D.
Enlisted on June 15, 1863, at Camp Tatnall, Florida. Appears on a roll of POW's and deserters that entered the military lines of the 16th U.S. Army Corps in April 1865, and was turned over to the Provost Marshal at Montgomery, Alabama, on May 5, 1865.

Bolton, William N., Pvt. Co. G.
Enlisted on November 14, 1861, at Dragoon Camp. Appears detached as a shoemaker on the September 12, 1863, company muster roll. He continues on the rolls as detached as a shoemaker through April 30, 1864. Paid $41.60 on March 4, 1863, for service from January 1 to February 28, 1863. Here he is shown as a Private in the Mobile Dragoons.

Bonifay, Felix J., Pvt./Corporal Co. D.
Enlisted on November 1, 1862, at Camp Tatnall, Florida. Muster Roll for September/October reports that he joined on November 1, 1863, at Camp Lomax, Florida. Promoted to 3rd Corporal from the ranks on January 1, 1864. POW surrendered at Citronelle, Alabama, on May 4, 1865, and paroled at Gainesville, Alabama, on May 14, 1865. Residence Pensacola, Escambia County, Florida.

Bonifay, M., Sergeant/Pvt. Co. C.
Enlisted on April 19, 1862, at Blakeley, Alabama. He appears on a list as a billing clerk with Surgeon's Certificate in the commissary department at Mobile, Alabama, for October 1, 1864. He appears on a list for the month of July 1864, as a wagon master at the military post of Mobile, Alabama, employed from December 10, 1863. Appears on a list of Confederate POW's on detached service in the Commissary Department CSA that were surrendered at Citronelle, Alabama, on May 4, 1865, and paroled at Meridian, Mississippi, on May 14, 1865. Residence Mobile, Alabama. He also appears on a roll of POW's of Co. C., 15th Confederate Cavalry that was surrendered on May 4, 1865, at Citronelle. * Pay vouchers and Special Order No. 96 assigning him to duty in Commissary Department is in his file.

Bonifay, R. H., Pvt. Co. D.
Enlisted on October 25, 1863, at Mobile, Alabama., by Lieutenant Rice for three years. Appears absent on detached service at Mobile by order of General Maury on a company muster roll for September/October 1863. November/December 1863, he is reported on the roll as absent with leave, thereafter he is shown as having deserted on January 5, 1864.

Bonner, A., Pvt. Co. K.
Appears on a roll of POW's of Company K, 15th Confederate Cavalry, CSA that were surrendered at Citronelle, Alabama, on May 4, 1865, and paroled at Gainesville, Alabama, on May 14, 1865. Residence Choctaw County, Alabama.

Bonner, Thomas, Pvt. Co. K.
Enlisted on March 17, 1862, at Washington County, Alabama. A Certificate of Disability is in his file and dated May 28, 1864. He was examined at Demopolis, Alabama. Appears on a roll of POW's of Company K, 15th Confederate Cavalry, CSA that were surrendered at Citronelle, Alabama, on May 4, 1865, and paroled at Gainesville, Alabama, on May 14, 1865. Residence Choctaw County, Alabama. He also appears on a roll of POW's on Tax in Kind duty 5th Congressional District of Alabama, CSA commanded by Captain T. C. Clark A. Q. M. that was surrendered at Citronelle on May 4, 1865. Here he is shown as having been paroled at Columbus, Mississippi, on May 18, 1865.

Bonnett, P. A., Pvt. Co. G.
Enlisted on June 2, 1863, at Camp Taylor. Appears as a deserter on a morning report of the Provost Marshal at New Orleans, Louisiana. Confined on March 16, 1864, by Captain Noyes, Provost Marshal, Ship Island, Mississippi. Signed a Oath of Allegiance to the USA at New Orleans, on March 17, 1864. Deserted from Bayou La Batre, Alabama on February 24, 1864. Complexion-dark, hair-brown, eyes-brown, 5 foot 8 inches.

Boon, Andrew J., Pvt. Co. C.
Enlisted on April 9, 1862, at Blakeley, Alabama. Appears on a roll of POW's and deserters from the CSA Army that entered the military lines of the 16th U.S. Army Corps during April 1865. Reported voluntarily and took the amnesty oath. Captured on April 18, 1865.

Boon, Cyrus, Pvt. Co. D.
Enlisted on March 16, 1863, at Camp Tatnall, Florida. Died on December 2, 1863, at Mobile, Alabama.

Boone, William J., Pvt. Co. B.
Enlisted on March 14, 1862, at Marianna, Florida. Appears absent on a September 12, 1863, company muster roll, detailed in Enrolling Office by order of General Maury from July 9. Appears on a list of POW's surrendered at Tallahassee, Florida, on May 10, 1865. Paroled on May 10, 1865, at Tallahassee, Florida.

Boroughs, Zed, Pvt. Co. A.
Enlisted on June 9, 1863, at Camp Lomax, Florida.

Bosarge, J. V., Pvt. Co. G.
Enlisted on September 13, 1862, at Dragoon Camp. Signed by his mark.

Bosarge, M., Pvt. Co. G.
Enlisted on March 1, 1862, at Dragoon Camp.

Boswell, James, Pvt. Co. L.
Appears on a record of CSA soldiers paroled at Headquarters of the 16th U.S. Army Corps at Montgomery, Alabama, on May 19, 1865. Hair-black, eyes-dark, complexion-dark, 6 foot 2 inches. His parole is in his file.

15TH CONFEDERATE CAVALRY

Bourg, A., Pvt. Co. G.
Enlisted on June 15, 1863, at Camp Taylor. Appears on a roll of POW's of divers companies and regiments (detached) CSA that were surrendered at Citronelle, Alabama, on May 4, 1865, and paroled at Meridian, Mississippi, on May 12, 1865. Residence New Orleans, Louisiana. He also appears on a roll of POW's of Co. G., 15th Confederate Cavalry that was surrendered on May 4, 1865, at Citronelle, on May 4, 1865.

Bowen, Joshua, Pvt. Co. D.
Enlisted on April 24, 1862, at Pensacola, Florida. POW captured on September 6, 1863, at Pensacola, Florida. Confined at the Custom House at New Orleans, Louisiana, from October 6, 1863. Exchanged at New Orleans on August 21, 1864.

Bowles, Nicholas A., Pvt. Co. B.
Enlisted on February 4, 1863, at Marianna, Florida. POW surrendered at Tallahassee, Florida, on May 11, 1865. Paroled on May 22, 1865, at Quincy, Florida.

Bowman, H. P., Pvt. Co. D.
Enlisted on September 24, 1862, at Camp Tatnall, Florida. Appears sick on a company muster roll for September 12, 1863, at home in Escambia County, Florida. Appears absent without leave since August 26, 1863, on the September/October 1863 muster roll. January/February roll reports that he deserted on August 26, 1863.

Bracken, R., Pvt. Co. C.
Enlisted on April 15, 1863, at Stockton, Alabama. Pvt. Robert Bracken, Co. C, 15th Confederate Cavalry appears on a roll of POW's of Company G and C, 12th Mississippi Cavalry, CSA that were surrendered at Citronelle, Alabama, on May 4, 1865, and paroled at Mobile, Alabama, on May 14, 1865. Residence Baldwin County, Alabama.

Bradley, Hobbs, Pvt./Corporal Co. D.
Enlisted on October 20, 1864, at Camp Tatnall, Florida.

Bradley, John, Pvt. Co. I.
Enlisted on March 9, 1863, at Conecuh County, Alabama. Signed a Parole of Honor at Mobile, Alabama on April 21, 1865. *A poor copy of his parole is in his file.

Bragh, J., Pvt. Co. C.
Enlisted on September 3, 1862, at Shell Banks [Alabama].

Brasfield, R. M., Sergeant/Pvt. Co. H.
Enlisted on September 22, 1862, at Mobile, Alabama. Reduced to the ranks from 2nd Sergeant on March 26, 1864.

Bray, Henry, Pvt. Co. I.
Enlisted on February 11, 1863, at Coneuch County, Alabama. Appears on a list of CSA soldiers paroled at Milton, Florida on July 4, 1865.

Bray, L. B., Pvt. Co. D.
Enlisted on May 1, 1863, at Camp Tatnall, Florida. Signed the Oath of Allegiance to the USA and received a Certificate of Amnesty at Milton, Florida, on June 7, 1865. He states on an Amnesty Oath Petition "I am 64 years of age. My home is in Santa Rosa Co. Fla. I volunteered in Co. D, 15th Confdt. Cav. April 15, 1663, and served until October 2, 1864,

at which time I deserted. I have taken no further part in the existing Rebellion." Signed by "X" on June 9, 1865. *The oath, petition and certificate are in his file.

Breighthing, F., Pvt. Co. G.
Appears on a roll of POW's of Company G, 15th Confederate Cavalry, CSA that were surrendered Citronelle, Alabama, on May 4, 1865, and paroled at Gainesville, Alabama, on May 14, 1865. Residence Marengo County, Alabama.

Brent, W. D., Pvt. Co. D.
Enlisted on October 12, 1863, at Halls Mill, Alabama. Appears present on extra duty as Adjutant's Clerk on bi-monthly muster rolls from November 1863, through June 30, 1864. POW captured by Cavalry forces under Brigadier General Lucas at Mount Pleasant, Alabama, on April 11, 1865. Forwarded as POW from Mobile, Alabama, to Ship Island, Mississippi. Received at Ship Island, on May 13, 1865. Forwarded to New Orleans, Louisiana, on June 8, 1865.

Bressingham, M., Pvt. Co. G.
Enlisted on July 30, 1864, at Mobile, Alabama.

Brewer, W. P., Pvt. Co. I.
Enlisted on December 7, 1863, at Halls Mill, Alabama. Appears absent sick in hospital in Mobile, Alabama, on bi-monthly muster rolls for December 31, 1863, through June 30, 1864. His name appears on a register of effects of deceased soldiers in 1864. Left $56.50. He is buried at Confederate Rest Magnolia Cemetery, Mobile, AL.

Brewton, E. G., Pvt. Co. D.
Enlisted on September 17, 1862, at Camp Tatnall, Florida. Appears present on bi-monthly muster rolls for November 1863 through February 1864. Appears present on special duty as a guide with companies near Pensacola, Florida.

Brisk, Isaac, Pvt. Co. F.
Enlisted on October 1, 1861, at Mobile, Alabama. Appears absent detached as a government saddler at Mobile, Alabama, from May 7, 1862, by order of General Forney on company muster rolls from September 1864 through June 1864.

Britton, D. M., Pvt. Co. K.
Enlisted on September 23, 1862, at Camp Forney. Appears on a roll of POW's of Company K, 15th Confederate Cavalry, CSA that were surrendered at Citronelle, Alabama, on May 4, 1865, and paroled at Gainesville, Alabama, on May 14, 1865. Residence Wayne County, Mississippi. *His December 11, 1863, pay voucher is in his file.

Britton, F. B., Pvt. Co. K.
Enlisted on September 23, 1862, at Camp Forney.

Broadous, W. see Brodiss, Willis

Brock, J. W., Pvt. Co. I.
Enlisted on December 27, 1862, at Santa Rosa, Florida. POW captured on April 11, 1865, at Mount Pleasant, Alabama, by U.S. Cavalry forces commanded by Brigadier General Lucas. Appears on a list of POW's forwarded from Mobile, Alabama, to Ship Island, Mississippi.

15TH CONFEDERATE CAVALRY

Brodiss, Alfred, Pvt. Co. H.
Enlisted on September 11, 1863, at Halls Mill, Alabama. Appears on a descriptive list for October 1, 1863, at Halls Mill, Alabama, as a teamster. Born-Jackson County, Mississippi, age-17, eyes-grey, hair-light, 5 foot 2 inches. He then appears present on muster rolls from December 31, 1863, through April 30, 1864. June 30, 1864, roll reports that he was transferred to Captain Tobin's Battery on May 22, 1864, by order of Colonel H. Maury.

Brodiss, Thomas, Pvt. Co. H.
Enlisted on June 14, 1863, at West Pascagoula, Mississippi. Muster roll for December 31, 1863, through April 30, 1864, reports that he deserted to the enemy on December 31, 1864.

Brodiss, Willis, Pvt. Co. H.
Enlisted on June 14, 1863, at West Pascagoula, Mississippi. Company muster roll for December 31, 1863, through April 30. 1964, reports that he was absent without leave from January 7, 1864, to May 20, 1864. "Came in under Gen. Polks Proclamation. No horse in Co. during the time." POW surrendered at Citronelle, Alabama, on May 4, 1865. Paroled at Mobile, Alabama, on June 8, 1865. Residence-Jackson, County, Mississippi, age-30, eyes-dark, hair-brown, 5 foot 9 inches.

Brogdon, W. J., Pvt. Co. E.
Enlisted on July 18, 1863, at Camp Lomax, Florida. POW captured on April 11, 1865, at Mount Pleasant, Alabama, by U.S. Cavalry forces commanded by Brigadier General Lucas. He appears on a list of POW's that were forwarded to Ship Island, Mississippi.

Brooks, B. C., Pvt. Co. I.
Enlisted on December 17, 1863, at Halls Mill, Alabama.

Brooks, James A., Sergeant Co. A.
Enlisted on March 7, 1862, at Station 3 on the P & G RR., Florida.

Brooks, J. F., Pvt. Co. A.
Enlisted on March 7, 1862, at Station 3 on the P & G RR., Florida. March/April 1864, muster roll reports that he was detailed for twenty days from April 21, 1864, to go after a horse by order of General Maury. Appears present on May/June 1864, muster roll.

Brooks, William, Pvt. Co. I.
Enlisted on January 13, 1863, at Conecuh County, Alabama. He is reported absent sick at home in Covington County, Alabama, since the first of May on a company muster roll for September 12, 1863.

Brosnaham, John Andrews, Contract Surgeon
Paid $146 February 6, 1863, for service December 8, 1862, through February 5, 1863. Served in Myers' Battalion Cavalry CSA in Jan. 1863. *His payment voucher is in his file.

Brown, Alexander, Pvt. Co. D.
Enlisted on September 24, 1862, at Camp Tatnall. A company muster roll for September 12, 1863, reports him present on extra duty since last muster as blacksmith in the Quarter Master's Department. November/December muster roll shows him absent without leave, extra duty? On the January/February 1864, roll and thereafter he is reported to have deserted on December 23, 1863.

Brown, David, T., Pvt. Co. E.
Enlisted on February 4, 1864, at Halls Mill, Alabama.

Brown, E. J., Pvt. Co. H.
Appears on a roll of POW's of detached duty and men belonging to General Forrest command whose regiments have sent in their rolls, commanded by Colonel W. N. Brown commanding post that surrendered at Gainesville, Alabama. Residence Gainesville, Sumpter County, Alabama. Paroled at Gainesville on May 11, 1865. *He is the subject of Special Order No. 106 of April 15, 1865, signed by himself and **D. T. Hollman**. This order is in his file but very difficult to read. It appears to be reassignment as a courier at Department Headquarters and states that his command is at Greenville, Alabama, 70 miles south of Montgomery, Alabama.

Brown, Everet, Pvt. Co. I.
Enlisted on September 20, 1863, at (Halls Mill) Mobile County, Alabama. * See **W. E. Brown**.

Brown, Franklin, Pvt. Co. H.
Enlisted on August 3, 1863, at West Pascagoula, Mississippi. A company muster roll for September/October 1863, reports that he was transferred, irregularly mustered and turned over to his command by Major Stead.

Brown, I. L., P. M.
Appears on a list of POW's that were surrendered at Tallahassee, Florida, on May 10, 1865. Paroled on May 17, 1865, at Madison, Florida.

Brown, J. I., Pvt. Co. A.
Enlisted on May 6, 1864, at Madison, Florida. Appears on a list of POW's that were surrendered at Tallahassee, Florida. Paroled on May 17, 1865, at Madison, Florida.

Brown, S. T., Pvt. Co. I.
POW captured at Mount Pleasant, Alabama, on April 11, 1865, by U.S. Cavalry forces under the command of Brigadier General T. J. Lucas. Forwarded from Mobile, Alabama, to Ship, Island, Mississippi.

Brown, W. E., Co. G, 3rd Regiment Confederate
Filed in error with Everet, Brown. He appears on a roll of POW's at Camp Douglas, Illinois. Captured at Murfreesboro, Tennessee, on January 1, 1862 [1863?]. A notation indicates that he may have been captured at the Battle of Stones River on January 7, 1863.

Bruner, M. J., Pvt. Co. K.
Enlisted on March 17, 1862, at Washington County, Alabama. Appears on a roll of POW's of Company K, 15th Confederate Cavalry, CSA that were surrendered at Citronelle, Alabama, on May 4, 1865, and paroled at Gainesville, Alabama, on May 14, 1865. Residence Choctaw County, Alabama.

Brunson, John R., Pvt. Co. B.
Enlisted on May 5, 1862, at Marianna, Florida. Appears on a list of POW's that were surrendered at Tallahassee, Florida, May 10, 1865. Paroled May 22, 1865, at Quincy, Fla.

Brunson, Joseph, Pvt. Co. B.
Enlisted on February 4, 1863, at Marianna, Florida. Appears on a list of POW's that were

surrendered at Tallahassee, Florida, on May 10, 1865. Paroled on May 22, 1865, at Quincey, Florida.

Brunson, William, Pvt. Co. B.
Enlisted on March 14, 1862, at Marianna, Florida. Admitted to Ross Hospital, Mobile, Alabama, on October 19, 1863, with debility. Sent to General Hospital, (Marianna, Florida) on October 24, 1863. March/April 1864, muster roll reports him discharged. Paid $369.12 as final payment on March 1, 1864, as follows. Pay as Private from May 1, 1863 to March 1, 1863 at $120 plus commutation for a horse 30 days at $120, plus commutation of clothing not drawn in kind at $128.72. His discharge reports him age-30, born-Edgefield District, South Carolina, eyes-hazel, hair-black, complexion-dark, 5 foot 11 inches, a school teacher by profession. He was discharged on March 1, 1864, at Bayou La Batre, Alabama, by reason of disability due to loss of vision of right eye and and partial loss of left in consequence of amaurosis. (loss of vision with no apparent pathologic condition of the eye) * His discharge and his certificate are in his file.

Bryan, A. S., Pvt. Co. H.
Enlisted on January 9, 1863, at Mobile, Alabama. The roll for December 31, 1863, through June 30, 1864, reports him discharged by order of General D. H.. Maury on June 7, 1864. Paid $171.17 on June September 7, 1864, for service, a horse and clothing from January 7, 1864, to June 5, 1864. Paid $62.80 for 5 months and 7 days pay, $62.80 for horse 157 days and $45.57 for commutation of clothing. Born in Rutherford County, Tennessee, age-36, eyes-blue, hair-dark, complexion-light, 6 foot. Discharged due to being a Justice of the Peace of Marengo County, Alabama, and by the order of General Maury. * His Certificate of Discharge is in his file.

Bryan, Daniel H., Sergeant Co. A.
Enlisted on April 7, 1862, at Montecello, Florida. Promoted from Corporal to 4th Sergeant on June 2, 1863. Appears on a list of POW's that were surrendered at Tallahassee, Florida, on May 10, 1865. Paroled on May 15, 1865, at Madison, Florida. Eyes-blue, hair-dark, complexion-dark, 5 foot 11 inches. *His parole is in his file.

Bryan, L. (Lawrence) L., Pvt. Co. C.
Enlisted on April 9, 1862, at Blakeley, Alabama. Appears on a list of POW's that were surrendered at Tallahassee, Florida, on May 10, 1865.

Bryan, R. U., Pvt. Co. K.
Enlisted on December 28, 1863, at Choctaw County, Alabama. Appears on a roll of POW's of Company K, 15th Confederate Cavalry, CSA that were surrendered at Citronelle, Alabama, on May 4, 1865, and paroled at Gainesville, Alabama, on May 14, 1865. Residence Choctaw County, Alabama.

Bryant, A. W., Pvt. Co. C.
Drew $144 pay on December 31, 1863, for service July 1 to December 31, 1863. Appears on a roll of POW's of Company C, 15th Confederate Cavalry, CSA that were surrendered at Citronelle, Alabama, on May 4, 1865, and paroled at Gainesville, Alabama, on May 14, 1865. Residence Baldwin County, Alabama.

Bryant, B. W., Pvt. Co. G.
Enlisted on January 1, 1864, at Mobile, Alabama

Bryant, H. W., Pvt. Co. C.
Enlisted on April 16, 1864, at Blakeley, Alabama. Detached on Special Order No. 11, Headquarters of the Gulf at Mobile, Alabama, on August 24, 1863. Muster rolls continue to report him thus until a roll for the period of December 31, 1863, through June 30, 1864. Here he is reported absent with leave. Appears on a register of paroled CSA POW's for the month of June 1865, by the Provost Marshal of the 16th U.S. Army Corps. Paroled June 9, 1865, at Montgomery, Alabama. Eyes-gray, hair-dark, complexion-dark, 5 foot 10 inches. *His parole and payment voucher are in his file.

Bryant, W. G., Pvt. Co. G.
Admitted to Ross Hospital, Mobile, Alabama, on January 7, 1865, with debilities. Sent to General Hospital at Greenville, Alabama, on February 6, 1865.

Bryars, C. (Cornelius), Pvt. Co. C.
Enlisted on October 31, 1862, at Camp Powell, Alabama. Appears on a list of CSA prisoners, that were paroled at Barrancas, Florida, on April 13, 1863. Taken at Perdido Bay on March 25, 1863. Age-28, eyes-blue, hair-light, complexion-light, 5 foot 10 inches, born-Baldwin County, Alabama, occupation-farmer. Appears absent, a paroled POW on company muster rolls from September 12, 1863, through October 31, 1863. He appears present thereafter through June 30, 1864. Appears on a roll of POW's of stragglers belonging to divers commands CSA that were surrendered at Meridian, Mississippi, in May 1865, and paroled at Mobile, Alabama, on May 19, 1865. Residence Baldwin County, Alabama.

Bryars, R. (Red) B. (Berry), Pvt. Co. C.
Enlisted on October 15, 1862, at Camp Powell, Alabama. He was elected State Legislator from Baldwin County, Alabama, and appears absent with leave on all muster rolls from September 12, 1863, through June 30, 1864. Mr. R. B. Bryars was elected and served in the Alabama Legislature from Baldwin County, Alabama in 1863. Born 1819, Died 1870. Buried in James Bryars Cemetery at Stockton, Alabama.

15TH CONFEDERATE CAVALRY

Bryars, W. L., Pvt. Co. C.
  Enlisted on April 15, 186_, at Stockton, Alabama. November/December 1863, company muster roll reports that he died on December 15.

Bryson, Henry, Pvt. Co. D.
  Enlisted on December 24, 1863, at Halls Mill, Alabama. Appears on a roll of stragglers paroled at Selma, Alabama, by Colonel William R. Marshall, 7th Minnesota Volunteers, in June of 1865.

Buck, W. J., Pvt. Co. C.
  Appears on a roll of POW's of Co. C., 15th Confederate Cavalry CSA that were surrendered at Citronelle, Alabama, on May 4, 1865, and paroled at Gainesville, Alabama, on May 14, 1865. Residence Mobile City, Alabama.

Bullock, Charles W., Pvt. Co. B.
  Enlisted on February 23, 1863, at Marianna, Florida. Appears present on extra duty by order of Colonel Maury on company muster rolls for September 1863, through June 30, 1864. He was reported as a waggoner for part of this time and without a horse for the entire period. Drew clothing on September 10, 1864.

Burdin, James F., Co. D.
  Appears on a roll of POW's at Fort Pickens, Florida, on January 8, 1865 until transferred on January 11, 1865.

Burgess, J., Pvt. Co. C.
  Enlisted on August 4, 1863, at Camp Powell, Alabama. POW captured on March 30, 1865, at his own house near Spanish Fort, Alabama, by 2nd Brigade, 2nd Division U.S. Army. "Claims to be a deserter from CSA." POW received at Ship Island, Mississippi, on April 1, 1865, from Lieutenant J. T. Turner, Provost Marshal at Dauphin Island, Alabama. Transferred from Ship Island to Vicksburg, Mississippi on May 1, 1865.

Burns, M. C., Pvt. Co. A.
  Enlisted on March 12, 1862, at Station No. 3 of the P & G RR, in Florida. March/April 1864 muster roll reports him detailed in Tobins Home Artillery on October 10, 1863, by order of Colonel H. Maury. May/June muster roll he is reported absent on sick furlough. A card in his file reports him discharged on Surgeon's Certificate of Disability.

Bush, R. H. see Rush, R. H.

Butler, A. H., Pvt. Co. E.
  Enlisted on September 18, 1861, at Milton, Florida.

Butler, C. H., Pvt. Co. A.
  Enlisted on May 4, 1864, at Madison, Florida.

Butler, James, Pvt. Co. A.
  Enlisted at Camp Lomax, Florida, on February 9, 1862. He signed a Oath of Amnesty on July 11, 1865, at Milton Florida. "I am 60 years of age my house is in Santa Rosa Co. Fla. I volunteered in Co. A, 15th Confd. Cav. Feby 9, 1863, and served until March 7, 1865. I have taken no further part in the existing Rebellion." He also signed a Oath of Allegiance the same day. Both are in his file.

Buzbee, B. S., Sergeant Co. A.
Enlisted on April 21, 1863, at Monticello, Florida. Appears on a roll of POW's of Company F, 15th Confederate Cavalry, CSA that were surrendered at Citronelle, Alabama, on May 4, 1865, and paroled at Gainesville, Alabama, on May 14, 1865. Residence Wacalla [Wakulla] County, Florida.

Burd, George, Pvt. Co. H.
Enlisted on December 4, 1862, at Mobile, Alabama.

C

Cain, R. P., Pvt. Co. C.
Enlisted on April 9, 1862, at Blakeley, Alabama. Appears on a roll of POW's of detachment of Company C, 15th Confederate Cavalry, CSA that were at Citronelle, Alabama, on May 4, 1865, and paroled at Gainesville, Alabama, on May 14, 1865. Residence Baldwin County, Alabama.

Callaway, John H., Sergeant/Pvt. Co. B.
Enlisted on March 14, 1862, at Marianna, Florida. Appears on a list of POW's that were surrendered at Tallahassee, Florida, on May 11, 1865. Surrendered on May 11, 1865, and paroled at Quincy Florida, on May 25, 1865. Here he is shown as a private.

Caller, E. M., Pvt. Co. C. filed with Collins, E. M.

Calloway, J. A., Pvt. Co. C.
Enlisted on April 15, 1862, at Stockton, Alabama. Appears on a roll of POW's as a member of Company C, 15th Confederate Cavalry, CSA that were surrendered at Citronelle, Alabama, on May 4, 1865, and paroled at Meridian, Mississippi, on May 11, 1865. Residence Baldwin County, Alabama.

Calloway, John G., Pvt. Co. C.
Enlisted on April 15, 1862, at Stockton, Alabama.

Cameron, Archibald, Pvt. Co. D.
Enlisted on May 1, 1862, at Pensacola, Florida. Appears on a September 12, 1863, company muster roll on extra duty as a guide by order of General Clanton.

Cameron, Daniel, Co. D.
His name appears on a register of claims of deceased soldiers from Arkansas and Florida which were filed for settlement. Enlisted on May 8, 1862, at Pensacola, Florida. Born-Santa Rosa, County, Florida, age-27, 5 foot 2 inches, complexion-fair, hair-light, eyes-blue, by profession a farmer, by **Martha Cameron**-widow. Paid $173.84 for service May 8, 1862, to September 19. 1862, bounty and clothing. *The settlement paper is in his file.

Cammack, A., Pvt. Co. C.
Appears on a roll of POW's of detachment of Company C, 15th Confederate Cavalry, CSA that were surrendered at Citronelle, Alabama, on May 4, 1865, and paroled at Gainesville, Alabama, on May 14, 1865. Residence Baldwin County, Alabama.

Campbell, Allen, Pvt. Co. I.
Enlisted on February 7,. 1863, at Conecuh, County, Alabama. He is reported as deserted on muster rolls December 31, 1863, through April 30, 1864.

15TH CONFEDERATE CAVALRY

Campbell, C. E., Pvt. Co. E.
Enlisted on May 8, 1862, at Warrington, Florida. His name appears on a roll of POW's captured at Mount Pleasant, Alabama, on April 11, 1865, by U.S. Cavalry forces under the command of Brigadier General T. J. Lucas. The roll is dated from Claiborne, Alabama. He is later reported on a list of POW's forwarded from Mobile, Alabama, to Ship Island, Mississippi.

Campbell, Charles, Pvt. Co. D.
Enlisted on May 1, 1862, at Pensacola, Florida. Appears absent, a paroled POW since April 13, 1862, on a company muster roll for September 12, 1863. Muster roll for September/October 1863, reports him present but absent without leave for two days since last muster [September 12, 1863?]. Reported absent without leave on November/December 1863, muster roll. The roll for January/February 1864, reports him as deserted on December 23, 1863. He is shown thus on all rolls thereafter.

Campbell, D. A., Corporal/Sergeant Co. E.
Enlisted on September 17, 1861, at Milton, Florida. Promoted from 2nd Corporal to 5th Sergeant on May 1, 1864.

Campbell, J. D., Pvt. Co. E.
Enlisted on May 3, 1862, at Warrington, Florida. Muster roll for March/April 1864, reports. "Deserted from Halls Mills, Ala. about 15 Jany. 64. Has probably gone to the enemy."

Campbell, J. S., Pvt. Co. F.
Enlisted on October 19, 1862, at Camp Withers, Alabama. Appears on a roll of POW's as a member of Company F, 15th Confederate Cavalry, CSA that were surrendered at Citronelle, Alabama, on May 4, 1865, and paroled at Gainesville, Alabama, on May 14, 1865. Residence Mobile County, Alabama.

Campbell, M., Pvt. Co. I.
Enlisted on October 4, 1862, at Santa Rosa, Florida. Muster roll for November/December 1864, reports him as deserted. Paid $134.13 on a descriptive list for clothing on April 14, 1864. [This man and **Malcom Campbell** following may be one and the same.]

Campbell, M. McL., Pvt. Co. E.
Enlisted on May 8, 1862, at Warrington, Florida.

Campbell, Malcom, Pvt. Co. I.
Enlisted on February 2, 186_, at Conecuh County, Alabama. Appears absent sick at home [in] Florida since July 6th on a company muster roll for September 12, 1863. Muster roll for September/October 1864, reports him absent without leave since October 1, 1863.

Campbell, R. H., Pvt. Co. F.
Enlisted on February 8, 1863, at Camp Withers, Alabama. Appears on a roll of POW's as a member of Company F, 15th Confederate Cavalry, CSA that were surrendered at Citronelle, Alabama, on May 4, 1865, and paroled at Gainesville, Alabama, on May 14, 1865. Residence Wayne County, Mississippi.

Campbell, Robert H., Pvt. Co. H.
Enlisted on June 5, 1863, at West Pascagoula, Jackson County, Mississippi.

Campbell, W. A., Pvt. Co. F.
Appears on a roll of POW's as a member of Company F, 15th Confederate Cavalry, CSA that were surrendered at Citronelle, Alabama, on May 4, 1865, and paroled at Gainesville, Alabama, on May 14, 1865. Residence Mobile, Mobile County, Alabama.

Campbell, W. P., Pvt. Co. E.
Enlisted on September 17, 1861, at Milton Florida.

Capers, Gabriel, Pvt. Co. A.
Enlisted on April 1, 1863, at Camp Lomax, Florida. Company muster roll for March/April 1864, reports that he deserted from Halls Mill, Alabama, on March 1, 1864.

Capp, Bishop, Pvt. Co. K., see **Cupp, Bishop**

Capp, M. J., Pvt. Co. K., see **Cupp, M. J.**

Caral, W. K., Pvt. Co. K., see **Carrell, W. K.**

Carbonnet, J. A., Pvt. Co. G. see **Charbonnet, J. A.**

Carley, J. F., Pvt. Co. H. see **Carllie, J. T.**

Carlie, J. T., Pvt. Co. H.
Enlisted on March 11, 1863, at Mobile, Alabama. POW captured at Ena, Mississippi, on December 6, 1864. Transferred from New Orleans, Louisiana, to Ship Island, Mississippi, on January 22, 1865. Received as a POW at Ship Island on January 25, 1865. Transferred to Vicksburg, Mississippi, on May 1, 1865.

Carlisle, Eli, Pvt. Co. D.
Enlisted January 1, 1863, at Camp Lomax, Florida. November/December 1863, muster roll reports him under arrest at Mobile, Alabama, absent without leave. "Ninety days since paid last." Appears absent without leave on a muster roll for January/February 1864.

Carman, W. H., Corporal, Co. A.
Enlisted on March 7, 1862, at Station 3 P & G Railroad, Florida. Promoted from Private to Corporal June 2, 1863. Appears on a list of POW's that were surrendered by Major General Sam Jones CSA to Brigadier General E. M. McCook USA at Tallahassee, Florida, on May 10, 1865. Paroled on May 15, 1865. Hair-dark, eyes-gray, complexion-light, 6 foot 2 inches. *His Oath of Allegiance is in his file.

Carney, James A., Pvt. Co. H.
Enlisted on May 14, 1862, at Mobile, Alabama. Appears on a roll of POW's of divers companies and regiments CSA that were surrendered at Citronelle, Alabama, on May 4, 1865, and paroled at Meridian, Mississippi, on May 17, 1865. Residence shown was Mobile, Alabama.

Carney, W. (William) M., Pvt. Co. H.
Enlisted on May 16, 1862, at Mobile, Alabama. Appears on a roll of POW's as a member of Company H, 15th Confederate Cavalry, CSA that were surrendered at Citronelle, Alabama, on May 4, 1865, and paroled at Gainesville, Alabama, on May 14, 1865. Residence Baldwin County, Alabama.

15TH CONFEDERATE CAVALRY

Carnley, George M., Pvt. Co. I.
Enlisted on October 4, 1862, at Santa Rosa, Florida. A muster roll for September 12, 1862, reports him absent without leave since May 8, 1863. November/December 1863, muster roll reports him deserted. On a roll for the period from December 31, 1863, through April 30, 1864, he is shown present on detached duty by order of Colonel Maury. On special duty with battery and no horse. May/June 1864 roll reports him transferred to Tobin's Battery on June 6, 1864. See also Tobin's Company, Tennessee, Artillery and Cawthon's Company, 6th Florida.

Carpenter, C. H., Pvt. Corporal Co. F.
Enlisted on September 16, 1862, at Camp Wither's, Alabama. September/October 1863, rolls reports that he has been detailed on October 31, 1863, to drive cattle in Baldwin County, Alabama, by order of General Maury. After March 1864, he is shown as 3rd Corporal. Appears on a roll of POW's as a member of Company F, 15th Confederate Cavalry, CSA that were surrendered at Citronelle, Alabama, on May 4, 1865, and paroled at Gainesville, Alabama, on May 14, 1865. Residence Baldwin County, Alabama. *There is also a card in his file showing **C. N. Carpenter**, Pvt. Co. I, 15th Regiment Confederate as a POW at Fort Delaware, Delaware, received from Gettsburg [Gettysburg?] in July 1863.

Carrell, W. H., Pvt. Co. K.
Enlisted on March 17, 1862, at Washington County, Alabama. Company muster roll for December 31, 1863, through April 30, 1864, reports him absent detached as a guard for commissary stores at Mobile, Alabama. Appears on a roll of POW's as a member of Company K, 15th Confederate Cavalry, CSA that were surrendered at Citronelle, Alabama, on May 4, 1865, and paroled at Gainesville, Alabama, on May 14, 1865. Residence shown was Choctaw County, Alabama.

Carroll, W. H. see **Carrell, W. H.**

Carrton, L. see **Cawthorn, L. F.**

Carrton, W. J., see **Cawthorn, William**

Carter, E. S. R., Pvt. Co. G.
Enlisted on July 30, 1861, at Dragoon Camp.

Carter, J. F., Pvt. Co. G.
Enlisted on May 19, 1863, at Camp Taylor. Appears on a roll of POW's as a member of Company G, 15th Confederate Cavalry, CSA that were surrendered at Citronelle, Alabama, May 4, 1865, and paroled at Gainesville, Alabama, May 14, 1865. Residence Jackson County, Mississippi.

Carter, J. P., Pvt. Co. G.
Enlisted on May 26, 1864, at Camp Taylor.

Carter, N. T., Pvt. Co. G.
He was enlisted on August 19, 1863, at Halls Mill, Alabama. He appears present under arrest on a company muster roll for September 12, 1863. September/October 1863, muster roll reports him present while the November/December 1863, roll shows him absent in arrest.

Carter, W. G., Pvt. Co. G.
   Enlisted on May 16, 1863, at Camp Taylor. *A requisition for 1 jacket and one pair of pants is in his file. Appears on a roll of POW's of 9 Regiment Mississippi Cavalry CSA that were surrendered at Meridian Mississippi, in May 1865, and paroled at Mobile, Alabama, on May 23, 1865. Residence Jackson County, Mississippi.

Carter, W. P., Co. G.
   Appears on a company muster roll as having been transferred to Major Steeds Command by command of General Maury. See petition in file of Pvt. Lewis Roberts.

Carter, W. W., Co. H.
   Enlisted on May 7, 1864, at Gonzalia, Florida. Appears on a roll of POW's of Berry's Regiment CSA that were surrendered at Citronelle, Alabama, on May 4, 1865, and paroled at Mobile, Alabama, on May 20, 1865. Residence Perry County, Mississippi.

Cartrett, H., Pvt. Co. C.

Cartright, Coatright, Henry R.
   Enlisted on December 28, 1863, at Halls Mill, Alabama.

Cartrett, J. V., Pvt. Co. C.
   Enlisted on April 15, 1862, at Stockton, Alabama. He appears absent as a paroled POW (Fort Pickens April 18, 1863) on a company muster roll for September 12, 1863. Muster roll for December 31, 1863, through June 30, 1864, reports that he died.

Carter, E. L., 1st Lieutenant Co. I.
   Enlisted on October 4, 1862, at Santa Rosa, Florida. Elected 1st Lieutenant on October 4, 1862. Paid $100 per month as a 1st Lieutenant. Resigned on December 19, 1863, as he was elected senator from Santa Rosa County, Florida. He appears on a roster of Co. I at Spring Hill on January 1, 1865. *His resignation and pay vouchers are in his file.

Cato, A., Pvt. Co. G.
   Enlisted on March 12, 1863, at Halls Mill, Alabama.

Cato, William, Pvt. Co. G.
   Enlisted on September 12, 1863, at Camp Taylor. He appears on a list of POW's. No Date. "Horse thief and spy. Captured by two companies of the 3 Michigan Cavalry stationed at Whistler, Ala. If any witnesses or proof of the facts are wanted send to Lt. Col. Richd Ritter 28 Ill Infty Vols. Comdg U.S. Forces at Whistler, Ala."

Caton, A. D., Pvt. Co. E.
   Signed a parole at the Headquarters of the 16th U.S. Army, Montgomery, Alabama, on June 2, 1865. Hair-dark, eyes-dark, complexion-fair, 5 foot 11 inches.

Cawthon, John K., Pvt. Co. B.
   Enlisted on February 13, 1863, at Marianna, Florida. Appears on a list of POW's that were surrendered at Tallahassee, Florida, on May 10, 1865. Surrendered and paroled at Quincy, Florida on May 11, 1865.

Cawthorn, L. F., Pvt. Co. I.
   Enlisted on April 21, 1864, at Santa Rosa, Florida. POW captured by a portion of Federal Troops under command of Brigadier General Asboth on a raid into the interior of Western

15TH CONFEDERATE CAVALRY

Florida and forwarded to New Orleans, Louisiana, on the steamer *Clinton* on October 8, 1864. He was captured at Walton, County, Florida, (Shoal River) (Marianna, Florida) on September 22, 1864. He appears on a roll of POW's at New Orleans, transferred to Ship Island, Mississippi, October 20, 1864. Appears on a roll of POW's at Ship Island, that were sent to New York on November 5, 1864. Received at Fort Columbus, New York Harbor from Ship Island on November 16, 1864. Appears on a roll, dated April 30, 1865, of POW's at Elmira, New York, who wish to take the Oath of Allegiance to the US. Joined (was committed to) Elmira Prison on November 20, 1864. "Was conscripted April 20, 1864. Has always been opposed to the rebellion. Desires to go to Pensacola, Florida." Hair-dark, eyes-blue, complexion-dark, 5 foot 7 ½ inch. Place of residence shown as Evergreen Depot, Alabama. Signed the Oath of Allegiance at Elmira, New York, and released June 23, 1865.

Cawthorn, William J., Pvt. Co. I.
Enlisted on April 21, 1864, at Santa Rosa, Florida. POW captured by a portion of Federal Troops under command of Brigadier General Asboth on a raid into the interior of Western Florida and forwarded to New Orleans, Louisiana, on the steamer *Clinton* on October 8, 1864. Captured at Walton, County, Florida, (Shoal River) (Marianna, Florida) on September 22, 1864. He appears on a roll of POW's at New Orleans, transferred to Ship Island, Mississippi, October 20, 1864. Appears on a roll of POW's at Ship Island, that were sent to New York on November 5, 1864. Received at Fort Columbus, New York Harbor from Ship Island on November 16, 1864. Transferred from Fort Columbus to Elmira Prison, New York, on November 19, 1864. Died at Elmira, New York of febris typhoid on February 26, 1865. His death record reports him to have been born in America, age-34, married and a resident of Washington County, Florida. He is shown as No. 1916 and buried at Elmira. Grave location No. 2347. * His death record is in his file.

Cazalas, John B., Pvt. Co. H.
Enlisted on September 4, 1862, at Mobile, Alabama. Appears on a roll of POW's as a member of Company H, 15th Confederate Cavalry, CSA that were surrendered at Citronelle, Alabama, on May 4, 1865, and paroled at Gainesville, Alabama, on May 14, 1865. Residence Mobile County, Alabama.

Chadwick, Issac J. G., Pvt. Co. G.
Enlisted on September 12, 1862, at Dragoon Camp. POW captured at Cedar Point, Mobile Bay, Alabama on March 2, 1865. He appears on a roll of Confederate prisoners forwarded from Dauphin Island, Alabama, on March 19, 1865, to the Provost Marshal at New Orleans, Louisiana. Confined at New Orleans on March 21, 1864, exchanged on May 11, 1865. Admitted to USA General Hospital No. 2, Vicksburg, Mississippi, on May 22, 1865 with acute diarrhoea. Died May 29, 1865.

Chalon, J. O., Pvt. Co. G.
Enlisted on June 15, 1863, at Camp Taylor. Appears on a roll of POW's paroled on May 22, 1865. Age-42, eyes-hazel, hair-black, complexion-dark, 6 foot, residence New Orleans, Louisiana.

Chapman, Reuben, Pvt. Co. H.
Enlisted on November 22, 1862, at Gainesville, Alabama.

Chapman, T. W., Pvt. Co. K.
Enlisted on April 19, 1863, at Halls Mill, Alabama. Appears on a roll of POW's as a member of Company K, 15th Confederate Cavalry, CSA that were surrendered at Citronelle,

Alabama, on May 4, 1865, and paroled at Gainesville, Alabama, on May 14, 1865. Residence Wayne County, Mississippi. Card in his file referrers to personal papers of **Jonathon Foscue** of McKellar's/White's Alabama Cavalry. Age-23, eyes-black, hair-black, complexion-dark, 6 foot 1 inch, born in Jasper, Mississippi. A farmer by occupation. See pay voucher in the file of **Pvt. Jonathon Foscue**.

Charbonnet, J. A., Pvt. Co. G.
Enlisted on June 24, 1863, at Camp Taylor.

Charbonnett, J. N., Pvt. Co. G.
Enlisted on June 10, 1863, at Camp Taylor.

Cherry, A. S., Pvt. Co. C.
Enlisted on October 31, 1862, at Camp Powell, Alabama. POW surrendered at Citronelle, Alabama, on May 4, 1865. Paroled at Mobile, Alabama, on June 7, 1865. Age-31, complexion-florid, eyes-grey, hair-sandy, 6 foot, residence Clarke County, Alabama.

Cherry, Josephus, Pvt. Co. H.
Enlisted on September 4, 1862, at Mobile, Alabama. His name appears on a roll of POW's of stragglers of various regiments CSA that were surrendered at Citronelle, Alabama, on May 4, 1865, and paroled at Mobile, Alabama, on May 21, 1865. Residence Mobile County, Alabama.

Cherry, W. H. H. (William Harrison?), Pvt. Co. C.
Enlisted on October 31, 1862, at Camp Powell, Alabama. POW surrendered at Citronelle, Alabama, on May 4, 1865. Paroled at Mobile, Alabama, on June 7, 1865. Age-24, complexion-fair, eyes-light, hair-sandy, 6 foot, residence Clarke County, Alabama.

Chesnut, A. H., Pvt. Co. K.
Enlisted on May 8, 1862, at Mobile, Alabama. Appears on a roll of POW's as a member of Company K, 15th Confederate Cavalry, CSA that were surrendered at Citronelle, Alabama, on May 4, 1865, and paroled at Gainesville, Alabama, on May 14, 1865. Residence Choctaw County, Alabama.

Chesnut, Jasper, Pvt. Co. I.
Enlisted on February 2, 1863, at Conecuh County, Alabama. Appears absent without leave since May 10, on a company muster roll for September 12, 1863. He appears absent in arrest on a company muster roll for September/October 1863. November/December 1863, muster roll reports that he was absent without leave since December 29, 1863. Reported to have deserted on the muster roll for the period December 31, 1863, through April 30, 1864.

Childress, John, Pvt. Co. F.
Enlisted on December 6, 1862, at Camp Withers. Muster roll for September/October 1863, reports him absent sick since September 3, 1863. November/December 1863, roll reports him discharged on December 4, 1863.

Chilldress, M., Pvt. Co. F.
Enlisted on May 20, 1862, at Camp Withers. Muster roll for September, October, November and December 1863, reports him absent detailed at Government Fishery from September 17, 1863, by order of General Maury. A company muster roll for March/April 1864, reports that he deserted on December 28, 1863.

Clanahan, G. W., Pvt. Co. K.
Enlisted on October 8, 1862, at Camp Forney. Appears on a roll of POW's as a member of Company K, 15th Confederate Cavalry, CSA that were surrendered at Citronelle, Alabama, on May 4, 1865, and paroled at Gainesville, Alabama, on May 14, 1865. Residence was Choctaw County, Alabama. A descriptive list found in the file of Pvt. **W. R. McKee** shows the following information on this man. Age-34, eyes-blue, hair-dark, complexion-fair, 5 foot 9 inches, born-Coweta County, Georgia, a farmer by occupation.

Clark, A. E., Pvt. Co. G.
Enlisted on September 23, 1862, at Dragoon Camp.

Clarke, D. C. (David), Pvt. Co. A.
Enlisted on March 7, 1862, at Station 3 P & G RR, Florida. Appears on a list of POW's that were surrendered at Tallahassee, Florida, on May 10, 1865. Paroled at Thomasville, Georgia, on May 16, 1865. * His signed parole and pay vouchers are in his file.

Clary, J. B., Pvt. Co. I.
Enlisted on October 4, 1862, at Santa Rosa, Florida. September/October 1863, muster roll reports him absent on detached service with the artillery since October 18, 1863. [There may be two men represented in this file.]

Clary, R. M., Sergeant/Pvt. Co. I.
Enlisted as 2nd Sergeant on October 4, 1862, at Santa Rosa, Florida. On the September/October 1863, company muster roll he appears absent on detached service in artillery and reduced to ranks from Sergeant on September 1.

Clements, H. W., Pvt. Co. E.
Enlisted on December 19, 1862, at Camp Lomax, Florida.

Clements, J. M., Corporal/Sergeant Co. E.
Enlisted as 1st Corporal on September 17, 1861, at Milton, Florida. Promoted from 1st Corporal to 4th Sergeant on May 1, 1864. POW captured on April 12, 1865, at Morvella, Alabama, by General Lucas' Command. He appears on a list of POW's forwarded from Mobile, Alabama, to Ship Island, Mississippi.

Cleveland, G. H., Pvt. Co. H.
Appears on a roll of POW's of divers companies and regiments of the CSA that were surrendered at Citronelle, Alabama, on May 4, 1865, and paroled at Meridian, Mississippi, on May 10, 1865. Residence Mobile, Alabama.

Cleveland, H. K., 2nd Lieutenant Co. H.
Enlisted on September 4, 1862, at Mobile, Alabama. He signs the September 12, 1863, company muster roll as commanding the company. Lieutenant Cleveland requisitioned for Captain Murrell's Company the following articles on December 5, 1863, at Camp Halls Mill, Alabama; 42 jackets, 44 pair of pants, 46 shirts, 30 pair of drawers, and 2 pair boots. He signs the December 31, 1863, through April 30, 1864, as present and Inspection and Mustering Officer. He appears on a roster of the 15th Confederate Cavalry at Pollard, Alabama, on May 12, 1864. Lieutenant Cleveland requisitioned corn and fodder for 94 animals at Pollard, Alabama, for the months of April, May and June, 1864. He appears on a roster of the 15th Confederate Cavalry at Camp Cumming on July 12, 1864. His name appears on a roster of the 15th Confederate Cavalry at Spring Hill, Alabama, on January 1,

1865. **There are numerous pay vouchers and requisitions in his file. Signed a Parole of Honor at Gainesville, Alabama, on May 14, 1865. This document is filed in error with **Pvt. W. F. Cleveland**, Co. H, below. See also the file of **Captain John W. Murrell**.

Cleveland, W. F., Pvt. Co. H.
He appears on a company muster roll for December 31, 1863, through April 30, 1864. His presence or absence is not stated. He appears absent on furlough on a company muster roll for December 31, 1863, through June 30, 1864. His name appears on a roll of POW's as a member of Company H, 15th Confederate Cavalry, CSA that were surrendered by at Citronelle, Alabama, on May 4, 1865, and paroled at Gainesville, Alabama, on May 14, 1865. Residence Mobile, County, Alabama.

Clements, J. M. (Clemmens), Corporal/Sergeant Co. E.
Enlisted on September 17, 1861, at Milton, Florida. Promoted from Corporal to 4th Sergeant on May 1, 1864. POW captured on April 12, 1865, at Morvella, Alabama, by General Lucas's Command. Appears on a roll of POW's forwarded from Mobile, Alabama, to Ship Island, Mississippi. No date shown.

Clifford, P. B. (Pierre Breaton), Pvt. Co. K.
Enlisted on August 25, 1862, at Pascagoula, Mississippi. Appears on a roll of POW's as a member of Company K, 15th Confederate Cavalry, CSA that were surrendered at Citronelle, Alabama, on May 4, 1865, and paroled at Gainesville, Alabama, on May 14, 1865. Residence Jackson County, Mississippi.

Cobb, A. J., Pvt./Corporal Co. D.
Enlisted on May 1, 1862, at Pensacola, Florida. Promoted from ranks to 2nd Corporal on January 1, 1864. March/April muster roll reports him on special duty near Bluff Springs, Florida. See file of **Pvt. Columbus Jernigan**. The two men exchanged regimental positions on February 3, 1863. See also file of **J. A. Cobb** below.

Cobb, B. W. T., Pvt. Co. D.
Enlisted on May 1, 1862, at Pensacola, Florida. Muster roll for September 12, 1863, reports him on extra duty as a guide by order of General Clanton. He does not appear under heading present on this roll. September/October 1863, muster roll reports him absent sick at home in Santa Rosa, Florida, "Having served on extra duty for 60 days since last muster." He appears absent without leave on a company muster roll for November/December 1863. January/February 1864, reports him present but having been absent without leave for 41 days since last paid (April 30, 1863). March/April 1864, muster roll reports him absent sick from injuries received by a fall from his horse. He appears present on a company muster roll for May/June 1864. Signed by his mark.

Cobb, F. H., 1st Sergeant Co. D.
Enlisted on May 1, 1862, at Pensacola, Florida. Promoted from 4th Corporal on July 1863.

Cobb, F. (Francis) M., Pvt. Co. E.
Enlisted on May 15, 1862, at Gonzalia, [Florida]. POW paroled at Milton, Florida, on June 22, 1865.

Cobb, J. A., Pvt. Co. D.
Enlisted on February 3, 1864, at Halls Mill, Alabama. Reported to have exchanged [places] with **Pvt. Columbia Jerrigan** of Co. D. 6th Alabama Cavalry. See also file of **A. J. Cobb**. He appears absent on a company muster roll for May/June 1864. Here he is shown on

leave. He is shown as deserted on a muster roll for the period December 31, 1863, to April 30, 1864.

Colbert, William, Pvt. Co. C.
Enlisted on April 9, 1863, at Blakeley, Alabama. He appears, absent from the company detailed on guide duty on Perdido Bay, on company muster rolls for September through December 31, 1863.

Coleman, Columbus [Cornelius], Pvt. Co. D.
Enlisted on April 3, 1863, at Pollard, Alabama. Company muster rolls from September 12, 1863 through February 29, 1864, reports him on detached service as a driver at Pollard, Alabama, since April 3, 1863, by order of General Canty. Paid $48 on November 14, 1863, for service July and August 1863. His signed pay voucher for this payment is in his file. Muster roll for March/April 1864, he is shown present on special duty near Bluff Springs, Florida. May/June 1864, he is shown present. On May 22, 1864, his name appears on a list of detailed soldiers employed in the Subsistence Department at Pollard, Alabama. Drew clothing on August 28, 1864. Here he signed by mark. He is identified as a driver and herdsmen for the 15th Confederate Cavalry. *

Coleman, C. P., Pvt. Co. G.
Enlisted on May 23, 1863, at Camp Taylor. September/October 1863, muster roll reports him ordered to be transferred to Major Steed's Command by General Maury.

Coleman, N., Pvt. Co. K.
Enlisted on August 25, 1862, at Pascagoula, Mississippi. POW surrendered at Citronelle, Alabama, on May 4, 1865. Paroled at Mobile, Alabama, on June 1, 1865. Residence Jackson County, Mississippi. Age-35, complexion-light, eyes-dark, hair-auburn, 5 foot 11 ½ inches.

Coleman, R. H., Pvt. Co. K.
Enlisted on March 17, 1863, at Washington County, Alabama. On a muster roll for May/June 1864, he is reported present.

Collins, E. M., Pvt. Co. C.
Enlisted on May 15, 1864, at Camp Powell, Alabama. His name appears on a roll of POW's as a member of Company C, 15th Confederate Cavalry, CSA that were surrendered at Citronelle, Alabama, on May 4, 1865, and paroled at Gainesville, Alabama, on May 14, 1865. Residence Clarke County, Alabama. Here his name is shown as **E. M. Caller**.

Collins, P., Pvt. Co. F.
Enlisted on October 1, 1861, at Mobile, Alabama. Admitted to Ross Hospital, Mobile, Alabama, on January 16, 1865, with febris intermittens. Returned to duty on March 11, 1865, remarks: Camp Correction. On January 16 his complaint was inflammation.

Collins, Spencer H., Pvt. Co. E.
Enlisted on April 9, 1863, at Camp Lomax, Florida. A muster roll for March/April 1864, reports that he was discharged on Surgeon's Certificate of Disability at Mobile, on January 2, 1864.

Collins, William, Pvt. Co. A.
Enlisted on September 10, 1863, at Mobile, Alabama. Drew clothing on September 7, 1864.

Combie, G. F., Pvt. Co. D.
　Enlisted on September 5, 1862, at Camp Tatnall, Florida. Drew clothing on August 28, 1864. Signs by his mark.

Commyns, Joseph, Pvt. Co. D.
　Enlisted on August 27, 1862, at Camp Tatnall, Florida. January/February 1864, muster roll reports that he deserted on January 13, 1864.

Commyns, Thomas, Pvt. Co. C.
　Enlisted on October 31, 1862?, at Camp Powell, Alabama. September/October 1863, muster roll reports that he Decd [?] September 26, 1863.

Cone, Arnold, Pvt. Co. A.
　Enlisted on April 15, 1862, at Monticello, Florida. Appears on a list of POW's that were surrendered at Tallahassee, Florida, on May 10, 1865. Paroled at Tallahassee, Florida, on May 24, 1865.

Connel, W. T., Pvt. Co. A.
　Enlisted on February 27, 1864, at Monticello, Florida. His name appears on a list of POW's that were surrendered at Tallahassee, Florida, on May 10, 1865. Paroled at Tallahassee, on May 17, 1865.

Connick, James, Pvt. Co. F.
　Enlisted on October 1, 1861, at Mobile, Alabama. Appears on a roll of POW's as a member of Company F, 15th Confederate Cavalry, CSA that were surrendered at Citronelle, Alabama, on May 4, 1865, and paroled at Gainesville, Alabama, on May 14, 1865. Residence Mobile County, Alabama.

Conroy, James, Pvt. Co. F.
　Enlisted on October 1, 1861, at Mobile, Alabama. September through December 1863, muster roll reports him absent detached on September 20, 1862, with Engineer Department at Mobile. March/April 1864, roll reports that he was discharged on December 6, 1863, for disability.

Conroy, John, Pvt. Co. K.
　Enlisted on June 18, 1862, at Bayou La Batre, Alabama.

Conway, C. W., Pvt. Co. C.
　Enlisted April 9, 1864, at Blakeley, Alabama or April 26, 1864, at Camp Powell, Alabama.

Cook, John W., Pvt. Co. B.
　Enlisted on March 14, 1862, at Marianna, Florida. Appears on a roll of POW's as a member of Company F, 15th Confederate Cavalry, CSA that were surrendered at Citronelle, Alabama, on May 4, 1865, and paroled at Gainesville, Alabama, on May 14, 1865. Residence Henry County, Alabama.

Cook, Seaborn, Pvt. Co. B.
　Enlisted on April 10, 1864, at Gonzalia, Florida. May/June muster roll shows that he enlisted at Pollard, Alabama, on April 30, 1864, and was never paid.

Cooler, William, Co. A.
　Appears on a receipt roll for clothing on September 7, 1864.

15TH CONFEDERATE CAVALRY

Coon, Louis, Pvt. Co. E.
Enlisted on March 1, 1863, at Camp Lomax, Florida. Signed by his mark "X", a parole at Montgomery, Alabama, on June 9, 1865, at the headquarters of the 16th U.S. Army Corp. Hair-dark, eyes-blue, complexion-dark, 5 foot 6 inches. His parole is in his file.*

Cooper, C., Co. C.
His name appears on a receipt roll for clothing on August 28, 1864.

Cooper, H. S., Pvt. Co. D.
Enlisted on April 24, 1862, at Pensacola, Florida. Drew clothing on August 28, 1864. He signed by his mark. Signed by name on a parole at Montgomery, Alabama, on May 30, 1865, at the headquarters of the 16th U.S. Army Corp. Hair-dark, eyes-dark, complexion-fair, 5 foot 10 inches. His parole is in his file. *

Cooper, J. B., Sergeant Co. D.
Enlisted at Pensacola, Florida, on April 24, 1862. He was captured by a detachment of 1st Florida, U.S. Cavalry and 2nd Me. Cavalry under the command of Colonel Spurling of 2nd Me. Cavalry, at Escambia County, (Pine Barren) Florida, on November 17, 1864. His name appears on a register of POW's confined at New Orleans, Louisiana, on November 21, 1864, and transferred to Ship Island, Mississippi, on December 10, 1864. Arrived at Ship Island December 13, 1864. Transferred from Ship Island to Vicksburg, Mississippi, May 1, 1865.

Cooper, Joseph, Pvt. Co. G.
Enlisted on July 30, 1861, at Dragoon Camp. Drew clothing on June 20, 1864. Signed by his mark. Appears on a roll of POW's as a member of Company G, 15th Confederate Cavalry, CSA that were surrendered at Citronelle, Alabama, on May 4, 1865, and paroled at Gainesville, Alabama, on May 14, 1865. Residence Mobile, Mobile County, Alabama.

Cooper, M. P., Pvt. Co. D.
Enlisted on April 24, 1862, at Pensacola, Florida. Drew clothing on August 28, 1864. Signed by his mark. Signed a parole at Mobile, Alabama, on April 31, 1865, at Mobile, Alabama. His parole is in his file.*

Cope, J. W., Pvt. Co. K.
Enlisted on August 18, 1863, at Halls Mill, Alabama. His name appears on a descriptive list for September 8, 1863, where he is shown as age-18, eyes-hazel, hair-dark, 5 foot 9 inches, a student by occupation, born in Wake, North Carolina. He was paid $50 bounty for signing.

Cotton, A. B., Pvt. Co. I.
Enlisted on October 4, 1862, at Santa Rosa, Florida. Muster roll for December 31, 1863, through April 30, 1864, reports that he deserted. He appears on a muster roll for Co. C Detachment of troops from Camp of Correction ordered to duty by Major General D. H. Maury and commanded by Major R. A. Harris at the mouth of Dog River, near Mobile, Ala., August 31, 1864. Shown as a member of Co. C. Harris' Battalion RO, Camp of Correction.

Cotton, F. S., Pvt. Co. I.
Enlisted on October 4, 1862, at Santa Rosa, Florida. Muster roll for December 31, 1863, through April 30, 1864, reports him present joined from desertion with no pay due. May/June 1864, muster he is shown present.

Cowley, John, Pvt. Co. F.
Enlisted on October 1, 1861, at Mobile, Alabama. Appears on a roll of POW's as a member

of Company F, 15th Confederate Cavalry, CSA that were surrendered at Citronelle, Alabama, on May 4, 1865, and paroled at Gainesville, Alabama, on May 14, 1865. Residence Mobile, Mobile County, Alabama.

Cox, Aurelius P., Pvt. Co. B.
Enlisted March 14, 1862, at Marianna, Florida. His name appears on a list of POW's surrendered at Quincy, Florida, on May 11, 1865. Paroled at Quincy, Florida, May 23, 1865.

Cox, J. M., Pvt. Co. I.
Enlisted on December 27, 1862, at Santa Rosa, Florida.

Crabtree, Samuel, Pvt./Bugler Co. H.
Enlisted on September 4, 1862, at Mobile, Alabama.

Craig, T. A., Pvt. Co. K.
See file of **Felix Oswald**, Pvt. Co. K, who is reported as a substitute for T. A. Craig. Enlisted on January 15, 1864, at Mobile. Alabama. Appears on a roll of POW's as a member of Company K, 15th Confederate Cavalry, CSA that were surrendered at Citronelle, Alabama, on May 4, 1865, and paroled at Gainesville, Alabama, on May 14, 1865. Residence Choctaw County, Alabama.

Crane, Lewis, Pvt. Co. E.
Enlisted on December 10, 1863, at Camp Lomax, Florida. His name appears on a roll of POW's as a member of Company F, 15th Confederate Cavalry, CSA that were surrendered at Citronelle, Alabama, on May 4, 1865, and paroled at Gainesville, Alabama, on May 14, 1865. Residence Santa Rosa County Florida.

Craven, A. S., Pvt. Co. H.
Enlisted on April 27, 1864, at Halls Mill, Alabama. Admitted to Ross Hospital, Mobile, Alabama, on January 5, 1865, with ulcer on leg. Drew clothing at Ross Hospital, Mobile, as a patient on March 5, 1865. Returned to duty on March 9, 1865.

Crawford, James, Pvt. Co. I.
Enlisted on October 4, 1862, at Santa Rosa, Florida.

Crawford, William, Pvt. Co. I.
Enlisted on October 4, 1862, at Santa Rosa, Florida. His name appears on a list of POW stragglers that were paroled at Selma, Alabama, during June 1865. Residence shown as Wilcox County, Alabama. There is a petition for amnesty dated June 23, 1865, at Pensacola, Florida, in his file. "I am thirty years of age - my home is in Walton County Fla. I served in the Confederate Army 15th Confederate Cavalry about nine months when I deserted and went to my home where I remained ever since. This is all the aid I have ever given to the Confederate Gov."..." Wm. Crawford." [There seems to be two men's files mixed here]

Crawford, Willis, Pvt. Co. I.
Enlisted on April 1, 1863, at Conecuh, County, Alabama. [see **Pvt. William Crawford** file above]

Creevey, Thomas, Sergeant Co. F.
Enlisted on October 1, 1861, at Mobile, Alabama. Signed a Parole of Honor on May 14, 1865, at Gainesville, Alabama. This parole is in his file. He is shown as a 2nd Lieutenant here. POW, a member of Company F, 15th Confederate Cavalry, CSA that were surrendered

at Citronelle, Alabama, on May 4, 1865, and paroled at Gainesville, Alabama, on May 14, 1865.*

Crosby, A. T., Pvt. Co. C.
Card in his file relative to Special Order 98/15, Captain Arrington's Co. A. Crosby, Aug., a Pvt. in Captain Cottrills Co. [Mobile} City Troop May 3, 1862. Discharged from Co. A. City Troops, Alabama Volunteers on March 26, 1863. Enlisted on May 13, 1863. POW captured at Blakeley, Alabama, on April 1, 1865. Admitted to Engineer Brigade Hospital, Mobile, Alabama, with gun shot wound. Confined at New Orleans, Louisiana, on May 1, 1865. Released on parole on May 17, 1865.

Crow, J. L., Pvt. Co. E.
Enlisted on November 2, 1862, at Camp Lomax, Florida. He appears on a roll of privates employed on extra duty as a carpenter May 23 through June 9, 1864, building Commissary Warehouse at Greenville, Alabama. His pay vouchers for $45 at $3 extra per day are in his file. Discharged due to disability caused by complete amarosis of left eye and partial of right plus chronic diarrhoea at Mobile, Alabama, on June 27, 1864. Age-54, eyes-blue, hair-light, complexion-fair, 5 foot 9 inches, a mechanic by profession. Born is Essex County, Virginia.*

Crowder, W. T., Pvt. Co. I.
Enlisted on October 4, 1862, at Santa Rosa, Florida. Appears absent without leave since July 3 on company muster rolls for September/October 1863. Reported to have deserted on November/December 1863, muster roll.

Crowell, David J., Pvt. Co. A.
Enlisted on March 7, 1862, at Station 3 of the P&G. RR, Florida. POW captured at Gonzalez Station Florida by the 91st N. Y. Volunteers on October 28, 1862. Born Barnwell, South Carolina, age-22, eyes-gray, hair-auburn, complexion-light, 5 foot 9 inches. Signed a parole "We of the Magnolia Dragoons, Florida Cavalry Confederate States Army, do solemnly swear that we will not serve in any capacity against the United States until we shall be regularly exchanged, nor will we give any information directly or indirectly to any enemy or enemies of the United States to the injury or prejudice of the said United States." at Escambia Florida, Fort Pickens, November 12, 1862. Appears present on company muster rolls from September 12, 1863, through January 1, 1864. Appears on a list of POW's that were surrendered at Tallahassee, Florida, on May 10, 1865. Paroled at Tallahassee, Florida, on May 18, 1865. A card in his file references personal papers of **William. C. Clark,** Pvt. Co. A, 30th Battalion Florida, Cavalry.*

Cruthirrds, W. D., Pvt. Co. H.
Enlisted on August 3, 1863, at West Pascagoula, Mississippi.

Cullen, P. H., Pvt. Co. H.
Enlisted on September 8, 1862, at Mobile, Alabama. His name appears on a list of soldiers employed in the Subsistence Department in the State of Alabama, at Montgomery, Alabama, on May 22, 1864. Month of July 1864, he is reported as employed as abstract clerk in various offices and bureaus at the Military Post of Mobile, Alabama. Appears October 1, 1864, on a list of men detailed as a clerk employed at Depot Commissary in Mobile, Alabama, by Major General Maury. "Has been on Surgeon's Certificate until 30th at which time he was re-examined and pronounced fit for field service. His detail has been extended until application which has been sent to Commissary General can be heard from. " He was listed among men on detached service in the Commissary Department that were surrendered

as POW's at Citronelle, Alabama, on May 4, 1865, and paroled at Meridian, Mississippi, on May 11, 1865. There is considerable paper work in his file. **

Cunningham, Pvt. Co. H.
Enlisted on September 15, 1863, at Mobile, Alabama.

Cunningham, F., Pvt. Co. K.
Enlisted on June 1, 1863, at Bayou La Batre, Alabama. His name appears on a roll of POW's that were stragglers surrendered at Citronelle, Alabama, in May 1865, and paroled at Meridian, Mississippi, on May 19, 1865. Residence Grand Bay, Alabama.

Cupp, Bishop, Pvt. Co. K.
Enlisted on April 25, 1862, at Mobile, Alabama. POW a member of Company K, 15th Confederate Cavalry, CSA that were surrendered at Citronelle, Alabama, on May 4, 1865, and paroled at Gainesville, Alabama, May 14, 1865. Residence Washington County, Ala.

Cupp, M. (Mike) J., Pvt. Co. K.
Enlisted on November 29, 1863, at Mobile, Alabama. POW a member of Company K, 15th Confederate Cavalry, CSA that were surrendered by Lt. General Richard Taylor at Citronelle, Alabama, on May 4, 1865, and paroled at Gainesville, Alabama, on May 14, 1865. Residence Washington County, Alabama.

Curran, C., Pvt. Co. G.
Enlisted January 15, 1862, at Dragoon Camp. Appears on a roll of CSA prisoners forwarded from Dauphin Island, Alabama, on March 19, 1865, to the Provost Marshal at New Orleans, Louisiana. He was captured at Mobile Bay. He is shown as a POW captured at Cedar Point, Louisiana, [Alabama?] on March 2, 1865. Confined at New Orleans. Louisiana, on March 21, 1865. Exchanged on May 11, 1865.

Cutts, Zach, Pvt. Co. I.
Enlisted on Oct. 4, 1862, at Santa Rosa, Florida. Shown absent without leave since July 1 on muster rolls for September/October 1863. November/December roll report him deserted.

Czarnowski, A., Pvt. Co. K.
Enlisted on September 21, 1863, at Halls Mill, Alabama. Paid on a descriptive list October 4, 1863. Age-18, eyes-grey, hair-light, complexion-fair, 5 foot 10 inches, a farmer by occupation. $50 enlistment bounty paid. He is shown as a POW a member of Company K, 15th Confederate Cavalry, CSA that were surrendered by at Citronelle, Alabama, on May 4, 1865, and paroled at Gainesville, Alabama, on May 14, 1865. Residence Mobile County, Alabama.

D

Dade, Morris H., Pvt. Co. H.
Enlisted on December 9, 1863, at Mobile, Alabama.

Dailey, M. H., Pvt. Co. D.
Enlisted on August 13, 1863, at Camp Tatnall, Florida. Muster roll for September/October 1863, reports that he was discharged on July 1, 1863, having furnished a substitute. See service record on his substitute **Pvt. Burrel Stevens**.

Dalive filed with Dolive.

15TH CONFEDERATE CAVALRY

Danell filed with Daniels.

Daniel, E. F., Pvt. Co. E.
Enlisted on August 15, 1863, at Camp Ward. Muster roll for September/October 1863, reports that he died of fever at his home in Butler County, Alabama on October 20, 1863.

Daniels, E. A., Co. C.
Drew clothing on August 28, 1864.

Daniels, Lawson, Pvt. Co. B.
Enlisted on March 14, 1862, at Marianna, Florida. POW captured by a portion of the Federal Troops under command of Brigadier General Asboth on the raid into the interior of Western Florida, at Shoal River on September 22, 1864. His name appears on a list of POW's received at New Orleans, Louisiana, in the five days ending October 12, 1864. Transferred to Ship Island, Mississippi, on October 20, 1864. Received at Ship Island on October 21, 1864, and sent to New York on November 5, 1864. Received at Fort Columbus, New York Harbor, from Ship Island on November 16, 1864. Received at Elmira, New York on November 20, 1864, from Fort Columbus. Died on April 14, 1865, of general debility at Elmira, N. Y. Grave No. 2708.

Daniels, William J., Pvt. Co. B.
Enlisted on February 6, 1863, at Campbellton, Florida. His name appears on a list of POW's that were surrendered at Tallahassee, Florida, on May 10, 1865. Paroled at Quincy, Florida, on May 11, 1865. One report shows parole date as May 23, 1865.

Daniels, W. J., Pvt. Co. G.
Enlisted on December 27, 1863, at Halls Mill, Alabama. Appears on receipt roll for pay as a tool inspector at Mobile, Alabama, drawing $3 per day for January through April 1864. POW surrendered at Citronelle, Alabama, on May 4, 1865. Paroled at Mobile, Alabama, on June 16, 1865. Residence-Monroe County, Alabama, age-33. complexion-dark, eyes-blue, hair-light, 5 foot 10 inches.

Dansby, L. L., Pvt. Co. K.
Enlisted on July 24, 1863, at Filley's Ferry, Mississippi. Age-18, eyes-grey, hair-light, complexion-fair, 5 foot 9 inches, born-Choctaw County, Alabama, a farmer by profession.

Dairdson, J. B., Pvt. Co. G.
Enlisted on July 30, 1861, at Dragoon Camp.

Davidson, Joseph, Pvt. Co. F.
Admitted to Ross Hospital, Mobile, Alabama, on October 3, 1863, with debility. Returned to duty on December 1.

Davis, A. J., Pvt. Co. C.
Enlisted on April 15, 1862, at Stockton, Alabama.

Davis, Benjamin, Pvt. Co. A.
Enlisted on May 6, 1863, at Camp Lomax, Florida.

Davis, B. N., 2nd Sergeant Co. C.
Enlisted on April 9, 1862, at Blakeley, Alabama. Age-40, eyes-blue, hair-dark, complexion-dark, 5 foot 11 inches, born-Marion Dist. South Carolina.

Davis, C. B., Pvt. Co. G.
   Enlisted on April 20, 1864, at Mobile, Alabama.

Davis, Charles W., 2nd Lieutenant Co. B.
   Enlisted on March 14, 1862, at Marianna, Florida. His Parole of Honor and considerable other paper work is in his file.**

Davis, D. L., Pvt. Co. I.
   Paroled at 16th U.S. Army Corps at Montgomery, Alabama, on June 7, 1865. Eyes-blue, hair-light, complexion-dark, 5 foot 9 inches. His parole is in his file.*

Davis, D. T., Pvt. Co. I.
   Paroled at 16th U.S. Army Corps at Montgomery, Alabama, on June 15, 1865. Eyes-blue, hair-dark, complexion-dark, 5 foot 9 inches. His parole is in his file.*

Davis, H., Bugler Co. D.
   Enlisted on April 24, 1862, at Pensacola, Florida.

Davis, H., Pvt. Co. F.
   POW a member of Company F, 15th Confederate Cavalry, CSA that were surrendered at Citronelle, Alabama, on May 4, 1865, and paroled at Gainesville, Alabama, on May 14, 1865. Residence Mobile County, Alabama.

Davis, H. D., Pvt. Co. C.
   Enlisted on April 15, 1862, at Stockton, Alabama.

Davis, J. B., Pvt. Co. G.
   Enlisted on March 15, 1862, at Dragoon Camp. Age-24, eyes-hazel, hair-light, complexion-light, 5 foot 8 inches, residence-Monroe County, Alabama.

Davis, J. F., Sergeant Co. C.
   Enlisted on April 9, 1862, at Blakeley, Alabama.

Davis, John, Pvt. Co. A.
   Enlisted on May 22, 1863, at Camp Lomax, Florida. His name appears on a muster roll August 31, 1864, for a detachment of troops from Camp of Correction, ordered to duty by Major General D. H. Maury and commanded by Major R. A. Harris at Mouth of Dog River, near Mobile, Alabama. Sent to Camp Correction February 10, 1864. March/April 1864, muster roll reports him charged with desertion. Sentenced to hard labor by Court Marshal in Mobile, Alabama.

Davis, John, T., Lieutenant/Captain AACS Co. B.
   Enlisted on March 14, 1862, at Marianna, Florida. Original Muster roll for September 12, 1863, reports him detailed as Quarter Master for Alabama and Florida Batt. Appointed to Captain and AACS on August 15, 1864, at Spring Hill. Considerable paper work is in his file.**

Davis, Joseph, Pvt. Co. C.
   POW a member of Company C, 15th Confederate Cavalry, CSA commanded by Captain T. C. Barlow that were surrendered by Lt. General Richard Taylor at Citronelle, Alabama, on May 4, 1865, and paroled at Gainesville, Alabama, on May 14, 1865. Residence Baldwin County, Alabama.

15TH CONFEDERATE CAVALRY

Davis, J. W., Pvt. Co. C.
Enlisted on May 11, 1864, at Camp Powell, Alabama.

Davis, L. F., Pvt. Co. K.
POW a member of Company K, 15th Confederate Cavalry, CSA that were surrendered at Citronelle, Alabama, on May 4, 1865, and paroled at Gainesville, Alabama, on May 14, 1865. Residence Baldwin County, Alabama.

Davis, Thomas, Pvt. Co. C.
Enlisted on June 1, 1863, at Camp Powell, Alabama. Muster rolls indicate that he deserted.

Davis, P. H., Pvt. Co. F.
Enlisted on October 1, 1861, at Mobile, Alabama. Discharged on December 6, 1863, for disability.

Dawkins, G. (George) W., Pvt. Co. A.
Enlisted on March 8, 1862, at Station 3, P & G RR, Florida. POW surrendered and paroled at Tallahassee, Florida on May 13, 1865.

Dawkins, (William) Henry, Pvt. Co. A.
Enlisted on March 7, 1862, at Station 3, P & G RR, Florida.

Dawson, J. A., Pvt. Co. G.
Enlisted on October 2, 1863, at Dragoon Camp.

Dawson, William O., Pvt. Co. G.
Enlisted on March 15, 1862, at Dragoon Camp.

Day, J. M., Pvt. Co. K.
Enlisted March 17, 1862, at Washington County, Ala. Residence Choctaw County, Ala.

Day, J. Roland, Pvt. Co. H.
Enlisted on October 12, 1863, at Clinton, Louisiana. He was transferred at the fight at Tunica Bend, La. from Scotts Louisiana Cavalry on March 4, 1864, where he was ranked a Corporal.

Deakel/Deekle see Deakle

Deakle, B., Pvt. Co. K.
Enlisted on June 26, 1863, at Bayou La Batre. Age-28, eyes-dark, hair-dark, complexion-dark, 5 foot 7 inches, born in Mobile County, Alabama. A farmer by occupation.

Deakle, E. A., Pvt. Co. G.
Enlisted on July 31, 1861, at Dragoon Camp.

Deakle, John, Pvt. Co. K.
Enlisted on June 24, 1863, at Bayou La Batre. Age-18, eyes-grey, hair-light, 5 foot 7 inches, born in Mobile County, Alabama. A farmer by occupation.

Deakle, J. W., Pvt. Co. G.
Enlisted on July 30, 1861, at Dragoon Camp (Mobile).

Deakle, Thomas E., Pvt. Co. H.
Enlisted on June 17, 1863, at West Pascagoula, Mississippi.

Deakle, William E., Pvt. Co. H.
Enlisted on August 7, 1863, at West Pascagoula, Mississippi.

Deakle, W. L., Pvt. Co. K.
Enlisted on August 19, 1862, at Pascagoula, Mississippi.

Deal, J. F., Pvt. Co. E.
Enlisted on January 25, 1863, at Camp Lomax, Florida. Detached as a teamster. Paroled at Montgomery in May 1865. Eyes-dark, hair-dark, complexion-fair, 6 foot. His parole is in his file.*

Dean, Richard, Pvt. Co. E/F.
Enlisted on September 17, 1861, at Milton, Florida. Shown on detached service to hunt deserters. POW captured at Claiborne, Alabama, on April 12, 1865.

DeBose see Dubose

DeCaussey, Marion, Pvt. Co. A.
Enlisted March 8, 1862, at Monticello, Florida. Eyes-dark, hair-dark, complexion-dark, 5 foot 5 inches. Signed a parole at Tallahassee, Fla., May 15, 1865. His parole is in his file.*

Dees, Arch, Pvt. Co. G.
Enlisted on September 16, 1863, at Dragoon Camp. Surrendered at Citronelle, Alabama, paroled at Meridian, Mississippi, on May 11, 1865.

Dees, L. C., Pvt. Co. G.
Enlisted on May 15, 1863, at Camp Taylor. Surrendered at Citronelle, Alabama, paroled at Gainesville, Alabama, on May 14, 1865.

Dees, Lemuel, Pvt. Co. K.
Enlisted on March 17, 1862, at Washington County, Alabama.

Dees, T. H., Pvt. Co. C.
Enlisted April 9, 1863, at Blakeley, Ala. POW paroled at Fort Pickens, Fla., April 18, 1863.

De LaRua, John, see LaRua, John De.

Deminick, R. H., see Denick, R. H.

Demott, Abram, Pvt. Co. A.
Enlisted on February 23, 1864, at Monticello, Florida. POW signed a parole at 16th U.S. Army headquarters in Greenville, Alabama, on April 22, 1865. Signed by his mark.

Denick, R. H., Pvt. Co. D.
Enlisted on April 24, 1862, at Pensacola, Florida. POW captured near Pollard, Alabama, on December 14, 1864. Confined at New Orleans, Louisiana, and sent to St. Lewis Hospital.

Denmark, J. M., Pvt. Co. H.
Enlisted on March 19, 1863, at Mobile, Alabama. Discharged due to physical disability.

15TH CONFEDERATE CAVALRY

Dering, John, D., Pvt. Co. B.
    Enlisted on March 14, 1862, at Marianna, Florida. POW surrendered at Citronelle, Alabama, paroled at Gainesville, Alabama, on May 14, 1865. Residence was Jackson County, Florida.

Devine, Thomas, Pvt. Co. H.
    Enlisted on June 1, 1863, at West Pascagoula, Mississippi. He was assigned to extra duty with Tolbins Battery of Artillery on February 15, 1864. Age-17, eyes-dark, hair-dark, complexion-light, 5 foot 6 inches, born-Mobile, Alabama. A farmer by occupation.

Diamond, J. C., Pvt. Co. D.
    Enlisted on April 24, 1862, at Pensacola, Florida. Signs by his mark.

Diamond, W. M., Corporal/Sergeant Co. D.
    Enlisted on April 24, 1862, at Pensacola, Florida. Promoted from 3rd Corporal to 5th Sergeant on January 1, 1864. Signs by his mark.

Dickson, N. B. (Dixon, Napoleon Bonaparte), Pvt. Co. I.
    Enlisted on February 22, 1864, at Halls Mill, Alabama.

Dickson, Thomas G., Pvt. Co. B
    Enlisted on June 15, 1864, at Marianna, Florida. POW surrendered at Tallahassee, Florida, paroled at Quincy, Florida, on May 22, 1865.

Diggs, William C., Pvt. Co. G.
    Enlisted on July 31, 1862, at Dragoon Camp. Muster rolls from September 1863, show him detached to work on Gun Boats.

Dill, W. A., Corporal/Sergeant Co. H.
    Enlisted on September 4, 1862, at Mobile, Alabama. POW surrendered at Citronelle, Alabama, paroled at Gainesville, Alabama, on May 14, 1865. Residence was shown as Baldwin County, Alabama.

Dimond, John, Pvt. Co. K.
    Enlisted on March 17, 1862, at Washington County, Alabama. (See reference in **R. M. Loper**, Pvt. Co. K, 15th Confederate Cavalry file.)

Ditmars, C. V., Pvt. Co. D.
    Enlisted on March 2, 1863, at Camp Tatnall, Florida. POW captured at Mount Pleasant, Alabama, on April 11, 1865.

Dittiss, Jacob M., Pvt. Co. H.
    Enlisted on April 1, 1863, at Mobile, Alabama. POW surrendered at Citronelle, Alabma, paroled at Gainesville, Alabama. Residence was in Greene County, Alabama.

Dixon, C. H., Pvt. Co. E.
    Enlisted on May 8, 1862, at Warrenton, Florida. September 1864, muster roll reports him detached to work on Gun Boat at Montgomery, Alabama. Reported to have deserted from Mobile, Alabama, while on detached duty as mechanic about January 15, 1864. "Has probably gone to the enemy at Pensacola Navy Yard."

Dixon, E., Pvt. Co. H.
    Enlisted on February 10, 1864, at Bayou La Batre, Alabama. POW surrendered at Citronelle,

Alabama, paroled at Gainesville, Alabama. Residence was shown as Lawrence County, Mississippi.

Dixon, G. W., Pvt. Co. E.
Enlisted on February 1, 1863, at Camp Lomax, Florida. On special duty as artilleryman.

Dixon, G. W., Pvt. Co. F.
Enlisted on June 22, 1864, at Gonzalia, Florida.

Dixon, H. H., Pvt. Co. E.
Enlisted on September 17, 1861, at Milton, Florida. Deserted from Halls Mill, Alabama, about December 12, 1863. "Has probably gone to Pensacola Navy Yard."

Dixon, N. B. (Napoleon Bonaparte) see **Dickson, N. B**.

Dixon, William H., Pvt. Co. I.
Enlisted on January 12, 1863, at Conecuh County, Alabama. He was admitted to Ross Hospital in Mobile, Alabama, on November 27, 1863, and died on December 19, 1863, of remitten fever, typhoid fever.

Dixon, W. J., Pvt. Co. E.
Enlisted on September 17, 1861, at Milton, Florida.

Dobson, N. H., Corporal/Sergeant Co. G.
Enlisted on September 15, 1861, at Dragoon Camp. POW surrendered at Citronelle, Alabama, paroled at Gainesville, Alabama.

Doby, James, M., Pvt./Assistant Surgeon/Captain F&S
Enlisted as a Private in Murrell's Partisan Rangers at Mobile, Alabama, September 4, 1862. Age-32, complexion-dark, eyes-blue, hair-dark, 5 foot 8 inches, a physician by occupation. Born in South Carolina. Commissioned as Assistant Surgeon on April 29, 1863. POW signed a Parole of Honor at Meridian, Mississippi, on May 13, 1865. His parole is in his file.*

Dolive, A., Pvt. Co. C.
Enlisted on April 15, 1862, at Stockton, Alabama. POW captured on April 18, 1865. Sent to Ship Island, Mississippi. Also show as POW surrendered at Citronelle, Alabama, paroled at Gainesville, Alabama. Residence Baldwin County, Alabama.

Dolive. J. L., Pvt. Co. C.
Enlisted on September 13, 1862, at Shell Banks, Alabama. POW captured in front of Blakeley, Alabama, on April 2, 1865. Surrendered at Citronelle, Alabama, paroled at Gainesville, Alabama, on May 14, 1865. Residence Mobile, Alabama.

Dolive, R. F., Sergeant Co. F.
Enlisted on February 20, 1862, at Camp Withers. Promoted from Corporal to 4th Sergeant on September 1, 1863. POW captured in front of Blakeley, Alabama, on April 2, 1865. Sent to Ship, Island, Mississippi.

Dolive, S., Private, Co. C.
Enlisted April 9, 1862, at Blakeley, Alabama. POW captured in front of Blakeley, Alabama, April 2, 1865. Sent to Ship, Island, Mississippi. Transferred to Vicksburg, Mississippi.

15TH CONFEDERATE CAVALRY

Dolive, Vanroy, Pvt. Co. C.
  POW surrendered at Citronelle, Alabama, paroled at Gainesville, Alabama, May 14, 1865. Residence was Baldwin County, Alabama.

Dolive, W. L., Pvt. Co. C.
  Enlisted on September 4, 1861, at Shell Banks, Alabama. POW surrendered at Citronelle, Alabama, paroled at Gainesville, Alabama, May 14, 1865. Residence was Baldwin County, Alabama.

Dolive, W. M., Pvt. Co. H.
  Enlisted on September 4, 1862, at Mobile, Alabama. He was shown on detached service as a clerk. POW surrendered at Citronelle, Alabama, paroled at Gainesville, Alabama, May 14, 1865. Residence was Mobile County, Alabama.

Donricourt, A., Pvt. Co. G.
  Enlisted on June 11, 1863, at Camp Taylor. POW.

Donricourt, J., Pvt. Co. G
  Enlisted on June 11, 1863, at Camp Taylor. POW surrendered at Citronelle, Alabama, paroled at Gainesville, Alabama, on May 14, 1865. Residence was New Orleans, Louisiana.

Dorghty, Thomas J., Pvt. Co. H.
  Enlisted on September 4, 1862, at Mobile, Alabama.

Douglas, William T., Pvt. Co. G.
  Enlisted on July 30, 1861, at Dragoon Camp (also shows Mobile, Alabama). Detached as a clerk for a time in the Engineering Department. POW surrendered at Citronelle, Alabama, paroled at Meridian, Mississippi, on May 16, 1865. Residence Mobile, Alabama.

Drew, J. A., Pvt. Co. C.
  Enlisted on October 10, 1862, at Shell Banks, Alabama. POW surrendered at Citronelle, Alabama, paroled at Gainesville, Alabama, on May 14, 1865. Residence Monroe County, Alabama.

Driskell, W. L., Pvt. Co. I.
  POW paroled at Montgomery, Alabama, on June 10, 1865. Hair-light, eyes-gray, complexion-light, 5 foot 6 inches.

Droesch, Frank, Pvt. Co. F.
  Enlisted on June 22, 1864, at Gonzalia, Florida. POW surrendered at Citronelle, Alabama, paroled at Gainesville, Alabama, on May 14, 1865. Residence Mobile, Mobile County, Alabama.

Drue, C., Pvt. Co. C.
  POW surrendered at Citronelle, Alabama, paroled at Gainesville, Alabama, on May 14, 1865. Residence Mobile, Mobile County, Alabama.

Drummond, H. F., 1st Lieutenant. Co. H.
  Enlisted on September 4, 1862, at Mobile, Alabama. He was assigned on detached duty as Provost Marshall of Biloxi and Pascagoula, Mississippi. There is considerable paper work in his file.**

Drury, J. F., Pvt. Co. E.
    Enlisted on September 17, 1861, at Milton, Florida.

DuBose, C. C., Pvt./Corporal Co. G.
    Enlisted on August 2, 1863, at Camp Murphy, records also show at Camp Taylor. POW surrendered at Citronelle, Alabama, paroled at Gainesville, Alabama, on May 14, 1864. Residence Mobile, Alabama.

Dubose, Jeptha, Pvt. Co. K.
    Enlisted on April 25, 1862, at Mobile, Alabama. POW surrendered at Citronelle, Alabama, paroled at Meridian, Mississippi, on May 10, 1864. Residence Choctaw, Alabama.

DuBuys, Lucian, Pvt. Co. G.
    Enlisted on June 26, 1863, at Camp Taylor. On detached service on gun boat. Transferred to Volunteer Navy.

Dudley, James B., Pvt. Co. B.
    Enlisted on March 14, 1862, at Marianna, Florida. POW surrendered at Quincy, Florida, on May 11, 1865, and paroled at Ouincy, Florida, on May 22, 1865.

Duncan, Peter, Pvt. Co. E.
    Enlisted on March 1, 1862, at Camp Perdido, Florida. He is shown on detached service as a courier. POW surrendered at Citronelle, Alabama, paroled at Gainesville, Alabama, on May 14, 1864. Residence Mobile, Alabama.

Dunham, W. T., Pvt. Co. I.
    Enlisted on June 13, 1864, at Santa Rosa, Florida.

Dupont, William, Pvt. Co. G.
    Enlisted on December 3, 1863, at Halls Mill, Alabama. Died at Ross Hospital, Mobile, Alabama, on September 17, 1864, of febris remittens congestiva. One gold ring and $72.25 delivered to his father.

Durant, C. L., Pvt. Co. C.
    POW surrendered at Citronelle, Alabama, paroled at Gainesville, Alabama, on May 14, 1864. Residence Baldwin County, Alabama.

Durant, N. B., Pvt. Co. C.
    Enlisted on May 26, 1864, at Camp Powell, Alabama. POW surrendered at Citronelle, Alabama, paroled at Gainesville, Alabama, May 14, 1864. His residence is shown as Baldwin County, Ala.

Durant, W. H., Pvt. Co. C.
    Enlisted on June 18, 1864, at Camp Powell, Alabama. POW surrendered at Citronelle, Alabama, paroled at Gainesville, Alabama, May 14, 1864. His residence is shown as Baldwin County, Ala..

Durden, James F., Pvt. Co,. D.
    Enlisted on April 24, 1862, at Pensacola, Florida. For a time he was on detached service as a guide near Pensacola to the 4th Alabama Cavalry. POW captured at Escambia County, Florida, on January 13, 1865. Sent to Ship Island, and on to Vicksburg, Mississippi.

15TH CONFEDERATE CAVALRY

Durden, Wyley, Pvt. Co.___.
    POW surrendered at Quincy, Florida on May 11, 1865. Paroled at Quincy on May 22, 1865.

Durett, Peter, Bugler. Co. G.
    Enlisted on August 2, 1861, at Mobile, Alabama.

Dykes, Calvin, Pvt. Co. B.
    Enlisted on March 20, 1864, at Marianna, Florida. POW paroled at Quincy, Florida, on May 22, 1865.

Dykes, George, R., Pvt. Co. B.
    Enlisted March 14, 1862, at Marianna, Florida. POW surrendered on May 11, 1865, at Quincy, Florida. Paroled on May 22, 1865, at Quincy.

Dykes, Jacob J., Pvt. Co. B.
    Enlisted on March 14, 1862, at Marianna, Florida. POW surrendered on May 11, 1865, at Quincy, Florida. Paroled on May 22, 1865, at Quincy.

Dykes, William H., Corporal Co. B.
    Enlisted on March 20, 1864, at Marianna, Florida. POW surrendered on May 11, 1865, at Quincy, Florida. Paroled at Quincy, Florida, on May 22, 1865.

E

Eastman, W., Pvt. Co. F.
    Enlisted on October 1, 1861, at Mobile, Alabama. POW surrendered at Citronelle, Alabama, paroled at Gainesville, Alabama, on May 14, 1864. Residence Mobile, Alabama.

Eddins, Hozea, Pvt. Co. A.
    Enlisted on June 1, 1863, at Camp Lomax, Florida. Deserted from Camp Ward, Alabama, on August 15, 1863.

Eddins, James, Pvt. Co. A.
    Enlisted on April 3, 1863, at Camp Lomax, Florida.

Edwards, Gabriel J., Pvt. Co. I/B.
    Enlisted on September 14, 1863, at Mobile County, Alabama. Transferred to Co. B. POW surrendered as a straggler at Selma, Alabama, in June 1865. Residence Wilcox County, Alabama.

Edwards, J. G. W., Pvt. Co. A.
    Enlisted April 1, 1863, at Camp Lomax, Florida. POW surrendered at Citronelle, Alabama, paroled at Meridian, Mississippi, Alabama, May 12, 1864. Residence shown as Mobile, Alabama.

Edwards, John W., Sergeant/2nd Lieutenant Co. B.
    Enlisted on March 14, 1862, at Marianna, Florida. Elected 2nd Lieutenant on August 15, 1864. POW captured at Mount Pleasant, Alabama, on April 11, 1865.

Egan, John, Pvt. Co. G.
    Enlisted on October 18, 1863, at Dragoon Camp.

Ellard, Francis, Pvt. Co. I.
Enlisted on October 4, 1862, at Santa Rosa, Florida. His records show that he deserted.

Elliot, Not S., Pvt. Co. A.
Enlisted on May 14, 1864, at Madison, Florida. POW captured at Mount Pleasant, Alabama, on April 11, 1865.

Elliot, Sebron, Pvt. Co. I.
Enlisted on May 19, 1864, at Santa Rosa, Florida.

Elliot, William, Pvt. Co. I.
Enlisted on October 4, 1862, at Santa Rosa, Florida.

Ellis, Green, Pvt. Co. D.
Enlisted on September 7, 1862, at Camp Tatnall, Florida.

Ellis, James, Pvt. Co. H.
POW surrendered at Citronelle, Alabama, paroled at Gainesville, Alabama, on May 14, 1864. Residence Mobile, Alabama.

Ellis, John, Pvt. Co. A.
Enlisted on April 1, 1863, at Camp Lomax, Florida. Detailed in Naval Department at Selma, Alabama, (Ordnance Department) February 15, 1864.

Ellis, John G., Corporal/Sergeant Co. I.
Enlisted on October 4, 1862, at Santa Rosa, Florida. Promoted to 4th Sergeant on September 1, 1863. Promoted to 1st Sergeant on December 1, 1863.

Ellis, W. J., Pvt. Co. D.
Enlisted on September 29, 1862, at Camp Tatnall, Florida. On extra duty as teamster with regimental headquarters in 1864.

Ely, Charles, H., Pvt. Co._.
POW surrendered at Quincy, Florida. Paroled on May 22, 1865, at Quincy.

Ely, J. C., Pvt. Co. H.
Enlisted on December 13, 1863, at Halls Mill, Alabama. Appears on a roll of POW's of the 9th Regiment of Mississippi Cavalry, CSA, surrendered at Meridian, Mississippi, in May 1865. Paroled at Mobile, Alabama, on May 23, 1865. Resident of Jackson County, Mississippi.

Emerson, George, Pvt. Co. F.
Enlisted on August 27, 1862, at Camp Withers.

Emmonds, G. W., Pvt. Co. D.
Enlisted on May 17, 1864, at Milton, Florida.

Emmonds, William, Pvt. Co. D.
Enlisted on May 17, 1864, at Milton, Florida.

Emmons, George, Pvt. Co. I.
Enlisted on October 1, 1862, at Conecuh, County, Alabama. He is also shown as enlisting

on October 4, 1862, at Santa Rosa, Florida. On June 1864, he is reported present to have "joined from desertion".

Enners, H. A., Pvt. Co. H.
Enlisted on September 4, 1864, at Mobile, Alabama.

Enterkin, William, Pvt. Co. D.
Enlisted on April 24, 1862, at Pensacola, Florida. Assigned on extra duty as a guide by order of General Clanton in 1863.

Entrican, James, Pvt. Co. A.
Enlisted on October 20, 1864, at Camp Lomax, Florida. In 1863 he is shown detailed as a guide for General J. H. Clanton. Deserted from Camp Lomax on October 10, 1863.

Etheridge, M. W., Pvt. Co. E.
Enlisted on September 17, 1861, at Milton, Florida.

Evans, J. L., 3rd Sergeant/Pvt. Co. K.
Enlisted on September 17, 1862, at Washington County, Alabama. June of 1864, he is reported sick in Choctaw County, Alabama. POW surrendered at Citronelle, Alabama, paroled at Gainesville, Alabama, on May 14, 1864. Residence Choctaw County, Alabama.

Evans, W. D., Pvt. Co. E.
Enlisted at Pitts Bridge, Florida.

Evans, William G., Pvt. Co. G.
Enlisted on May 19, 1863, at Camp Taylor. POW surrendered at Citronelle, Alabama, paroled at Gainesville, Alabama, on May 14, 1864. Residence Jackson County, Mississippi.

Ewing, John, Pvt. Co. F.
Enlisted on May 20, 1862, at Camp Withers. On detached service at Government Fishery. Deserted on December 28, 1863.

Ezell, C. P., Pvt. Co. C.
Enlisted on September 1, 1863, at Stockton, Alabama. POW surrendered at Citronelle, Alabama, paroled at Gainesville, Alabama, May 14, 1864. Residence Clarke County, Ala.

F

Fairbanks, Ellis, Pvt. Co. K.
Enlisted on September 5, 1863, at Halls Mill, Alabama. His name appears on a roll of POW's of the 9th Regiment of Mississippi Cavalry, CSA, surrendered at Meridian, Mississippi, in May 1865. Paroled at Mobile, Alabama, on May 23, 1865. Residence Jackson County, Mississippi, Age-40, eyes-blue, hair-light, complexion-fair, 6 foot 1 inch, a farmer by occupation.

Fairly, P. M., Pvt. Co. K.
Enlisted on January 19, 1864, at Pascagoula, Mississippi.

Faith, L. H., Pvt. Co. K.
Enlisted on October 8, 1863, at Mobile, Alabama. Age-17, eyes-grey, hair-dark, complexion-fair, 5 foot 8 inches, a farmer, born in Alabama. POW surrendered at Citronelle,

Alabama, paroled at Gainesville, Alabama, on May 14, 1864. Residence Washington County, Alabama.

Famous, Edwin, Pvt. Co. F.
Enlisted on August 27, 1862, at Camp Withers. POW surrendered at Citronelle, Alabama, paroled at Gainesville, Alabama, on May 14, 1864. Residence Mobile County, Alabama.

Farrish, John, Pvt. Co. D.
Enlisted on November 1, 1862, at Camp Tatnall, Florida. He deserted on August 26, 1863.

Farley, Thomas, Pvt. Co. K.
POW surrendered at Citronelle, Alabama, paroled at Meridian, Mississippi, on May 12, 1864. Residence Jackson County, Mississippi.

Farnel, J. M., Pvt. Co. G.
Enlisted on July 30, 1861, at Mobile, Alabama.

Farnel, William, H., Pvt. Co. G.
Enlisted on March 22, 1862, at Dragoon Camp.

Farragut, N. G., Pvt. Co. G.
Enlisted on July 1, 1863, at Camp Taylor. POW captured in April 1865, forwarded from Mobile, Alabama, to Ship Island, Mississippi.

Farragut, W. J., Pvt. Co. G.
Enlisted on July 1, 1863, at Camp Taylor.

Farragut, W. J., Pvt. Co. I.
Enlisted on October 4, 1862, at Santa Rosa, Florida. June 1864. He is reported to have deserted.

Faulk, John, Pvt. Co. A.
Enlisted on June 1, 1863, at Camp Lomax, Florida.

Feagin, A. B., Pvt. Co. I.
POW paroled at Montgomery, Alabama, on June 20, 1865. Eyes-gray, hair-auburn, complexion-dark, 5 foot 10 inches. His parole is in his file.*

Feagin, A. P., 1st Lieutenant Co. E.
Enlisted on December 16, 1861, at Camp Perdido, Florida. Appointed 1st Lieutenant on May 7, 1862. In 1864 he is on special duty as Assistant Surgeon. There is paper work in his file.*

Feagin, J. E., Pvt. Co. E.
Enlisted on November 16, 1862, at Camp Lomax, Florida.

Fergerson, T. W., Pvt. Co. C.
Enlisted on October 31, 1862, at Camp Powell, Alabama. On September 12, 1863, company muster roll he is shown absent a prisoner paroled April 18, 1863, from Fort Pickens. Surrendered at Meridian, Mississippi, among stragglers, paroled at Mobile, Alabama, on May 19, 1865. Residence Quitman, Mississippi.

15TH CONFEDERATE CAVALRY

Ferrell, W. F., Pvt. Co. H.
Transferred from Captain Rodes Company on July 5, 1863.

Fickland, Charles, Pvt. Co. C.
Enlisted on October 31, 1862, at Camp Powell, Alabama. POW surrendered at Citronelle, Alabama, paroled at Gainesville, Alabama, May 14, 1864. Residence Baldwin County, Ala.

Fickland, Thomas, Pvt. Co. C.
Enlisted on April 15, 1862, at Stockton, Alabama.

Fickling see Fickland

Fields, John, Pvt. Co. K.
Enlisted on August 14, 1862, at Pascagoula, Mississippi. POW surrendered at Citronelle, Alabama, paroled at Gainesville, Alabama, on May 14, 1864. Residence Jackson County, Alabama [Mississippi?].

Fields, W. H., Pvt. Co. I.
Enlisted on October 4, 1862, at Conecuh, County, Alabama.

Files, James L., Pvt. Co. B.
Enlisted on January 26, 1864, at Greenville, Alabama. POW captured at Mount Pleasant, Alabama. on April 11, 1865. Paroled at Montgomery, Alabama, on June 16, 1865. Hair-dark, eyes-hazel, complexion-fair, 6 foot 1 inch. His parole is in his file.*

Fillingim, V., Pvt. Co. D.
Enlisted on October 30, 1862, at Camp Tatnall, Florida. Assigned to extra duty as a guide by General Clanton. Deserted on January 1, 1864. Residence Escambia County, Florida.

Fincher, J. T., Pvt. Co. E/I.
Enlisted on March 1, 1862, at Camp Perdido, Florida. Transferred from Captain Leigh's Co. E to Captain Amos' Co. I on October 22, 1863. POW captured at Mount Pleasant, Alabama, on April 11, 1865.

Finck, F., Pvt. Co. F.
Enlisted on October 1, 1861, at Mobile, Alabama. He deserted about January 15, 1864.

Findley, Benjamin L., Pvt. Co. B.
Enlisted on March 14, 1862, at Marianna, Florida. Detailed as an orderly by General Maury. During October and November he was paid as a courier at Mobile. POW surrendered on May 11, 1865, at Quincy, Florida. Paroled at Quincy, Florida, on May 23, 1865. There is considerable paper work in his file.**

Finlayson, John L., Pvt. Co. B.
Enlisted on March 16, 1862, at Marianna, Florida. Detailed as a hospital clerk by order of General Forney on September 15, 1862. POW surrendered on May 11, 1865, at Quincy, Florida. Paroled at Quincy, Florida, on May 22, 1865. There is paperwork in his file.*

Fitts, C., Pvt. Co. G.
POW surrendered at Citronelle, Alabama, paroled at Gainesville, Alabama, on May 14, 1864. Residence McClellan, [McMullen?] County, Texas.

Fitzgerald, T. H., Pvt. Co. F.
Enlisted on November 26, 1862, at Camp Withers.

Flaherty, John, Pvt. Co. C.
Enlisted on April 9, 1862, at Blakeley, Alabama. Absent without leave and then absent in arrest at Mobile. Employed at General Hospital Nott at Mobile as a Nurse on April 1, 1864. Appears on a list of POW's that were nurses or patients of Moore Hospital surrendered at Citronelle, Alabama on May 4, 1865. Paroled at Meridian, Mississippi, on May 16, 1864. Residence Baldwin County, Alabama.

Flanders, George, Pvt. Co. C.
POW surrendered at New Orleans, Louisiana, on May 26, 1865. Paroled at Alexandria, Louisiana, on June 19, 1865. Residence New Orleans.

Fleming, A. L., Pvt. Co. E.
POW captured on November 17, 1864, at Escambia County, Florida, by a detachment of 1st Florida Cavalry and 2nd Me. Cavalry. Transferred to Ship Island, Mississippi, December 10, 1864, and arrived there on December 13. He was transferred to Vicksburg, Mississippi, on May 1, 1865.

Fleming, E. D., Pvt. Co. I.
Enlisted on December 28, 1862, at Santa Rosa, Florida. POW paroled on June 8, 1865, at Montgomery, Alabama. Hair-light, eyes-grey, complexion-fair, 5 foot 8 inches. His parole is in his file.

Fleming, George, Pvt. Co. I.
Enlisted on December 18, 1862, at Santa Rosa, Florida. Reported absent without leave. Sentenced to hard labor for 12 months by Court Marshal in Mobile, Alabama. Sent to camp of correction on February 10, 1864.

Fleming, J. W., Pvt. Co. H.
Enlisted on September 22, 1862, at Mobile, Alabama. Detached as a courier for General Cumming. Muster roll for April 30, 1864, he was reported missing during the siege of Vicksburg, Mississippi, while acting as courier. Muster roll for June 30, 1864, reports that he died.

Fleming, R. P., Corporal Co. E.
Enlisted on September 17, 1861, at Milton, Florida. Promoted from 3rd to 1st Corporal on May 1, 1864. POW captured on November 17, 1864, at Escambia County, (Pine Barren) Florida, by a detachment of 1st Florida Cavalry and 2nd Me. Cavalry. Appears on a register of POW's at New Orleans, Louisiana, confined November 21, 1864. Transferred to Ship Island, Mississippi, December 10, 1864, arrived there on Dec. 13. Transferred to Vicksburg, Mississippi, on May 1, 1865.

Fleming, T. J., Pvt./Corporal Co. I.
Enlisted on December 27, 1862, at Santa Rosa, Florida. POW paroled at Montgomery, Alabama, on June 5, 1865. Hair-light, eyes-hazel, complexion-fair. 6 foot. His parole is in his file.*

Fletcher, J. F. L., Pvt. Co. C.
Enlisted on April 15, 1862, at Stockton, Alabama.

15TH CONFEDERATE CAVALRY

Floyd, Stephen, Pvt. Co. I.
Enlisted on March 9, 1863, at Conecuh County, Alabama.

Flurry, Joseph, Pvt. Co. H.
Enlisted on July 6, 1863, at West Pascagoula, Mississippi. Transferred to another regiment.

Ford, H. P., Corporal Co. G.
Enlisted on July 30, 1861, at Mobile, Alabama.

Fort, D. A., Pvt. Co. G.
Enlisted on January 6, 1862, at Dragoon Camp.

Foscue, Jonathan, Pvt. Co. K.
Enlisted on March 7, 1863, at Halls Mill, Alabama. POW surrendered at Citronelle, Alabama, and paroled at Gainesville, Alabama, on May 14, 1864. Residence Clarke County, Alabama. Age-39, eyes-blue, hair-dark, complexion-fair, 5 foot 10 inches, born-Jones County, North Carolina. A farmer by occupation. Pay voucher with descriptions of **Jonathan Foscue, J. J. Goode** and **T. W. Chapman** are in his file.*

Foster, Henry, Pvt. Co. E.
Enlisted on November 1, 1862, at Camp Lomax, Florida. Assigned on special duty with artillery service from October 10, 1863.

Foster, S. H., Pvt. Co. G.
Enlisted on July 22, 1863, at Camp Murphry. POW surrendered at Citronelle, Alabama, May 4, 1865. Paroled at Gainesville, Alabama, May 16, 1864. Residence Monroe County, Miss.

Fowler, William, Pvt. Co. I.
Enlisted on January 27, 1864, at Halls Mill, Alabama. POW among stragglers paroled at Selma, Alabama, during June 1865. Residence Monroe County, Alabama.

Fox, J. A., Pvt. Co. K.
Enlisted on March 17, 1862, at Washington County, Alabama.

Fox, W. W., Pvt. Co. K.
Enlisted on October 16, 1862, at Halls Mill, Alabama. POW surrendered on May 4, 1865, at Citronelle, Alabama. Paroled at Gainesville, Alabama, on May 14, 1865. Residence Choctaw County, Alabama.

Frader, J. W. see Frater J. W.

Franklin, Olis, Pvt. Co. G.
Enlisted on September 12, 1862, at Dragoon Camp. Muster roll for December 31, to April 30, 1864, reports that he was transferred to the Navy by order of Major General Maury. See special order 128/11.

Frater, J. W., Pvt./Corporal Co. E.
Enlisted on September 17, 1861, at Milton, Florida. POW captured on November 17, 1864, by a detachment of 1st Florida Cavalry and 2nd Me. Cavalry at Escambia County, (Pine Barren) Florida. Confined at New Orleans, Louisiana, on November 21, 1864. Transferred to Ship Island, Mississippi, on December 10, 1864. Transferred from Ship Island to Vicksburg, Mississippi, on May 1, 1865.

Freeman, James, Pvt. Co. A.
Enlisted on April 18, 1862, at Monticello, Florida. POW surrendered on May 10, 1865, at Tallahassee, Florida. Paroled at Albany, Georgia. Signed a Parole by his mark "X" at Albany. Hair-dark, eyes-blue, complexion-dark, 5 foot 11 inches. His parole is in his file.*

Frisbee, David, Pvt. Co. A.
Enlisted on March 8, 1862, at Monticello, Florida. POW paroled at Montgomery, Alabama, on May 31, 1865. Signed a parole at Montgomery. Hair-dark, eyes-dark, complexion-dark, 5 foot 8 inches. His parole is in his file.*

Fukeway, Henry, Pvt. Co. I.
Enlisted on October 4, 1862, at Santa Rosa, Florida.

Fulford, J. W., Pvt. Co. C.
Enlisted on September 23, 1862, at Shell Banks, Alabama. Detached by reason of special order No. 11. from Headquarters of the Gulf at Mobile. August 24, 1863. POW surrendered on May 4, 1865, at Citronelle, Alabama. Paroled at Gainesville, Alabama, on May 14, 1865. Residence Baldwin County, Alabama.

Fulford, W. F., Pvt. Co. F.
Enlisted on December 8, 1862, at Camp Withers. Detailed to Government Fishery on September 17, 1863, by order of General Maury.

Fuqua, James, Pvt. Co. E.
Enlisted on September 17, 1861, at Milton, Florida. May/June 1864, muster roll reports that he deserted about March 1, 1864, while on sick furlough.

G

Gabel, John J., Pvt. Co. C.
Enlisted on April 9, 1862, at Blakeley, Alabama. Detached by reason of special order No. 11. Headquarters of the Gulf at Mobile, dated. August 24, 1863. There is a pay voucher in his file.*

Gabel, M. V., Pvt. Co. C.
Enlisted on May 12, 1862, at Camp Powell, Alabama. POW surrendered on May 4, 1865, at Citronelle, Alabama. Paroled at Gainesville, Alabama, on May 14, 1865. Residence Baldwin County, Alabama.

Gabreal, Thomas, Pvt. Co. F.
Enlisted on January 17, 1862, at Camp Withers. Detailed on September 17, 1863, at Government Fishery by order of General Maury. March/April 1864, muster roll reports that he deserted on December 28, 1863.

Gabzer, W. W. see Gelzer

Galle, Lewis, Pvt. Co. K.
Enlisted on May 1, 1863, at Bayou La Batre, Alabama. Detached on conscript duty during early months of 1864. He appears on a list of men employed at the Military Post of Mobile, Alabama, during July 1864. He is shown here as Yard Sergeant in Major Harris Camp of Correction. There is paper work in his file.*

15TH CONFEDERATE CAVALRY

Gamble, Job, Musician/Bugler Co. A.
Enlisted on April 19, 1862, at Monticello, Florida. He is also shown as having enlisted at Station 3, P&G RR, Florida. POW surrendered at Tallahassee, Florida, on May 10, 1865. Paroled at Tallahassee, on May 17, 1865.

Gammoge, D. Y., Co. E.
Drew clothing on September 2, 1864.

Gardner, A., Pvt. Co. G.
POW surrendered on May 4, 1865, at Citronelle, Alabama. Paroled at Gainesville, Alabama, on May 14, 1865. Residence Selma, Dallas County, Alabama.

Gardner, John, 1st Lieutenant Co.. D.
Elected April 24, 1862, at Spring Hill. Resigned on September 21, 1863.

Garner, W. J., Sergeant Co. D.
Enlisted on April 24, 1862, at Pensacola, Florida. Promoted from 4th to 3rd Sergeant on January 1, 1864. POW captured on November 17, 1864, by a detachment of 1st Florida Cavalry and 2nd Me. Cavalry at Escambia County, (Pine Barren) Florida. Confined at New Orleans, Louisiana, on November 21, 1864. Transferred to Ship Island, Mississippi, on December 10, 1864. Transferred from Ship Island to Vicksburg, Mississippi, May 1, 1865.

Garrett, George, O., Pvt. Co. H.
Enlisted on September 4, 1862, at Mobile, Alabama. He was detailed to the artillery in September 1863. Transferred to Captain Tobin's Battery on January 26, 1864, by order of General Maury.

Gaskins, S. J., Pvt. Co. I.
Enlisted on October 4, 1862, at Santa Rosa, Florida. Muster rolls show him absent without leave. November/December 1862, report shows that he deserted.

Gayle, F. P., Pvt. Co. G.
Enlisted on July 30, 1861, at Mobile, Alabama. Transferred to 5th Regiment S. C. Cavalry by order of Secretary of War. His December 5, 1863, request for transfer is in his file with endorsements and referrals from Major General D. H. Maury, Commanding General P. G. T. Beauregard and others.**

Gazzam, George, G., Brevet 2nd Lieutenant Co. G.
Enlisted on March 17, 1862, at Dragoon Camp. Signs muster roll for April 30, 1864, as commanding company and Inspecting and mustering officer. Appointed Jr. 2nd Lieutenant on March 10, 1863. He requisitioned 127 shirts on December 31, 1863, at Halls Mill, Alabama. There are a number of pay vouchers and requisitions in his file.**

Gelzer, W. W., Corporal Co. A.
Enlisted on March 7, 1862, at Station 3, P&G RR, Florida. Promoted from Private to Corporal in June 2, 1863. POW surrendered on May 10, 1865, at Tallahassee, Florida. Paroled at Tallahassee, Florida, on May 16, 1865. Hair-dark, eyes-hazel, complexion-dark, 5 foot 8 inches. His parole is in his file. *

Gentry, J. W., Pvt. Co. C.
Enlisted on April 15, 1861, at Stockton, Alabama. Company muster roll for June 30, 1864, reports that he died.

George, William, H., Pvt. Co. G.
   Enlisted on March 29, 1862, at Dragoon Camp. POW surrendered on May 4, 1865, at Citronelle, Alabama. Paroled at Gainesville, Alabama, on May 14, 1865. Residence Mobile County, Alabama.

Gibson, David, Pvt. Co. H.
   POW surrendered on May 4, 1865, at Meridian, Mississippi. Paroled at Mobile, Alabama, on May 22, 1865. Residence Green County, Mississippi. He is also shown as belonging to Co. G or C of the 12th Mississippi Cavalry CSA.

Gibson, John, Pvt. Co. H.
   Enlisted on December 17, 1862, at Mobile, Alabama. POW surrendered at Citronelle, Alabama, on May 4, 1865. Paroled at Mobile, Alabama, on June 1, 1865. Residence Green County, Mississippi. Description; hair-brown, eyes-black, complexion-light, 5 foot 6 inches, Age-27.

Gibson, M. C., Pvt. Co. H.
   Enlisted on September 8, 1862, at Mobile, Alabama. Transferred to the Navy on April 9, 1864, by order of General D. H. Maury.

Gibson, William S., Pvt. Co. H.
   Enlisted December 15, 1862, at Mobile, Ala. POW surrendered at Citronelle, Alabama, May 4, 1865. Paroled at Mobile on June 20, 1865. Residence Green County, Mississippi. Hair-dark, eyes-dark, complexion-dark, 5 foot 10 inches, Age-35, occupation-farmer.

Gilbert, B. T., Pvt. Co. K.
   Enlisted on March 17, 1862, at Washington County, Alabama. POW captured at Claiborne, Alabama, on April 12, 1865, by U. S. Calvary Forces under the command of Brigadier General T. J. Lucas. Forwarded from Mobile, Alabama, to Ship Island, Mississippi.

Gilbert, John B., Pvt./Trumpeter Co. B.
   Enlisted on March 20, 1862, at Marianna, Florida. Signed an Oath of Allegiance to the USA at Military Prison in Louisville, Kentucky on September 28, 1863. "Gave himself up at Blys Ferry on September 9. Claimed to be a conscript. To remain in the north."

Gilbert, L. Y., Pvt. Co. _.
   POW surrendered at Tallahassee, Florida, on May 10, 1865. Paroled at Quincy, Florida, on May 22, 1865.

Gilley, P., Pvt. Co. G.
   Enlisted on February 3, 1864, at Halls Mill, Alabama. POW surrendered at Citronelle, Alabama, on May 4, 1865. Paroled at Gainesville, Alabama, on May 14, 1865. Residence Mobile, County, Alabama.

Gillis, J. L., Pvt. Co. I.
   Enlisted on December 27, 1862, at Santa Rosa, Florida.

Gilly, J., Pvt. Co. G.
   Enlisted on March 30, 1862, at Dragoon Camp. POW surrendered at Citronelle, Alabama, on May 4, 1865. Paroled at Gainesville, Alabama, on May 14, 1865. Residence Mobile, County, Alabama.

15TH CONFEDERATE CAVALRY

Gingles, J. W., Farrier Co. D.
Enlisted on October 17, 1862, at Cavalry Camp, (Camp Tatnall, Florida).

Gipson, J. G., Pvt. Co. I.
Enlisted on October 4, 1862, at Santa Rosa, Florida. Muster rolls dated April 30, 1864, and June 30, 1864, reports him detached to Tobins' Battery, no horse.

Glass, I. T., Wagon Master
POW surrendered at Tallahassee, Florida, on May 10, 1865. Paroled at Madison, Florida, on May 18, 1865.

Godwin, J. M., Pvt. Co. D.
Enlisted on April 3, 1863, at Pollard, Alabama. Appears on a list of soldiers employed in the Substance Department at Montgomery, Alabama, on May 22, 1864. POW captured at Mount Pleasant near Claiborne, Alabama, on April 11, 1865, by U. S. Calvary Forces under the command of Brigadier General T. J. Lucas. Forwarded from Mobile, Alabama, to Ship Island, Mississippi. There is a pay voucher in his file.*

Godwin, Wiley, Pvt. Co. D.
Enlisted on May 17, 1864, at Milton, Florida.

Goff, Daniel, Pvt. Co. H.
Enlisted on July 21, 1863, at West Pascagoula, Mississippi.

Goff, George see Gorff, George

Goff, James, Pvt. Co. H.
Enlisted on June 15, 1863, at West Pascagoula, Mississippi.

Goff, J. M., Pvt. Co. H.
POW surrendered in May 1865, at Meridian, Mississippi. Paroled at Mobile, Alabama, on May 23, 1865. Residence Jackson County, Mississippi. He is also shown as belonging to the 9th Mississippi Cavalry CSA.

Goff, Justin, Pvt. Mobile Dragoons.
Issued a Certificate of Disability on May 5, 1862, at Bayou La Batre due to phyhisis pulmonis. Enlisted in Captain William Boyles Company of the Mobile Dragoons at Bayou La Batre, Alabama, on March 29, 1862. Born Jackson County, Mississippi, age-23, hair-back, eyes-blue, complexion-light, 6 foot, by occupation a farmer. His Certificate of Disability is in the file of **J. M. Goff** above.*

Goff, L. P., Pvt. Co. H.
Enlisted on September 1, 1862, at Camp Forney. POW captured at Jackson County, Mississippi, on December 25, 1864. Confined at New Orleans on December 25, 1864. Transferred to Ship Island, Mississippi, on January 22, 1864. Applied to take the Oath of Allegiance to the USA at Ship Island. Transferred to Vicksburg, Mississippi, May 1, 1865.

Goff, Moses, Pvt. Co. G.
Enlisted on May 22, 1863, at Camp Taylor. POW surrendered in May 1865, at Meridian, Mississippi. Paroled at Mobile, Alabama, on May 23, 1865. Residence Jackson County, Mississippi. He is also shown as belonging to the 9th Mississippi Cavalry CSA. See J. M. Goff above.

Goff, Stephen, Pvt. Co. K.
  POW surrendered at Citronelle, Alabama, on May 4, 1865. Paroled at Gainesville, Alabama, on May 14, 1865. Residence Jackson County, Mississippi.

Golden, Tim, Pvt. Co. G.
  Enlisted on October 16, 1861, at Dragoon Camp.

Gonzales, C. B., Pvt. Co. D.
  Enlisted on September 6, 1862, at Camp Tatnall, Florida. On detached service as Forage Master with the Quarter Master Department at Greenville, Alabama. POW captured at Mount Pleasant, near Claiborne, Alabama, on April 11, 1865, by U.S. Cavalry forces. Forwarded from Mobile to Ship Island, Mississippi.

Gonzales, M. F., Captain & AQM
  Appointed Captain and AQM at Halls Mill, Alabama, on June 1, 1863. D. W. Waples was appointed AQM on March 24, 1864, which relieved Captain Gonzales of this duty. There are considerable requisitions and other paper work in his file. In addition he signs many other requisitions found in these files as Assistant Quarter Master CSA.**

Goode, J. J., Pvt. Co.
  Enlisted on March 7, 1863, at Halls, Mill, Alabama. Age-32, hair-dark, complexion-fair, eyes-blue, 5 foot 9 inches, born-Clarke County, Alabama. A lawyer by occupation. See pay voucher in the file of **Pvt. Jonathan Foscue**. Note: This man does not have a roster file in the 15th Confederate Cavalry service records.

Goode, Philip, Pvt. Co. G.
  Enlisted on February 11, 1862, at Halls Mill, Alabama. POW surrendered at Citronelle, Alabama, on May 4, 1865. Paroled at Mobile, Alabama, on June 16, 1865. Age-21, complexion-fair, eyes-blue, hair-red, residence-Monroe County, Alabama.

Goodman, Robinson, Pvt. Co. A.
  Enlisted on March 1, 1864, at Madison, Florida. POW surrendered at Tallahassee, Florida, on May 10, 1865. Paroled at Madison, Florida, on May 20, 1865.

Goodman, Iverson, Pvt. Co. I.
  Enlisted on October 4, 1862, at Santa Rosa, Florida. Signed an Amnesty Oath and a Oath of Allegiance to the USA, at Pensacola, Florida, on July 8, 1865. "I am twenty seven years of age - my home is in Walton County Fla - I served in the 1st Fla & 15th Confederate Cavalry since May 1861 up to April 1865. I left my Company and returned home where I have since remained. I was not paroled. This is all the service I have rendered to the Confederate Govt." Signed by "X" his mark. These documents are in his file. *

Gordon, A. A., Sergeant Co. K.
  Enlisted on March 17, 1862, at Washington County, Alabama. POW surrendered at Citronelle, Alabama, on May 4, 1865. Paroled at Gainesville, Alabama, on May 14, 1865. Residence Choctaw County, Alabama.

Gordon, A. J. Jr., Pvt. Co. C.
  Enlisted on October 6, 1862, at Shell Banks, Alabama. POW surrendered at Citronelle, Alabama, on May 4, 1865. Paroled at Gainesville, Alabama, on May 14, 1865. Residence Baldwin County, Alabama.

15TH CONFEDERATE CAVALRY

Gordon, A. J. Sr., Pvt. Co. C.
Enlisted on August 1, 1862, at Mount Pleasant, Alabama. Drew clothing on August 28, 1864.

Gordon, Albert A., Pvt. Co. B.
Enlisted on April 6, 1864, at Atlanta, Georgia.

Gordon, F. M., 2nd Lieutenant Co. I.
Enlisted as Jr. 2nd Lieutenant on October 4, 1862, at Santa Rosa, Florida. Commissioned on October 4, 1862. Promoted to 2nd Lieutenant on December 19, 1863. POW captured at Shoal River, Florida, on September 22, 1864, on a raid of Federal Troops under the command of Brigadier General Asboth into the interior of Western Florida. Confined at New Orleans, Louisiana, before October 10, 1864. Sent to Fort Lafayette, New York Harbor, confined there on October 20, 1864. He appears on a list of POW's at Fort Warren, Massachusetts, on December 21, 1864. Released on June 12, 1865. There are pay vouchers in his file.*

Gorff, George, Pvt. Co. F.
Enlisted on February 10, 1863, at Camp Withers. He is shown as a POW.

Gould, B. G., Pvt. Co. F.
Enlisted on October 1, 1861, at Mobile, Alabama.

Gould, Emerson S., Pvt. Co. F.
Enlisted on July 15, 1862, at Camp Withers.

Gould, L. D., Pvt. Co. F.
Enlisted on October 1, 1861, at Mobile, Alabama. POW captured at Claiborne, Alabama, on April 11, 1865. Sent to Ship Island, Mississippi.

Graham, Daniel, Pvt. Co, A.
Enlisted on March 7, 1862, at Station 3, P&G RR, Florida. POW surrendered at Tallahassee, Florida, on May 10, 1865. Paroled on May 15, 1865. He is also shown as POW surrendered at Citronelle, Alabama, on May 4, 1865. Paroled at Mobile, Alabama, on June 13, 1865. Residence Jefferson County, Florida, age-32, hair-dark, eyes-grey, complexion-dark, 5 foot 10 inches. There is a signed parol in his file at Tallahassee, Florida, on May 15, 1865. Daniel S. Graham, 5 foot 10 inches, hair-dark, eyes-grey, complexion-dark.*

Graham, John, Pvt. Co. G.
Enlisted on May 16, 1863, at Camp Taylor. Transferred to Major Steeds's Command by order of General Maury.

Graham, T. J., Pvt. Co. G.
Enlisted August 25, 1861, at Dragoon Camp. Navy transfer by order of General Maury.

Graham, T. M., Co. B.
Company B, Alabama & Florida Battalion Cavalry formerly Steed Battalion Coast Defense Troop. See personal papers of **Lewis, Roberts** Co. B. Alabama & Florida Battalion Cavalry.

Graham, William, Pvt. Co. F.
Enlisted on September 29, 1862, at Camp Withers.

Granade, I. N., Pvt. Co. K.
POW surrendered at Citronelle, Alabama, on May 4, 1865. Paroled at Gainesville, Alabama, on May 14, 1865. Residence Washington County, Alabama.

Grant, Stephen C., 1st Sergeant/Pvt. Co. B.
Enlisted as 1st Sergeant on March 14, 1862, at Marianna, Florida. He is shown as a private after October 1863. POW detailed in Ordnance Department at Macon, Mississippi, surrendered at Citronelle, Alabama, on May 4, 1865. Paroled at Columbus, Mississippi, on May 18, 1865.

Grantham, J. P., 1st Sergeant/2nd Lieutenant Co. A.
Enlisted on March 7, 1862, at Station 3, P&G RR, Florida. Promoted from 1st Sergeant to Lieutenant on September 11, 1863. Detailed as Officer of Guard batteries at Pollard and Montgomery, Alabama, on April 24, 1864, by order of Colonel Maury. POW surrendered at Tallahassee, Florida, on May 10, 1865. Paroled at Tallahassee, on May 15, 1865. Hair-light, eyes-grey, complexion-fair, 6 foot 3 inches. His Oath of Allegiance to the USA and several pay vouchers are in his file.**

Grater, C. F., Pvt. Co. G.
Enlisted on June 6, 1863, at Camp Taylor. He appears on a register of sick POW's at City Hospital, Mobile, Alabama. No date given.

Gray, S. P., 1 Sergeant/Jr. 2nd Lieutenant Co. F.
Enlisted on October 16, 1862, at Camp Withers. Promoted to Jr. 2nd Lieutenant on January 14, 1864. POW signed a Parole of Honor at Gainesville, Alabama, on May 14, 1865. His parole and a pay voucher are in his file.*

Green, E. B., Pvt. Co. H.
POW signed a parole at the Headquarters of the 16th U.S. Army Corp in Montgomery, Alabama, on June 8, 1865. Hair-light, eyes-blue, complexion-dark, 5 foot 8 inches. His parole is in his file.

Greene, James H., Sergeant/2nd Lieutenant. Co. E.
Enlisted on September 17, 1861, at Milton, Florida. Promoted from 3rd to 1st Sergeant on May 1, 1864. Shown as a 2nd Lieutenant POW, paroled at Montgomery, Alabama, on May 6, 1865. Hair-light, eyes-blue, complexion-fair, 5 foot 7 inches. His Parole of Honor is in his file.*

Greene, John, Pvt. Co. I.
Enlisted on January 27, 1864, Halls Mill, Alabama.

Greene, W. W., 2nd Lieutenant Co. I.
Enlisted on October 4, 1862, at Santa Rosa, Florida. Signs the November/December company muster roll as commanding the company. Promoted to 1st Lieutenant on December 19, 1863. May/June muster roll reports him absent in arrest or confinement.

Milton, Florida, September 18, 1864.

"I hereby certify that on Sunday night the 11th day of September 1864, one Sorrel Horse the property of the Confederate States & then in my possession, broke loose from his halter tied to a stake & strayed. I have used every means to find him without being successful. I also certify that the said horse did not get loose by any neglect or mismanagement on my part."

>W. W. Greene
>1st Lt. Co. I
>15th Con. Regt. Cavalry

"I hereby certify that the above statement of Lt. Greene is correct & true, & that he has used every exertion to find the lost Horse; & that it was not through any neglect or mismanagement on the part of Lt. Greene that the said horse got away."

>F. M. Gordon
>2nd Lt. Co. I
>15th Conf. Regt. Cavalry

Lieutenant Greene drew 10 shirts and 9 caps at Halls Mill on December 20, 1863. On February 15, 1864, he received 300 pounds of salt pork and 800 pounds of fodder at Shubuta. [Mississippi] On March 22, 1864, he drew 41 jackets, 42 pair of pants, 42 pair of shoes, 38 shirts and 10 blankets, at Halls Mill, Alabama. The requisitions, lost horse letter and a number of pay vouchers in his file.**

Greenwood, A., Pvt. Co. C.
Enlisted April 9, 1862, at Blakeley, Alabama. POW surrendered at Citronelle, Alabama, May 4, 1865. Paroled Gainesville, Ala., May 14, 1865. Residence Baldwin County, Ala.

Greenwood, Ignatious, Pvt. Co. C.
POW surrendered at Citronelle, Alabama, on May 4, 1865. Paroled at Gainesville, Alabama, on May 14, 1865. Residence Baldwin County, Alabama.

Greenwood, John, Pvt. Co. C.
Enlisted on March 8, 1863, at Camp Powell, Alabama. POW surrendered at Citronelle, Alabama, on May 4, 1865. Paroled at Gainesville, Alabama, on May 14, 1865. Residence Baldwin County, Alabama.

Greenwood, J. S., Pvt. Co. C.
Enlisted on September 1, 1861, at Shell Banks, Alabama. POW surrendered at Citronelle, Alabama, on May 4, 1865. Paroled at Gainesville, Alabama, on May 14, 1865. Residence Baldwin County, Alabama.

Greenwood, Wm. H. H., Pvt. Co. C./Sergeant Major, Field and Staff
Enlisted on July 15, 1861, at Shell Banks, Alabama. POW surrendered at Citronelle, Alabama, on May 4, 1865. Paroled at Gainesville, Alabama, on May 14, 1865. Residence Baldwin County, Alabama. Here he is shown as Sgt. Major.

Grey, B., Pvt. Co. H.
Enlisted on September 7, 1863, at Halls Mill, Alabama.

Grey, John B., Pvt. Co. H.
Enlisted on July 1, 1863, at West Pascagoula, Mississippi. Transferred due to irregularly mustered over to his proper command by Major Steed.

Grey, Thomas, A., Pvt. Co. H.
Enlisted on June 15, 1863, at West Pascagoula, Mississippi. Transferred due to irregularly mustered and turned over to his proper command by Major Steed.

Grice, B. F., Pvt. Co. E.
Enlisted on November 9, 1862, at Camp Lomax, Florida. POW he appears on a list of CSA soldiers paroled at Milton, Florida, on June 28, 1865.

Grice, Caper, Pvt. Co. E.
Enlisted on March 15, 1864, at Halls Mill, Alabama. POW he appears on a list of CSA soldiers paroled at Milton, Florida, on June 28, 1865.

Grice, Jacob, Pvt. Co. I.
Enlisted on March 9, 1863, at Conecuh, County, Alabama. POW he appears on a list of CSA soldiers paroled at Milton, Florida, on June 28, 1865.

Grice, T. J., Pvt. Co. E.
Enlisted on March 12, 1863, at Camp Lomax, Florida. Muster roll for September 12, 1863, reports him detailed to assist the A. A. Surgeon since July 1862. Later muster rolls shows him on special duty as hospital steward.

Griffin, J. F., Pvt. Co. H.
Enlisted on June 6, 1863, at Mobile, Alabama. Discharged from this regiment by reason of having received appointment of 2nd Lieutenant in Major Gus' Battalion.

Griffin, Joseph, Pvt. Co. D.
Enlisted at Camp Tattnall, Florida, on January 1, 1863. He is also shown as having enlisted on January 1, 1863, at Camp Lomax, Florida. He is reported to have died on December 3, 1863, at Mobile, Alabama.

Grimes, J. J., Pvt. Co. D.
Enlisted on April 24, 1862, at Pensacola, Florida. May/June 1864 muster roll reports him absent in Guard House in Mobile, Alabama. POW signed a parole at the headquarters of the 16th U.S. Army Corps in Montgomery, Alabama, on May 30, 1865. Hair-dark, eyes-light, complexion-dark, 6 foot, signed by "X."

Grimes, P. L., Pvt. Co. K.
Enlisted on December 26, 1862, at Mobile, Alabama. POW surrendered at Citronelle, Alabama, on May 4, 1865. Paroled at Gainesville, Alabama, on May 14, 1865. Residence Washington County, Alabama.

Grimes, William, Pvt. Co. D.
Enlisted on May 1, 1863, at Camp Tatnall, Florida. He is reported to have deserted on August 26, 1863.

Grist, John H., Pvt. Co. H.
Enlisted on September 4, 1862, at Mobile, Alabama. POW surrendered at Citronelle, Alabama, on May 4, 1865. Paroled at Gainesville, Alabama, on May 14, 1865. Residence Baldwin County, Alabama.

Grist, J. R., Pvt. Co. C.
Enlisted on August 1, 1863, at Camp Powell, Alabama. POW captured the night of April 8, 1865, at Blakeley, Alabama. Note on this POW roll "Orderly to General Liddell."

Grovis, W. M., Pvt. Co. K.
Enlisted on September 9, 1863, at Halls Mill, Alabama. Discharged on September 30, 1863.

15TH CONFEDERATE CAVALRY

Grubbs, E., Pvt. Co. D.
Enlisted on April 24, 1862, at Pensacola, Florida. He is reported to have deserted on December 23, 1863.

Guillot, Jules, Pvt. Co. H.
Enlisted on September 4, 1862, at Mobile, Alabama. Reported to have deserted on September 63, 1863, "suppose to have gone to the enemy."

Gillot, Maxwell, Pvt. Co. H.
Enlisted on February 8, 1863, at Mobile, Alabama.

Gunter, John, Pvt. Co. D.
Enlisted on October 20, 1862, at Camp Tatnall, Florida. Reported to have deserted on August 20, 1863.

H

Haas, George, Pvt. Co. F.
Enlisted on October 1, 1861, at Mobile, Alabama.

Hadley, J. T., Pvt. Co. C.
Enlisted on October 31, 186_, at Camp Powell, Alabama. Reported to be absent without leave.

Hairston, J. E., Corporal Co. B.
POW surrendered at Citronelle, Alabama, on May 4, 1865. Paroled at Meridian, Mississippi, on May 17, 1865. Residence Lowndes County, Mississippi.

Hadley, Michael, Pvt. Co. B.
Enlisted on March 14, 1862, at Marianna, Florida. Assigned to extra duty as waggoner on August 15, 1863, by order Colonel Maury for several months.

Hall, C. T., Pvt./Corp. Co. H.
Enlisted on May 25, 1862, at Bayou La Batre, Alabama. POW surrendered at Citronelle, Alabama, on May 4, 1865. Paroled at Mobile, Alabama, on June 13, 1865. Residence- Baldwin County, Alabama, age-21, hair-fair, eyes-gray, complexion-light, 5 foot 2 inches. On March 1, 1864, at Mobile, Alabama, he requisitioned and drew fodder for 6 horses for 27 days for a squad of six men and horses on secret service. He signed here as a Corporal.*

Hall, H. A., Pvt. Co. C.
Enlisted on April 3, 1864, at Pollard, Alabama. POW surrendered at Citronelle, Alabama, on May 4, 1865. Paroled at Gainesville, Alabama, on May 14, 1865. Residence Baldwin County, Alabama.

Hall, James, Pvt. Co. A.
Enlisted on July 8, 1863, at Pollard, Alabama. Discharged on May 31, 1864, by Medical Examining Board at General Hospital, Greenville, Alabama. His discharge shows that he enlisted at Camp Lomax, Florida, on June 20, 1863. Born Baldwin County, Georgia, age-67, 5 foot 10 inches, complexion-dark, eyes-dark, hair-grey, a farmer by occupation. Discharged due to general debility. "He was recd. as a substitute and has never done any duty with his command."

Hall, James, Corporal Co. D.
Enlisted on May 1, 1862, at Pensacola, Florida. He is shown as having deserted on December 16, 1863.

Hall, James W., Pvt. Co. D.
Enlisted on September 14, 1863, at Halls Mill, Alabama. Reported on several muster rolls on extra duty in Quartermasters Department. There is a letter of recommendation in his file for appointment as A. Q. M. It is written from Brooklyn, Alabama, on October 26, 1864, by Jackson Maston of Florida and attest to J. W. Hall's qualifications and character. Mr. Maston states that Hall is between 40 and 45 years in age and unfit for active duty. There is also a letter signed by Governor John Milton of Florida, and James Abinrombic, Senator of 1st District of Florida, and a State Representative from Escambia County, Florida, all asking Secretary of War James A. Siddon to consider James Hall for Quarter Master. It appears that the Q. M. General declined the appointment. ** These and other documents are in his file.

Hall, L. H., Bugler/Pvt. Co. C.
Enlisted on July 1, 1862, at Camp Powell, Alabama. He is also shown as having enlisted at Camp Withers on February 19, 1862. His records report him as bugler through December 31, 1863, thereafter he is shown as Private. His name appears on a list of POW's captured by the 16th U.S. Army Corps at Greenville, Alabama, on April 20, 1865. Turned over to the Assistant Provost Marshal at Montgomery, Alabama, on May 5, 1865.

Hall, S. H., Bugler/Pvt. Co. C.
There may be two men represented in the above file.

Hall, Starkes, Pvt. Co. I.
Enlisted on October 7, 1862, at Conecuh County, Alabama. He is also shown as having enlisted the same date at Santa Rosa, Florida.

Hall, William E., Sergeant/Pvt. Co. H.
Enlisted on September 4, 1862, at Mobile, Alabama. Reported on detached service by order of General Maury. Reduced to ranks from 4th Sergeant on December 11, 1863. POW surrendered at Citronelle, Alabama, on May 4, 1864. Paroled at Mobile, Alabama, on June 7, 1865. Age-29, hair-light, eyes-gray, complexion-fair, 5 foot 10 inches, a resident of Baldwin County, Alabama.

Hall, William, Pvt. Co. I
Enlisted on October 4, 1862, at Conecuh County, Alabama. He is also reported to have enlisted on the same date at Santa Rosa, Florida.

Hall, W. P., Pvt. Co. C.
Enlisted on July 1, 1862, at Camp Powell, Alabama. He is also shown as having enlisted at Camp Withers on October 23, 1862. POW surrendered at Citronelle, Alabama, on May 4, 1865. Paroled at Gainesville, Alabama, on May 14, 1865. Residence Baldwin County, Alabama.

Hallett, L. J., 1st Lieutenant/Captain Co. G.
Enlisted as 1st Lieutenant on July 30, 1862, at Mobile, Alabama. His Commission dates from May 19, 1862. He was paid $100 per month as 1st Lieutenant. He signs the November/December 1863, muster roll as commanding the company. Lt. Hallett requisitioned on December 8, 1863, at Halls Mill, Alabama, 128 jackets, 122 pair pants, 136 shirts, 126 pair drawers, 126 caps. He signs the January/February/March/April muster rolls

as Acting Adjutant. Lt. Hallett requisitioned 250 grain sacks and 34 lbs. of rope on February 12, 1864, at Halls Mill, Alabama. "Sacks are required to make nose bags & corn wallets and the rope for a picket rope of the use of the company." On March 25, 1864, he requisitioned 41 pair of pants, 42 jackets, 21 pair shorts, 37 shirts and 6 blankets at Halls Mill, Alabama. On March 31, 1864, he requisitioned 52,452 lbs. of corn and 30,597 lbs. of fodder for 141 horses for 31 days, at Halls Mill, Alabama. Promoted to Captain on November 15, 1864. POW signed a Parole of Honor at Gainesville, Alabama, on May 12, 1865. This and several requisitions and pay vouchers in his file. **

Halley, E. (Holley?), E., Pvt. Co. F.
POW paroled at the headquarters of the 16th U.S. Army Corps at Montgomery, Alabama, on June 16, 1865. Eyes-gray, hair-dark, complexion-dark, 5 foot 8 inches.

Halter, Thomas, A., Pvt. Co. C.
POW a member of Quarter Master Department CSA, surrendered at Citronelle, Alabama, on May 4, 1865. Paroled at Mobile, Alabama, on May 23, 1865. Residence Mobile, Alabama.

Hamilton, Benjamin, Pvt. Co. H.
Enlisted on March 4, 1863, at Mobile, Alabama. Admitted to Ross Hospital, Mobile, Alabama, on September 18, 1863, with hernia. He was furloughed on November 17, 1863, for 30 days. He was discharged by reason of physical disability by order of General Maury. Age-35, 5 foot 7 inches, complexion-fair, eyes-grey, hair-dark, by occupation a farmer. Discharged and paid $141 for service and clothing on January 1, 1864, at Halls Mill, Alabama. His Certificate for Discharge is in his file.*

Hammond, A. F., Pvt. Co. A.
Enlisted on May 2, 1863, at Camp Lomax, Florida. POW surrendered at Meridian Mississippi, on May 4, 1865. Paroled at Mobile, Alabama, on May 22, 1865. Residence Essex County, Massachusetts. Here he is shown as a member of 15th Confederate Cavalry but on a roll of POW's of Co. F, 2nd Mississippi Cavalry Reserves commanded by Colonel E. A. Case.

Hammond, John T., Pvt. Co. C.
Enlisted on April 15, 1862, at Stockton, Alabama. POW surrendered at Meridian Mississippi, on May 4, 1865. Paroled at Mobile, Alabama, on May 22, 1865. Residence Baldwin County, Alabama.

Handley, John, Co. F.
His papers are filed with Pvt. **Hanley, John**, Co. I 1st Battalion Confederate Infantry.

Hanborn, John, Pvt. Co. F.
Enlisted on November 24, 1862, at Camp Withers. Reported absent sick in hospital on several muster rolls.

Hannon, Thomas, 1st Lieutenant Co. F.
Enlisted on May 7, 1862. Elected 1st Lieutenant on May 7, 1862. His name appears as 1st Lieutenant of Co. A, City Troop, Battalion, Alabama Cavalry at Fort Morgan, Alabama, in October and November 1862. He signs the September 12, 1863, muster roll as commanding the company. His pay was $100 per month as 1st Lieutenant. On September 16, 1863, at Halls Mill, Alabama, he requisitioned corn for 97 horses. On this requisition a note explains that there was no fodder to be obtained to fill his request. He was charged with "drunkenness

on duty" on October 11, 1863, at Camp Moore, Halls Mill, Alabama. The offence took place on or about the 28th of August 1863, at or near Halls. Mill, Alabama. The specification against him was signed by Captain E. T. Arrington, Co. F. Witnesses were Captain John H. Marshal, Co. A, Captain John T. Davis, Co. B, Lieutenant Kenney Cleveland, Co. H, Sergeant Crevy, [Thomas Creevey] Co. F, and Private Rufus Campbell, Co. F. Charges were preferred against him by Colonel Maury and his trial set for October 23. He resigned on October 19, 1863. Captain Arrington's specifications against Captain Hannon and his resignation are in his file. **

Hanson, P. H., Pvt. Co. F.
Enlisted on September 1, 1862, at Camp Withers. He is reported as having been on detached duty at the Government Fisheries on September 17, 1863, by order of General Maury. He is reported to have deserted on December 23, 1863.

Harnverson, William, Pvt. Co. D. see **Haverson, William**.

Hardaway, S. D., Corporal/Sergeant Co. H.
Enlisted on September 4, 1863, at Mobile, Alabama. September/October muster roll reports him detailed to the artillery. There after he is shown as present. Promoted to 5th Sergeant from 1st Corporal on December 11, 1863. POW surrendered at Citronelle, Alabama, on May 4, 1865. Paroled at Gainesville, Alabama, on May 14, 1865. Residence Mobile County, Alabama.

Harman, M. D., Pvt. Co. H.
Enlisted on September 4, 1863, at Mobile, Alabama. Detailed to the artillery by order of General Maury. Detached on October 21, 1863. Paid $139.84 at Mobile, Alabama, for four months service, paid for he and his horse and clothing on January 1, 1864. POW in detached CSA service surrendered at Meridian Mississippi, on May 4, 1865. Paroled at Meridian, Mississippi, on May 13, 1865. Residence Quitman Mississippi. His pay voucher is in his file.*

Harmond or Harmon see Harman.

Harney, J. C., Pvt. Co. H.
Enlisted on March 23, 1863, at Mobile, Alabama. Detached on September 25, 1863, by General Maury to the Engineer Department. January/April 1864, muster roll reports "Deserted from that place supposed to have gone to Havana." A pay voucher for $48 on November 2, 1863, is in his file.

Haroldson, Jesse, Pvt. Co. E.
Enlisted at Pitts Bridge, Florida. No date given.

Harris, D. W., Pvt. Co. C.
POW surrendered at Citronelle, Alabama, on May 4, 1865. Paroled at Gainesville, Alabama, on May 14, 1865. Residence Baldwin County, Alabama.

Harris, J. L., 3rd Sergeant Co. C.
Enlisted May 3, 1862, at Stockton, Alabama. POW surrendered at Citronelle, Alabama, on May 4, 1865. Paroled at Gainesville, Alabama, on May 14, 1865. Residence Baldwin County, Alabama. (There is a note in his file relative to information furnished by **Mrs. Myrtle Boazman** of Mobile, Ala. She says **John Lewis Harris** enlisted at Fort Morgan, Alabama, served for one year, was discharged and re-enlisted under Captain Barlow.)*

15TH CONFEDERATE CAVALRY

Harris, L. J., Pvt. Co. C.
Enlisted on October 29, 1862, at Camp Powell, Alabama. POW surrendered at Citronelle, Alabama, on May 4, 1865. Paroled at Gainesville, Alabama, on May 14, 1865. Residence Baldwin County, Alabama.

Harrison, J. T., Pvt. Co. K.
Enlisted on July 1, 1863, at Bayou La Batre, Alabama. Age-17, eyes-black, hair-dark, complexion-fair, 5 foot 3 inches, born-Choctaw County, Alabama, a farmer by occupation. POW captured April 11, 1865, at Mount Pleasant, Alabama, by U.S. Cavalry forces. His name appears on a list of POW's forwarded from Mobile, Alabama, to Ship Island, Mississippi. He also appears on a roll of men of Co. K, 15th Confederate Cavalry that were surrendered at Citronelle, Alabama, on May 4, 1865. Paroled at Gainesville, Alabama, on May 14, 1865. Residence Choctaw County, Alabama. His descriptive list and record of $50 bounty pay is to be found in the file of **Pvt. J. F. Hutchinson** of Co. K.

Harrison, G., Pvt. Co. B.
His name appears on a roll of POW's captured on April 27, 1865, at Greenville, Alabama, by 3rd Brigade of U.S. Cavalry. Paroled at Greenville, Alabama.

Harrold, J. W., Pvt. Co. K.
His name appears on a roll of stragglers paroled at Selma, Alabama, in June 1865. Residence reported to be Bibb County, Alabama.

Hart, Abraham, Pvt. Co. I.
Enlisted on October 4, 1862, at Santa Rosa, Florida. POW captured at Mount Pleasant, Alabama, by U.S. Cavalry forces on April 11, 1865. His name appears on a list of POW's forwarded from Mobile, Alabama, to Ship Island, Mississippi.

Hart, Charles H., Pvt. Co. G.
Enlisted on October 17, 1861, at Dragoon Camp. Appears on a list of men on detached service in Commissary Department that were surrendered at Citronelle, Alabama, on May 4, 1865. Paroled at Meridian, Mississippi, on May 11, 1865. Residence Mobile, Alabama. His file contains a note that his detail requested to heard cattle April 1865, and to see the personal papers of **W. T. Edwards** Major & C.S. *

Hart, David, Pvt. Co. A.
Enlisted on May 12, 1864, at Monticello, Florida. POW captured at Mount Pleasant, Alabama, by U.S. Cavalry forces on April 11, 1865. His name appears on a list of POW's forwarded from Mobile, Alabama, to Sand Island, Mississippi. There is a pay voucher in his file in the amount of $48.40 for service of he and his horse in May and June 1863.

Hart, D. E., Pvt. Co. I.
Enlisted on June 4, 1864, at Santa Rosa, Florida.

Hart, Jacob, Pvt. Co. A.
Enlisted on January 4, 1864, at Halls Mill, Alabama. POW surrendered at Tallahassee, Florida, on May 10, 1865. Paroled at Tallahassee, Florida, on May 17, 1865.

Hart, Joshua, Pvt. Co. I.
Enlisted on October 4, 1862, at Santa Rosa, Florida. September 12, 1863. Muster rolls reports him on detached service since June 26, herding cattle by order of General Cantey. November/December 1863, roll reports him dead.

Hart, Reuben, Pvt. Co. I.
Enlisted on October 4, 1862, at Santa Rosa, Florida. September 12, 1863, muster rolls reports him on detached service since June 26, herding cattle by order of General Cantey. His name appears on a list of detached soldiers employed in the Subsistence Department at Montgomery, Alabama, on May 22, 1864, stationed at Pollard, Alabama.

Hartwell, T. C., Pvt. Co. F.
POW surrendered at Citronelle, Alabama, on May 4, 1865. Paroled at Gainesville, Alabama, on May 14, 1865. Residence Mobile, Mobile County, Alabama.

Harvey, George W., Pvt. Co. G.
Enlisted on February 26, 1862, at Dragoon Camp. Admitted to Ross Hospital, Mobile, Alabama, on January 14, 1864, with catarrh (cerebritis). Died on January 16, 1864. Company muster roll for December 31, 1863/April 30, 1864, reports that he died on January 16, 1864.

Harvey, James H., Corporal, Co. B.
Enlisted on March 20, 1862, at Marianna, Florida. Company muster roll for September 12, 1863, reports him detailed in the enrolling office on May 10, 1863, by order of General Maury. Promoted from 2nd to 1st Corporal on November 1, 1863. There is a pay voucher in the amount of $24 for service for May and June 1863, in the Marianna Dragons. *

Harvey, John H., Pvt. Co. B.
Enlisted on May 3, 1862, at Marianna, Florida. Company muster roll for September 12, 1863, reports him detailed in the enrolling office by order of General Maury. Subsequent rolls report him present. POW captured at Mount Pleasant, Alabama, by U.S. Cavalry forces on April 11, 1865. His name appears on a list of POW's forwarded from Mobile, Alabama, to Ship Island, Mississippi.

Harvey, W. J., Sergeant Co. B.
POW surrendered at Citronelle, Alabama, on June 1, 1865. Paroled on June 2, 1865, at Mobile, Alabama. Age-34, hair-black, eyes-dark, complexion-dark, 5 foot 11 inches, residence shown as Marianna, Florida.

Hassell, F. M., Corporal/Sergeant Co. I.
Enlisted on October 4, 1862, at Santa Rosa, Florida. He was promoted to 4th Sergeant on November 1, 1863.

Hastan, N. H., Pvt. Co. E. see Horton, N. H.

Hastie, J. H. Jr., Pvt. Co. C.
Enlisted on April 9, 1862, at Blakeley, Alabama. POW surrendered at Citronelle, Alabama, on May 4, 1865. Paroled at Gainesville, Alabama, on May 14, 1865. Residence Baldwin County, Alabama.

Hatter, T. A., Pvt. Co. C.
Enlisted on May 12, 1862, at Stockton, Alabama. His name appears on a list of soldiers employed in the Commissary Department at Mobile, Alabama for the month of July 1864. He is shown here as a miller at Otis Mill.

Haven, Charles, Pvt. Co. G.
Enlisted May 16, 1863, at Camp Taylor. Company muster roll for September 1863, reports

15TH CONFEDERATE CAVALRY

him present under arrest. September/October muster roll reports him ordered transferred to Major Steeds Command by General Maury. See petition in file of Pvt. **Lewis Roberts**.

Havens, H. C., Corporal/Pvt. Co. H.
Enlisted on September 4, 1862, at Mobile, Alabama. He is shown as 3rd Corporal on September/October 1863, muster roll, thereafter he is shown as Private. Assigned extra duty as Forage Master for the regiment. Pay due as Corporal from December 11, 1863.

Havens, Jeff, Pvt. Co. H.
Enlisted on June 3, 1864, at Mobile, Alabama.

Havens, John F., Pvt. Co. H.
Enlisted on September 4, 1862, at Mobile, Alabama.

Havens, W. L., Pvt. Co. H.
Enlisted on December 3, 1862, at Mobile, Alabama. Admitted to Ross Hospital, Mobile, Alabama, on January 9, 1864, with catarrh. Furloughed for 30 days on January 17, 1864.

Haverson, William, Pvt. Co. D.
Enlisted on April 24, 1862, at Pensacola, Florida.

Hawkins, J. R., Pvt. Co. A.
Enlisted on March 12, 1863, at Camp Lomax, Florida. He appears present on a muster roll at General Hospital, Greenville, Alabama, from March 1 to August 31, 1864. POW captured at Greenville, Alabama, on April 27, 1865, by U.S. Cavalry. He was paroled at Greenville, Alabama.

Hawkins, Thomas, Pvt. Co. K.
Enlisted on March 18, 1863, at Halls Mill, Alabama. POW surrendered at Citronelle, Alabama, on May 4, 1865. Paroled at Gainesville, Alabama, on May 14, 1865. Residence Washington County, Alabama.

Hawthorn, J. R., Pvt. Co. E.
Enlisted on January 27, 1864, at Halls Mill, Alabama. POW captured at Escambia County Florida by a detachment of 1st Florida and 2nd Maine Cavalry on November 17, 1864. He was confined at New Orleans, Louisiana, on November 21, 1864, and transferred to Ship Island, Mississippi, on December 10, 1864. Received at Ship Island on December 13, 1864, and transferred to Vicksburg, Mississippi, on May 1, 1865.

Hays, G., Pvt. Co. F.
POW surrendered at Citronelle, Alabama, on May 4, 1865. Paroled at Gainesville, Alabama, on May 14, 1865. Residence Mobile, Mobile County, Alabama.

Helveston, Philip, Pvt. Co. H.
Enlisted on September 4, 1862, at Mobile, Alabama.

Hemphill, S. L., Pvt./Corporal Co. I.
Enlisted on October 4, 1862, at Santa Rosa, Florida. He was promoted to 3rd Corporal on September 1, 1863, from the ranks.

Henderson, Robert, Pvt. Co. D.
Enlisted on April 25, 1862, at Pensacola, Florida. Company muster roll of September 12,

1863, reports him absent without leave since August 26, 1863. September/December muster roll reports him having deserted on August 26.

Henderson, William, Pvt. Co. D.
Enlisted on April 24, 1862, at Pensacola, Florida. Company muster roll of September 12, 1863, reports him absent without leave since August 26, 1863. September/December muster roll reports him having deserted on August 26.

Hendrix, T. D., Pvt. Co. G.
Enlisted on July 30, 1861, at Mobile, Alabama.

Henley, J. D., Pvt. Co. E.
Enlisted on April 9, 1862, at Camp Perdido, Florida.

Henson, J., Pvt. Co. C.
His name appears on a roll of POW's of Cos. G and C, 12th Regiment Mississippi Cavalry CSA, that were surrendered at Citronelle, Alabama, on May 4, 1865. Paroled at Mobile, Alabama, on May 22, 1865. Residence Baldwin County, Alabama.

Herrington, V. J., Pvt./Corporal Co. G.
Enlisted on August 11, 1862, at Dragoon Camp. POW surrendered at Citronelle, Alabama, on May 4, 1865. Paroled at Mobile, Alabama, on May 30, 1865. Residence Jackson County, Mississippi. Age-35, eyes-dark, hair-dark, complexion-dark, 6 foot.

Hester, James T., Pvt. Co. A.
Enlisted March 1, 1863, at Camp Lomax, Florida. Admitted to Ross Hospital, Mobile, Alabama, with Chronic Rheumatism October 19, 1863. Furloughed 30 days on October 31.

Hester, Thomas, Pvt. Co. D/A.
Enlisted in Company D on February 1, 1863, at Camp Tatnall, Florida. Transferred to Company A on September 1, 1863. November/December 1863, muster roll reports him on duty with Maury's Horse Artillery.

Hester, W. T., Pvt. Co. A.
Enlisted on June 9, 1863, at Camp Lomax, Florida.

Hetzell, Peter, Pvt. Co. F.
Enlisted on August 27, 1862, at Camp Withers. January through June 1864, he is reported to be detailed as a courier to General Maury. POW captured on April 9, 1865, at Blakeley, Alabama. His name appears on a list of POW's received at Ship Island, Mississippi, on April 15, 1865. Transferred to Vicksburg, Mississippi, on May 1, 1865.

Heyts, C., Pvt. Co. F.
POW surrendered at Citronelle, Alabama, on May 4, 1865. He was paroled at Meridian, Mississippi, on May 9, 1865. Residence Alabama.

Hetzler, P. see **Hetzell, Peter**

Hickman, Berry, Pvt. Co. E.
Enlisted on May 26, 1862, at Camp Perdido, Florida. March/April 1864, company muster roll reprots that he "Deserted from Halls Mill, Alabama, about 25 Dec. 63, and has probably gone to the enemy at Pensacola Navy Yard."

15TH CONFEDERATE CAVALRY

Hildreth, L. A., Pvt. Co. H.
Enlisted on September 4, 1862, at Mobile, Alabama. POW surrendered at Citronelle, Alabama, on May 4, 1865. Paroled at Gainesville, Alabama, on May 14, 1865. Residence Marengo County, Alabama.

Hill, T. J., 2nd Lieutenant Co. G.
Enlisted on July 30, 1861, at Mobile, Alabama. His commission was from May 19, 1862. He signed the September/November 1863, company muster roll as commanding the company. November/December muster roll reports him absent without leave. December 31, 1863/April 30, 1864, roll reports him present under arrest. He requisitioned 20 pair of shoes on February 28, 1864, for Captain Marshall's Co. G. Regimental Roster for January 1, 1865, at Spring Hill, shows him as 1st Lieutenant, promoted on November 15, 1864. There are a number of pay vouchers and requisitions signed by Lt. Hill in his file. **

Hines, G. W., Pvt. Co. A.
Enlisted at Station 3 on P & G RR, Florida. Company muster roll for March/April 1864, reports him as Regimental Color Bearer.

Hines, J. T., Pvt. Co. A.
Enlisted on April 10, 1864, at Halls Mill, Alabama. POW surrendered at Tallahassee, Florida, on May 10, 1865. Paroled at Tallahassee, Florida, on May 15, 1865.

Hines, J. W., Pvt. Co. _.
POW surrendered Tallahassee, Fla., May 10, 1865. Paroled Tallahassee, Fla. May 18, 1865.

Hinlason, J. L., Pvt. Co. B. see **Finlayson, John L**.

Hinote, G. B., Pvt. Co. E.
Enlisted on July 10, 1863, at Camp Morgan, Florida. Transferred to Co. E February 1, 1864, from Captain J. C. Keyser's Co. I, 6th Alabama Regiment Cavalry in exchange for **W. A. Whitmire** of Company E.

Hinson, John, Pvt. Co. C.
Enlisted on April 15, 1862, at Stockton, Alabama.

Hobbs, B. F., Pvt. Co. D.
Enlisted on April 24, 1862, at Pensacola, Florida. January/February 1864, muster roll reports that he deserted on January 19, 1864.

Hobley, William, Pvt. Co. E.
Appears on a list of POW's stragglers surrendered at Selma, Alabama, in June 1865. Residence Wilcox County, Alabama.

Hoffins, G., Pvt. Co. F. see **Hofheins, George**

Hofheins, George, Pvt. Co. F.
Enlisted on October 1, 1861, at Mobile, Alabama. Admitted to Ross Hospital, Mobile, Alabama, with debility on September 24, 1863. Returned to duty on November 1, 1863. Admitted to Ross Hospital, Mobile, Alabama, on October 18, 1864, with febris intermittens tert. Sent to General Hospital Nidelet on December 5, 1864. His name appears on a roll of POW's and deserters captured at line of march in Alabama, on April 18, 1865, by the 16th U.S. Army Corps. He reported voluntarily and took the Amnesty Oath.

Holdsworth, A., Pvt. Co. G.
Enlisted on October 17, 1861, at Dragoon Camp. Admitted to Ross Hospital, Mobile, Alabama, on September 3, 1864, with neuralgia. Furloughed for 60 days on September 17.

Holland, John, Pvt. Co. D.
Enlisted on April 20, 1864, at Pollard, Alabama. Signs by his mark.

Holland, W. T., Bvt. 2nd Lieutenant/1st Lieutenant Co. F.
Entered State Service on May 7, 1862. 2nd Lt. William Holland appears on a field return from Harbor Brigade at Fort Morgan, Alabama. He is shown with Co. A. City Troop, absent at Camp Withers. Elected 2nd Lieutenant on May 7, 1862. He signs the September/December 1863, company muster rolls as commanding the company. Lt. Holland requisitioned for Co. F, at Halls Mill on December 20, 1863; 37 jackets, 40 pair pants, 50 caps and 100 shirts. In December 1863, he requisitioned corn and fodder for 51 horses. Promoted to 1st Lieutenant on January 12, 1864. He was paid $100 per month as Lieutenant. He signed a Parole of Honor at Gainesville, Alabama, on May 14, 1865. He signs as Captain commanding Co. F. This document and other vouchers, paper work and requisitions are in his file. **

Holley, E., Pvt. Co. F. see **Halley, E.**, Pvt. Co. F.

Hollinger, A., Pvt. Co. C.
Enlisted on April 9, 1862, at Blakeley, Alabama. Company muster roll for December 31, 1863, through June 30, 1864, reports him as having deserted.

Hollinger, C. A., Pvt. Co. H.
POW surrendered at Citronelle, Alabama, on May 4, 1865. Paroled at Gainesville, Alabama, on May 14, 1865. Residence Mobile County, Alabama.

Hollman, J. D., Pvt. Co. D.
Enlisted on April 24, 1862, at Pensacola, Florida. Company muster roll for January/February 1864, reports that he deserted on December 23, 1863.

Holly, A. D., Pvt. Co. I.
Enlisted on June 1, 1864, at Santa Rosa, Florida.

Holman, J. D., Pvt. Co. D. see **Hollman, J. D.**

Holmes, J. W., Pvt. Co. E. see **Holms, J. W.**

Holmes, O. S., Assistant Surgeon, Field and Staff.
Commission or appointment dates from August 31, 1862. His name appears on muster rolls September 1863, through April 1864. He was paid $110 per month as Assistant Surgeon. Field and Staff muster roll from December 31, 1863, through June 30, 1864, reports that Assistant Surgeon Holmes relieved from duty. **Dr. Doby** assigned in his stead. There are several requisitions and pay vouchers in his file.**

Holmes, Thomas G., Pvt. Co. C.
Enlisted on September 1, 1863. His place of enlistment is shown as Mobile, Blakeley and Camp Powell, Alabama. POW surrendered at Citronelle, Alabama, on May 4, 1865. Paroled at Gainesville, Alabama, on May 14, 1865. Residence Baldwin County, Alabama.

15TH CONFEDERATE CAVALRY

Holmes, J. W., Pvt. Co. E.
Enlisted on October 26, 1862, at Camp Lomax, Florida. Drew clothing on September 2, 1864.

Holston, S. W., Pvt. Co. K.
Enlisted on May 8, 1862, at Mobile, Alabama.

Horton, N. H., Pvt. Co. E.
Enlisted on August 25, 1862, at Camp Lomax, Florida. Signed a parole at Headquarters of the 16th U.S. Army Corps at Montgomery, Alabama on June 5, 1865. Hair-dark, eyes-hazel, complexion-dark, 5 foot 8 inches. His parole is in his file.

Houseman, G. O., Pvt. Co. D.
Enlisted on April 24, 1862, at Pensacola, Florida. Drew clothing on August 28, 1864.

Houston, S. J., Pvt. Co. A.
Enlisted on June 11, 1862, at Camp Tatnall, Florida. POW surrendered at Tallahassee, Florida, on May 10, 1865. Paroled on May 17, 1865.

Howard, Harrison, Pvt. Co. A.
Enlisted on April 13, 1863, at Camp Lomax, Florida. Drew clothing on September 7, 1864.

Howard, J. P., Pvt. Co. D.
Enlisted on April 11, 1864, at Santa Rosa, Florida.

Howard, William, Pvt. Co. I.
Enlisted on April 4, 1863, at Conecuh County, Alabama. Company muster roll for September/October 1863, reports him absent without leave since August 5. November/December roll reports him having deserted.

Howard, W. L., Pvt. Co. K.
Enlisted on March 17, 1862, at Washington, County, Alabama. POW surrendered at Citronelle, Alabama, on May 4, 1865. Paroled at Gainesville, Alabama, on May 14, 1865. Residence Choctaw County, Alabama.

Hubbard, Francis M., Pvt. Co. C.
Enlisted on April 15, 1862, at Stockton, Alabama. Admitted to Ross Hospital, Mobile, Alabama, on October 19, 1863, with intermittent fever. Returned to duty on November 1. Company muster roll for November/December 1863, reports him absent without leave. Roll for December 31, 1863, through June 1864, reports him as having deserted.

Hubbell, G. L., Pvt. Co. G.
Enlisted on July 30, 1861, at Mobile, Alabama. POW surrendered at Citronelle, Alabama, on May 4, 1865. Paroled at Gainesville, Alabama, on May 14, 1865. Residence Mobile, Mobile County, Alabama.

Hubbell, O. E., Pvt. Co. G.
Enlisted on May 22, 1862, at Dragoon Camp. POW surrendered at Citronelle, Alabama, on May 4, 1865. Paroled at Meridian, Mississippi, on May 10, 1865. Residence Mobile, Alabama.

Huggins, Burrell (Burl), Pvt. Co. D.
  Enlisted on April 24, 1862, at Pensacola, Florida. Died December 6, 1863, at Mobile, Ala.

Huggins, J. B., Pvt. Co. G.
  Enlisted on July 30, 1861, at Mobile, Alabama. His file contains a POW record that is too dark to read.*

Huggins, Jesse, Pvt. Co. G.
  Enlisted on April 24, 1862, at Pensacola, Florida. September/October company muster roll reported him on extra duty as a guide by order of General Clanton. POW surrendered at Citronelle, Alabama, on May 4, 1865. Paroled at Gainesville, Alabama, on May 14, 1865. Residence Washington County, Alabama.

Hughes, Griffith, Pvt. Co. G.
  Enlisted in Mobile Dragoons on July 30, 1861, at Mobile, Alabama. Age-34, eyes-blue, hair-light, complexion-florid, 5 foot 6 inches, born-Balla Wales, occupation-gardener. September through December 1863, company muster rolls report him detailed as a teamster. Drew clothing on September 10, 1864.

Hughs, R. S., Pvt. Co. E.
  Enlisted on March 13, 1863, at Camp Lomax, Florida. Signed a parole at headquarters of 16th U.S. Army Corps, Montgomery, Alabama, on June 8, 1865. Hair-black, eyes-blue, complexion-dark, 5 foot 7 inches.

Hughs, T. M., Pvt. Co. E.
  Enlisted on December 24, 1862, at Camp Lomax, Florida. POW captured in Escambia County, Florida, by a detachment of 1st Florida Cavalry and 2nd Maine Cavalry on November 17, 1864. Confined at New Orleans, Louisiana, on November 21, 1864. Transferred to Ship Island, Mississippi, on December 10, 1864. Received at Ship Island on December 13, and transferred to Vicksburg, Mississippi, on May 1, 1865.

Hugonin, P., Pvt. Co. G.
  Enlisted on July 1, 1861, at Mobile, Alabama. September 12, 1863, through April 30, 1864, company muster rolls report him detached as a courier to the Chief of Artillery. Age-29, eyes-black, hair-black, complexion-dark, 5 foot 3 inches, born in New Orleans, Louisiana. There are a considerable number of pay vouchers in his file. He was paid $12 per month plus $12.40 for his horse. **

Hunter, Isaac, S., Pvt. Co. E.
  Enlisted on March 20, 1862, at Camp Lomax, Florida. Discharged by Medical Board at General Hospital Moore, Mobile, Alabama, on May 12, 1864. Unable to perform his military duty due to the development of numerous fatty tumors through muscular tissue and over his body generally. Born in Irwin County, Georgia, age-29, 5 foot 8 inches, eyes-grey, complexion-light, hair-dark, a miller by occupation. His Certificate of Disability is in his file.*

Hunter, Joseph T., Pvt. Co. B.
  Enlisted on March 14, 1862, at Marianna, Florida. September/October 1863, company muster roll reports him detailed for Provost Duty by order or General Maury from June 17, 186?. POW surrendered on May 11, 1865, at Quincy, Florida. Paroled at Quincy, Florida, on May 22, 1865. There is a pay voucher in his file.*

15TH CONFEDERATE CAVALRY

Hurring, C. B., Pvt. Co._.
POW surrendered on May 10, 1865, at Tallahassee, Florida. Paroled at Quincy, Florida, on May 22, 1865.

Huse, J., Pvt. Co. G.
Admitted to Ross Hospital, Mobile, Alabama, on October 26, 1864, with febris congestia, febris remittens. He is reported to have died on October 29, 1864.

Hutchison, Frascis S., Pvt./Corporal Co. H.
Enlisted on September 4, 1862, at Mobile, Alabama. Promoted to 3rd Corporal from ranks on December 18, 1863. He appears as 2nd corporal on later muster rolls. Admitted to Ross Hospital, Mobile, Alabama, on October 21, 1864, with febris intermittens quot. Sent to General Hospital Heustis on November 30, 1864.

Hutchinson, J. F., Pvt. Co. K.
Enlisted on November 1, 1863, at Mobile, Alabama. Age-17, eyes-grey, hair-light, complexion-fair, 5 foot 8 inches, born-Clarke County, Alabama, a student by occupation. POW surrendered at Citronelle, Alabama, on May 4, 1865. Paroled at Gainesville, Alabama, on May 14, 1865. Residence Choctaw County, Alabama. He was paid $50 joining bounty. here is a descriptive list and account of bounty for he, **J. T. Harrison**, **Samuel Mallet** and **S. T. Lyons** in his file. See the individual entries for their descriptions.

Hutton, J. G., Pvt. Co. D/Ordnance Sergeant F&S.
Enlisted on August 20, 1862, at Camp Tatnall, Florida. Appointed Ordnance Sergeant on June 1, 1863. POW who's name appears on a parole of POW's at Headquarters of Cavalry forces M. D. W. M. [Medical Dept.?] near Greenville, Alabama. Paroled at Headquarters of the 16th U.S. Army Corps at Montgomery, Alabama, on June 2, 1865. Hair-light, eyes-blue, complexion-fair. 5 foot 11 inches. His parole is in his file*.

I

Infinger, Clark, Pvt. Co. I.
Enlisted on October 4, 1862, at Santa Rosa, Florida. September /October 1863, muster roll reports him absent without leave, since February 28. November/December 1863, and later rolls report him to have deserted.

Ingalls, William, Pvt. Co. F.
Enlisted on October 1, 1861, at Mobile, Alabama. September /December 1863, company muster roll reports him on detached service from February 23, 1863, to work on floating battery by order of General Marshall. His detail is shown thus on muster rolls through June 1864. POW surrendered at Citronelle, Alabama, on May 4, 1865. Paroled at Gainesville, Alabama, on May 14, 1865. Residence Mobile, Mobile County, Alabama.

Ingram, James J., Pvt. Co. A.
He is shown to have enlisted on May 10, 1864, at Pollard, Alabama. He drew clothing on September 7, 1864.

Innerarity, James, Pvt. Co. G.
Enlisted on November 29, 1862, at Halls Mill, Alabama. His name appears on a roll of POW's of stragglers surrendered and paroled at Selma, Alabama, on May 28, 1865. Residence Mobile, Alabama.

Irwin, Joseph, Pvt. Co. B.
Enlisted on March 14, 1862, at Marianna, Florida. POW surrendered at Tallahassee, Florida, on May 10, 1865. Paroled at Tallahassee, Florida, on May 23, 1865.

J

Jackson, B. R., Pvt. Co. G.
POW captured on March 2, 1865, at Cedar Point, Alabama by U.S. Army. Confined at New Orleans, Louisiana, on March 21, 1865. Exchanged on May 11, 1865.

Jackson, William J., Pvt. Co. E.
Enlisted on April 2, 1864, at Pollard, Alabama. Admitted to Ross Hospital, Mobile, Alabama, on March 23, 1865, with phthisis [tuberculosis]. Sent to General Hospital at Meridian on April 2, 1865.

Jenkins, E. P., Bugler/Chief Bugler
Enlisted on March 17, 1862, at Washington County, Alabama. POW captured at Mount Pleasant, Alabama, on April 11, 1865, by U.S. Cavalry forces. POW surrendered at Citronelle, Alabama, on May 4, 1865. Paroled at Gainesville, Alabama, on May 14, 1865. Residence Choctaw County, Alabama.

Jennett, Frank, Pvt. Co. H.
Enlisted on January 16, 1863. November/December 1863, company muster roll reports him on detached service as courier to General Maury. There are several pay vouchers in his file. He was paid $3 per day less 60 cents per day for rations for 54 days on November 21, 1863, at Mobile, Alabama, for a total of $129.60. **

Jernigan, Benjamin, Pvt. Co. D.
Enlisted on November 1, 1862, at Camp Tatnall, Florida. Drew clothing on August 28, 1864. Signed by his mark.

Jernigan, Columbus, Pvt. Co. D.
Enlisted on April 24, 1863, at Pensacola, Florida. Exchanged with **Pvt. J. A. Cobb** of Captain Orm's Company, 6th Alabama Cavalry, on February 3, 1864. See the files of **J. A. Cobb** and **A. J. Cobb** of the 15th.

Jernigan, David, Pvt. Co. E.
Enlisted on July 27, 1863, at Camp Lomax, Florida. Discharged at Mobile, Alabama, on November 22, 1863, for being a minor and enlisting without the consent of his parents. His discharge is in his file.*

Jernigan, Edward, Pvt. Co. D.
Enlisted on May 1, 1863, at Pensacola, Florida. There is a pay voucher in his file. He was paid $48 on November 14, 1863, for two months service for he and his horse. *

Jernigan, Elijah, Pvt. Co. D.
Enlisted on April 13, 1863, at Pollard, Alabama. Detailed as a cow driver at Pollard, Alabama. There is a pay voucher in his file.

Jernigan, James S., Bugler/Pvt. Co. E.
Enlisted on September 12, 1861, at Milton, Florida. Reduced to the ranks from Bugler on February 24, 1864, by order of Lt. Colonel Myers. POW signed a parole at Headquarters

of the 16th U.S. Army Corps at Montgomery, Alabama, on May 25, 1865. Hair-light, eyes-blue, complexion-light, 5 foot 5 inches. His parole is in his file.*

Jernigan, J. E., Pvt. Co. E.
Enlisted on September 17, 1861, at Milton, Florida. March/April 1863, company muster roll reports him on special duty as a courier for Colonel Maury since March 1, 1864. Drew clothing on September 10, 1864.

Jernigan, Joseph, Pvt. Co. D.
Enlisted on October 25, 1862, at Camp Tatnall, Florida. Company muster rolls in 1864, report him absent without leave for 50 days and then assigned as courier at Pollard, Alabama.

Jernigan, N. B., Pvt. Co. E.
Enlisted on April 9, 1862, at Camp Perdido, Alabama . September 12, 1863, company muster roll reports him detailed as a courier at Pollard, Alabama, by order of General Marshall since December 15, 1862. September/October, November/December company muster rolls reports him detailed as wagon master since December 15, 1863, by order of General Marshall. There are pay vouchers in his file.*

Jernigan, Silas, Pvt. Co. I.
Enlisted on November 1, 1863, at Halls Mill, Alabama. POW signed a parole at Headquarters of the 16th U.S. Army Corps at Montgomery, Alabama, on June 21, 1865. Hair-light, eyes-blue, hair-dark, 5 foot 4 inches. His parole is in his file.*

Jewett, T. S., Pvt. Co. G.
Enlisted on June 25, 1863, at Camp Taylor. POW surrendered at Citronelle, Alabama, on May 4, 1865. Paroled at Gainesville, Alabama, on May 14, 1865. Residence New Orleans, Louisiana.

Johnson, A. J., Pvt. Co. D.
Enlisted on January 16, 1863, at Camp Tatnall, Florida. September 12, 1863, company muster roll reports him absent without leave since August 26, 1863. September/October 1863, muster roll reports him to have deserted.

Johnson, Batts M., Pvt. Co. A.
Enlisted on July 2, 1863, at Pollard, Alabama. September 12, 1863, company muster roll he is reported on detached service as guide for General Clanton. Later he is shown present, absent without leave since December 20, 1863, and present but dismounted. Drew clothing on September 10, 1864.

Johnson, B. M., Pvt. Co. E.
Enlisted on October 13, 1861, at Camp Perdido, Alabama. Discharged on May 1, 1863, having furnished a substitute. in the person of **D. J. Turvin**. There is a letter of inquiry in his file.* see the file of **D. J. Turvin**.

Johnson, C. A., Pvt. Co. D.
Enlisted on May 1, 1862, at Pensacola, Florida. September/ October company muster roll reports him on scout duty for 50 days since last muster. Drew clothing on August 28, 1864. There is a pay voucher in his file.*

Johnson, G. Z. (Grabiel Z.), Pvt. Co. H.
Enlisted on September 1, 1862, at Mobile, Alabama. He appears on a list of POW's and

deserters that entered the lines of the 16th U.S. Army Corps during April 1865. " Captured April 18, 1865, on the line of march and took the Amnesty Oath. Reported Voluntarily".

Johnson, Hardy, Pvt. Co. A.
Enlisted on March 1, 1864, at Marianna, Florida. POW surrendered on May 11, 1865, at Tallahassee, Florida. Paroled at Quincy, Florida, on May 20, 1865.

Johnson, James, Pvt. Co. C.
Enlisted on April 9, 1862, at Blakeley, Alabama. Drew clothing on August 28, 1864.

Johnson, J. M., Pvt. Co. C.
POW surrendered at Citronelle, Alabama, on May 4, 1865. Paroled at Mobile, Alabama, on June 7, 1865. Residence Monroe County, Alabama. Age-23, complexion-fair, eyes-yellow, hair-brown, 6 foot 1 inch.

Johnson, John, A., Corporal Co. E.
Enlisted on September 17, 1861, at Milton, Florida. May/June 1864, company muster roll reports him promoted from 4th to 2nd Corporal on May 1, 1864, on special duty in blacksmith shop. POW captured at Escambia County, Florida, (Pine Barren, Florida) by a detachment of 1st Florida and 2nd Maine Cavalry on November 17, 1864. Confined at New Orleans, Louisiana, on November 21, 1864. Transferred to Ship Island, Mississippi on December 10, 1864. Admitted to USA General Hospital No. 2, Vicksburg, Mississippi, from steamer on May 6, 1865, with acute diarrhoea on May 6, 1865. Returned to duty [prison] on May 12, 1865.

Johnson, J. P., Pvt. Co. C.
POW surrendered at Citronelle, Alabama, on May 4, 1865. Paroled at Mobile, Alabama, on June 7, 1865. Residence Monroe County, Alabama. Age-20, complexion-light, eyes-grey, hair-sandy, 6 foot.

Johnson, J. S., Pvt. Co. I.
Enlisted on October 1, 1863, at Mobile, Alabama. Admitted to Ross Hospital, Mobile, Alabama, on July 19, 1864, with debilitas [feebleness]. Returned to duty on July 23.

Johnson, P., Pvt. Co. G.
Enlisted on November 18, 1861, at Dragoon Camp. Drew clothing on September 10, 1864.

Johnson, R. S., Pvt. Co. D.
Appears on a roll of POW's that were captured by a detachment of 1st Florida and 2d Maine Cavalry at Pine Barren in Escambia County, Florida, on November 17, 1864. Confined at New Orleans, Louisiana, on November 21, 1864. Transferred to Ship Island, Mississippi, on December 10, 1864. Transferred from Ship Island to Vicksburg, Mississippi, on May 1, 1865. Admitted from steamer to USA General Hospital No. 2, Vicksburg on May 6, 1865 with acute diarrhoea. Age-17. Returned to duty [prison] on May 12, 1865.

Johnson, William A. J., Pvt. Co. D.
Enlisted on April 2, 1863, at Camp Tatnall, Florida. Admitted to Ross Hospital, Mobile, Alabama, on January 9, 1864, with gonorrhea. Returned to duty on January 18, 1864. Died on February 3, 1864, in camp.

Johnson, W. C., Pvt. Co. E.
Enlisted on April 1, 1864, at Pollard, Alabama. Drew clothing on September 2, 1864.

15TH CONFEDERATE CAVALRY

Johnson, William, Pvt. Co. E.
Enlisted on July 8, 1863, at Camp Lomax, Florida. He appeared on several muster rolls as having no horse since July 18, 1863. May/June company muster roll reports him assigned to special duty as a artillery man since February 1, 1864. Admitted to Ross Hospital, Mobile, Alabama, on September 11, 1864, with febris intermittens. He was returned to duty on September 15.

Johnson, W. J., Pvt. Co. E.
Enlisted on September 17, 1861, at Milton, Florida. September 12, 1863, company muster roll reports him detailed to work on gunboat at Montgomery, Alabama, by order of General Buckner since April 3, 1863. He is shown thus on subsequent muster roll until June 30, 1864. A descriptive list of October 13, 1863, at Halls Mill, Alabama, reports him as follows; Age-33, eyes-blue, hair-dark, complexion-fair, 5 foot 9 inches, a mechanic by occupation, born-Pike County, Alabama. Paid $96.80 on February 19, 1864, at Mobile, Alabama, for service and horse. Paid $218.13 on March 3, 1864, at Mobile, for service and clothing. POW captured at Milton, Florida, by a detachment of 2nd Maine Cavalry on December 24, 1864. Confined at New Orleans, Louisiana, on December 27, 1864. Transferred to Ship Island, Mississippi, on January 22, 1865. Applied to take the Oath at Ship Island. Transferred from Ship Island to Vicksburg, Mississippi, on May 1, 1865. There are two pay vouchers in his file.*

Johnston, F. C., Pvt. Co. D.
Enlisted on April 24, 1862, at Pensacola, Florida. September 12, company muster roll reports that he was a paroled POW since April 13, 1863. He appears present but dismounted for a partial time on muster rolls until June 30, 1864. His name appears on a register of paroles given at Columbus, Mississippi, on May 21, 1865. There are two very hard to read documents in his file.*

Johnston, Henry, W., Pvt. Co. D.
Enlisted on May 1, 1862, at Pensacola, Florida. His name appears on a register of paroles given at Columbus, Mississippi, on May 21, 1865. There are several pay vouchers in his file some are from General Hospital at Greenville, Alabama, where he was a patient.*

Johnston, Mack, T., Pvt. Co. E.
Enlisted on March 16, 1864, at Halls Mill, Alabama. He was reported absent sick on company muster rolls from March to June 30, 1864.

Jones, Aaron, Pvt. Co. G.
Enlisted on July 12, 1861, in Mobile Dragoons at Mobile, Alabama. Company G muster roll for September 12, 1863, reports him on detached service as orderly to General Beauregard. He is shown thus on muster rolls through April 30, 1864. Admitted to Episcopal Church Hospital, Williamsburg, Virginia, on June 3, 1864, with lumbago.

Jones, Alexander, Pvt. Co. I.
Enlisted on April 30, 1864, at Santa Rosa, Florida. Reported present on May/June 1864, company muster roll.

Jones, E. C., Sergeant/Pvt. Co. G.
Enlisted on July 30, 1861, at Mobile, Alabama. Muster rolls report him as 4th Sergeant until April 30, 1864. Drew clothing on September 10, 1864. He is reported as a private at surrender. POW surrendered at Citronelle, Alabama, on May 4, 1865. Paroled at Gainesville, Alabama, on May 14, 1865. Residence Mobile, Mobile County, Alabama.

Jones, Henry W., Pvt. Co. C.
Enlisted on April 15, 1862, at Stockton, Alabama. POW surrendered at Citronelle, Alabama, on May 4, 1865. Paroled at Mobile, Alabama, on June 13, 1865. Age-18, complexion-dark, eyes-gray, hair-light, 5 foot 5 inches. There is also a prisoner **H. Jones** surrendered at Citronelle, paroled at Gainesville, with residence shown as Monroe County, Alabama. There may be two men represented in this file.

Jones, J. (John) B., Pvt. Co. C.
Enlisted on October 10, 1862, at Shell Banks, Alabama. POW surrendered at Citronelle, Alabama, on May 4, 1865. Paroled at Gainesville, Alabama, on May 14, 1865. Residence Monroe County, Alabama.

Jones, J. C., Pvt./Sergeant Co. I.
Enlisted on October 4, 1862, at Santa Rosa, Florida. Company muster rolls report him absent on detached service since November 18, 1862, with Quarter Master at Mobile, Alabama. Promoted to 5th Sergeant on December 1, 1863, and back with his company. POW captured at Greenville, Alabama, on April 25, 1865. Paroled at Greenville. [Hospital?] There are several pay vouchers in his file.*

Jones, J. L., Pvt. Co. D.
Enlisted on April 24, 1862, at Pensacola, Florida. January/February 1864, muster roll reports him on extra duty as ambulance driver. He drew clothing on August 28, 1864.

Jones, John, Pvt. Co. D.
Enlisted on April 24, 1862, at Pensacola, Florida. He is reported on company muster rolls as absent without leave and then reported to have deserted on December 26, 1863.

Jones, John, Pvt. Co. H.
Enlisted on December, 3, 1863, at Mobile, Alabama. His name appears on a roll of POW's of 9th Regiment Mississippi Cavalry, CSA that were surrendered at Meridian Mississippi, in May 1865, and paroled May 23, 1865, at Mobile. Residence Jackson County, Miss.

Jones, Josiah, Pvt. Co. D.
Enlisted on April 24, 1862, at Pensacola, Florida. Drew clothing on August 28, 1864.

Jones, L. A., Blacksmith Co. D.
Enlisted on April 24, 1862, at Pensacola, Florida. Appointed smith [blacksmith] on May 1, 1862. Company muster roll for March/April 1864, reports him on duty with regimental headquarters at Pollard, Alabama. Drew clothing on June 18, 1864, at Pollard, Alabama.

Jones, Lewis, Pvt. Co. D.
Enlisted on April 24, 1862, at Pensacola, Florida. Admitted to Ross Hospital, Mobile, Alabama, on October 10, 1863, with congestive fever. Sent to General Hospital, Greenville, Alabama, on October 29, 1863. Drew clothing on August 28, 1864, and signed by his mark. His name appears on a list of POW's paroled at Milton, Florida, on June 29, 1865.

Jones, M. B., Pvt. Co. E.
Enlisted on November 5, 1863, at Camp Perdido. Drew clothing on September 2, 1864.

Jones, M. J., Pvt. Co. K.
Enlisted Sept., 1, 1862, at Camp Forney. He appears present on rolls as late as June 30, 1864.

15TH CONFEDERATE CAVALRY

Jones, S. C., Pvt. Co. E.
Enlisted on November 5, 1861, at Camp Perdido, Florida. Drew clothing on September 2, 1864.

Jones, T. M., Pvt. Co. K.
Enlisted on September 5, 1862, at Camp Forney. Drew clothing on August 28, 1864.

Jones, W. H., Pvt./Sgt. Co. A.
Enlisted on March 31, 1862, at Monticello, Florida. Muster roll for November/December 1863, reports him dismounted on duty with Maury's Horse Artillery. Mounted on February 9, 1864. Drew clothing on September 7, 1864. Appears on a list of POW's surrendered at Tallahassee, Florida, on May 10, 1865. Here he is shown as a Sergeant paroled at Thomasville, Georgia, on May 18, 1865. His parole is in his file. Hair-dark, eyes-hazel, complexion-dark, 6 foot.*

Jones, Willis, Pvt. Co. E.
Enlisted on October 12, 1863, at Camp Lomax, Florida. Drew clothing on September 2, 1864.

Jonte, Joseph, Pvt. Co. G.
Enlisted on June 23, 1863, at Camp Taylor. Drew clothing on June 20, 1864.

Jordan, A. J., Pvt. Co. I.
Enlisted on October 4, 1862, at Santa Rosa, Florida. Appears present on May/June 1864 company muster roll.

Jordan, J. E., Pvt. Co. I.
Enlisted on October 27, 1862, at Santa Rosa, Florida. Appears on company muster rolls as absent without leave since December 29, 1863. Muster roll for May/June 1864, reports that he deserted.

Jordan, J. H., Pvt. Co. K.
Enlisted on September 12, 1862, at Washington County, Alabama. Drew clothing on August 28, 1864. POW surrendered at Citronelle, Alabama, on May 4, 1865. Paroled at Meridian, Mississippi, on May 13, 1865. Residence Winchester, Mississippi.

Jordan, M. V. B., Pvt. Co. D.
Enlisted on September 11, 1862, at Camp Tatnall. He appears on muster rolls as in detached service at Pollard, Alabama from before September 11, 1862, until February 29, 1864. Muster roll for May/June 1864, reports him on special duty. Drew clothing on June 26, 1864, at Pollard, Alabama.

Jordan, Thomas, E., Pvt. Co. D.
Enlisted on September 6, 1862, at Camp Tatnall. He appears on muster rolls as in detached service as Postmaster at Pollard, Alabama, from before September 11, 1862, until June 30, 1864. POW captured at Little Escambia River near Pollard, Alabama, on December 17, 1864. Captured by a detachment of 2 Maine Cavalry and 1st Florida Cavalry. Transferred to Ship Island, Mississippi, on January 22, 1865. Received at Ship Island on January 25, 1864. Applied to take the Oath of Allegiance to the USA. Returned to New Orleans, Louisiana, on April 1, 1865. Residence Conecuh County, Alabama. Complexion-light, hair-light, eyes-blue, 5 foot 9 1/2 inches. Took the Oath and paroled at New Orleans on May 23, 1865.

Jordan, W. McR., 1st Lieutenant and Adjutant F&S

His name appears on a register of the 3rd Florida Batallion in June of 1863. Appointed as 1st Lieutenant in the 15th Alabama Cavalry on June 1, 1863, Halls Mill, Alabama. Appointed Adjutant in the 15th Cavalry on June 15, 1864. Appears on a list of POW's and deserters entering the lines of the 16th U.S. Army Corps during the month of April 1865. Captured at Greenville, Alabama, by Colonel Spurling's U.S. Cavalry on April 30. Shown as a POW turned over to Provost Marshal at Montgomery. Paroled at Montgomery, Alabama, on May 6, 1865. Note in his file to see the personal papers of **Pvt. Michael Ward**, Company R, 1st Florida Volunteers. Signed a parole at Headquarters of the 16th U.S. Army Corp in Montgomery, Alabama on May 6, 1865. Hair-light, eyes-blue, complexion-fair, 5 foot 10 1/2 inches. This parole is in his file. The following letter is also in his file.

>   Richmond, Va.
>   August 19, 1862
>
> Sir
>
> I am desirous of receiving the appointment of Drill Master in one of the Conscript Camps of Alabama and have the fortune of a recommendation from General Forney and hourly expect it by telegraph and I now respectfully address this my application for the position.
>
> As it would be gratifying to me to know if I would get it upon the Generals recommendation. I respectfully ask of you a reply at your earliest convenience.
>
> I enlisted in the service of my State before I knew of the Secession Ordinance being passed and afterward enlisted in the Confederate service for twelve months. I was in the battle of Shiloh with General Anderson's staff, and he made considerable mention of my conduct in his report. H. R. B. Hinton - Congressman from my State has been in the service in the same regiment with myself and will recommend me [????]fully for the position that I ask for.
>
>   I rem yrs vy Respectfully
>   W. Mc R. Jordan

On March 25, 1864, at Halls Mill, Alabama Lt. Jordan requisitioned for the staff of the regiment the following: four jackets, four pair pants, five pair shoes, six shirts, three blankets. There are considerable other documents in his file including letters, requisitions, pay vouchers, etc.**

Jorden, H. C., Pvt. Co. F.

Enlisted on May 7, 1863, at Camp Withers, Alabama, for three years. Admitted to Ross Hospital, Mobile, Alabama, on March 24, 1865, with gonorrhea. Returned to duty on April 7, 1865.

Jumonville, Albert, Pvt. Co. G.

His name appears on a roll of POW's of divers companies and regiments (detached) that were surrendered at Citronelle, Alabama, on May 4, 1865, and paroled at Meridian, Mississippi, on May 12, 1865. Residence shown as New Orleans, Louisiana.

Jumonville, F., Pvt. Co. G.

Enlisted on December 14, 1863, at Halls Mill, Alabama. His name appears on a roll of POW's of divers companies and regiments (detached) that were surrendered at Citronelle, Alabama, on May 4, 1865, and paroled at Meridian, Mississippi, on May 12, 1865. Residence shown as New Orleans, Louisiana. He also appears on a roll of POW's surrendered at Citronelle and paroled at Gainesville, Alabama, on May 14, 1865.

15TH CONFEDERATE CAVALRY

Jumonville, G., Pvt. Co. G.
Enlisted on June 14, 1863, at Camp Taylor. POW surrendered at Citronelle, Alabama, on May 4, 1865, and paroled at Gainesville, Alabama, on May 14, 1865. His residence is shown as New Orleans, Louisiana.

K

Keely, E. see **Kelly, Edward**

Kellam, E. L., Pvt. Co.. H.
Enlisted on February 13, 1863, at Mobile, Alabama. On a company muster roll he is reported to have deserted on January 12, 1864, and has since been captured and sentenced by Court Marshal to hard labor during the war. His name appears on a descriptive list as having enlisted at Choctaw Bluff, Alabama, on February 13, 1863. Description; eyes-dark, hair-dark, complexion-light, age-27, 6 foot 2 inches, a farmer, born in Monroe [County] Alabama.

Kelley, William, J., Pvt. Co. D.
Enlisted on May 10, 1864, at Milton, Florida. POW captured by U.S. Cavalry at Mount Pleasant, Alabama, on April 11, 1865. Forwarded from Mobile, Alabama, to Ship Island, Mississippi.

Kelly, Edward, Pvt. Co. D.
Enlisted on April 15, 1863, at Camp Tatnall. [Some records show that he enlisted at Camp Lomax.] POW captured by U.S. Cavalry at Mount Pleasant, Alabama, on April 11, 1865. Received at Ship Island, Mississippi, on May 13, 1865. Transferred from Ship Island to New Orleans, Louisiana, on June 8, 1865.

Kelly, John T., Pvt. Co. D.
Paid $73.60 on November 28, 1862, at the time of discharge from the 3rd Battalion Florida Cavalry on October 2, 1862, at Camp Tatnall, Florida. Born in Cumberland County, North Carolina, age-47, 5 foot 8 inches, complexion-dark, eyes-blue, hair-black, by profession a jailor. Enlisted in the Florida Cavalry on September 17, 1861, at Milton, Florida. His Discharge is in his file. Enlisted in Co. D of the 15th Confederate Cavalry on January 1, 1863, at Camp Tatnall. [Some records show that he enlisted at Camp Lomax.] He is reported to have deserted on December 29, 1863.*

Kelly, Joseph, see **Kelley, William J.**

Kemp. U., Pvt. Co. F.
Enlisted on January 26, 1863, at Camp Withers for three years or the war. Admitted to Ross Hospital, Mobile, Alabama, on October 30, 1863, with chronic diarrhoea. Returned to duty on November 4, 1863.

Kendall, J. F., Pvt. Co. I.
His name appears on a register of paroled soldiers for June 1865. POW paroled on June 20, 1865, at headquarters of the 16th U.S. Army Corps at Montgomery, Alabama. Hair-light, eyes-blue, complexion-light, 5 foot 10 inches. His parole is in his file.*

Kendall, J. K., Pvt. Co. I.
Enlisted on March 5, 1862, at Conecuh County, Alabama. His name appears on a register of paroled soldiers for June 1865. POW paroled on June 20, 1865, at Headquarters of the

16th U.S. Army Corps at Montgomery, Alabama. Description; hair-light, eyes-blue, complexion-fair, 5 foot 11 inches. His parole is in his file.*

Kendrix, R., Pvt. Co. I.
Enlisted on October 1, 1862, at Camp Withers, Alabama, for three years or the war. September/November 1863, company muster roll shows him on detached service in the Government Fishery at Mobile, Alabama, since September 1, 1863, by order of General Maury. He appears on a descriptive list due $89 for clothing not drawn in kind on January 25, 1864, at Halls Mill, Alabama. Age-43, born-New York, eyes-dark, hair-black, complexion-dark, 5 foot 7 inches, a seaman by occupation. He was paid $145.60 at Mobile, on February 11, 1864, for his horse 184 days at 40 cents per day and six months service at $12 month. Descriptive list and pay voucher are in his file.*

Kennedy, James, Pvt. Co. I.
Enlisted on October 4, 1862, at Santa Rosa, Florida for the war. Company muster rolls report him absent without leave since December 23, 1863, and later as having deserted.

Kennedy, W. D., Pvt. Co. E.
Enlisted on October 20, 1863, at Halls Mill, Alabama. March/April 1864, company muster roll reports him on special duty at Pollard, Alabama, as Purser, since April 1, 1863. Drew clothing on June 20, 1864, at Pollard, again on September 2, 1864, no location given.

Kennedy, William, Pvt. Co. I.
Enlisted on October 4, 1862, at Santa Rosa, Florida. September 12, 1862, muster roll reports him absent without leave since July 20. He is reported later as sick at home, and absent without leave. Company muster roll January/April 1864, reports that he enlisted at Conecuh County, Alabama, and joined from desertion with pay due from April 1, 1864. POW captured on April 11, 1865, at Mount Pleasant, Alabama, by a detachment of the U.S. Cavalry.

Kent, George, Pvt. Co. G.
Enlisted on July 30, 1861, at Mobile, Alabama. Muster rolls from September 12, 1863. until April 30, 1864, reports him absent, detailed to work on Gun Boats.

Kent, J. H., Pvt. Co. K.
Enlisted on September 1, 1862, at Bladon Springs, Alabama. Drew clothing on August 28, 1864. POW surrendered at Citronelle, Alabama, on May 4, 1865. Paroled at Gainesville, Alabama, on May 14, 1865. Residence Choctaw County, Alabama.

Key, R. Morris, Pvt. Co. H.
Enlisted on September 4, 1862, at Mobile, Alabama, for the war. Muster rolls report him absent on detached service by order of General Mackall, on January 27, 1863. Signed a Parole of Honor at Meridian, Mississippi, on May 11, 1865. His parole and pay vouchers are in his file.*

Kilcrease, E. B., Co. F.
Drew clothing on August 29, 1864.

Kilcrease, John, Corporal/Pvt. Co. F.
Enlisted on April 15, 1862, at Stockton, Alabama, for three years or the war. Promoted to 4th Corporal on September 1, 1863, and 3rd Corporal on September 17, 1863. Drew clothing on August 29, 1864. POW surrendered on May 4, 1865, at

15TH CONFEDERATE CAVALRY

Citronelle, Alabama, paroled at Mobile, Alabama, on June 13, 1865. Age-32, complexion-dark, eyes-black, hair-grey, 5 foot 10 inches. Residence Baldwin County, Alabama.

Killcrease, Joshua, Pvt. Co. F.
Enlisted on May 1, 1864, at Canal [Canoe?]Station for three years. Drew clothing on August 29, 1864. POW surrendered on May 4, 1865, at Citronelle, Alabama, paroled at Mobile, Alabama on June 13, 1865. Age-30, 5 foot 10 inches, complexion-dark, eyes-gray, hair-gray, residence-Baldwin County, Alabama.

Kilpatrick, A., Pvt. Co. K.
POW surrendered at Citronelle, Alabama, on May 4, 1865. Paroled at Gainesville, Alabama, on May 14, 1865. Residence Clarke County, Alabama.

Kilpatrick, G. H., j Pvt. Co. K.
Enlisted on September 15, 1862, at Bladon Springs, Alabama, for the war. Appears on a descriptive list at Halls Mill, Alabama, on September 8, 1863. Age-27, eyes-blue, hair-grey, complexion-fair, 6 foot 2 inches, born-Clarke County, Alabama, a farmer by occupation. Drew clothing on August 28, 1864. POW surrendered at Citronelle, Alabama, on May 4, 1865. Paroled at Gainesville, Alabama, on May 14, 1865. Residence Clarke County, Alabama.

King, Issac. P., Pvt. Co. B.
Enlisted on March 14, 1862, at Marianna, Florida, for three years or the war. Drew clothing on September 10, 1864. POW surrendered at Tallahassee, Florida, on May 10, 1865. Paroled at Quincy, Florida, on May 10, 1865.

King, M., Pvt. Co. C.
Enlisted on June 7, 1864, at Camp Powell, Alabama. Drew clothing on August 28, 1864.

Kirk, James, Pvt. Co. H.
Enlisted on September 4, 1862, at Mobile, Alabama, for the war. On detached service by order of General Mackall on December 16, 1862. Died in General Hospital at Mobile on January 16, 1864. There are two pay vouchers in his file.

Kirkland, Green, B., Pvt. Co. B.
Enlisted on March 14, 1862, at Marianna, Florida, for three years or the war. His name appears on a report of furloughs granted by the Medical Examining Board to Disabled Camp, Lauderdale, Mississippi, for the week ending January 31, 1865. Wound in right leg. Residence-Millwood, Jackson, County [Mississippi?]. Note: "unfit for any duty. To await authority to be retired."

Kirkland, William, M., Pvt. Co. D.
Enlisted on May 10, 1864, at Milton, Florida, for three years. May/June 1864, muster roll reports him on special duty and dismounted since enlisting. Drew clothing on August 28, 1864. He signed by his mark. POW surrendered at Citronelle, Alabama, on May 4, 1865. Paroled at Gainesville, Alabama, on May 14, 1865. Residence Fulford County, Georgia.

Kitchem, S. E., Pvt. Co. C.
Drew clothing on August 28, 1864. POW surrendered at Citronelle, Alabama, on May 4, 1865. Paroled at Gainesville, Alabama, on May 14, 1865. Residence Baldwin County, Alabama.

Kling, Frank, Pvt. Co. K.
  Enlisted on March 17, 1862, at Washington County, Alabama for the war. May/June 1864, muster roll reports him on extra daily duty as a blacksmith. Drew clothing June 19, 1864, at Pollard, Alabama. Drew clothing on August 28, 1864. There is a document in his file for pay as a blacksmith at Camp Forney, East Pascagoula, Mississippi.*

Klopner, L., Pvt. Co. F.
  Enlisted on October 1, 1861, at Mobile, Alabama, for three years or the war. Company muster rolls after September/October 1863, report him detached on May 7, 1862, as a blacksmith on the gunboat Baltic, by order of General Forney. Detached under Special Order No. 154, June 2, 1864.

Klotz, John, Pvt. Co. F.
  Enlisted on August 27, 1862, at Mobile, Alabama, for three years or the war. He is reported on detached service of muster rolls. Drew clothing on August 29, 1864.

Knight, Ben R., Pvt. Co. D.
  Enlisted on August 26, 1862, at Camp Tatnall, Florida, for three years. The September 12, 1863, company muster roll reports him absent sick at hospital, and on extra duty as a wagon master since last muster. He is reported on several rolls as sick in hospital in Greenville, Alabama. Discharged on Surgeons Certificate of Disability on October 13, 1864, at General Hospital, Greenville, Alabama. Age-33, hair-dark, eyes-blue, 5 foot 7 inches, complexion-fair, a City Marshal by occupation. Born in Richmond, North Carolina. His Certificate of Disability is in his file.*

Knighton, Al R., Pvt. Co. A.
  Enlisted on March 15, 1862, at Monticello, Florida, for three years. Drew clothing on September 7, 1864. Admitted to Ross Hospital, Mobile, Alabama, in September 1863, with interrmitten fever and in December 1863, with catarrh. POW surrendered at Tallahassee, Florida, on May 10, 1865. Eyes-blue, hair-light, complexion-fair, 5 foot 9 inches. His Oath of Allegiance is in his file.*

Koenig, F., Pvt. Co. F.
  Enlisted on January 12, 1863, at Camp Withers, for three years or the war.

Kragh, Julius, Pvt. Co. C.
  Enlisted on September 3, 186[2?], at Shell Banks, Alabama, for three years or the war. Detached by reason of Special Order No. 243, from Headquarters of the Department of the Gulf on October 8, 1862. Paid $48 on March 3, 1864, for service November 1, 1863, to February 29, 1864.

Krebs, A. R., Pvt. Co. G.
  Enlisted on May 26, 1863, at Camp Taylor for July 30, 1864, or the war. Drew clothing on June 20, 1864.

Krebs, H. M., Pvt. Co. H.
  Enlisted on September 8, 1863, at Halls Mill, Alabama, for the war. Drew clothing on September 7, 1864.

15TH CONFEDERATE CAVALRY

L

Lacoast, Hicklin, Pvt. Co. F.
Enlisted on May 26, 1862, at Camp Withers, for three years or the war. Drew clothing on August 29, 1864. POW surrendered at Citronelle, Alabama, on May 4, 1865. Paroled at Gainesville, Alabama, on May 14, 1865. Residence Mobile, Mobile County, Alabama.

Ladnier, A., Pvt. Co. G.
POW surrendered at Citronelle, Alabama, on May 4, 1865. Paroled at Gainesville, Alabama, on May 14, 1865. Residence Mobile County, Alabama.

Ladnier, John, Pvt. Co. G.
Enlisted on September 22, 1863, at Dragoon Camp for July 30, 1864, or the war. Drew clothing on September 4, 1864. Admitted to Ross Hospital, Mobile, Alabama, in July 1864, with rubeola.

Lamas, J. L., Pvt. Co. G.
Enlisted on September 15, 1861, at Dragoon Camp for July 30, 1864, or the war. September 12, 1863, and all company muster rolls through April 30, 1864, reports him absent, detached to work on gun boat.

Lambert, A. D., Pvt. Co. G.
Enlisted on June 10, 1863, at Camp Taylor, for July 30, 1864, or the war. Drew clothing on June 30, and September 4, 1864. POW surrendered at Citronelle, Alabama, on May 4, 1865. Paroled at Gainesville, Alabama, on May 14, 1865. Residence is shown as New Orleans, Louisiana.

Lambert, C. W., Corporal Co. G.
Enlisted on April 12, 1862, at Dragoon Camp, for July 30, 1864, or the war. September/October 1864, company muster roll reports him transferred to Captain Travers Company of 7 Alabama Cavalry.

Lamey, A., Pvt. Co. G.
Enlisted on September 23, 1862, at Dragoon Camp for July 30, 1864, or the war. Drew clothing on June 20, 1864, (signed by his mark) and September 4, 1864. POW surrendered at Citronelle, Alabama, on May 4, 1865. Paroled at Gainesville, Alabama, on May 14, 1865. Residence Mobile County, Alabama.

Lance, W. G., Pvt. Co. I.
Enlisted on June 13, 1864, at Santa Rosa, Florida, for the war. He signed a parole at Headquarters of 16th U.S. Army Corps, Montgomery, Alabama, on June 17, 1864. Hair-grey, eyes-blue, complexion-fair, 5 foot 10 inches. His parole is in his file.*

Land, Benjamin F., Pvt. Co. B.
Enlisted on March 14, 1862, at Marianna, Florida, for three years or the war. He was admitted in September 1863, to Ross Hospital, Mobile, Alabama, with spinal irritation. Sent to General Hospital on October 31, 1863. Drew clothing on September 10, 1864.

Land, Henry G., Pvt. Co. B.
Enlisted on May 3, 1862, at Marianna, Florida, for three years or the war. POW surrendered on May 11, 1865, at Tallahassee, Florida. Paroled at Quincy, Florida, on May 24, 1865.

Land, James C., Farrier/Pvt. Co. B.
Enlisted on May 3, 1862, at Marianna, Florida, for three years or the war. POW surrendered on May 11, 1865, at Tallahassee, Florida. Paroled at Quincy, Florida, on May 24, 1865.

Land, S. W., Pvt. Co. A.
Enlisted April 7, 1864, at Marianna, Florida, for the war. May/June 1864, muster roll reports him present detailed as farrier. POW surrendered on May 11, 1865, at Tallahassee, Florida. Paroled at Quincy, Florida, on May 23, 1865. Here he is show as **Land, Stephen, W.**

Lang, Charles, Pvt. Co. F.
Enlisted on October 1, 1861, at Mobile, Alabama. for three years or the war. Company muster roll for September 12, 1863, reports that he is absent detached service with Volunteer Navy. Discharged at Halls Mill, Alabama on September 8, 1863, by reason of being transferred to CSN on September 8, 1863. Paid $140 for service and commutation of clothing not drawn. Born in Germany, age-37, eyes-hazel, hair-brown, complexion-fair, 5 foot 6 inches, by profession a sailor. His discharge is in his file.*

Langley, A. B., Pvt. Co. I.
Enlisted on October 1, 1862, at Santa Rosa, Florida, for the war. Company muster rolls show him present, absent on scout, absent without leave and finally in April 1864 he is reported to have deserted.

La Rue, John De, Pvt. Co. D.
Enlisted on August 21, 1862, at Camp Tatnall for three years. Company muster roll for January/February 1864, reports him on extra duty as Colonel's Orderly. Drew clothing on August 28, 1864. POW surrendered at Citronelle, Alabama, on May 4, 1865. Paroled at Gainesville, Alabama, on May 14, 1865. His residence is shown as Greenville, Butler County, Alabama.

Lassiter, Amos, Pvt. Co. I.
Enlisted on October 4, 1862, at Santa Rosa, Florida, for the war. First company muster roll on September 12, 1863, reports him a POW since December 25, 1862. November/December 1852, company muster roll reports him as deserted.

Lassiter, J. T., Pvt. Co. I.
Enlisted on October 1, 1862, at Santa Rosa, Florida, for the war. First company muster roll of September 12, 1863, reports him absent without leave since August 20. November/December 1863, muster roll reports him as deserted.

Latimer, E. R., Pvt./Corp. Co. H.
Enlisted on September 11, 1863, at Halls Mill, Alabama, for the war. Promoted to 4th Corporal from the ranks on March 26, 1864. Drew clothing on September 7, 1864.

Latimore, see Latimer above.

Lattimer, Edwin R., see Latimer above.

Laurendine, J., Pvt. Co. K.
Enlisted on July 1, 1863, at Bayou La Batre, Alabama, for the war. Substitute for Sgt. **J. M. Williams**, mustered in on March 17, 1862. He is shown as having drawn clothing on September 4, 1864.

Laurendine, J. H., Pvt. Co. G.
Enlisted on July 30, 1861, at Mobile, Alabama, for July 30, 1864, or the war. Appears present on a company muster roll for December 31, 1863, to April 30, 1864.

Laurendine, J. W., Pvt. Co. G.
Enlisted on February 23, 1862, at Dragoon Camp, for July 30, 1864, or the war. His name appears on a descriptive list of the Mobile Dragoons, Alabama, at Bayou La Batre, Alabama, for August 8, 1862. Age-17, eyes-grey, hair-dark, complexion-dark, 6 foot, a farmer born in Mobile, Alabama. Drew clothing on June 20, 1864.

Lawrance, Richard A., Pvt. Co. ?
His name appears on a list of POW's surrendered on May 11, 1865, at Tallahassee, Florida. Paroled at Quincy, Florida, on May 23, 1865.

Lawrence, Thomas, G., Pvt. Co. B.
Enlisted on September 1, 1862, at Marianna, Florida, for three years or the war. Drew clothing on September 10, 1864. POW surrendered on May 11, 1865, at Tallahassee, Florida. Paroled at Quincy, Florida, on May 23, 1865.

Laws, Thomas, Pvt. Co. F.
Enlisted on October 1, 1861, at Mobile, Alabama, for three years or the war. Drew clothing on August 29, 1864. POW surrendered at Citronelle, Alabama, on May 4, 1865. Paroled at Gainesville, Alabama, on May 14, 1865. Residence Mobile, Mobile County, Alabama.

Leavins, M., Pvt. Co. C.
Enlisted on June 3, 1863, at Camp Powell for three years or the war. He appears absent with leave and absent sick on company muster rolls from November 1863, until the last roll on June 30, 1864.

Ledder, J., Pvt. Co. F.
POW surrendered at Citronelle, Alabama, on May 4, 1865. Residence Baldwin County, Alabama. Paroled at Meridian, Mississippi, on May 17, 1865.

Lee, G. M., see **Leigh, George M.**

Lee, J. J., Pvt. Co. D.
Enlisted on August 22, 1863, at Camp Ward for three years. March/April 1864, company muster roll reports him on special duty near Bluff Springs, Alabama. Drew clothing on August 28, 1864. Signed by his mark.

Lee, T. G., Pvt. Co. K.
Enlisted on October 8, 1863, at Mobile, Alabama, for the war. Paid $50 bounty for signing. Drew clothing on August 28, 1864. POW surrendered at Citronelle, Alabama, on May 4, 1865. Paroled at Gainesville, Alabama, on May 14, 1865. Residence Choctaw County, Alabama. Age-18, eyes-dark, hair-black, complexion-dark, 5 foot 8 inches, a farmer born in Barbour County, Alabama.

Leigh, George M., Pvt. Co. E.
Enlisted on January 30, 1864, at Halls Mill, Alabama. Drew clothing on September 2, 1864. POW captured by a detachment of 1st Florida Cavalry and 2nd Maine Cavalry at Escambia County, Florida, on November 17, 1864. Appears on a register of POW's confined at New Orleans, Louisiana, on November 21, 1864. Transferred to Ship Island, Mississippi, on

December 10, 1864. Transferred from Ship Island to Vicksburg, Mississippi, on May 1, 1865. Admitted to USA General Hospital No. 2 at Vicksburg on May 6, 1865, with acute diarrhoea. Returned to duty [prison] on May 12, 1865.

Leigh, N. R., Captain Co. E.
Enlisted on September 17, 1861, at Milton, Florida, for three years. Elected Captain on May 6, 1862. Appears on a roster of company E, 15th Confederate Cavalry at Spring Hill on January 1, 1865. On November 1, 1863, Captain Leigh requisitioned at Halls Mill, Alabama, 95 jackets, 97 pair pants, 108 shirts, 97 pair drawers, 98 caps. Almost six months later on March 25, 1864, Captain Leigh requisitioned again at Halls Mill, Alabama, 42 jackets, 42 pair pants, 23 pair shoes, 45 shirts, 42 blankets, "As the men are in want of the above articles." These requisition as well as many other requisitions and pay vouchers are in his file. He was paid $140 per month as a Captain.**

Leines, A., Pvt. Co. F.
Enlisted on April 12, 1862, at Camp Withers for three years or the war. March/April 1864, company muster roll reports that he deserted about January 25, 1864.

Lemons, N., Pvt. Co. D.
Enlisted on April 24, 1862, at Pensacola, Florida. He appears on the first muster roll on September 12, 1863, on extra duty as a teamster with Quarter Master Department. Rolls continue to report him thus through April 1864. He drew clothing on June 20, 1864, at Pollard and again on August 28, 1864, and signed by his mark. The latter draw shows no location.

Lenard, W. A., Pvt. Co. E.
Enlisted on September 17, 1861, at Milton, Florida for three years. Company muster roll for September 12, 1863, reports that he deserted about August 12, 1863, and went to the enemy at Pensacola, Florida.

Letford, John, Pvt. Co. F.
Enlisted on December 14, 1861, at Camp Withers, for three years or the war. Drew clothing on August 29, 1864.

Levins, John, Pvt. Co. D.
Enlisted on April 24, 1862, at Pensacola, Florida, for three years. Muster rolls from September 12, 1863, report him absent without leave since August 26, 1863. He is reported as deserted August 26, 1863, on the May/June 1864, muster roll.

Lewis, Calvin, Pvt. Co. C.
Enlisted on October 16, 1862, at Camp Powell, for three years or the war. Admitted to Ross Hospital, Mobile, Alabama, on September 20, 1863, with acute diarrhoea. Sent to General Hospital on September 21, 1863. (Remarks: Point Clear) He is reported absent in General Hospital, Mobile, Alabama, on company muster rolls for September through December 1863. POW captured in front of Blakeley, Alabama, on April 2, 1865. (One reference card indicates that he was captured on March 24, 1865.) Received at Ship Island, Mississippi, on April 4, 1865. Transferred to Vicksburg, Mississippi, on May 1, 1865.

Lewis, Freeman see **Lewis, J. F.** Co. F.

Lewis, Green, Pvt. Co. G.
Enlisted on July 30, 1861, at Mobile, Alabama. for July 30, 1864, or the war. Drew clothing

on September 4, 1864. His name appears on a list of prisoners and deserters forwarded by the Provost Marshal of the U.S. 3d Division 13th A. C. McIntosh Bluffs, Alabama on May 9, 1865, to Provost Marshal General Military Division West Mississippi. Appears on a roll of POW's of detailed men that were surrendered at Citronelle, Alabama, on May 4, 1865. Paroled at Mobile, Alabama, on May 14, 1865. His residence is shown as Mobile County, Alabama.

Lewis, G. W., Pvt. Co. E.
Drew clothing September 2, 1864. POW captured at Pine Barren, Florida. POW captured on 1864, at Pine Barren, Escambia County, Florida, by a detachment of 1st U.S. Florida Cavalry and 2nd Maine Cavalry. Confined at New Orleans, Louisiana, on November 21, 1864. Transferred to Ship Island, Mississippi, on December 10, 1864. Transferred from Ship Island to Vicksburg, Mississippi, on May 1, 1865.

Lewis, J. F., Corporal/Pvt. Co. F.
Enlisted on October 1, 1861, at Mobile, Alabama, for three years or the war. Drew clothing on August 29, 1864. POW captured at Liberty, Mississippi, on November 18, 1864. Received at Ship Island, Mississippi, from New Orleans, Louisiana, on December 13, 1864. The name Pvt. **Freeman Lewis** appears on a roll of POW and deserters that entered the Military Lines of the 16th U.S. Army Corps voluntarily during the month of April 18, 1865, at line of march Alabama. Took the Oath of Amnesty. There are likely two individuals records in this file.

Lewis, W. F., Pvt. Co. E.
Enlisted on September 17, 1861, at Milton, Florida, for three years. Drew clothing on September 2, 1864.

Lewis, W. H., Pvt. Co. E.
Enlisted on September 17, 1861, at Milton, Florida, for three years. September 12, 1863, company muster roll reports him absent, detached as a guide for 5th Regiment Alabama Cavalry at Pollard, Alabama, since August 24, 1863. POW captured at Pensacola, Florida on September 9, 1863. His name appears on a return of POW's confined at Fort Pickens, Florida.

Libby, F. E., Pvt. Co. K.
Appears on a roll of POW's that were surrendered at Citronelle, Alabama, on May 4, 1865. Paroled at Gainesville, Alabama, on May 14, 1865. His residence is shown as Baldwin County, Alabama.

Lindsay, Elisha F. see **Lindsey, Elisha F.**

Lindsey, Elisha F., Pvt. Co. B.
Enlisted on March 14, 1862, at Marianna, Florida, for three years or the war. Drew clothing on September 10, 1864. He appears on a list of sick and wounded POW's at City Hospital, Mobile, Alabama. Died on April 27, 186_[5?], of chronic diarrhoea.

Lins, John, Pvt. Co. K.
Enlisted on March 17, 1862, at Washington County, Alabama, for the war. Drew clothing on August 28, 1864.

Linsday, E. F. see **Lindsey, Elisha F.**

Linson, W. T., Pvt. Co. K.
Enlisted on May 5, 1864, at Baldwin County, Alabama, for three years. Drew clothing on August 28, 1864. Appears on a roll of POW's that were surrendered at Citronelle, Alabama, on May 4, 1865. Paroled at Gainesville, Alabama, on May 14, 1865. Residence Baldwin County, Alabama.

Livingston, G. J., Pvt. Co. I.
Enlisted on October 4, 1862, at Santa Rosa, Florida, for the war. He is reported absent without leave since February 28, 1864, on a company muster roll and finally reported as having deserted.

Livingston, S. J., Pvt. Co. I.
Enlisted on October 4, 1862, at Santa Rosa, Florida, for the war. He is reported absent without leave since July 1, 1863, on a company muster roll and finally reported as deserted.

Lockart, Perry, J., Pvt. Co. B.
Enlisted on February 25, 1863, at Hodgson's Landing, Florida, for three years or the war. Drew clothing on September 10, 1864. POW surrendered on May 11, 1865, at Tallahassee, Florida. Paroled at Quincy, Florida, on May 23, 1865.

Lockey, Joseph B., Pvt. Co. B.
Enlisted on March 14, 1862, at Marianna, Florida, for three years or the war. Drew clothing on September 10, 1864. POW surrendered on May 11, 1865, at Tallahassee, Florida. Paroled at Quincy, Florida, on May 25, 1865. Paid $15 at Mobile, Alabama, on March 31, 1863, for commutation of rations while on detached duty from March 3 to March 23, 1863, for carrying the body of a deceased soldier to Jackson County, Florida,

Long, Edwin D., Pvt. Co. B.
Enlisted on September 12, 1862, at Mobile, Alabama, for three years or the war. September 12, 1863, company muster roll reports him absent on detail as Hospital Clerk since September 15, 1862. Other rolls report him present or on detached service through June 30, 1864. There are pay vouchers in his file. He was a POW surrendered on May 11, 1865, at Tallahassee, Florida. Paroled at Quincy, Florida, on May 23, 1865.

Long, F. B., Pvt. Co. C.
Enlisted on April 9, 1862, at Blakeley, Alabama, for three years. Drew clothing on August 28, 1864.

Long, J. N., Pvt. Co. H.
Enlisted on February 1, 1864, at Halls Mill, Alabama, for three years. Drew clothing on August 29, 1864. POW surrendered at Citronelle, Alabama, on May 4, 1865. Paroled at Gainesville, Alabama, on May 14, 1865. Residence Mobile County, Alabama.

Long, Oscar P., Pvt. Co. B.
Enlisted on February 8, 1863, at Marianna, Florida, for three years or the war. Drew clothing on September 10, 1864. He was a POW surrendered on May 11, 1865, at Tallahassee, Florida. Paroled at Quincy, Florida, on May 22, 1865.

Long, T. B., Pvt./Sergeant Co. I.
Enlisted on February 12, 1863, at Conecuh County, Alabama, for the war. Promoted to 2nd Corporal on September 1, 1863, from the ranks. Admitted to Ross Hospital, Mobile, Alabama, with int. fever quo. on December 13, 1863. He was given a medical 30 day

furlough from December 22, 1863. Signed a parole at Headquarters of the 16 U.S. Army Corps on June 14, 1865. Eyes-hazel, hair-dark, complexion-fair, 6 foot 2 inches. His parole is in his file. Here he is shown with rank of Sergeant.*

Long, T. R., Brevet 2nd Lieutenant Co. K.
Enlisted on May 16, 1862, as Brevet Jr. 2nd Lt. at Mobile, Alabama, for the war. A September/October 1863, roll shows his rank as 3rd Lieutenant. Elected to 2nd Lieutenant on December 27, 1862. Elected to Jr. 2nd Lieutenant on March 30, 1863. Signed a Parole of Honor at Gainesville, Alabama, on May 14, 1863. His parole is in his file. There are a number of requisitions and pay vouchers in his file. **

Loper, G. H., Pvt. Co. K.
Enlisted on March 17, 1862, at Washington County, Alabama, for the war. He was a POW surrendered at Citronelle, Alabama, on May 4, 1865. Paroled at Gainesville, Alabama, on May 14, 1865. Residence Washington County, Alabama.

Loper, H., Pvt. Co. K.
Enlisted on January 16, 1864, at Halls Mill, Alabama, for the war. POW surrendered at Citronelle, Alabama, on May 4, 1865. Paroled at Gainesville, Alabama, on May 14, 1865. Residence Washington County, Alabama.

Loper, R., Pvt. Co. K.
Enlisted on January 16, 1864, at Halls Mill, Alabama, for the war. **R. M. Loper**, Pvt. Co. K, was detailed on September 24, 1864, for duty in Commissary Department at Moible, Alabama. POW surrendered at Citronelle, Alabama, on May 4, 1865. He was paroled at Gainesville, Alabama, on May 14, 1865. Residence Washington County, Alabama. (See personal papers of **John Diamond**, Co. K., 15th Confederate Cavalry.)

Lord, John, Sergeant Co. H.
Enlisted on September 4, 1862, at Mobile, Alabama, for the war. Promoted to 4th Sergeant from 5rd Sergeant December 11, 1863. Drew clothing on September 7, 1864. POW surrendered at Citronelle, Alabama, on May 4, 1865. Paroled at Gainesville, Alabama, on May 14, 1865. Residence Clarke County, Mississippi.

Louis, C., Pvt. Co. C see **Lewis, Calvin**

Low, C. B., Pvt. Co. I.
Enlisted on September 4, 1863, at Mobile, Alabama, for the war. Signed a parole at the Headquarters of the U.S. 16th Army Corps at Montgomery, Alabama, on May 26, 1865. Hair-dark, eyes-grey, complexion-fair, 5 foot 10 inches. His parole is in his file.

Lumsden, A. McD, Pvt. Co. C.
Enlisted on April 9, 1862, at Mobile, Alabama, in Captain Barlow's Baldwin Rangers for three years or the war. Drew clothing on September 13, 1864. There are a number of pay vouchers in his file. **

Lumsden, Frank, Pvt. Co. H.
Enlisted on October 7, 1863, at Halls Mill, Alabama, for the war. Drew clothing on September 10, 1864. POW surrendered at Citronelle, Alabama, on May 4, 1865. Paroled at Gainesville, Alabama, on May 14, 1865. His residence is shown as Baldwin County, Alabama.

Lundy, James, Pvt. Co. H.
Enlisted on September 26, 1863, at Halls Mill, Alabama, for the war. Admitted to Ross Hospital, Mobile, Alabama, on December 14, 1863, with acute rheumatism. Returned to duty on January 20, 1864. He drew clothing on September 7, 1864, and appears on a descriptive roll for pay and clothing on September 30, 1863, at Halls Mill. Age-17, eyes-blue, hair-light, complexion-fair, 5 foot 10 inches, born-Green County, Miss., a farmer.

Lundy, W. C., Pvt. Co. I.
Enlisted on October 4, 1862, at Santa Rosa, Florida, for the war. POW captured at Andalusia, Alabama, on March 23, 1865, by U.S. Cavalry under the command of Brigadier General T. J. Lucas. Received at Ship Island, Mississippi, on April 4, 1865. Transferred from Ship Island to Vicksburg, Mississippi, on May 1, 1865.

Lumsford, J. P., Pvt. Co. I.
Enlisted on October 4, 1862, at Santa Rosa, Florida, for the war. Company muster roll for September 12, 1863, reports him sick at home in Conecuh County, Alabama, since July 3. Other muster rolls report him present through June 30, 1864.

Lumsford, William, Pvt. Co. I.
Enlisted on October 4, 1862, at Santa Rosa, Florida, for the war. First company muster roll for September 12, 1863, reports him on detached service since June 26, herding cattle on orders of General Canty. His name appears on a list of soldiers from the Mobile District that are employed in the Substance Department in the State of Alabama. He is reported to be employed at Pollard, Alabama. Cow Driver. Muster rolls report him present through June 30, 1864.

Lurty, J. G., Pvt. Co. E.
Company muster roll for March/April 1864, reports him absent without leave. Transferred to this company from 4th La. Regiment Infantry on March 20, 1864. May/June 1864, muster roll reports him absent without leave.

Luther, J. F., Pvt. Co. K.
Enlisted on August 27, 1862, at Pascagoula, Mississippi, for the war. His name appears on a descriptive list for pay and clothing at Mobile, Alabama, on October 9, 1863. Age-28, eyes-grey, hair-dark, complexion-fair, 5 foot 11 inches, born Autauga County, Alabama, a farmer by occupation. Drew clothing on August 28, 1864. POW surrendered at Citronelle, Alabama, on May 4, 1865. Paroled at Gainesville, Alabama, on May 14, 1865. Residence Jackson County, Mississippi.

Luther, William, Pvt. Co. G.
Enlisted on October 10, 1861, at Dragoon Camp for July 30, 1864, or the war. Company muster rolls September 12, 1863, through April 30, 1864, report him absent detached as a shoemaker. Signed with his mark. Paroled at the Headquarters of the U.S. 16th Army Corps at Montgomery, Alabama, on May 19, 1865. Hair-light, eyes-blue, complexion-fair, 5 foot 8 inches. His parole is in his file.*

Lyon, Jasper N., Pvt. Co. K.
Enlisted on August 19, 1862, at Pascagoula, Mississippi, for the war. He appears absent sick on a company muster roll dated June 30, 1864.

Lyons, James T., Pvt. Co. F.
Enlisted on December 24, 1862, at Camp Withers for three years or the war. Drew clothing

15TH CONFEDERATE CAVALRY

on August 29, 1864. Admitted to Ross Hospital, Mobile, Alabama, on October 14, 1864, with syphilis consecutiva. Returned to duty on November 12, 1864.

Lyons, S. P., Pvt. Co. K.
Enlisted on December 26, 1863, at Mobile, Alabama, for three years or the war. His name appears on a letter addressed to Captain J. Lovell, A. A. General P. M. [US] Dept. Army and Division of West Mississippi., signed by Captain S. E. Hawkins, 8th Iowa Infantry. "Deserted from his command near Clairborne, Alabama, April 10, 1865. Claims to have been conscripted and forced into the army. His home is in Mobile. Desires to take the Oath of Amnesty and remain at home."

Lyons, S. T., Pvt. Co. K.
This man only appears on the descriptive list and there is no service record filed with the records of the 15th Confederate Cavalry. Age-41, eyes-grey, hair-?, complexion-dark, 5 foot 2 inches, born-Jackson County, Mississippi, a butcher by occupation. His descriptive list and record of bounty pay is to be found in the file of Pvt. **J. F. Hutchinson** of Co. K. He was paid $50 bounty.

Lyons, W., Pvt. Co. F.
Enlisted on October 1, 1861, at Mobile, Alabama, for three years or the war. Some muster rolls report him on detached service with the Commissary Department at Mobile. Company muster roll for May/June 1864, reports him present.

M

MacDonald, John, Pvt. Co. F.
Enlisted on October 1, 1861, at Mobile, Alabama, for three years or the war. Drew clothing on August 29, 1864. Admitted to Ross Hospital, Mobile, Alabama, on October 16, 1864, with febris intermittens quot. Returned to duty on October 21, 1864. POW surrendered at Citronelle, Alabama, on May 4, 1865. Paroled at Gainesville, Alabama, on May 14, 1865. Residence Mobile, Mobile County, Alabama.

Magaha, John, Pvt. Co. D.
Enlisted on June 2, 1864, at Milton, Florida, for the war. Drew clothing on August 28, 1864. POW surrendered at Citronelle, Alabama, on May 4, 1865. Paroled at Gainesville, Alabama, on May 14, 1865. Residence Santa Rosa, Florida.

Magahahan, John see **Magaha, John**

Mallett, C, Pvt. Co. K.
Enlisted on September 1, 1862, at Camp Forney, Jackson County, Mississippi, for the war. May/June 1864, company muster roll reports him present.

Mallett, Samuel, Pvt. Co. K.
Enlisted on December 12, 1863, at Mobile, Alabama, for the war. Drew clothing on August 28, 1864. His name appears on a roll of POW's of Companies G and C, 12th Mississippi Cavalry, commanded by Captain James Lyons that were surrendered at Citronelle, Alabama, on May 4, 1865. Paroled at Mobile, Alabama, on May 23, 1865. Residence Jackson County, Mississippi. Age-17, eyes-grey, hair-dark, complexion-fair, 5 foot 7 inches, born-Jackson County, Mississippi, a farmer by occupation. He appears on a descriptive list and record of bounty pay found in the file of **Pvt. J. F. Hutchinson** of Co. K. He was paid $50 bounty.

Malley, Vincent, Pvt. Co. H.
Enlisted on June 17, 1863, at West Pascagoula, Mississippi, for the war. September/October company muster roll reports that he was transferred to "his proper comman." due to irregularly attending muster.

Malone, Ephriaim, Pvt. Co. E.
Enlisted on November 15, 1862, at Camp Lomax, Florida, for three years. First company muster roll reports him absent detailed as a guide for the 5th Regiment Alabama Cavalry since August 30, 1862. Other muster rolls report him present through June 30, 1864. Drew clothing on September 2, 1864.

Mancil, Bryant, Pvt. Co. E.
Enlisted on January 26, 1863, at Camp Lomax, [Florida] for three years. Admitted to Ross Hospital, Mobile, Alabama, on February 12, 1864, with rubeola. Returned to duty on February 22, 1864. Drew clothing on September 2, 1864.

Maniac see **Moniac**

Maning see **Manning**

Mann, J. W., Pvt. Co. E.
Enlisted on September 17, 1861, at Milton, Florida, for three years. His name appears on a hospital muster roll for November/December 1863, as a patient at General Hospital Moore, Mobile, Alabama, Admitted to Ross Hospital, Mobile, Alabama, with measles complicated by pneumonia on February 26, 1864. Returned to duty on March 10, 1864. Drew clothing on September 2, 1864. POW surrendered at Citronelle, Alabama, on May 4, 1865. Paroled at Gainesville, Alabama, on May 14, 1865. Residence Santa Rosa, Florida.

Mann, W. J., Pvt. Co. H.
Enlisted on September 4, 1862, at Mobile, Alabama, for the war. Company muster roll for September/December 1863, reports that he was transferred to Captain Winston's Battery by order of General Maury.

Manning, M. C., Pvt. Co. E.
Enlisted on September 13, 1863, at Camp Lomax, Florida, for three years. First muster roll on September 12, 1863, reports him absent sick at Greenville Hospital, since February 18, 1862. He is reported to have died of chronic diarrhoea in Butler County, Alabama on September 15, 1863.

Manning R. G., Pvt. Co. A.
Enlisted on April 7, 1862, at Monticello, Florida, for three years. Pvt. **Richard G. Manning** of Co. A, 15th Cavalry was admitted to Ross Hospital, Mobile, Alabama, on September 22, 1863, with int. fever tert. Returned to duty on September 24, 1863. Drew clothing on September 7, 1864. POW surrendered on May 10, 1865, at Tallahassee, Florida. Paroled at Tallahassee, Florida, on May 10, 1865.

March, George W., Pvt. Co. H.
Enlisted on Mazy 11, 1864, at Mobile, Alabama, for the war. Drew clothing on September 7, 1864. POW surrendered at Citronelle, Alabama, on May 4, 1865. Paroled at Gainesville, Alabama, on May 14, 1865. Residence Mobile, Mobile County, Alabama. There is a pay voucher in his file.

Markham, George, Sergeant Co. G.
Enlisted March 5, 1862, at Dragoon Camp for July 30, 1864, or the war. Some company muster rolls show him on detached service. His name appears on a roll of non-commissioned officers and privates, in September 1864, employed on extra duty at Mobile, Alabama, by Major Henry St. Paul, Chief of River Transportation, by order of General D. H. Maury. Nature of service is reported as Pilot Steamer, *Ariel*. Age-42.

Markham, W. B., Pvt. Co. H.
Enlisted on September 4, 1862, at Mobile, Alabama, for the war. Company muster roll for December 31, 1863, to April 30, 1864, reports that he was transferred to the Navy on April 9, 1864, by order of General Maury.

Marshall, John H., Captain Co. G.
Enlisted on July 30, 1861, at Mobile, Alabama, for July 30, 1864, or the war. He signs the muster roll certificate as Inspector or Mustering Officer. He appears absent sick on muster rolls from September 1863, through April 30, 1864. Roster of Company G, 15th Confederate Cavalry at Pollard, Alabama, on May 12, 1862, reports him as having received his commission on May 19, 1862, by election. Captain Marshall was wounded in a skirmish with Federals on October 20, 1863, at Shieldsboro, Miss. His name appears on a register of Medical Director's Office, Richmond, Virginia, as having been received on July 11, 1864, and appears again on a similar register as received from Huguenot Springs Hospital, on September 6, 1864. He was given a 30 day furlough. Surgeon's Certificate at Huguenot Springs dated July 9, 1864, recommends a 30 day furlough, "As he is suffering from a gunshot wound of the right shoulder, with paralysis of the arm, from the effects of which he has suffered since October 21, 1862." Here his address is shown as Company G, 15th Confederate Cavalry, PO at Petersburg, Virginia. Company roster for January 1, 1865, at Spring Hill, reports him on the retired list as of June 15, 1964. Succeeded by **L. J. Hallett**. There is considerable requisitions and pay vouchers in his file. **

Marshall, William H., Pvt. Co. E.
Enlisted on September 12, 1862, at Camp Lomax, Florida, for three years. Company muster rolls for November 1863, through April 30, 1864, reports him on special duty as a blacksmith since December 15, 1863. Drew clothing on September 2, 1864.

Marston, Samuel J., Pvt. G.
Enlisted on March 16, 1863, at Halls Mill, Alabama, for July 30, 1864, or the war. Company muster rolls after September 1863, report him on detached service in the Signal Corps. His extra duty muster rolls report him as a Signal Operator. Paid $24 per month. He appears on the rolls as late as May 1864. There are several pay vouchers in his file. **

Martin, Samuel, Pvt. Co. A.
Enlisted on May 15, 1864, at Monticello, Florida, for the war. Drew clothing on September 7, 1864. POW surrendered on May 10, 1865, at Tallahassee, Florida. Paroled at Tallahassee, Florida, on May 26, 1865.

Martin, James, Pvt. Co. H.
Enlisted on June 16, 1863, at West Pascagoula, Mississippi, for the war. September/December 1863, company muster roll reports his transfer due to "irregularly mustered and tuned over to his proper command."

Mashbun, Dennis, Pvt. Co. E.
Drew clothing on September 2, 1864. [There is a letter in his file as follows:]

Office Pro. Marshal
Barrancas, Fla. Oct.27, 1864,

Dennis Mashbun Co. E, 15th Confederate Cav. states that on the 20th day of Sept 1864 he deserted his Reg then stationed at the Tensas River doing picket duty. "I went to the Regiment sick it was in camp at Greenwood - with the exception of Capt. Amos Co. stationed at Milton. and one Co. on the Perdido River." He remained with the Regt four days and then started for home in Santa Rosa Co. some one hundred miles distant from the Regt. I see no troops on the way and knows nothing of the intended movements of the Rebels. He remained at Home about four weeks and then started for the Federal lines which he entered Oct 26, 1864 ."the above is a true copy"

Geo. W. Maynare
Capt & Dist Pro. Mar.

Mask, J. J., Sergeant/Pvt. Co. E.
Enlisted on September 17, 1861, at Milton, Florida, for three years. Fist company muster roll for September 12, 1863, reports him on detached service as a machinist since February 1862, by order of General Jones. May/June 1964, he continues to be shown on detached service as a machinist and reduced to the ranks from 2nd Sergeant by his own consent on May 1, 1864. Drew clothing on September 2, 1864.

Mason, B. W., Pvt. Co. G.
Enlisted on December 27, 1862, at Halls Mill, Alabama, for July 30, 1864, or the war. He appears absent with leave on company muster rolls from September 1863, to April 30, 1864. His name appears on a roll of POW's of stragglers, CSA, surrendered on May 4, 1865, by Lt. General R. Taylor and paroled at Selma, Alabama, during June 1865.

Mason, F. O., Pvt. Co. A.
Enlisted on April 5, 1862, at Monticello, Florida, for three years. Company muster roll for September 12, 1863, report him detached in Naval Service. November/December 1863, muster roll reports that he deserted from Montgomery Naval Yard, exact date not known.

Mason, H. C., Pvt. Co. K.
Enlisted on September 8, 1862, at Halls Mill, Alabama, for the war. Appears on a descriptive list for pay and clothing on October 4, 1863. Born-Wilcox County, Alabama, age-17, eyes-hazel, hair-black, complexion-dark, 5 foot 11 inches, a farmer by occupation. Drew clothing on August 28, 1864. POW surrendered at Citronelle, Alabama, May 4, 1865. Paroled at Gainesville, Alabama, on May 14, 1865. Residence Choctaw, County, Ala.

Mason, Hugh C., see **Mason, H. C.**

Mason, N. M., see **Mayson, N. M.**

Mason, T. J., Pvt./Corporal Co. K. also below

Mason, T. Jefferson, Pvt. Co. D. Murphy's Battalion, Alabama Cavalry CSA
Enlisted on April 17, 1862, at Mobile, Alabama, for the war. Early muster rolls in the fall of 1863, report him absent on detached service. Drew clothing on August 28, 1864. POW surrendered at Citronelle, Alabama, on May 4, 1865. Paroled at Gainesville, Alabama, on May 14, 1865. Residence Choctaw, County, Alabama.

Mathers, S. M., Pvt. Co. A.
Enlisted on March 11, 1862, at Tallahassee, Florida, for the war. Company muster roll for

15TH CONFEDERATE CAVALRY

December 1863, reports him absent without leave. Roll for March/April 1864, reports that he deserted from Halls Mill, Alabama, on December 29, 1863. His name appears on the roll of POW's surrendered on May 10, 1865, at Tallahassee, Florida. Paroled at Tallahassee, Florida, on May 17, 1865.

Mathews, Henry, Pvt. Co. ?
His name appears on the roll of POW's surrendered on May 11, 1865, at Tallahassee, Florida. Paroled at Quincy, Florida, on May 24, 1865.

Mathews, John, Pvt. Co. B.
Enlisted on March 14, 1862, at Marianna, Florida, for three years or the war. Drew clothing on September 10, 1864. POW surrendered on May 10, 1865, at Tallahassee, Florida. Paroled at Quincy, Florida, on May 11, 1865.

Mauldin, A. J., Pvt./Sergeant Co. G.
Enlisted on May 24, 1863, at Camp Taylor for July 30, 1864, or the war. Drew clothing on September 4, 1864. POW surrendered at Citronelle, Alabama, on May 4, 1865. Paroled at Gainesville, Alabama, on May 14, 1865. Residence Marengo County, Alabama.

Maury, Henry, Colonel/Brigadier General Field and Staff
Colonel Maury served the Confederate States as Captain of 1st Alabama Artillery, Colonel 2nd Alabama Infantry and Lt. Colonel of the 32nd Alabama Infantry. Early on from correspondence in his file he was arrested and confined at close quarters at Fort Morgan by order of General Braxton Bragg while serving as Colonel of the 2nd Alabama Infantry. His cousin Major General Dabney H. Maury states in a telegram on March 4, 1864, to Confederate President Jefferson Davis that Colonel Maury's "habits are now exemplary. He has given me his word never during the war to touch Liquor." On March 6, 1861, Colonel Henry Maury writes as Captain of Artillery "If I can obtain a commission as Captain in the [CSA] Navy, I shall prefer it to anything else, as most of my life has been spent at sea. ....[if there] shall be no room in the Navy for me, please ask the President to retain me in the Artillery or Ordnance Department as I am better instructed in those services than anything else." On April 1, 1861, Alabama Governor A. B. Moore writes to L. P. Walker, Confederate Secretary of War at Montgomery, Alabama, "Captain H. Maury has been of great service as Ordnance Officer at Ft. Morgan since it's capture. His Appointment to the position recommended [Captain of Artillery] by Col. [William J.] Hardee [Colonel Commanding Fort Morgan, later to become Lt. General] would be highly gratifying to me." On October 29, 1862, from Mobile, George N. Stewart writes: "Col. Maury was one of the very first who took up arms in the war. He was one of those who volunteered to seize Fort Morgan and did aid in taking and holding it. He offered to seize Fort Pickens, and has his men ready to do it, and would have done it if he had been permitted to do so. He was elected Colonel of the Second Regiment of Alabama Volunteers by an overwhelming vote, although he did not belong to the regiment. He gave to that regiment great reputation. He put Fort Morgan in its powerful state of defense, mounted it's guns, and for a part of the time was in command of that command." His commission as Colonel in the 15th Confederate Cavalry dates from September 24, 1863. He appears present at September/October 1864, Field and Staff muster at Halls Mill, Alabama. He appears on an inspection report of the Brigade commanded by Colonel Isaac W. Patton at Pollard, Alabama, on June 30, 1864. He signed a Parole of Honor at Gainesville, Alabama. on May 12, 1865. His parole is in his file. There are several letters testamentary to his good character and etc. Several letters recommend him as Brigadier General of Cavalry. Henry's cousin, Major General Dabney Maury was persistent in recommending Harry as is reflected by the following telegram.

Recd. at Richmond Mch 64

By telegraph from Mobile March 2, 1864.
His Excy Jeff Davis,
          Genl. Higgins has been compelled by chronic dysentery and paralysis to give up his command. I ask for Col. Harry Maury to be appointed Brigadier to command that line. His qualifications are extraordinarily. He is a sailor and knows the whole ground well. I have more than a thousand effectives and three brigades for duty. Two thousand shots have been fired at Fort Powell, [located at Grant's Pass north of Dauphin Island] it is now better than on the first day. That line can be held, I believe by a rigorous Commander. The shallow water and the winds interrupt the enemy much. Please answer.
                        (Signed) D. H. Maury
                                Maj. Genl.

[Brigadier General Richard L. Page was appointed to fill General Edward Higgins position. In spite of all the recommendations and persistence of his relative. Henry (Harry) Maury remained a Colonel until the very end of the war. In his memoirs General Dabney Maury states that Harry (Henry) finally was made Brigadier General near the end of the war.] There is considerable paper work, letters, pay vouchers and requisitions in his file. **

Maxwell, W. D., Pvt. Co. D.
    Enlisted on April 24, 1862, at Pensacola, Florida, for three years. On muster rolls he appears, dismounted, on scout, and on extra duty with the artillery Drew clothing on August 28, 1864. Appears on a list of paroled POW's for the month of June 1865, by Provost Marshal of the 16th U.S. Army Corps. [Montgomery]

May, Asel, Pvt. Co. K.
    Enlisted as a private in D. McKellars Mounted Alabama Company on September 15, 1862 for three years at Choctaw County, Alabama. Discharged by reason of disability on April 1, 1863, at Halls Mill, Alabama. Born-Sumpter County, Alabama, age-19, five foot 11 inches, complexion-fair, eyes-grey, hair-light, a farmer by occupation. Paid $50 bounty on April 20, 1863, plus $164.30 for service and his horse. He signs a transfer "the within amount to Mss. Houston and Simons for collection". Enlisted on November 26, 1863, at Mobile, Alabama, for the war. Drew clothing on August 28, 1864. POW surrendered at Citronelle, Alabama, on May 4, 1865. Paroled at Gainesville, Alabama, on May 14, 1865. Residence Clarke County, Alabama.

May, Charles, Pvt. Co. K.
    Enlisted on September 15, 1862, at Bladon Springs, Alabama, for the war. He appears on muster rolls in detached service and on furlough. May/June 1864, company muster roll reports him present. POW surrendered at Citronelle, Alabama, on May 4, 1865. Paroled at Gainesville, Alabama, on May 14, 1865. Residence Clarke County, Alabama. A descriptive list found in the file of Pvt. **W. R. McKee** shows further information on this man. Age-24, eyes-hazel, hair-auburn, complexion-dark, 6 foot, born-Sumpter County, Alabama, a farmer.

Mayo, F. B., Pvt. Co. E.
    Enlisted on September 17, 1861, at Milton, Florida, for three years. Drew clothing on September 2, 1864.

Mayo, Mark, Pvt. Co. E.
    Enlisted on September 12, 1861, at Milton, Florida, for three years. Drew clothing on September 2, 1864.

15TH CONFEDERATE CAVALRY

Mayson, F. R., Pvt. Co. E.
Enlisted on June 5, 1863, at Camp Lomax, Florida, for three years. Drew clothing on September 2, 1864.

Mayson, M. M., Pvt. Co. E.
Enlisted on September 17, 1861, at Milton, Forida, for three years. Company muster roll for March/April 1864, reports him sick in Hospital at Greenville, Alabama. He appears on a hospital muster roll for July/August 1864, as a patient at General Hospital in Marion, Alabama. Drew clothing on September 2, 1864. POW captured near Pollard, Alabama, on December 14, 1864, by 2nd Maine Cavlary, the 1st Florida Cavalry, 82, 86 and 97th U.S. Infantry under the command of Colonel Robinson of the 97th U.S. Infantry. One report shows capture at Little Escambia River, Florida. Confined at New Orleans, Louisiana, on December 27, 1864, transferred to Ship Island, Mississippi, on January 22, 1865. Applied to take the Oath of Allegiance to the USA at Ship Island. Transferred from Ship Island to Vicksburg, Mississippi, on May 1, 1865.

McAgaya, John see **Magaha, John**

McAnulty, E. H. or McA Nutly see **McNulty, E. H.**

McCalister, P. A., Pvt. Co. H.
Enlisted on April 5, 1864, at Mobile, Alabama, for the war. Muster rolls from December 31, 1863, to June 30, 1864, report him absent without leave.

McCarty, T., Pvt. Co. K.
Enlisted on August 18, 1862, at Pascagoula, Mississippi, for the war. Admitted to Ross Hospital, Mobile, Alabama, on April 5, 1864, with dysentery. Returned to duty on May 7, 1864. He appears on a hospital muster roll for March to August 1864. Died at Greenville, Alabama. on September 12, 1864. Left one military jacket and $5.

McCaskeal, W. C. see **McCaskill, W. C.**

McCaskial, D. E. see **McCaskial, E. D.**

McCaskial, E. D., Pvt. Co. I.
Enlisted on February 1, 1864, at Halls Mill, Alabama. He appears present on Muster rolls from December 31, 1863, through June 30, 1864.

McCaskill, E. D. see **McCaskial, E. D.** above

McCaskill, W. C., 1st Sergeant/2nd Lieutenant Co. I.
Enlisted on October 4, 1862, at Santa Rosa, Florida, for the war. Promoted to 3rd Lieutenant on December 1, 1863. Elected to fill position of Jr. 2nd Lieutenant on May 12, 1864, at Pollard, Alabama. Commission to date from January 1, 1864. Admitted to Ross Hospital, Mobile, Alabama, on January 13, 1864, with catarrh. Returned to duty on January 19, 1864. Died on October 24, 1864. There is a pay voucher for Lieutenant McCaskill and a tax in kind receipt for corn in his file for **J. W. Andrews** of Baldwin County, Alabama.

McClellan, William, Pvt. Co. I.
Company muster rolls for September/October 1863, report him absent with out leave August 11, 1863. November/December 1863, muster roll reports him as deserted.

McCloud, John, Pvt. Co. A.
   Drew clothing on September 7, 1864.

McConnell, Charles, Pvt. Co. C.
   Drew clothing on August 28, 1864. POW surrendered at Citronelle, Alabama, on May 4, 1865. Paroled at Mobile, Alabama, on June 21, 1865. Residence-Baldwin County, Alabama, age-20, complexion-sallow, eyes-gray, hair-light, 5 foot 8 inches.

McCrary, G. G., Pvt. Co. F.
   Enlisted on April 3, 1863, at Camp Withers [Mississippi], for three years or the war. Appears on detached service in Mobile, Alabama on September 12, 1863, thereafter he appears present on muster rolls. Drew clothing on August 29, 1864.

McCurdy, F. M., Pvt. Co. D.
   Enlisted on April 24, 1862, at Pensacola, Florida, for three years. Company muster roll for September 12, 1863, reports him on extra duty since August 26, by order of General Clanton. The next roll in September/October reports him on scout on extra 50 days since last muster. Muster rolls from November 1863, through June 30, 1864, report him absent without leave for 38 days. On August 28, 1864, he drew clothing and signed by his mark.

McCurdy, G. W., Pvt. Co. D.
   Enlisted on April 24, 1862, at Pensacola, Florida, for three years. Between September 1863, and June 30, 1864, he is reported on muster rolls as present, on scout, dismounted for 20 days, dismounted for 90 days on special duty near Bluff Springs, Florida, and present but dismounted for 151 days. Drew clothing on August 28, 1864. Signs by his mark.

McDavid, A. J., Pvt. Co. C.
   Enlisted on April 9, 1862, at Blakeley, Alabama, for three years or the war. Drew clothing on August 28, 1864. POW captured at Mount Pleasant, Alabama, April 11, 1865, by U.S. Cavalry. He appears on a list of POW's forwarded from Mobile, Ala., to Ship Island, Miss.

McDavid, J. (John) E., Pvt. Co. D.
   Enlisted on May 8, 1862, at Pensacola, Florida, for three years. Muster rolls from September 1863, report him present, on scout, absent without leave and finally deserted on December 20, 1863. Strangely he then appears as a POW surrendered at Citronelle, Alabama, on May 4, 1865. Paroled at Gainesville, Alabama, May 14, 1865. Residence Baldwin County, Ala.

McDavid, J. F., Pvt. Co. C.
   Enlisted on May 11, 1864, at Camp Powell, Alabama, for three years. POW surrendered at Citronelle, Alabama, on May 4, 1865. Paroled at Gainesville, Alabama, on May 14, 1865. Residence Baldwin County, Alabama.

McDavid, R. M., 2nd Lieutenant Co. C.
   A Field Return for Baldwin Rangers at Brigade Headquarters, Fort Morgan, Alabama, for October 2, 1862, reports him present as 2nd Lieutenant. Company muster roll for September 12, 1863, reports that he enlisted for three years or the war but no location is shown. September/October 1863, muster roll he signs as commanding company. On March 30, 1864, he signs a requisition for corn and fodder for 112 horses at Halls Mill, Alabama, and signs as commanding company. Muster roll of May 12, 1864, at Pollard, Alabama, reports that his commission dates from April 18, 1862. He signed a Parole of Honor at Gainesville, Alabama, on May 14, 1865. His parole is in his file. There is considerable other paper work in his file. **

15TH CONFEDERATE CAVALRY

McDavid, R. T., Pvt. Co. D.
Enlisted on September 29, 1862, at Camp Tatnall, Florida, for three years. Company muster rolls from September report him sick at home at Santa Rosa, Florida. (since August 20, 1863). Muster rolls after January 1864, report him as having deserted as of January 1, 1864.

McDavid, W. H. H., 1st Sergeant Co. C.
Enlisted on April 9, 1862, at Blakeley, Alabama, for three years. Drew clothing on June 20, and August 28, 1864. POW surrendered at Citronelle, Alabama, on May 4, 1865. Paroled at Gainesville, Alabama, on May 14, 1865. Residence Baldwin County, Alabama.

McDonald, A. J., Pvt./Quartermaster Sergeant Co. H/Field and Staff
Enlisted on September 4, 1862, at Mobile, Alabama, for the war. Muster rolls report him on extra duty. Transferred to Field and Staff as Quartermaster Sergeant on January 19, 1864. Drew clothing on September 10, 1864.

McDonald, D., Pvt. Co. K.
Enlisted on September 1, 1862, at Camp Forney, Mississippi, for three years. Two out of seven company muster rolls report him absent without leave. Others show him present. **David McDonald** appears as a POW of 9 Regiment Mississippi, Cavalry CSA that was surrendered at Meridian, Mississippi, in May 1865. Paroled at Mobile, Alabama, on May 23, 1865. Residence Jackson County, Alabama.

McDonald, G. A., Pvt. Co. G.
Enlisted on April 5, 1862, at Dragoon Camp for July 30, 1864, or the war. Drew clothing in June 1864. POW surrendered at Citronelle, Alabama, on May 4, 1865. Paroled at Gainesville, Alabama, on May 14, 1865. Residence Jefferson County, Mississippi.

McDonald, A., Pvt. Co. C.
Enlisted on May 9, 1864, at Camp Powell, Alabama, for three years.

McEarthern see **McEathern**

McEathern, William, Pvt. Co. K.
Enlisted on March 17, 1862, at Washington County, Alabama, for the war. Admitted to Ross Hospital, Mobile, Alabama, with chronic dysenteria, on November 20, 1863. Returned to duty on December 17, 1863. Drew clothing on August 28, 1864. POW surrendered at Citronelle, Alabama, on May 4, 1865. Paroled at Gainesville, Alabama, on May 14, 1865. Residence Choctaw County, Alabama.

McFarland, John, Pvt. Co. H.
POW surrendered at Citronelle, Alabama, on May 4, 1865. Paroled at Gainesville, Alabama, on May 14, 1865. Residence Jackson County, Mississippi.

McGill, J. P., Pvt. Co. C.
Enlisted on April 16, 1862, at Blakeley, Alabama, for three years or the war. He appears present on a muster roll on June 30, 1864.

McGowin, J. L., Pvt./Corporal Co. I.
Enlisted on January 13, 1862, at Conecuh County, Alabama. He was promoted to 4th Corporal from the ranks on September 1, 1863. He appears present on a muster roll on June 30, 1864.

McGraw, J. L., Pvt. Co. D.
 He appears on a list of POW's paroled at Headquarters of the 16th U.S. Army Corps at Montgomery, Alabama, on My 24, 1865. Hair-dark, eyes-blue, complexion-fair, 5 foot 6 inches. His parole is in his file.*

McGriff, Richard R., Pvt. Co. B.
 Enlisted on March 14, 1862, at Marianna, Florida, for three years or the war. First company muster roll on September 12, 1863, reports him detailed for Provost Duty on June 17, by order of General Maury. A later muster roll for March/April 1864, reports him detached on January 28, 1864, by order of General Maury. There is a Form 3 in his file that shows him employed as a special detective at Shubuta, Mississippi, for Major R. M. Cox, PACS, Assistant Provost Marshal, General, from February 26 to April 12, 1864. There are several monthly pay vouchers in his file for he and the use of his horse at Selma and Mobile Alabama, in late 1863, and early 1864. Age-36, eyes-dark, hair-brown, complexion-light, 5 foot 8 inches, born in Henry County, Alabama, a farmer by occupation. There is considerable paperwork in his file. **

McKay, P., Sergeant Co. F.
 Enlisted on October 1, 1861, at Mobile, Alabama, for three years or the war. Drew clothing on August 29, 1864. Paid $0.40 per day at Knoxville, on extra duty in the Signal Corps from March 1, to April 30, 1863.

McKee, W. R., Pvt. Co. K.
 Enlisted on September 1, 1862, at Camp Forney, Mississippi, for the war. He appears on detached service on two company muster rolls. Drew clothing on August 28, 1864. POW surrendered at Citronelle, Alabama, on May 4, 1865. Paroled at Gainesville, Alabama, on May 14, 1865. Residence Washington County, Alabama. Descriptive list in his file shows him: Age-21, eyes-grey, hair-dark, complexion-dark, 5 foot 8 inches, born-Chambers County, Alabama, a farmer by occupation. This descriptive list contains the data on two other solders, Pvt. **C. May** and Pvt. **G. W. Clanahan**, see their files for details.

McKellar, Duncan, Captain Co. K.
 Enlisted on March 17, 1862, at Washington County, Alabama, for the war. Served with Murphy's Battalion Alabama Cavalry. Served as 1st Lieutenant for a time and promoted to Captain of Co. K, 15th Confederate Cavalry on December 27, 1862. His commission dates from March 17, 1862. He appears present on company muster rolls from September 12, 1863, through June 30, 1864, with the exception of on sick leave of absence for 60 days from May 12, 1864. He was admitted twice to Ross Hospital, Mobile, Alabama, with phthisis pheumonialis. In September 1863, he requisitioned corn for 78 horses at Halls Mill, Alabama, it was reported that there was no fodder on hand or to be obtained. In the 3rd Quarter of 1863, he requisitioned 50 carbines, 50 slings, 1000 rifle cartridges, 1000 musket caps and one packing box. In the 4th quarter of 1863, Captain McKellar requisitioned; 109 jackets, 12 pair pants, 24 shirts, 24 pair drawers, 11 caps, 109 pair boots.

McKellar, J. C., Pvt. Co. K.
 Enlisted on March 17, 1862, at Washington County, Alabama, for the war. Company muster rolls report him absent, detached, on furlough for 40 days and present. POW surrendered at Citronelle, Alabama, on May 4, 1865. Paroled at Gainesville, Alabama, on May 14, 1865. Residence Choctaw County, Alabama.

McKey see **Mckee**

15TH CONFEDERATE CAVALRY

McKinnon, John P., Sergeant Co. H.
    Enlisted on October 29, 1862, at Mobile, Alabama, for the war. Drew clothing on September 7, 1864. Admitted to Ross Hospital, Mobile, Alabama, for 10 days in November 1864, with febris intermittens. POW surrendered at Citronelle, Alabama, on May 4, 1865. Paroled at Gainesville, Alabama, May 14, 1865. Residence Mobile, Mobile County, Ala.

McLaughlin see **McLoughlin**

McLean, J. G., Pvt. Co. I.
    Enlisted on April 10, 1864, at Santa Rosa, Florida, for the war. He appears on company muster rolls from December 31, 1863, through June 30, 1864.

McLean, John H., Pvt. Co. H.
    Enlisted on December 18, 1863, at Halls Mill, Alabama, for the war. Company muster rolls report him absent on detached duty by order of Colonel Jennifer from January 1, 1864. POW captured at Mount Pleasant, Alabama, by U.S. Cavalry on April 11, 1865.

McLean, W. F., Pvt. Co. I.
    Enlisted on July 21, 1863, at Santa Rosa, Florida, for the war. He appears on company muster rolls from September 12, 1863, through June 30, 1864.

McLellan, Charles, Pvt. Co. A.
    Enlisted on March 8, 1862, at Monticello, Florida, for three years. Muster rolls report him present, dismounted, and on extra duty as a teamster at various times. Drew clothing on September 7, 1864.

Mclillan, William see **McClellan, William**

McLoughlin, D., Pvt. Co. K.
    Enlisted January 6, 1864, at Halls Mill, Ala. for the war. Drew clothing August 28, 1864.

McLoughling, E., Pvt. Co. K.
    Enlisted on March 17, 1862, at Washington County, Alabama, for the war. Drew clothing on August 28, 1864. POW surrendered at Citronelle, Alabama, on May 4, 1865. Paroled at Gainesville, Alabama, on May 14, 1865. Residence Choctaw County, Alabama.

McMillan, Duncan, Pvt. Co. E.
    Enlisted on November 15, 1862, at Camp Lomax, Florida, for three years. Drew clothing on September 2, 1864.

McMillan, M., Pvt. Co. F.
    Enlisted on May 1, 1864, at Canoe Station, Alabama, for three years. Drew clothing on August 29, 1864.

McMillan, Neill, Pvt. Co. E.
    Enlisted on July 17, 1863, at Camp Lomax, Florida, for three years. Company muster roll reports that he deserted from Halls Mill, Alabama, about December 18, 1863. "Has probably gone to the Pensacola Navy Yard."

McNealy, Charles, Pvt. Co. B.
    Enlisted on February 13, 1863, at Marianna, Florida, for three years or the war. Drew clothing on September 10, 1864. POW.

McNeil, Charles, Pvt. Co. D.
  POW captured on April 11, 1865, at Mount Pleasant, Alabama, by U.S. Cavalry forces.

McNulty, E. H., Pvt. Co. F.
  Enlisted on October 1, 1861, at Mobile, Alabama, for three years or the war. Drew clothing on August 29, 1864. POW surrendered at Citronelle, Alabama, on May 4, 1865. Paroled at Gainesville, Alabama, on May 14, 1865. Residence Mobile, Mobile County, Alabama.

McNulty, John, Pvt. Co. F.
  Enlisted on October 1, 1861, at Mobile, Alabama, for three years or the war. Drew clothing on August 29, 1864.

McQueen, D. W., Pvt. Co. D.
  Only a reference envelope exist in his file.

McRay, Loch, 1st Sergeant/Pvt. Co. E.
  Enlisted on September 17, 1861, at Milton, Florida, for three years. First company muster roll on September 12, 1863, and subsequent rolls report him absent detailed on April 8, 1863, to work on gunboat at Montgomery, Alabama, by order of General Buckman. May/June 1864, reports him absent detailed as above but reduced to ranks by his own consent on May 1, 1864. Drew clothing on September 2, 1864.

McVoy, B. O., Pvt./Corporal, Co. F.
  Enlisted on October 1, 1861, at Mobile, Alabama, by three years or the war. Promoted to 4th Corporal on September 17, 1863. Drew clothing on August 29, 1864. POW captured by U.S. Cavalry forces at Greenville, Alabama, on April 27, 1863. Admitted to Ross Hospital, Mobile, Alabama, on March 24, 1865, with dysentery. Returned to duty on March 28, 1865. Paroled at Greenville.

McVoy, George W., Pvt. Co. F.
  Enlisted on August 3, 1862, at Camp Withers, Mississippi, for three years or the war. Several company muster rolls report him absent sick in General Hospital, Mobile, Alabama. Drew clothing on August 29, 1864. Medical cards report him admitted to Ross Hospital, Mobile, Alabama, and hospital at Greenville, Alabama, with primary syphilis and gonorrhea.

McVoy, Joseph, 1st Sergeant/2nd Lieutenant Co. H.
  Enlisted on September 4, 1862, Mobile, Alabama, for the war. Drew clothing on September 2, 1864. Elected 2nd Lieutenant on November 5, 1864. He signed a Parole of Honor at Gainesville, Alabama, on May 14, 1865. His parole is in his file. There is a requisition in his file for rations for 10 horses for two days at Leakesville, [Mississippi] on February 15, 1864.

McVoy, Thomas, Pvt. Co. A.
  Enlisted on March 20, 1864, at Halls Mill, Alabama, for three years. Drew clothing on September 7 and 10, 1864. POW captured at Pine Barren, Escambia County, Florida, by U.S. Cavalry on November 17, 1864. Confined at New Orleans, Louisiana, on November 21, 1864. Transferred to Ship Island, Mississippi, on December 10, 1864. Transferred from Ship Island to Vicksburg, Mississippi, on May 1, 1865.

McVoy, W. H., Pvt. Co. A.
  Enlisted on November 1, 1862, at Camp Tatnall, Florida, for three years. Drew clothing on September 7, 1864. POW captured at Pine Barren, Escambia County, Florida, by U.S.

15TH CONFEDERATE CAVALRY

Cavalry on November 17, 1864. Confined at New Orleans, Louisiana, on November 21, 1864. Transferred to Ship Island, Mississippi, on December 10, 1864. Transferred from Ship Island to Vicksburg, Mississippi, on May 1, 1865.

McWhorter, C. J., Pvt. Co. H.
Enlisted on August 5, 1863, at Meridian, Mississippi, for the war. He appears on a descriptive list for September 30, 1863, at Halls Mill, Alabama. Age-33, eyes-gray, hair-gray, complexion-dark, 5 foot 10 inches, born- Barnwell District, South Carolina, a farmer by occupation. POW captured at Mount Pleasant, Alabama, on April 11, 1865, by U.S. Cavalry forces. Received at Ship Island, Mississippi, on May 13, 1865, from Provost Marshal, Mobile, Alabama. Transferred from Ship Island to New Orleans, Louisiana, on June 8, 1865.

McWhorter, D. O., Pvt. Co. H.
Enlisted on September 4, 1862, at Mobile, Alabama, for the war. Drew clothing on September 7, 1864. Appears on a list of POW's of detailed men of the Subsistance Department CSA that were surrendered at Citronelle, Alabama, on May 4, 1865. Paroled at Gainesville, Alabama, on May 14, 1865. Residence Sumpter County, Alabama.

McWhorter, John, Pvt. Co. B.
Enlisted on February 23, 1864, at Greenville, Alabama, for the war. Drew clothing on September 10, 1864. POW captured at Mount Pleasant, Alabama, by U.S. Cavalry on April 11, 1865.

McWhorter, William W., Pvt. Co. B.
Enlisted on March 1, 1864, at Greenville, Alabama, for the war. POW captured at Mount Pleasant, Alabama, by U.S. Cavalry on April 11, 1865.

Michael, George J., Pvt. Co. G.
Enlisted on May 24, 1863, at Camp Taylor, for the July 30, 1864, or the war. POW captured at Blakeley, Alabama, the night of April 8, 1865, by U.S. Forces. Here he is shown as a clerk for General Liddell.

Michael, William E., Pvt. Co. G.
Enlisted on May 28, 1863, at Camp Taylor, for July 30, 1864, or the war. Drew clothing on September 4, 1864. POW surrendered at Citronelle, Alabama, on May 4, 1865. Paroled at Gainesville, Alabama, on May 14, 1865. His residence is shown as Marengo County, Alabama.

Middleton, D. W., Pvt. Co. D.
Enlisted on September 1, 1863, at Camp Ward for three years. Died on November 24, 1863, at Mobile, Alabama.

Mikell, Frank A., Pvt. Co. A.
Enlisted on March 8, 1862, at Camp Monticello, Florida for three years. He was paid $225 for his horse that was killed in action by the enemy at Gonzalez, Florida, on October 28, 1862. He was paid on December 24, 1863, at Halls Mill, Alabama by Quartermaster Captain Gonzalez. A letter stating the loss and value plus a pay voucher is in his file. Drew clothing on September 7, 1864. POW surrendered at Tallahassee, Florida, on May 10, 1865. Paroled at Tallahassee on May 15, 1865. Eyes-blue, hair-light, complexion-dark, 5 foot 8 inches. His parole is in his file.*

Miles, John P., Pvt. Co. C.
Enlisted on April 9, 1862, at Blakeley, Alabama, for three years. Drew clothing on August 28, 1864. His file reports that he was detailed for a time.

Miller, Henry H., Pvt. Co. I.
Enlisted on October 4, 1862, at Santa Rosa, Florida, for the war. He appears present on a company muster roll for May/June 1863.

Miller, James B., Pvt. Co. I.
Enlisted on October 4, 1862, at Santa Rosa, Florida, for the war. First company muster roll for September 12, 1863, reports him present sick in quarters. Later he is shown absent on scout and yet later present. April 30, 1864, he is shown present.

Miller, John B., Pvt. Co. I.
Enlisted on October 4, 1862, at Santa Rosa, Florida, for the war. First company muster roll for September 12, 1863, reports him absent a POW since December 25, 1862. November/December 1863, company muster roll reports that he deserted.

Miller, Richard, Pvt. Co. I.
Enlisted on October 4, 1862, at Santa Rosa, Florida, for the war. First company muster roll for September 12, 1863, reports him absent without leave since August 25. November/December 1863, company muster roll reports him present. Muster rolls from December 31, 1863, and June 30, 1864, report him absent sick.

Miller, T. R., Pvt. Co. E.
Enlisted on September 17, 1861, at Milton, Florida, for three years. Drew clothing on September 2, 1864. POW captured near Pensacola, Escambia County, Florida, on November 17, 1864, by a detachment of U.S. Cavalry. Confined at New Orleans, Louisiana, on November 21, 1864, transferred to Ship Island, Mississippi, on December 10, 1864. Transferred from Ship Island, to Vicksburg, Mississippi, on May 1, 1865.

Miller, W. R., Corporal Co. A.
Enlisted at Station 3 on P & G Railroad, Florida, for three years. Signed a parole at Thomasville, Georgia, on May 16, 1865. Hair-dark, 5 foot 8 inches, eyes-hazel, complexion-florid.

Mills, A. O., Pvt. Co. K.
Enlisted on September 1, 1862, at Camp Forney, Mississippi, for the war. POW surrendered at Citronelle, Alabama, on May 4, 1865. Paroled at Gainesville, Alabama, on May 14, 1865. Residence Choctaw County, Alabama.

Mills, J. C., Pvt. Co. K.
Enlisted on August 5, 1863, at State Line, Mississippi, for the war.

Mills, Lang, Pvt. Co. H.
Enlisted on August 2, 1863, at West Pascagoula, Mississippi, for the war. Drew clothing on September 7, 1864. He appears on a descriptive list at Halls Mill, Alabama, for October 1, 1864. Here he is shown; age-18, eyes-blue, hair-light, complexion-fair, 5 foot 8 inches, born Green County, Mississippi, a farmer by occupation. POW surrendered at Citronelle, Alabama, on May 4, 1865. Paroled at Mobile, Alabama, on June 17, 1865. Residence Green County, Alabama [Mississippi?]. Age-19, eyes-blue, hair-sandy, complexion-fair, 5 foot 10 inches. [He must have grown two inches from October 1864, to June 1865?]

15TH CONFEDERATE CAVALRY

Mills, Z. T., Pvt. Co. K.
POW surrendered at Citronelle, Alabama, on May 4, 1865. Paroled at Gainesville, Alabama, on May 14, 1865. Residence Choctaw County, Alabama.

Milstead, George B., Pvt. Co. C.
Enlisted on April 16, 1862, at Blakeley, Alabama, for three years or the war. Drew clothing on August 28, 1864.

Milstead, J. E., Pvt. Co. C.
Enlisted on October 15, 1862, at Camp Powell, Alabama, for three years or the war. Appears on company muster rolls from September 1863, until June 30, 1864.

Milton, J. P., Pvt. Co. I.
Enlisted on October 4, 1862, at Santa Rosa, Florida, for the war. Appears absent without leave on September 1863, company muster roll but present from December 31, 1863, through June 30, 1864.

Mims, D. McD., Pvt. Co. E.
Enlisted on May 8, 1862, at Warrington, Florida, for three years. He appears present on company muster rolls for September/December 1863, but absent without leave on November/December 1863, rolls. March/April company muster roll reports him deserted from Halls Mill, Alabama, about January 1, 1864. "He has probably gone to the enemy at Pensacola Navy Yard."

Mims, T. B., Pvt. Co. E.
Enlisted on August 30, 1862, at Camp Lomax, Florida, for three years. First company muster roll on September 12, 1863, reports him absent without leave since August 12, 1862. September/October 1863, company muster roll reports him as deserted from August 12, 1863, "whereabouts not known."

Mints, J. J., Pvt. Co. E.
Enlisted on May 1, 1862, at Warrington, Florida, for three years. He appears present on company muster rolls from September 1863, through June 1864. Drew clothing on September 2, 1864. POW captured by a detachment of U.S. Cavalry on November 17, 1864, at Pine Barren, Escambia County, Florida. He was confined at New Orleans, Louisiana, on November 21, 1864. Transferred to Ship Island, Mississippi, on Dec. 10, 1864. Transferred from Ship Island to Vicksburg, Mississippi, on May 1, 1865.

Mitchell, Charles, J., Pvt. Co. H.
Enlisted on December 9, 1863, at Mobile, Alabama, for the war. He appears absent without leave on company muster rolls from November 1863, through June 30, 1864. His name then appears on a receipt roll for clothing issued on September 10, 1864.

Mitchell, James, Pvt. Co. C.
Enlisted on April 15, 1862, at Stockton, Alabama, for three years or the war. He appears present on early company muster rolls and on December 31, 1863, through June 30, 1864, he is reported absent, and detached as a teamster by order of Colonel H. Maury. Drew clothing June 14, and August 28, 1864.

Mitternight, C. C., Pvt. Co. ?
POW captured by U.S. Cavalry forces on December 17-18, 1864, Near Pollard, Alabama, at Little Escambia, River. Confined at New Orleans, Louisiana, on December 27, 1864.

Transferred to Ship Island, Mississippi, on January 22, 1865. Transferred from Ship Island, to Vicksburg, Mississippi, on May 1, 1865.

Mizell, James, Pvt. Co. H.
Enlisted on August 5, 1863, at West Pascagoula, Mississippi, for the war. Company muster roll for September/October 1863, reports that he irregularly mustered and was transferred and turned over to his proper command.

Mobley, W. M., Assistant Surgeon, Field and Staff
Commission dates from March 19, 1863. His name appears on a Field and Staff muster roll for September/October 1863, at Halls Mill, Alabama, as present. POW captured at Wayside Hospital, Fort Blakeley, Alabama, on April 9, 1865. Arrived at Ship Island, Mississippi, on April 16, 1865. Transferred from Ship Island, on April 28, and confined on April 30, 1865, at New Orleans, Louisiana. Forwarded to Vicksburg, Mississippi, on May 1, 1865.

Molett, J. D., Pvt. Co. G.
Enlisted on February 10, 1864, at Halls Mill, Alabama, for July 30, 1864, or the war. Company muster roll for December 31, 1863, through April 30, 1864, reports him absent without leave. Drew clothing on June 20, 1864. In a September 2, 1864, letter at camp near Mobile, he and Pvt. **Joseph A. Ulmer**, write to the Secretary of War CSA and apply to be named to the position of Cadet after having served as Privates for four years, as they desire to remain in the country's service after the war. The letter is in his file.*

Moniac, D. A., Pvt. Co. C.
Enlisted on February 1, 1864, at Halls Mill, Alabama, for three years. Company muster roll for December 31, 1863, through June 30, 1864, reports him on detached service as wagon master by order of Colonel H. Maury. Drew clothing on June 10 and September 10, 1864. POW surrendered at Citronelle, Alabama, on May 4, 1865. Paroled at Gainesville, Alabama, on May 14, 1865. Residence Baldwin County, Alabama.

Moniac, George, Pvt. Co. C.
Enlisted on October 1, 186?, at Shell Banks, Alabama, for three years or the war. Muster roll for September/October 1864, report him present but in November/December 1863, he is shown as absent without leave. He was admitted to Ross Hospital, Mobile, Alabama, on October 5, 1863, with intermitten fever. Furloughed from hospital on October 25, for 25 days. Company muster roll for December 31, 1863, through June 30, 1864, he is reported to have deserted.

Moniac, J. R., Pvt. Co. C.
Enlisted on April 9, 186?, at Blakeley, Alabama, for three years or the war. He appears on company muster rolls from September 12, 1863, through June 30, 1864. The December 31, 1863 to June 30, 1864, reports that he joined at Camp Powell, on May 24, 1864.

Moniac, M., Pvt. Co. C.
He was enlisted on April 9, 1862, at Blakeley, Alabama, for three years. Company muster rolls from September 12, 1863, report him absent without leave, present or presence not stated. Final Regimental Muster roll from December 30, 1863, to June 30, 1864, reports him deserted.

Montague, G., Pvt. Co. F.
Detailed on Special Order No. 115 by order of General Maury. Transferred from Co. G, 17th Alabama Regiment to Co. F, 15th Regiment Confederate Cavalry on April 15, 1864.

15TH CONFEDERATE CAVALRY

He appears on a roll of non-commissioned officers and privates employed on extra duty during August 1864. His duty is shown as a courier.

Montomery, F., Pvt. Co. C.
Enlisted on August 11, 1863, at Camp Powell, for three years. Drew clothing on August 28, 1864. POW surrendered at Citronelle, Alabama, on May 4, 1865. Paroled at Gainesville, Alabama, on May 14, 1865. Residence Baldwin County, Alabama.

Moore, D. S., Pvt. Co. E.
Enlisted on July 19, 1863, at Camp Lomax, Florida, for three years. Company muster rolls from September 1863, through April 30, 1864, report him sick in hospital in Mobile, Alabama. May/June 1864, muster he is shown present. He was admitted to Ross Hospital, Mobile, Alabama, on February 20, 1864, with rubeola. Returned to duty on May 7, 1864. [Carried forward monthly on the hospital register for March, April and May as complain of diarrhoea.] Drew clothing on September 2, 1864. POW captured near Pensacola, Escambia County, Florida, on November 17, 1864, by U.S. Cavalry. Confined at New Orleans, Louisiana, on November 21, 1864. Transferred to Ship Island, Mississippi, on December 10, 1864. Transferred from Ship Island to Vicksburg, Mississippi, on May 1, 1865. Admitted from steamer to USA Hospital No. 2, at Vicksburg with acute diarrhoea. Returned to duty on May 31, 1865. Age-38. Admitted from M. Bar. (Military Barracks?) again to Hospital No. 2, on June 1, 1865, with chronic diarrhoea. Died June 1, 1865.

Moore, James, A., Pvt. Co. A.
Enlisted on March 15, 1862, at Monticello, Florida, for three years. He is reported on detached service by order of General Maury from December 21, 1863, to January 6, 1864. Company muster roll for March/April 1864, reports that he died on January 9, 1864.

Moore, Lenard, Pvt. Co. B/E.
Drew clothing on September 10, 1864. He appears on a roll of POW stragglers that were paroled in Selma, Alabama, in June 1865. Here he is reported as a Private in Co. E., 15th Confederate Cavalry and a resident of Wilcox County, Alabama.

Moore, S. P., Pvt. Co. I.
Enlisted on October 4, 1862, at Santa Rosa, Florida, for the war. He appears on company muster rolls as absent without leave, absent on scout, absent on detached service and present from September 1863 through June 1864. He appears May 22, 1864, on a list of detailed soldiers employed by the commissary agent at Pollard, Alabama.

Moore, L. D., Pvt. Co. I.
Enlisted on January 12, 1863, at Conecuh County, Alabama, for the war. He appears on company muster rolls from September 1863, through June 30, 1864.

More, F. A., Pvt. Co. H.
POW surrendered at Citronelle, Alabama, on May 4, 1865. Paroled at Gainesville, Alabama, on May 14, 1865. Residence Mobile County, Alabama.

Morre, Robert, L., Pvt. Co. K.
His name appears on a descriptive list in the file of **Private Daniel Taylor**, Co. K. He is shown as: age-36, eyes-hazel, hair-dark, complexion-dark, 5 foot 8 inches, born-Anson County, North Carolina, a carpenter by trade. Enlisted on January 28, 1863, by Captain McKellar at Halls Mill, Alabama, for the war.

Morgan, James, Pvt. Co. E.
    Appears on a detachment of CSA surrendered by Lt. General Taylor in May 1865, and paroled at Demopolis, Alabama, on June 23, 1865. Residence Brownsville, Tennessee.

Morgan, Samuel, Pvt. Co. D.
    Enlisted on April 24, 1862, at Pensacola, Florida, for three years. Company muster roll for March/April 1864, report him a courier near Pensacola to Pollard and dismounted for 20 days in last pay period. Drew clothing on August 28, 1864. POW captured at Pine Barren, Escambia County, Florida, by U.S. Cavalry forces on November 17, 1864. Confined at New Orleans, Louisiana, on November 21, 1864. Transferred to Ship Island, Mississippi, on December 10, 1864. Transferred from Ship Island to Vicksburg, Mississippi, May 1, 1865.

Morgan, T. J., Pvt. Co. H.
    POW surrendered at Citronelle, Alabama, on May 4, 1865. Paroled at Gainesville, Alabama, on May 14, 1865. Residence Perry County, Alabama.

Morgan, W. A., Jr. 2nd Lieutenant Co. D.
    His commission dated from April 24, 1862. Appears present on first company muster roll for September 12, 1863. He requisitioned for Co. D at Halls Mill, Alabama, on October 20, 1863; 106 jackets, 98 pants, 98 shirts, 98 drawers, 98 caps, 14 pair boots, "as the clothing previously drawn are worn out". Promoted to 2nd Lieutenant on January 12, 1864. March/April 1864, the muster roll he signs as commanding the company. On June 30, 1864, he requisitions corn and fodder for 78 horses at Pollard, Alabama. On July 22, 1864, at Camp Cumming he requisitioned 6 mess pans, 6 camp kettles and 2 skillet lids "as the company is very short on cooking utensils" and he signs as commanding the company. There are considerable requisitions and pay vouchers in his file. **

Morrison, Allen, Pvt. Co. I.
    Enlisted on October 4, 1862, at Santa Rosa, Florida, for the war. He appears on first company muster roll for September 12, 1863, at absent without leave. September/October 1863, muster roll he is reported to have died, with pay due from April 30 to October 20.

Morrison, Berry, Pvt. Co. I.
    Enlisted on May 5, 1863, at Conecuh County, Alabama, for the war. November/December 1863, company muster roll reports him detached as a nurse at hospital, Mobile, Alabama. He appears present on May/June 1864, muster roll.

Morrison, Finley, Pvt. Co. I.
    Enlisted on October 4, 1862, at Santa Rosa, Florida, for the war. He appears company on muster rolls from September 12, 1863, through June 30, 1864.

Morrison, Miles, Pvt. Co. I.
    Enlisted on October 4, 1862, at Santa Rosa, Florida, for the war. First company muster roll for September 12, 1863, reports him on detached service since June 26, herding cattle by orders of General Cantey. November/December 1863, muster roll reports him dead.

Morton, George, Pvt. Co. F.
    Enlisted on January 30, 1863, at Camp Withers, Mississippi, for three years or the war. Admitted to Ross Hospital, Mobile, Alabama, on November 13, 1863, with gonorrhea. Returned to duty on December 15, 1863. He appears present on company muster roll for May/June 1864.

15TH CONFEDERATE CAVALRY

Mosby, John K., Pvt. Co. H.
Enlisted on August 19, 1863, at Mobile, Alabama, for the war. He appears on a descriptive list at Halls Mill, Alabama, on September 30, 1863. Age-19, eyes-blue, hair-dark, complexion-fair, 6 foot 3 inches. He appears on a roll of POW's of Mitchell's Company Mississippi Cavalry CSA commanded by Captain J. B. Mitchell, that was surrendered at Citronelle, Alabama, on May 4, 1865. Paroled at Meridian, Mississippi, on May 15, 1865. Residence Kemper County, Alabama [Mississippi?].

Mosby, William H., Pvt. Co. H.
Enlisted on September 4, 1862, at Mobile, Alabama, for the war. He appears on a report of furloughs granted by Medical Examining Board at Disabled Camp, Lauderdale, Mississippi, on March 14, 1864, for 60 days due to hemorrhoids. Residence Sanderdale, Mississippi. POW surrendered at Citronelle, Alabama, on May 4, 1865. Paroled at Gainesville, Alabama, on May 14, 1865. Residence Kemper County, Mississippi.

Mosely, R. F., Pvt. Co. I.
Enlisted on January 27, 1864, at Halls Mill, Alabama, for the war. He appears on May/June 1864, company muster roll as present and never having been paid.

Mosley, R. R., Pvt. Co. F.
He signed a parole on June 6, 1864, at Headquarters of the 16th U.S. Army Corps in Montgomery, Alabama. Hair-dark, eyes-dark, complexion-fair, 5 foot 10 inches. His parole is in his file.*

Moss, Zacharia, Austin, Pvt. Co. Co. A.
Enlisted in Magnolia Dragoons on March 7, 1862, at Station 3, P & G RR, Florida, for three years. He appears on a list of CSA prisoners paroled at Pensacola, Florida, on November 12, 1862. Age-37, eyes-grey, hair-dark, complexion-sallow, 5 foot 7 inches, born-Lancaster District, South Carolinia, a farmer by occupation. He was captured at Gonzalez Station, Florida, by 91st NY Vols. After signing a Parole of Honor he was paroled at Fort Pickens, Escambia County, Florida, on November 12, 1862. March/April 1864, muster roll reports he is absent detailed for 20 days from April 23, to go after a horse. POW surrendered at Tallahassee, Florida, on May 10, 1865. He is shown as having been paroled at Tallahassee on May 17, 1865.

Mouye, Benjamin see **Moye, Benjamin**

Moye, Benjamin, Pvt. Co. D.
Enlisted on April 23, 1863, at Camp Tatnall, Florida, for three years. First muster roll of September 12, 1863, through December 31, 1863, report him absent without leave since August 26, 1863. March/April 1864, and subsequent muster rolls report him as deserted on August 26, 1863.

Mull, Henry, Pvt. Co. D.
Enlisted on September 3, 1862, at Camp Tatnall, Florida, for three years. First company muster roll for September 12, 1863, report him absent without leave since August 15, 1863. He is shown on only one other roll of September/October 1863, and he is reported deserted as of August 10, 1863.

Mundray, James, Pvt. Co. B.
Drew clothing on September 10, 1864.

Murphy, John, Pvt. Co. E.
Enlisted on January 20, 1863, at Halls Mill, Alabama, for the war. Company muster rolls from September 1863, through June 30, 1864, report him detached, detached as nurse in Hospital Moore, detached substitute for **Sergeant E. D. Pittman**, mustered in March 1, 1862. He appears on a list of men employed at the Military Post of Mobile, Alabama, as a nurse, from September 2, 1863, unfit for field duty. He is shown as a nurse for **Surgeon L. L. Nidelet**, at General Hospital Ross [Mobile, Alabama]. Paid $19 per month. Drew clothing on March 26, 1864. Admitted to Ross Hospital, Mobile, Alabama, on November 9, 1864, with varicose veins. Returned to duty on April 12, 1865.

Murphy, J. P., Pvt. Co. E.
Enlisted on September 17, 1861, at Milton, Florida, for three years. Drew clothing on September 12, 1864.

Murphy, W., Pvt. Co. I.
His name appears on a register of paroled CSA soldiers that were paroled on June 16, 1865, by Provost Marshal of 16th U.S. Army Corps at Montgomery, Alabama. Hair-dark, eyes-dark, complexion-fair, 5 foot 9 inches. His parole is in his file.

Murray, Joshua, Pvt. Co. K.
Enlisted on September 1, 1862, at Camp Forney, Mississippi, for the war. He was admitted twice to Ross Hospital, Mobile, Alabama, with intermitten fever on October 21, 1863, and November 17, 1863. Drew clothing on August 28, 1864.

Murrell, John W., Captain Co. H.
Enlisted on September 4, 1862, at Mobile, Alabama, for the war. His commission dates from his election on September 4, 1862. On September 11, 1862, at Mobile, Captain Murrell requisitioned one pair of scales and one butcher knife for his company. Captain Murrell requisitioned hay and fodder for 62 horses and 8 mules for 15 days on January 1, 1863, at Mobile, Alabama. He requisitioned hay and fodder for 21 horses for 8 days on February 22, 1863, at Mobile, Alabama. "This requisition is for the use of a squad of twenty men in command of Lt. Cleveland, who were ordered to Mt. Vernon....." January 13, 1863, at Mobile, he requisitioned 50 curry combs. On March 1, 1863, at Mobile, he requisitioned food for 11 horses for the use of a squad of men sent to Baldwin County under Lt. Cleveland for 12 days. On August 9, 1863, at Mobile, he requisitioned 12 Enfield rifles, 40 bridles, 10 saddles, 10 blankets, one .58 cal. rifle, and 1 one .58 carbine. By September 16, 1863, his company animal count had risen to 108 horses and 2 mules as shown on his monthly feed requisition at Halls Mill, Alabama. He notes here that there was no fodder on had to or to be obtained. March 25, 1864, he requisitioned 42 pair pants, 42 jackets, 19 pair shoes, 35 shirts and 6 blankets. On June 17, 1864, Captain Murrell requisitioned 1 battery wagon, 1 field forge, 2 limbers, 1 tar bucket and 2 water buckets, at Columbus, Georgia. There is an undated requisition for 5 kegs of powder and 250 pounds of lead. His rate of pay as Captain is shown as $140 month. He signed a Parole of Honor at Gainesville, Alabama, on May 14, 1865. His parole and many other documents are in his file. **

Myers, Daniel, Pvt. Co. F.
Enlisted on May 9, 1863, at Camp Withers, Mississippi, for three years or the war. Company muster roll for September/October 1863, reports him sick at home since May 16, 1863. December roll reports him present. Discharged on December 6, 1863, as being disabled. The official date of his discharge was January 5, 1864.

15TH CONFEDERATE CAVALRY

Myers, John R., Pvt. Co. H.
    Enlisted on March 21, 1863, at Mobile, Alabama, for the war. Company muster roll dated June 30, 1864, reports him absent sick.

Myers, T. J., Lt. Colonel Field and Staff.
    He applied in June 1862 for position of Lieutenant of Infantry. The following letter is among several in his file.

                                          Pollard, Alabama
                                          April 30th 1863

Secy. S. H. Mellon [?]
A A Genl.
        Secy.
                Your favor of the 15th Inst. is received and I hasten to reply. I am commander of a detachment of Florida Cavalry composed of Capt. R. H. Partridge's Company, from middle Florida, Captain J. B. Vaughn's from Escambia County, north Florida, and Captain N. R. Leigh's Company from Santa Rosa County. I was placed in command nearly a year ago by an order of Genl. Forney: have been retained by the officers succeeding him. My Command petitions for organization and to have me appointed to command, which was recommended by the Genl. and forwarded. I have been recommended for appointment by Gen. Canty and by Genl. Buckhanan, previously by Genl. Jones and Forney. I have forwarded all the papers to the department, some of them through the Honorable A. E. Alexander, Senator from Florida, as I was fearful that they had miscarried. My situation is and has been unpleasant, having no commission and having to command a lot of cav. men: the officers of which have given me no little trouble. I most certainly [fold in paper renders the text unreadable] I have been in the service since the very beginning of our struggle. I was an older soldier, a member of the Palmetto Regt. in Mexico: where I received wounds that have disabled me for life. Although I am exempt from military duty I insist upon doing my duty to my country. Your earnest attention to my case is respectfully solicited by Your humble Servt.
                                      T. J. Myers Capt.
                                      Commd Lilett Fla.
                                          Cavalry
                                        Pollard, ALa.

His commission dates from his appointment on September 24, 1863. It was confirmed on February 17, 1864. His rate of pay as Lt. Colonel is $185 per month. There is considerable paper work in his file much can not be read due to poor quality of the photocopies. **

Myers, Theodore L., Pvt. Co. H.
    Enlisted on September 19, 1863, at Halls Mill, Alabama, for the war. Pvt. Myers was hospitalized twice at Ross Hospital, Mobile, Alabama. He appears on a descriptive list for pay and clothing for September 30, 1863, at Halls Mill. Age-18, eyes-blue, hair-light, complexion-fair, 5 foot 8 inches, born-Perry County, Mississippi, a farmer by occupation. POW surrendered at Citronelle, Alabama, on May 4, 1865. Paroled at Gainesville, Alabama, on May 14, 1865. Residence Perry County, Alabama [Mississippi?].

Myles, A., Pvt. Co. C.
    POW surrendered at Citronelle, Alabama, on May 4, 1865. Paroled at Gainesville, Alabama, on May 14, 1865. Residence Baldwin County, Alabama.

Myles, John, Pvt. Co. C.
Enlisted on April 9, 1862, at Blakeley, Alabama, for three years or the war. Drew clothing on August 28, 1864. POW surrendered at Citronelle, Alabama, on May 4, 1865. Paroled at Gainesville, Alabama, on May 14, 1865. Residence Baldwin County, Alabama.

Myles, Joseph, Pvt. Co. C.
Drew clothing on August 28, 1864.

Myrick, Littleton, Pvt. Co. B.
Enlisted on March 14, 1862, at Marianna, Florida, for three years or the war. September/October 1863, company muster roll reports him absent, wounded in action on November 8, 1863. Muster rolls February through June 1864, report him on detached service from February 22, 1864, by order of General Maury.

N

Napp, Stephen, Pvt. Co. K.
Enlisted on May 8, 1862, at Mobile, Alabama, for the war. He appears on detached service on September through December 1863, company muster rolls. Drew clothing August 8, 1864. POW surrendered at Citronelle, Alabama, on May 4, 1865. Paroled at Gainesville, Ala., May 14, 1865. Residence Choctaw County, Ala. There is a pay voucher in his file.*

Naulty, C. H., Farrier/Pvt. Co. G.
Enlisted as farrier on August 2, 1861, for July 30, 1864, or the war. Subsequent rolls report him as Private. Drew clothing on June 10 and September 10, 1864. POW surrendered at Citronelle, Alabama, on May 4, 1865. Paroled at Gainesville, Alabama, on May 14, 1865. Residence Mobile, Mobile, County, Alabama.

Needham, E. W., Pvt. Co. K.
Enlisted on March 17, 1862, at Washington County, Alabama, for the war. He appears on company muster rolls as present, absent sick and detached from September 1863, through June 30, 1864. Drew clothing on August 28, 1864. He appears present on a hospital muster roll from March 1 to August 31, 1864, at General Hospital, Greenville, Alabama. Drew clothing on September 19, 1864, at General Hospital, Greenville.

Neely, James, Pvt. Co. D.
Enlisted on April 24, 1862, at Pensacola, Florida, for three years. He appears on special duty at Pollard, Alabama, and dismounted for 45 days on company muster rolls from September 1863, through June 30, 1864. Admitted to Ross Hospital, Mobile, Alabama, with neuralgia on January 9, 1864. Returned to duty on January 14, 1864.

Nelson, A. W., Pvt. Co. F.
Enlisted on January 1, 1862, at Camp Withers, Mississippi, for three years or the war. September 1863, company muster roll reports him absent detailed at Government Fishery on September 17, 1863, by order of General Maury. March/April 1864, muster roll reports that he deserted on December 28, 1863.

Nelson, C., Pvt. Co. F.
Enlisted on January 12, 1862, at Camp Withers, Mississippi, for three years or the war. September 1863, company muster roll reports him absent on detached service at Mobile, Alabama. March/April 1864, muster roll reports that he transferred to CSA Navy in February.

15TH CONFEDERATE CAVALRY

Nelson, G. W., Pvt. Co. F.
Enlisted on April 5, 1862, at Camp Withers, Mississippi, for three years. September/October 1863, company muster roll reports that he was reduced to ranks from 4th Sergeant on September 1, 1863, and detailed at Government Fishery by order of General Maury. Drew clothing on August 29, 1864.

Nelson, J. D., Pvt. Co. F.
Enlisted on June 17, 1862, at Camp Withers, Mississippi, for three years or the war. He appears present on company muster rolls from September 1863, through June 1864.

Nelson, J. N., Pvt. Co. H.
Enlisted on December 3, 1863, at Halls Mill, Alabama, for the war. Drew clothing on September 7, 1862. He appears on a roll of Quarter Master Department CSA that were surrendered at Citronelle, Alabama, on May 4, 1865. Paroled at Mobile, Alabama, on May 23, 1865. Residence Mobile, Alabama.

Nelson, S., Corporal/Pvt. Co. F.
Enlisted on January 17, 1862, at Camp Withers, Mississippi, for three years or the war. September/October 1863, company muster roll reports him reduced to the ranks from 3rd Corporal and detailed to the Government Fisheries on September 17, 1863, by order of General Maury. March/April 1864, muster roll reports that he deserted on December 28, 1863.

Nelson, M. L., Pvt. Co. H.
POW surrendered at Citronelle, Alabama, on May 4, 1865. Paroled at Mobile, Alabama, on June 8, 1865. Residence Jackson County, Mississippi. Age-22, hair-light, complexion-dark, eyes-grey, 6 foot.

Nelson, T. F., Pvt. Co. F.
Enlisted on January 31, 1862, at Camp Withers, Mississippi, for three years or the war. September/October 1863, company muster roll reports him detailed to Government Fisheries on September 17, 1863, by order of General Maury. March/April 1864, muster roll reports that he deserted on December 28, 1863.

Nelson, William, Pvt. Co. H.
Enlisted on September 7, 1863, at Halls Mill, Alabama, for the war. He appears on a descriptive list for pay and clothing at Halls Mill, Alabama, on September 30, 1863. Age-19, eyes-dark, hair-grey, complexion-dark, 6 foot 3 inches, born-Jackson County, Mississippi, a farmer by occupation. POW surrendered at Citronelle, Alabama, on May 4, 1865. Paroled at Gainesville, Alabama, on May 14, 1865. Residence Baldwin County, Alabama.

Nevill, Hugh, Pvt. Co. F.
Enlisted on October 1, 1861, at Mobile, Alabama, for three years or the war. He appears present on muster rolls from September 1863, through June 1864. Drew clothing on August 29, 1864.

Newbold, H. L., Pvt. Co. F.
Enlisted on October 1, 1861, at Mobile, Alabama, for three years or the war. He appears present on muster rolls from September 1863, through June 1864. Drew clothing on June 15, 1864 and August 29, 1864. POW surrendered at Citronelle, Alabama, on May 4, 1865. Paroled at Gainesville, Alabama, on May 14, 1865. Residence Mobile, Mobile County, Alabama.

Newman, J. J., Pvt. Co. F.
Enlisted on November 24, 1862, at Camp Withers, Mississippi, for three years or the war. March/April 1864, company muster roll reports that he was transferred from 15th Confederate Cavalry to Tobin's Artillery on December 1, 1863.

Newton, Charles A., Pvt./Bugler Co. E.
Enlisted on February 4, 1864, at Halls Mill, Alabama, for three years. Drew clothing on September 2, 1864. POW captured by a detachment of U.S. Cavalry forces at Pine Barren, Escambia County, Florida, on November 17, 1864. He appears on a list of POW's confined at New Orleans, Louisiana. Transferred from New Orleans to Ship Island, Mississippi, on December 10, 1864. Transferred from Ship Island, to Vicksburg, Mississippi, on May 1, 1865. His name, **C. A. Newton**, appears on a record of CSA soldiers paroled at Headquarters of 16th U.S. Army Corps, Montgomery, Alabama. Paroled on May 25, 1865. Hair-dark, eyes-blue, complexion-dark, 5 foot 5 inches. His parole is in his file.*

Nicholl see **Nichols**

Nichols, D. R., Pvt. Co. H.
Enlisted on March 11, 1863, at Mobile, Alabama, for the war. He appears present on muster rolls from September 1863, through June 1864. POW surrendered at Citronelle, Ala., May 4, 1865. Paroled at Gainesville, Ala., May 14, 1865. Residence Perry County, Miss.

Nichols, J. W., Pvt. Co. H.
Enlisted on March 11, 1863, at Mobile, Alabama, for the war. He appears, sick in quarters, absent, sick in hospital and absent sick on company muster rolls from September 1863, through June 30, 1864.

Nicholson, D. N., Pvt. Co. E.
His name appears on a receipt for clothing on September 2, 1864.

Nixon, H. G., Pvt. Co. E.
Enlisted on September 17, 1863, at Milton, Florida, for three years. September 1863, through June 1864, company muster rolls report him on special duty as a teamster since August 1862. Drew clothing on June 20, 1863 and September 2, 1864. POW surrendered at Citronelle, Alabama, on May 4, 1865. Paroled at Gainesville, Alabama, on May 14, 1865. Residence shown as Pike County, Alabama.

Nobles, W. D., Pvt. Co. A.
Enlisted on January 4, 1863, at Camp Tatnall, Florida, for 3 years. He appears present on company muster rolls from September 12, 1863, through November 30, 1863. November/December company muster roll reports him absent without leave since December 30, 1863. March/April muster roll report him absent in confinement charged with desertion. May/June 1864, muster roll reports him absent sentenced to hard labor by Court Marshal at Mobile, Alabama. His name appears on a muster roll of Co. C, Camp of Correction, ordered to duty by Major General D. Maury and commanded by Major R. A. Harris at the Mouth of Dog River near Mobile. This roll is dated August 31, 1864. Drew clothing on August 24, 1864.

Noel, Benjamin, Pvt. Co. H.
Enlisted on September 4, 1862, at Mobile, Alabama, for the war. He was discharged with a Surgeon's Certificate of Disability on January 8, 1864. Age-23, 5 foot 8 inches, eyes-grey, hair-black, complexion-dark, born-Mobile, Alabama, a farmer by occupation. His discharge is in his file.*

15TH CONFEDERATE CAVALRY

Nolley, Ruben McD., Pvt. Co. C.
Enlisted on September 1, 186?, at Mobile, Alabama, for three year or the war. Admitted to Ross Hospital, Mobile, Alabama, on September 20, 1863, with acute dysentery. September 11, 1863, company muster roll reports that he died on September 30, 1863.

Norris, B. H., Pvt. Co. G.
Enlisted on August 19, 1863, at Halls Mill, Alabama, for July 30, 1864, or the war. Drew clothing on September 4, 1864.

Norris, E. L., Pvt. Co. E.
Enlisted on November 10, 1862, at Mobile, Alabama, for three years. First company muster roll of September 12, 1863, reports him present and without horse from April 25 to May 19, 1863. September/October 1863 muster roll reports him present on special duty as Ordnance Sergeant. The remainder of muster rolls on file through June 30, 1864, report him on special duty in Ordnance Office since October 1, 1863. Drew clothing on September 2, 1864.

Norris, Frank J., 1st Sergeant/2nd Lieutenant Co. G.
Enlisted on July 30, 1861, at Mobile, Alabama, for July 30, 1864, or the war. A register shows him serving in the Baldwin Rangers from September 1 to October 15, 1862. Elected 2nd Sergeant Co. G, 15th Confederate Cavalry on September 3, 1864. Drew clothing on June 10 and September 4, 1864. A POW, he signed a Parole of Honor at Selma on June 19, 1865. He signs as Frank J. Norris, 1st Lieutenant Co. G, 15th Regiment Confederate Cavalry. His parole is in his file.*

Norris, H. C., Pvt. Co. G.
Enlisted on October 19, 1862, at Halls Mill, Alabama, for July 30, 1864, or the war. He was given a 30 day furlough from December 1, 1863, at Ross Hospital, Mobile, Alabama, due to illness caused by acute diarrhoea. Muster roll from December 31, 1863, through April 30, 1864, report him present. POW surrendered at Citronelle, Alabama, on May 4, 1865. He was paroled at Gainesville, Alabama, on May 14, 1865. Residence Monroe County, Alabama.

Norris, S. L., Pvt. Co. G.
Enlisted on March 22, 1862, at Dragoon Camp, for July 30, 1864, or the war. POW surrendered at Citronelle, Alabama, on May 4, 1865. Paroled at Gainesville, Alabama, on May 14, 1865. Residence Monroe County, Alabama.

Norton, D. C., Pvt. Co. H.
Enlisted on September 4, 1862, at Mobile, Alabama, for the war. Drew clothing on December 9, 1864. POW captured at Blakeley, Alabama, on April 9, 1865. Arrived at Ship Island, Mississippi, on April 15, 1865. Transferred from Ship Island to Vicksburg, Mississippi, on May 1, 1865. He appears on a list of POW's of divers companies commanded by Major G. B. Gerald that were surrendered at Citronelle, Alabama, on May 4, 1865. Paroled at Meridian, Mississippi, on May 9, 1865. Residence Alabama.

O

Odam see **Odom**

Oder, T. O., Pvt. Co. A.
Enlisted on March 16, 1862, at Station 3, P & G RR, Florida, for three years. March/April 1864, company muster roll reports him absent without leave since April 22, 1864. May/June

1864, roll reports him present but dismounted since last muster. Drew clothing on September 7, 1864. POW surrendered at Tallahassee, Florida, on May 10, 1865. Paroled at Tallahassee on May 15, 1865. Hair-light, eyes-dark, complexion-fair, 5 foot 8 inches. His parole is in his file.*

Odom, A. J., Pvt. Co. E.
Enlisted May 12, 1862, at Oak Fields, Florida, for three years. Drew clothing September 2, 1864. POW captured by U.S. Cavalry forces near Pensacola, Escambia County, Florida, November 17, 1864. Confined at New Orleans, November 21, 1864. Transferred to Ship Island, Mississippi, December 10, 1864. Transferred to Vicksburg, May 1, 1865.

Odom, W. J., Pvt. Co. E.
Enlisted on April 1, 1863, at Camp Lomax, Florida, for three years. Drew clothing on September 2, 1864.

Oliver, J. W., Pvt. Co. C.
Enlisted on October 31, 1862, at Camp Powell, Alabama, for three years. His name appears on a roll of POW's and deserters that entered the military lines of the U.S. 16th Army Corps. Captured on line of march on April 18, 1864, "reported voluntarily and took the Amnesty Oath". Paroled on May 9, 1865, at Headquarters of the 16th U.S. Army Corps at Montgomery, Alabama. His parole is in his file.*

Oliver, S. A., Pvt. Co. K.
Enlisted on August 24, 1862, at Pascagoula, Mississippi, for the war. Company muster rolls from September 1863, through June 1864, report him absent detached, present and present, on daily extra duty as a teamster. Drew clothing on June 26, 1864, at Pollard, Alabama. He signed with his "X".

Orrell, A. G., Pvt. Co. H.
Enlisted on December 28, 1863, at Halls Mill, Alabama, for the war. Drew clothing on September 7, 1864.

Orrell, C. C., Pvt. Co. G.
Enlisted on March 6, 1862, at Dragoon Camp, for July 30, 1864, or the war. Drew clothing on June 20, and September 4, 1864. POW surrendered at Citronelle, Alabama, on May 4, 1865. Paroled at Gainesville, Alabama, on May 14, 1865. Residence Mobile County, Alabama.

Orrell, P. H., Pvt. Co. G.
Enlisted on January 12, 1862, at Dragoon Camp, for July 30, 1864, or the war. Drew clothing on June 20, September 10, 1864. POW surrendered at Citronelle, Alabama, on May 4, 1865. Paroled at Gainesville, Alabama, on May 14, 1865. Residence Mobile County, Alabama.

O Shea, C., Pvt. Co. F.
Enlisted on August 27, 1862, at Camp Withers, Mississippi, for three years or the war. March/April 1864, company muster roll reports him as transferred to CS Navy in February.

Oswald, Felix, Pvt. Co. K.
Enlisted on February 22, 1863, at Halls Mill, Alabama, for the war. May/June 1864, muster roll reports him as a substitute for **T. A. Craig**, Co. K, mustered in September 1, 1862. Drew clothing on August 28, 1864.

15TH CONFEDERATE CAVALRY

Oswald, Marion, Pvt. Co. B.
Enlisted on March 14, 1862, at Marianna, Florida, for three years or the war. Early muster rolls from September through December 1863, report him absent sick. Admitted to Ross Hospital, Mobile, Alabama, on November 16, 1863, with gonorrhea. He was returned to duty on January 14, 1864. He then is reported present on rolls through June 1864. Drew clothing on September 20, 1864. POW captured at Mount Pleasant, Alabama, on April 11, 1865, by U.S. Cavalry forces.

Owens, Asbury, Pvt. Co. I.
Enlisted on January 31, 1863, at Conecuh County, Alabama, for the war. First muster roll for September 12, 1863, reports him absent without leave since 25th instant. September/October 1863, roll reports him present but no horse since July 2, "hold back 1 month pay." November/December 1863, roll reports him absent without leave since December 29, 1863. January/ April muster roll reports him deserted.

Owens, C. D., Pvt. Co. K.
POW signed a parole at the Headquarters of the 16th U.S. Army Corps in Montgomery, Alabama, on May 8, 1865. Hair-brown, eyes-blue, complexion-fair, 5 foot 3 inches. His parole is in his file.*

Owens, E. H., Pvt. Co. I.
Enlisted on February 12, 1862, at Conecuh County, Alabama, for the war. September/October 1863, company muster roll reports him present. November/December muster roll reports him absent with leave on 40 day furlough. Muster roll for December 31, 1863, through April 30, 1864, reports him absent in arrest. May/June 1864, shows him absent in arrest in Mobile, Alabama. Admitted to Ross Hospital, Mobile, Alabama, on July 20, 1864, with pneumonia typhoides. Died on July 22, 1864, and left no effects.

Owens, J. B., Pvt. Co. I.
Enlisted on November 12, 1862, at Conecuh County, Alabama, for the war. Company muster rolls for September/October 1863, report him absent without leave since August 25, 1863. November/December 1863, muster roll reports him as deserted.

Owens, J. E., Pvt. Co. E.
Enlisted on January 12, 1863, at Camp Lomax, Florida, for three years. First company muster roll of September 12, 1863, reports him absent without leave since August 21, 1862, but next roll for September/October 1863, and thereafter show him present through June 30, 1864. Drew clothing on September 2, 1864. He was admitted twice to Ross Hospital, Mobile, Alabama, once for bronchitis and later for febris intermittens.

Owens, William, Pvt. Co. I.
Enlisted on November 12, 1862, at Conecuh County, Alabama, for the war. First company muster roll of September 12, 1863, reports him absent without leave since July 5. The next roll for September/October 1863, reports him present but no horse since July 3, "hold back one month pay." Regimental Muster Roll for November/December 1863, reports him deserted.

P

Pace, Nat, Pvt. Co. B.
Enlisted on February 6, 1863, at Campbellton, Florida, for three years or the war. First company muster roll of September 12, 1863, reports him absent detailed on May 13, in the

Enrolling Office, by order or General Maury, thereafter he is shown present through June 30, 1864. Drew clothing on September 10, 1864.

Padgett, N. A., Co. F.
His name appears on a receipt roll for clothing on August 29, 1864.

Padron, Andre, Pvt. Co. H.
Enlisted on June 5, 1863, at Jackson County, Mississippi, for the war. September/October 1863, muster roll reports him present, detailed to the artillery, no horse from October 1, 1863. On February 15, 1864, he was detailed to Tobins Battery by order of General Maury. He appears on a descriptive list at Halls Mill, Alabama, for October 1863. Age-33, eyes-dark, hair-dark, complexion-dark, 5 foot 5 inches, born-New Orleans Parish, Louisiana, a clerk by occupation.

Parazine, F., Pvt. Co. C.
Enlisted on October 24, 1862, at Camp Powell, Alabama, for three years. He appears present on muster rolls from September 1863, through June 1864. Drew clothing on August 28, 1864. POW surrendered at Citronelle, Alabama, on May 4, 1865. Paroled at Gainesville, Alabama, on May 14, 1865. His residence is shown as Mobile, Mobile County, Alabama.

Parker, B. W., Pvt. Co. E.
Enlisted on September 16, 1862, at Camp Lomax, Florida, for three years. Muster rolls from September through October 1863, report that he was without a horse from May 1, 1863. Drew clothing on September 2, 1864. POW surrendered at Citronelle, Alabama, on May 4, 1865. Paroled at Gainesville, Alabama, May 14, 1865. Residence Butler (?) County, Alabama.

Parker, E., Pvt. Co. C.
POW surrendered at Citronelle, Alabama, on May 4, 1865. Paroled at Gainesville, Alabama, on May 14, 1865. Residence Baldwin County, Alabama.

Parker, Elisha, Pvt. Co. E.
Enlisted on May 12, 1862, at Greenville, Alabama, for three years. Muster rolls from September 12, 1863, through June 1864, report him absent sick at home or sick at a Mobile, Alabama hospital. He was admitted to Ross Hospital, Mobile, with chronic rheumatism on October 19, 1863, for 8 days and sent to hospital at Greenville, Alabama. POW surrendered at Citronelle, Alabama, on May 4, 1865. Paroled at Gainesville, Alabama, on May 14, 1865. Residence Butler County, Alabama. There are several pay vouchers in his file.*

Parker, George, Pvt. Co. E.
POW captured at Pine Barren, Escambia County, Florida, November 17, 1864, by a detachment of U.S. Cavalry. [One card indicates that G. W. Parker was captured on September 24, 1864, at Marianna, Florida.] Confined on November 21, 1864, at New Orleans, Louisiana. Transferred to Ship Island, Mississippi, on December 10, 1864. Transferred to Vicksburg, Mississippi, on May 1, 1865. There may be more than one man represented in this file perhaps **G. M. Parker** or **G. W. Parker**.

Parker, H. T., Pvt. Co. E.
Enlisted on May 17, 1862, at Gonzalia, Florida, for three years. He is reported present on muster rolls from September 1863, through June 1864. He drew clothing on September 2, 1864.

15TH CONFEDERATE CAVALRY

Parker, John, W., Pvt. Co. B.
Enlisted on February 6, 1863, at Campbellton, Florida, for three year or the war. He is reported present on muster rolls from September 1863, through June 1864. Drew clothing on September 10, 1864. POW surrendered at Citronelle, Alabama, on May 4, 1865. Paroled at Gainesville, Alabama, on May 14, 1865. Residence Butler County, Alabama.

Parker, J. T., Pvt. Co. E.
Enlisted on September 17, 1861, at Milton, Florida, for three years. First company muster roll for September 12, 1863, reports him absent, detailed as Forage Master by order or General Cantey since July 20, 1863. Muster rolls continue to record him thus through June 1864. Drew clothing on September 2, 1864.

Parker, J. W., Pvt. Co. E.
Enlisted on February 5, 1863, at Camp Lomax, Florida, for three years. Drew clothing on September 2, 1864. POW captured by a detachment of U.S. Cavalry on November 17, 1864, at Pine Barren, Escambia County, Florida. Confined at New Orleans, Louisiana, on November 21, 1864. Transferred to Ship Island, Mississippi, on December 10, 1864. Transferred to Vicksburg, Mississippi, on May 1, 1865.

Parker, L. B., Pvt. Co. D.
Enlisted on April 15, 1864, at Mobile, Alabama, for three years. Company muster roll for May/June 1864, reports him absent without leave.

Parker, Noah, Pvt. Co. E.
Enlisted on May 12, 1862, at Greenville, Alabama, for three years. Company muster rolls from September 1863, through June 1864, report him present, present on special duty as a teamster, and present on special duty as a artillery man. Drew clothing on September 2, 1864. POW surrendered at Citronelle, Alabama, on May 4, 1865. Paroled at Gainesville, Alabama, on May 14, 1865. Residence Butler County, Alabama.

Parker, P. T., Pvt. Co. E.
Enlisted on September 17, 1861, at Milton, Florida, for three years. Company muster rolls from September 1863, through June 1864, report him present, present on special duty as a artillery man, absent with leave ("Has had no horse since November 1, 1863."), absent without leave, and present. Admitted to Ross Hospital, Mobile, Alabama, on July 16, for 9 days with febris intermittens. POW captured at Little Escambia River, Florida, near Pollard, Alabama, on December 17, 1864, by a detachment U.S. Cavalry forces. Confined at New Orleans, Louisiana, on December 27, 1864. Received at Ship Island, Mississippi, on January 25, 1865, and applied to take the Oath of Allegiance to the USA. Transferred to Vicksburg, Mississippi, on May 1, 1865. The following letter is in his file.

Jan. 5, 1865

Col Hood, Sir
I wish to have a chance to get out of this place by taking the oath to the U. S. Government. I came in to your lines at bluff Springs, Fla. I had not arms and intended to come to the Navy yard the first chance. I have a brother living there an has been there for 15 months. I came in to your troops the 12 of Dec./64/ and it would be very hard on me to be held a prisoner an Exchanged back to the Confederates when I am where I wish to remain. I........... lived and I wish to take

the Oath as I came into your troops and gave up and the Rebels know it. Your Obt. Servant P. T. Parker.
 [It does not appear that the letter had any effect.]

Parker, Samuel, Pvt. Co. E.
 Enlisted on September 17, 1861, at Milton, Florida, for three years. Company muster rolls from September 1863, through June 1864, report him present, sick in hospital in Mobile and present again. Drew clothing on September 2, 1864. He was admitted to Ross Hospital, Mobile, Alabama, on October 19, 1863, with debility for 7 days. POW surrendered at Citronelle, Alabama, on May 4, 1865. Paroled at Gainesville, Alabama, on May 14, 1865. Residence Butler County, Alabama. There are several pay vouchers in his file. **

Parker, S. M. C. H., Pvt. Co. E.
 Enlisted on January 10, 1863, at Camp Lomax, Florida, for three years. Drew clothing on September 2, 1864. POW captured at Mount Pleasant, Alabama by a U.S. Cavalry forces on April 12, 1865. He appears on an undated list of POW's sent from Mobile, Alabama, to Ship Island, Mississippi. Here he is shown as having been captured at Movella, [Maubila] Alabama.

Parker, W. H., Pvt. Co. E.
 Enlisted on September 17, 1861, at Milton, Florida, for three years. He appears present on company muster rolls from September 1863, through June 1864. Drew clothing on September 2, 1864.

Parker, W. M., Pvt. Co. E.
 Enlisted on September 17, 1861, at Milton, Florida, for three years. Promoted from the ranks to 4th Corporal on May 1, 1864. Drew clothing on September 2, 1864. POW captured on December 17, 1864, at Little Escambia River, Florida, (near Pollard, Alabama) by U.S. Cavalry forces. Confined at New Orleans, Louisiana, on December 27, 1864. Transferred to Ship Island, Mississippi, on January 22, 1865. Applied to take the Oath of Allegiance to the U.S. at Ship Island. Transferred to Vicksburg, Mississippi, on May 1, 1865.

Parker, William, Pvt. Co. K.
 Enlisted on March 17, 1862, at Washington County, Alabama, for the war. He appears on company muster rolls from September 1863, through June 1864, as absent, detached and later present. Drew clothing on August 28, 1864. POW captured by U.S. Cavalry forces at Mount Pleasant, Alabama, on April 12, 1865. There is a pay voucher in his file.*

Parker, William H., Pvt. Co. C.
 Enlisted on October 29, 1862, at Camp Powell, for three years. Admitted to Ross Hospital, Mobile, Alabama, on February 27, 1864, for 6 days with rubeola with complications. POW surrendered at Citronelle, Alabama, on May 4, 1865. Paroled at Gainesville, Alabama, on May 14, 1865. Residence Butler County, Alabama.

Parks, I. D., Pvt. Co. ?
 POW surrendered at Tallahassee, Florida, on May 10, 1865. Paroled at Quincy, Florida, on May 24, 1865.

Parrenote, A. E., Pvt. Co. I.
 Enlisted on January 22, 1864, at Halls Mill, Alabama, for the war. Company muster rolls show him present and on extra daily duty. Drew clothing at Pollard, Alabama, on June 10, 1864. His name appears on a roll of POW's and deserters of CSA that entered the Military

15TH CONFEDERATE CAVALRY

Lines of the 16th U.S. Army Corp. Captured at Greenville, Alabama, on April 20, 1865. Turned over to the Assistant Provost Marshal at Montgomery, Alabama.

Parris see **Purvis**

Partridge, B. S., Pvt. Co. K.
Enlisted on July 30, 1863, at Farley's Ferry, Mississippi, for the war. His name appears on a descriptive list at Halls Mill, Alabama, on September 12, 1863. Age-22, eyes-grey, hair-dark, complexion-fair, 5 foot 9 inches, born-Mobile County, Alabama, a tinner by trade.

Partridge, B. W., Pvt. Co. A.
Enlisted on April 18, 1862, at Monticello, Florida, for three years. Transferred from Co. H, 3rd Florida Regiment on April 15, 1862. "Due infantry pay from December 31, 1861, to April 15, 1862." He appears present on company muster rolls from September 1863, through June 1864. Drew clothing on September 7, 1864. POW surrendered at Tallahassee, Florida, on May 10, 1865. Paroled at Tallahassee, Florida, on May 10, 1865.

Partridge, R. H., Captain Co. A, Major Field and Staff.
Enlisted as Captain of Co. A. on March 7, 1862, at Station 3 of the P & G. RR for three years. His commission as Major dates from September 24, 1863. POW surrendered at Tallahassee, Florida, on May 10, 1865. Paroled at Tallahassee, Florida, on May 10, 1865. One record note reports him paroled at Tallahassee on May 24. He was paid $140 per month as Captain and $162 as Major. There are a considerable number of requisitions for food for his horse and other paper work in his file.**

Partridge, Thomas, Pvt. Co. K.
Admitted to Ross Hospital, Mobile, Alabama, on March 20, 1865, with epilepsy. Returned to duty on April 10, 1865.

Pate, Isaiah, Pvt. Co. I.
Enlisted on October 4, 1862, at Santa Rosa, Florida, for the war. His muster rolls report him absent without leave, absent on scout and for the most part present from September 12, 1863, through June 1864.

Paulk, A. H., Pvt. Co. I.
Enlisted on December 27, 1862, at Santa Rosa, Florida, for the war. Company muster rolls report him absent without leave, present with no horse from August 25 to October 24, 1863, absemt detached as waggoner for General Gonzales, present sick in quarters with no horse since March 1, 1864, and finally present on June 30, 1864.

Payne, Joseph, Pvt. Co. E.
Enlisted on April 1, 1863, at Camp Lomax, Florida, for three years. Admitted to Ross Hospital, Mobile, Alabama, with chronic ulcer for 9 days on October 19, 1863. Admitted again to Ross Hospital on November 2, 1863, with gunshot wound. Sent to general hospital on November 3, 1863.

Payne, William, Pvt. Co. C.
Enlisted on April 15, 1862, at Stockton, Alabama, for three years. Drew clothing on August 28, 1864.

Peacock, Leroy, Pvt. Co. A.
Enlisted on May 11, 1864, at Monticello, Florida, for the war. He is shown present on

company muster roll for June 1984. Drew clothing on September 7, 1864. POW surrendered at Tallahassee, Florida, on May 10, 1865. Paroled at Tallahassee, Florida, on May 10, 1865.

Peaden, Jackson, Pvt. Co. I.
Enlisted on June 25, 1863, at Santa Rosa, Florida, for the war. September 1863, muster roll reports him absent without leave since July 21, thereafter he is reported present through June 30, 1864. Admitted with jaundice to the Ross Hospital, Mobile, Alabama, on January 5, 1864. Returned to duty on February 2, 1864.

Peaden, Samuel, Pvt. Co. I.
Enlisted on June 25, 1863, at Conecuh County, Alabama, for the war. September 1863, muster roll reports him absent without leave since July 21. November/December 1863, muster roll he is reported to have deserted.

Peagler, George W., Pvt. Co. B.
Enlisted on January 26, 1864, at Greenville, Alabama, for the war. Drew clothing on September 10, 1864.

Peagley, Gideon J., Pvt. Co. B.
Admitted to Ross Hospital, Mobile, Alabama, on March 21 1865, with febris intermittens. Returned to duty on March 28, 1865. Drew clothing March 28, 1865.

Pearce, A. J., Pvt. Co. G.
Enlisted on March 22, 1862, at Dragoon Camp for July 30, 1864, or the war. Company muster rolls from September 12, 1863, report him first as absent on detached service, then present through April 30, 1864. POW surrendered at Citronelle, Alabama, on May 4, 1865. Paroled at Demopolis, Alabama, on June 2, 1865. His residence is shown as Marengo County, Alabama.

Pearce, A. M., Pvt. Co. E.
Enlisted on September 2, 1863, at Camp Lomax, Florida, for three years. Appears on a hospital muster roll dated August 31, 1864, at General Hospital, Greenville, Alabama. Here he is shown as **Asa M. Pearce** who enlisted on May 8, 1862, at Greenville, Alabama. Muster rolls from September 12, 1863, through April 30, 1864, report him absent without horse since July 1, 1863, absent without leave and finally present.

Peavy, W. A., Pvt. Co. E.
Enlisted on September 17, 1861, at Milton, Florida, for three years. Drew clothing on September 2, 1864. Appears on a record of CSA POW's paroled at Headquarters of 16th U.S. Army Corps in Montgomery during May 1865. Hair-dark, eyes-blue, complexion-fair, 5 foot 10 inches.

Peebles, W. E., Pvt. Co. H.
Enlisted on September 4, 1862, at Mobile, Alabama, for the war. September/October 1863, company muster roll reports him detached to the artillery and no horse. Later he is shown as present.

Peeler, W. F., Pvt. Co. A.
Enlisted on April 18, 1862, at Monticello, Florida, for three years. Drew clothing on September 9, 1864. POW surrendered at Tallahassee, Florida, on May 10, 1865. Paroled at Tallahassee, Florida, on May 20, 1865.

15TH CONFEDERATE CAVALRY

Pelham, J. A., Pvt. Co. K.
Enlisted on August 8, 1863, at Halls Mill, Alabama, for the war. Age-43, eyes-blue, hair-dark, complexion-fair, 5 foot 11 inches, born Dallas County, Alabama, a pilot by occupation. Company muster rolls report him absent detached as a pilot by General D. H. Maury. Extra duty rolls report his assignment as a pilot at Mobile, Alabama. POW surrendered at Citronelle, Alabama, on May 4, 1865. Paroled at Gainesville, Alabama, on May 14, 1865. Residence Washington County, Alabama.

Pelt, John J., Pvt. Co. ?
His name appears on a roll of POW's surrendered at Tallahassee, Florida, on May 10, 1865. Paroled at Quincy, Florida, on May 11, 1865.

Perrenot, George F., 2nd Lieutenant Co. E.
Enlisted on September 17, 1861, at Milton, Florida, for three years. His commission dates from September 17, 1861. His file indicates that the was re-elected upon reorganization of the company on May 7, 1862. November December 1863, company muster roll reports him absent on special duty in Adjutant's office. March through June 1864, muster rolls report him on special duty as commissary [officer]. On October 31, 1864, he resigned as 2nd Lieutenant at Greenwood's [Plantation] Baldwin County, Alabama. It was recommended and approved by his superiors. His resignation and other paper work is in his file. *

Perryman, Walter D., Pvt. Co. E.
Enlisted on September 3, 1863, at Mobile, Alabama, for three years. Company muster roll for May/June 1864, reports that he is absent detached as a distiller (in Medical Department) since September 3, 1863, by order of General Maury. He appears on April 23, 1865, on a parole of POW's at Headquarters of Cavalry forces M. D. W. M. near Greenville, Alabama.

Peterson, J. J., Pvt. Co. G.
He drew clothing on June 20, 1864. POW surrendered at Citronelle, Alabama, May 4, 1865. Paroled at Gainesville, Alabama, on May 14, 1865. His residence is shown as Greene County, Alabama.

Philabart, B., Pvt. Co. F.
Enlisted on September 6, 1862, at Camp Withers, Mississippi, for three years or the war. Admitted to Ross Hospital, Mobile, Alabama, on October 23, 1863, with debility. Returned to duty on December 1, 1863. Muster rolls report that he deserted about January 15, 1864.

Philips, John, Pvt. Co. I.
Enlisted on May 25, 1864, at Santa Rosa, Florida, for the war.

Phillips, John L., Pvt. Co. H.
Enlisted on September 4, 1862, at Mobile, Alabama, for the war. September/October company muster roll reports that he was detailed to the artillery and had no horse from October 21, 1863. Transferred to Captain Tobins Battery on April 2, 1864, by order of General Maury.

Phistol see **Pistole**

Piburn see **Pybrun**

Pickens, S. J., Pvt. Co. K.
Enlisted on March 17, 1862, at Washington County, Alabama, for the war. Company muster

rolls from September 1863, through April 30, 1864, report him absent detached, and absent detached at Halls Mill, Alabama. May/June 1864, he is reported present. Drew clothing on August 28, 1864. POW surrendered at Citronelle, Alabama, on May 4, 1865. Paroled at Gainesville, Alabama, on May 14, 1865. Residence Clarke County, Alabama.

Pierce, Pvt. Co. H.
Enlisted on September 1, 1863, at Halls Mill, Alabama, for the duration of the war. No first name given.

Pierce, E. W., 2nd Lieutenant Co. F.
Elected 2nd Lieutenant on May 7, 1862. POW signed a Parole of Honor at Gainesville, Alabama, on May 14, 1865. His parole is in his file. There are a considerable amount of pay vouchers and requisitions in his file.**

Pierce, Franklin, Pvt. Co. H.
Enlisted on August 1, 1863, at West Pascagoula, Mississippi, for the war. Company muster roll for September/October 1863, reports that he was transferred due to irregularly mustering and "turned over to his proper command."

Pierce, George, Pvt. Co. H.
Enlisted on July 21, 1863, at West Pascagoula, Mississippi, for the war. Company muster roll for September/October 1863, reports that he was transferred due to irregularly mustering and "turned over to his proper command."

Pierce, Jerry, Co. F
His name appears on a receipt for clothing on August 29, 1864.

Pierce, Larkin, Pvt. Co. H.
Enlisted on August 3, 1863, at West Pascagoula, Mississippi, for the war. Company muster roll for September/October 1863, reports that he was transferred due to irregularly mustering and "turned over to his proper command."

Pierce, Lewis, Pvt. Co. H.
Enlisted on August 3, 1863, at West Pascagoula, Mississippi, for the war. Company muster roll for September/October 1863, reports that he was transferred due to irregularly mustering and "turned over to his proper command."

Pierson, M., Pvt. Co. H.
POW surrendered at Citronelle, Alabama, on May 4, 1865. Paroled at Gainesville, Alabama, on May 14, 1865. Residence Greenville, Butler County, Alabama.

Pipkin, Nathan, Pvt. Co. I.
Enlisted on October 4, 1862, at Santa Rosa, Florida, for the war. Company muster roll for September 12, 1863, reports him absent without leave since July 3. Muster roll for September/ October 1863, dated October 31, 1863, shows that he was present. November/December muster roll again reports him absent without leave this time since December 29, 1863. Muster roll from December 31, 1863, through April 30, 1864, reports that he deserted.

Pipkin, Sampson, Pvt. Co. I.
Enlisted on March 9, 1863, at Conecuh County, Alabama, for the war. Company muster roll for September 12, 1863, reports him present, sick in quarters. Muster roll for September/

15TH CONFEDERATE CAVALRY 147

October 1863, dated October 31, 1863, shows that he was absent without leave since October 24. November/December muster roll again reports him absent without leave this time since December 29, 1863. Muster roll from December 31, 1863, through April 30, 1864, reports that he deserted.

Pippins, Abijah, Pvt. Co. B.
Enlisted on July 10, 1862, at Mobile, Alabama, for three years or the war. September through December 1863, company muster rolls report him present. On January/February 1864, muster roll he is reported present on extra duty as a carpenter of the regiment since December 10, by order of Colonel Maury. Drew clothing June 15 and September 10, 1864.

Pistole, A., Pvt. Co. F.
Enlisted on June 28, 1864, at Canoe, Station, Alabama, for three years. Drew clothing on August 29, 1864. POW surrendered at Citronelle, Alabama, on May 4, 1865. Paroled at Meridian, Mississippi, on May 10, 1865. Residence Mobile, Alabama.

Pistole, George, Pvt. Co. F.
Enlisted on June 22, 1864, at Gonzalia, Florida, for three years. Drew clothing on August 29, 1864. Admitted to Ross Hospital, Mobile, Alabama, on March 24, 1865 for three days with lumbago. POW captured on April 11, 1865, at Mount Pleasant, Alabama.

Pittman, E. D., Pvt. Co. K.
Enlisted February 2, 1864, at Waynesboro, Mississippi, for three years. Drew clothing on August 28, 1864. POW surrendered at Citronelle, Alabama, on May 4, 1865. Paroled at Gainesville, Alabama, on May 14, 1865. Residence Wayne County, Mississippi.

Pittman, E. D., Sgt. see file of **Murphy, John**, Pvt. Co. E.

Pittman, Robert J., 2nd Lieutenant Co. B.
Enlisted on March 14, 1862, at Marianna, Florida, for three years or the war. His commission dates from his election on November 20, 1862. He was paid $90 per month as 2nd Lieutenant. In August 1864, at Blakeley, he requisitioned feed for 91 horses for Captain Smith's Company B. There are a number of pay vouchers and requisitions in his file.**

Pitts, John, Pvt. Co. I.
Enlisted on June 22, 1864, at Santa Rosa, Florida, for the war. POW captured by U.S. forces under the command of U.S. Brigadier General Asboth on September 27, 1864, at Marianna, Florida. Forwarded as prisoner on board the Steamer *Clinton* on October 8, 1864, to New Orleans, Louisiana. Received at New Orleans, between October 10, and October 15, 1864. Transferred to Ship Island, Mississippi, on October 21, 1864. Died at Ship Island of pneumonia on November 22, 1864, grave No. 33. He was scheduled to be sent to New York on November 5, 1864, but was reported to be sick in hospital at Ship Island, so did not make the trip and died instead in the Federal prison.

Pitts, Thomas, Pvt. Co. I.
Enlisted on April 30, 1864, at Santa Rosa, Florida, for the war. He is reported present on company muster rolls through June 30, 1864.

Plash, P., Pvt. Co. F.
Enlisted on May 29, 1862, at Camp Withers, Mississippi, for three years or the war. He appears on detached service to run the schooner *Geo Brown* from Mobile to Bon Secour Bay on September 1, 1863, through July 1864.

Plummer, J. L., Pvt./2nd Corporal Co. K.
Enlisted on July 2, 1862, at Bayou La Batre, Alabama, for the war. Drew clothing on August 28, 1864. POW surrendered at Citronelle, Alabama, on May 4, 1865. Paroled at Gainesville, Alabama, on May 14, 1865. Residence Wayne County, Mississippi. His name appears on a descriptive list dated July 2, 1864, at Bayou La Batre. He is shown as age-23, eyes-grey, hair-dark, complexion-dark, 5 foot 10 inches, born-Charlestown South Carolina, a farmer by occupation.

Pollard, J. C., Pvt. Co. G.
Enlisted on October 19, 1861, at Dragoon Camp for July 30, 1864, or the war. Company muster rolls report him on detached service as a courier for General Maury. For several months from December 1863, he is reported as courier for Assistant Adjutant General. POW surrendered at Citronelle, Alabama, on May 4, 1865. Paroled at Gainesville, Alabama, on May 14, 1865. Residence Mobile County, Alabama. There are several pay vouchers and requisitions for horse feed in his file.

Pope, Charles, H., Pvt. Co. A.
Enlisted on September 15, 1863, at Mobile, Alabama, for three years. Company muster rolls indicate that he was detailed in the Quarter Master Department. Drew clothing on June 26 and September 7, 1864. POW surrendered at Citronelle, Alabama, on May 4, 1865. Paroled at Gainesville, Alabama, on May 14, 1865. His residence is shown as Mobile County, Alabama.

Porter, C. J., Pvt. Co. A.
Enlisted on April 18, 1862, at Monticello, Florida, for three years. He appears present on company muster rolls from September 1863, through June 1864. Drew clothing on June 10 and September 7, 1864. POW surrendered at Tallahassee, Florida, on May 10, 1865. Paroled at Tallahassee, Florida, on May 17, 1865.

Posey, William, Pvt. Co. F.
Enlisted on January 29, 1863, at Camp Withers, Mississippi, for three years or the war. Drew clothing on August 29, 1864. His name appears on a roll of POW's and deserters of the CSA that entered the military lines of the 16th U.S. Army Corps on April 18, 1865. It was reported that he entered voluntarily and took the Amnesty Oath.

Powe, R. A., 2nd Lieutenant/1st Lieutenant Co. K.
Enlisted on March 17, 1862, at Washington County, Alabama, for the war. His commission is dated from March 17, 1862. He was promoted to 1st Lieutenant on December 27, 1862. Lt. Powe was paid $90 per month as a 2nd Lieutenant and $100 per month as a 1st Lieutenant. On March 15, 1864, at Halls Mill, Alabama he signs a requisition stating that there are 122 men in the company. The requisition is for 120 caps, 1 jacket, 1 pair pants and 1 pair shoes. The uniform was designated for Pvt. W. Beard. On March 20, 1864, at Halls Mill he requisitioned 41 pair pants, 41 jackets, 40 pair shoes, 37 shirts and 7 blankets. A POW he signed a Parole of Honor at Gainesville, Alabama, on May 14, 1865. His parole is in his file. There are a considerable number of requisitions and pay vouchers in his file.**

Powell, A. H., Pvt. Co. E.
Enlisted on January 27, 1864, at Halls Mill, Alabama, for three years. Company muster roll for May/June 1864, reports him present on special duty to buy fodder for the regiment. His name appears on a roll of POW stragglers paroled at Selma, Alabama, during June 1865. Residence shown as Wilcox County, Alabama.

15TH CONFEDERATE CAVALRY

Powell, B. F., Pvt. Co. G.
Enlisted on September 12, 1862, at Dragoon Camp for July 30, 1864, or the war. Company muster roll for December 31, 1863, through April 30, 1864, reports that he was transferred to the CSA Navy by order of Major General Maury.

Powell, Elbert J., Corporal Co. B.
POW surrendered at Citronelle, Alabama, May 4, 1865. Paroled Gainesville, Ala., May 14, 1865. Residence Clarke County, Ala., age-17, eyes-hazel, hair-black, 5 foot 7 1/2 inches.

Powell, W. J., Pvt. Co. K.
Enlisted on March 17, 1862, at Washington County, Alabama, for the war. He appears present on a company muster roll December 31, 1863, through June 30, 1864. POW surrendered at Citronelle, Alabama, on May 4, 1865. Paroled at Gainesville, Alabama, on May 14, 1865. Residence Choctaw County, Alabama.

Powers, Henry see **Powers Richard H.**

Powers, Richard H., Pvt. Co. B.
Enlisted on April 6, 1864, at Atlanta, Georgia, for the war. Drew clothing on September 10, 1864. His name appears on a Parole April 24, 1865, at Headquarters of U.S. Cavalry forces M. D. W. M. near Greenville, Alabama. [hospital?]

Powers, W. A., Pvt. Co. B.
He appears on a roll of POW stragglers that were paroled at Selma, Alabama, during June 1865. Residence-Butler County, Alabama.

Preslar, W. A., Pvt. Co. E.
Enlisted on December 24, 1862, at Camp Lomax, Florida, for three years. Company muster rolls report him present September 1863, through June 1864. Drew clothing on September 3, 1864. POW captured at Pine Barren, Escambia County, Florida, by a detachment of U.S. Cavalry on November 17, 1864. Confined at New Orleans, Louisiana, on November 21, 1864. Transferred to Ship Island, Mississippi, on December 10, 1864. Transferred from Ship Island to Vicksburg, Mississippi, on May 1, 1865.

Presler, William, Pvt. Co. E.
Drew clothing on September 2, 1864.

Price, C. A., Pvt. Co. H.
Enlisted on February 9, 1864, at Mobile, Alabama, for the war. He appears present on company muster rolls from December 1863, through June 1864.

Price, J. A., Pvt. Co. C.
Enlisted on April 9, 186[2?], at Blakeley, Alabama, for three years or the war. He appears absent without leave on two muster rolls for September/October and November/December 1863. Muster roll for December 31, 1863, through June 1864, reports him absent sick. Admitted to Ross Hospital, Mobile, Alabama, with debilitas for 3 days on June 11, 1864. Drew clothing on August 28, 1864.

Pritchett, L. W., Pvt. Co. I.
Enlisted on December 27, 1862, at Santa Rosa, Florida, for the war. November/December 1864, company muster roll reports that he joined on December 26, 1862, at Conecuh County, Alabama, and that he transferred to 57th Regiment of Alabama Volunteers.

Pruett, A. J., Farrier
Enlisted on April 16, 1862, at Blakeley, Alabama, for three years. Muster rolls report that he is on detached service as Regimental Farrier by order of Colonel H. Maury. Admitted to Ross Hospital, Mobile, Alabama, on March 3, 1865, with chronic rheumatism. Sent to General Hospital (in Selma, Alabama?) on March 16, 1865.

Purvis, G. M., Pvt. Co. E.
POW captured at Pine Barren, Escambia County, Florida, on November 17, 1864, by a detachment of U.S. Cavalry. He appears on a register of POW's confined on November 21, 1864, at New Orleans, Louisiana, that were transferred to Ship Island, Mississippi, on December 10, 1864. Transferred from Ship Island to Vicksburg, Mississippi, on May 1, 1865.

Purvis, J. N., Pvt. Co. E.
Drew clothing on September 2, 1864.

Purvis, John E., Pvt. Co. G.
Enlisted on June 11, 1862, at Dragoon Camp, for July 30, 1864, or the war. He appears present on company muster rolls from September 12, 1863, through April 30, 1864. POW surrendered at Citronelle, Alabama, on May 4, 1865. Paroled at Gainesville, Alabama, on May 14, 1865. Residence Mobile, Mobile County, Alabama.

Purvis, R., Pvt. Co. G.
Enlisted on July 30, 1861, at Mobile, Alabama, for July 30, 1864, or the war. He appears present on company muster rolls from September 12, 1863, through April 30, 1864. POW surrendered at Citronelle, Alabama, on May 4, 1865. Paroled at Gainesville, Alabama, on May 14, 1865. Residence Mobile, Mobile County, Alabama.

Purvis, Thomas, Pvt. Co. E.
Enlisted on February 12, 1863, at Camp Lomax, Florida for three years. Company muster roll for September 1863, through June 30, 1864, report him present on special duty as a teamster. Drew clothing on June 20, 1864, at Pollard, Alabama, and again September 11, 1864, at a unspecified location.

Pybrurn, Archibald, Pvt. Co. I.
Enlisted December 17, 186?, at Santa Rosa, Florida, for the war. Company muster rolls for September/October 1863, report him absent without leave since August 25. November/December muster roll reports that he enlisted Oct. 4, 1862, at Santa Rosa and has deserted.

Q

Quinn, Michael, Pvt. Co. F.
Enlisted on August 27, 1862, at Camp Withers, [Mississippi] for three years or the war. A index card in his file indicates that he was a member of Co. A, City Troop, Mobile, Alabama, Mounted Volunteers and transferred to the Navy, September 7, 1863.

R

Rabassa, J. D., Pvt. Co. G.
Enlisted on June 14, 1863, at Camp Taylor, for July 30, 1864, or the war. Two company muster rolls September through December 1863, report him absent without leave. Muster roll for December 31, 1863, through April 30, 1864, report him present. Drew clothing on

15TH CONFEDERATE CAVALRY 151

June 20, 1864. He appears on a roll of Confederate POW's sick at City Hospital, Mobile, Alabama, on May 11, 1865.

Rabby, Alf Jr., Pvt. Co. G.
Enlisted on July 30, 1861, at Mobile, Alabama, for July 30, 1864, or the war. He appears present on company muster rolls from September 1863, through April 30, 1864. POW surrendered at Citronelle, Alabama, on May 4, 1865. Paroled at Gainesville, Alabama, on May 14, 1865. Residence Mobile, Mobile County, Alabama. A index card in his file indicates that his detail requested to herd cattle in April 1865. The card also states to see personal papers of **W. T. Edwards**.

Rabby, Alfred, Pvt. Co. G.
Enlisted on July 30, 1861, at Mobile, Alabama, for July 30, 1864, or the war. He appears present on company muster rolls from September 1863, through April 30, 1864. Drew clothing on June 20, 1864. POW surrendered at Citronelle, Alabama, on May 4, 1865. Paroled at Meridian, Mississippi, on May 11, 1865.

Rabby, E., Pvt. Co. G.
Enlisted on July 30, 1861, at Mobile, Alabama, for July 30, 1864, or the war. He appears present on company muster rolls from September 1863, through April 30, 1864. He was admitted to Ross Hospital, Mobile, Alabama, for 8 days in July 1864, with rubeola. POW surrendered at Citronelle, Alabama, on May 4, 1865. Paroled at Gainesville, Alabama, on May 14, 1865. Residence Mobile, Mobile County, Alabama.

Rabby, Henry, 2nd Lieutenant Co. H.
Enlisted on September 4, 1862, at Mobile, Alabama, for the war. His commission as Jr. 2nd Lieutenant dates from September 4, 1862. He was admitted to Ross Hospital, Mobile, Alabama, for 10 days in January 1864, with lumbago. Resigned on November 3, 1864. He was paid $90 per month as a 2nd Lieutenant. There are a number of pay vouchers in his file.** His resignation is filed in error with **Henry Rabby Jr.** and appears in that file.

Rabby, Henry Jr., Pvt. Co. H.
Enlisted on September 4, 1862, at Mobile, Alabama, for the war. He appears present on company muster rolls from September 1863, through June 30, 1864. Drew clothing on September 7, 1864.

Rabby, John, Sergeant Co. G.
Enlisted on July 30, 1861, at Mobile, Alabama, for July 30, 1864, or the war. He appears present on company muster rolls from September 1863, through April 30, 1864. Drew clothing on September 4, 1864. POW surrendered at Citronelle, Alabama, on May 4, 1865. Paroled at Gainesville, Alabama, on May 14, 1865. His parole is in his file.*

Rabby, Peter, Pvt. Co. H.
Enlisted on September 9, 1862, at Halls Mill, Alabama, for the war. He appears present on company muster rolls from September through December 1863. Muster roll for December 31, 1863, through April 30, 1864, reports him on detached service by order of General Maury. He appears on a receipt roll at Mobile, Alabama, for April 1864, as a watchman, paid $3 per day. He signed by his mark.

Rabby, T., Pvt. Co. G.
Drew clothing on June 20, 1864. POW surrendered at Citronelle, Alabama, on May 4, 1865. Paroled at Gainesville, Alabama, May 14, 1865. Residence Mobile County, Alabama.

Rain, Benton C., Sergeant Co. K.
Enlisted on March 17, 1862, at Washington County, Alabama, for the war. He appears absent on detached service on company muster rolls and absent on furlough for 40 days from April 25, 1864. In May/June 1864 muster roll his is reported present. Drew clothing on August 28, 1864. Admitted to Ross Hospital, Mobile, Alabama, for 2 days in September 1864, with a hernia. POW surrendered at Citronelle, Alabama, on May 4, 1865. Paroled at Gainesville, Alabama, on May 14, 1865. Residence - Washington County, Alabama.

Ramsey, G. Mc, Pvt. Co. A.
Enlisted on March 12, 1862, at Montgomery, Alabama, for three years. Muster rolls in September/October 1863, report him as dismounted and on November/December roll he is shown as absent on detached service until January 28, 1864, by order of General Maury and still dismounted. March through June 1864, he is reported present and dismounted. Drew clothing on June 26, 1864, at Pollard, Alabama. POW surrendered at Tallahassee, Florida, on May 10, 1865. Paroled at Tallahassee, Florida, on May 23, 1865.

Randle, J. K., Pvt. Co. G.

Randall, John, Co. G.
Enlisted on July 30, 1861, at Mobile, Alabama, for July 30, 1864, or the war. Muster rolls for September through December 1863, report him absent sick. December 31, 1863, through April 1864, rolls report him present. Drew clothing on September 16, 1864. [A **John Randall** of Co. G was shot and wounded near Eight Mile Creek Bridge in Whistler, Alabama, just Northwest of Mobile, on April 18, 1865. He died the same day from his wounds. This was once reported by local papers to be the last death east of the Mississippi in this War Between the States conflict.] Buried in Section 21, Magnolia Cemetery Mobile, Alabama.

Rathbone, J. D., Pvt. Co. F.
Enlisted on October 1, 1861, at Mobile, Alabama, for three years or the war. Company muster rolls report him absent on detached service since March 21, 1863, working on floating battery Mobile by order General Mackall. May/June 1864, roll reports him detailed by special order #154 by order of General Maruy. Drew clothing on August 29, 1864.

Raum, J. M., Pvt. Co. G.
Enlisted on May 29, 1863, at Camp Taylor, for July 30, 1864, or the war. Company muster rolls report him present from September 1863, through April 30, 1864. Admitted to Ross Hospital, Mobile, Alabama on August 20, 1864, with febris intermittens. Returned to duty on August 24, 1864.

Ray, John H., Pvt. Co. D.
Enlisted on April 15, 1863, at Camp Tallnall, by Captain Vaughn for three years. Company muster roll for September/October 1863, report him on scout. Muster rolls from November 1863, through June 30, 1864, report him present. Drew clothing August 28, 1864. His name appears on a roll of POW's that were stragglers paroled at Selma, Alabama, in June 1865. Residence shown as Wilcox County, Alabama.

Ray, S. F., Pvt. Co. D.
Enlisted on April 24, 1862, at Pensacola, Florida, by Captain Vaughn for three years. Shown on September 12, 1863, as not present on extra duty by order of General Clanton. Company muster roll for September/October 1863, reports him present on extra duty for 60 days. November/December 1863, muster roll reports him absent without leave, thereafter he is

15TH CONFEDERATE CAVALRY

reported as having deserted on December 29, 1863. In December his name appears on a receipt roll for pay as an overseer at $2.40 per day. He signed at Mobile with his mark "X".

Reaves, T. L., Pvt. Co.?
His name appears on a list of POW's surrendered to Brigadier General E. M. McCook by Major General Sam Jones CSA at Tallahassee, Florida, on May 10, 1865. Paroled at Quincey, Florida, on May 22, 1865.

Reddick, Columbus, Pvt. Co. I.
Enlisted on October 4, 186? at Santa Rosa, Florida, by Captain Amos for the war. Muster roll for September 12, 1863, reports that he deserted on July 21, 1863.

Reed, D. J., Pvt. Co. H.
Enlisted on March 11, 1863, at Mobile by Captain Murrell for the war. Company muster rolls from September 1863, through June 30, 1864, report him present. Admitted to Ross Hospital, Mobile, Alabama, on May 2, 1864, with febris intermittens. Returned to duty on May 5, 1864.

Reed, Thomas see Reid, Thomas D.

Refords, Perry see Rhoads Berry

Regers, J. F. see Rogers, J. F.

Register, Ezekiel A. Pvt. Co. B.
Enlisted on March 20, 1862, at Marianna, Florida, by Colonel J. J. Finley for three years or the war. Company muster rolls from September 1863, through June 30, 1864, reports him present. Drew clothing on September 10, 1864. POW captured by U.S. Cavalry forces at Mount Pleasant, Alabama, on April 11, 1865. His name appears on a list of POW's forwarded from Mobile, Alabama to Ship Island, Mississippi.

Reid, John, Pvt. Co. G.
His name appears on a list of POW's surrendered by Lt. General R. Taylor CSA to Major General E. R. S. Canby at Citronelle, Alabama, on May 4, 1865. He was paroled at Gainesville, Alabama on May 14, 1863. Residence shown as Marion in Perry County, Alabama.

Reid, Thomas, D. Pvt. Co. F.
Enlisted on February 14, 1861, at Montgomery, Alabama, by Lt. Berry for 3 years or the war. Company muster rolls for September 1863, through June 1864, report him present. He is reported to have re-enlisted for the war on February 14, 1864. Drew clothing on August 29, 1864. His name appears on a roll of POW's surrendered at Meridian, Mississippi on May 4, 1865, and paroled at Mobile, Alabama. He is show as a member of Companies K or C of 12th Regiment Mississippi Cavalry CSA under the command of Captain James Lyles. POW surrendered by Lt. General R. Taylor CSA to Major General E. R. S. Canby at Citronelle, Alabama, on May 4, 1865. Residence - Marion in Perry County, Alabama.

Reily, W. J. see Riley W. J.

Reira, Albert, Pvt. Co. D.
Enlisted on August 20, 1862, at Camp Tatnall, Florida, by Captain Vaughn for three years. On the Company muster roll for September 12, 1863, he is reported absent sick at Greenville,

Alabama, Hospital since last muster. November/December muster roll reports that he was discharged on December 18, 1863. Certificate of Discharge shows him to be age-21, complexion-dark, eyes-hazel, hair-black, 5 foot 11 inches tall, a merchant by occupation. He was paid $214.85 in back pay and commutation for clothing and his horse on February 4, 1864, at Halls Mill, Alabama.*

Reira, Anthony, Pvt. Co. D.
Enlisted on January 1, 1863, at Camp Tatnall, Florida, by Captain Vaughn for three years. Company muster rolls for September 1863, through December 1863, report him absent sick at hospital. Muster rolls for January 1864 through June 1864, report him present. Drew clothing on August 28, 1864.

Renald, Nocholas see Renauld, Nicholas

Renalud, Nicholas, Pvt. Co. F.
Enlisted on October 1, 1861, at Mobile, Alabama, by Major Hessie for three years or the war. Company muster roll for September 12, 1863, reports him absent sick. Company muster roll for September/October 1863, through June 1864, report him present. Drew clothing on August 29, 1864. Admitted to Ross Hospital, Mobile, Alabama, on October 15, 1864, with febris intermittens. Sent to General Hospital on December 5, 1864. His name appears on a roll of POW's of detailed men of the Quartermaster's Department, commanded by Major Thomas Peters that were captured at Mobile, Alabama and were surrendered by Lt. General R. Taylor CSA to Major General E. R. S. Canby at Citronelle, Alabama, on May 4, 1865. Residence shown as Mobile, Alabama.

Renfro, J. G. see Renfroe, J. C.

Renfroe, J. G., Pvt. Co. E.
Enlisted on August 15, 1863, at Camp Ward, Alabama, by Major T. J. Myers for three years. Company muster rolls from September 12, 1863, through June 30, 1864, report him present. On March/April 1864, muster roll he is reported present on extra duty as a teamster since March 15. Drew clothing on September 2, 1864. His name appears on a roll of POW's captured at Little Escambia River, Florida, on December 17, 1864. Appears on a register of POW's at New Orleans, Louisiana, on December 27, 1864, transferred to Ship Island, Mississippi, on January 22, 1865. Transferred from Ship Island, Mississippi, to Vicksburg, Mississippi, on May 1, 1865.

Rerai, Anthony see Reira, Anthony

Reviere, Tally L. see Riviere Talionis L.

Revirs, W. see Rivers, William

Rhoades, M. W. see Hohde, N. M.

Rhode, N. M., Pvt. Co. E.
Drew clothing on September 2, 1864. His name appears on a roll of POW's captured at Pine Barren Escambia County, Florida, on November 17, 1864. His name appears on a register of POW's at New Orleans, Louisiana, on November 21, 1864, transferred to Ship Island, Mississippi, on December 10, 1864. Transferred from Ship Island, Mississippi, to Vicksburg, Mississippi, on May 1, 1865.

15TH CONFEDERATE CAVALRY

Rhoads, Berry, Pvt. Co. A.
    Enlisted on July 8, 1863, at Pollard, Alabama, by Captain Partridge for three years. Company muster roll for September/October 1863, report him present. Company muster roll for November/December 1863, report him on duty in Maury's Horse Artillery. From March 1864 through June 1864, he is reported present on muster rolls. Drew clothing on September 2, 1864. POW paroled at Montgomery, Alabama, at Headquarters of the 16th Army Corps, Office of the Provost Marshal on June 6, 1865. Eyes-hazel, hair-black, complexion-dark, 5 foot 8 inches, signed by his mark "X".

Rice, W. P., 2nd Lt. Co. D.
    Company muster roll for September 12, 1863, reports him present and signs the roll as commanding the company. Company muster rolls from September 1863, through February 1864, report him present and in command of the company. On March 25, 1864, at Camp Halls Mill, Alabama, he drew, 41 pair pants, 41 jackets, 30 pair shoes, 38 shirts, and 12 blankets for Company D. Company muster roll for March/April 1864, report him absent on furlough. Muster roll for May/June 1864, report him on special duty. Promoted to 1st Lieutenant on January 12, 1864. POW paroled at Montgomery, Alabama, at Headquarters of the 16th Army Corps, Office of the Provost Marshal on June 21, 1865. Eyes-blue, complexion-fair, hair-dark, 6 foot 2 inches. **

Richards, A. J., Pvt. Co. C.
    Enlisted on October 31, 1862, at Camp Powell by Captain Barlow for three years or the war. Company muster roll for September 12, 1863, reports him present but muster roll for September/October 1863, reports him absent sick. Admitted to Ross Hospital, Mobile, Alabama, on October 11, 1863, with intermitten fever. Furloughed for 25 days on October 31, 1863. He is reported present from November 1, 1863, through June 30, 1864.

Richardson, G. W., Pvt. Co. E.
    Enlisted on January 1, 1863, at Camp Lomax, Florida, by Captain Leigh for three years. Company muster rolls for September/October 1863, report him absent without leave since August 12, 1863. He is show as deserted, whereabouts unknown.

Richardson, John T, Corporal/Sergeant Co. H.
    Enlisted on March 1, 1862, as 3rd Corporal at Clinton, Alabama, by N. M. Carpenter for the war. Company muster roll for September/October 1863, report him present, detailed to the artillery. November/December 1863, muster roll reports him absent on furlough, promoted to 1st Corporal from 2nd Corporal on December 11, 1863. Muster roll for December 31, 1863, through April 30, 1864, reports him present, promoted from 1st Corporal to 5th Sergeant on March 26, 1864. He is shown as present through June 30, 1864. Drew clothing on September 7, 1864.

Richburg, H. C., Pvt. Co. C.
    Enlisted on April 15, 1863, at Stockton, Alabama, by Captain Barlow. Company muster rolls from September 12, 1863, through December 31, 1863, report him present. Company muster roll for December 31, 1863, through June 30, 1864, report him absent on detail with Tobins Battery (of artillery) by order of Colonel Maury. Admitted to Ross Hospital, Mobile, Alabama, on February 28, 1864, with rubeola. Returned to duty on March 5, 1864. Admitted to Ross Hospital, Mobile on September 11, 1864, with febris intermittens. Returned to duty on September 14, 1864.

Richburg, J. S., Pvt. Co. C.
    Enlisted on April 5, 1863, at Dragoon Camp, by Captain Boyles for July 30, 1864, or the war.

Company muster roll for September 12, 1864, reports him absent on detached service. Muster rolls from September 1863, through April 30, 1864, report him present. "No horse since December 31, 1863."

Richerson, Elias, Pvt. Co. C.
Enlisted on May 16, 1862, at Stockton, Alabama, by Captain Barlow. Company muster roll for September 12, 1863, reports him present. Muster roll for September/October 1863, reports him absent with leave. Muster roll for November/December 1863, reports him absent in General Hospital, Mobile, Alabama. Admitted to Ross Hospital, Mobile, on December 24, 1863, with pneumonia. Returned to duty on January 24, 1864. Shown present from December 31, 1863, through June 30, 1864. Drew clothing on August 28, 1864.

Richerson, S.[Stephen] B.[Beasley], Pvt./5th Sergeant Co. C.
Enlisted on October 31, 1862, at Camp Powell, Alabama, by Captain Barlow for three years or the war. Company muster rolls from September 12, 1863, through June 30, 1864, report him present. Drew clothing on August 28, 1864. POW surrendered by Lt. General R. Taylor CSA to Major General E. R. S. Canby at Citronelle, Alabama, on May 4, 1865. Paroled at Gainesville, Alabama, on May 14, 1864. Residence shown as Baldwin County, Alabama. Born December 9, 1834. Died June 2, 1898. Buried in Richerson Cemetery, Stockton, Alabama.

Richie, L. J. see Ritchie, L. J.

Riera, Albert see Reira, Albert

Riera, Anthony see Reira, Anthony

Riley, E. G., Pvt. Co. I.
Enlisted on June 1, 1864, at Santa Rosa, Florida, by Captain Amos for the war. Company muster roll for May/June 1864, reports him present. POW captured at Mount Pleasant, Alabama, on April 11, 1865.

Riley, E. J. see Riley, E. G.

Riley, W. J., Pvt. Co. E.
Enlisted on September 26, 1862, at Camp Lomax, Florida, by Captain Leigh for three years. Company muster roll for September 12, 1862, reports him present. Muster rolls for September/October and November/December 1863, report him absent sick in hospital in Mobile, Alabama. Muster rolls from March through June 1864, report him present. Drew clothing on September 2, 1864. POW surrendered by Lt. General R. Taylor CSA to Major General E. R. S. Canby at Citronelle, Alabama, on May 4, 1865. Paroled at Gainesville, Alabama, on May 14, 1864. Residence shown as Butler County, Alabama.

Riley, W. J., Pvt. Co. I.
Enlisted on February 6, 1863, at Conecuh County, Alabama, by Captain W. B. Amos for the war. He appears present on company muster rolls from September 12, 1863, through June 30, 1864. POW captured at Andalusia, Alabama, on March 23, 1865. Confined at Ship Island, Mississippi, April 4, 1865. Transferred from Ship Island to Vicksburg, Mississippi, on May 1, 1865.

Riner, R. P., Pvt. Co. D.
Enlisted on April 24, 1862, at Pensacola, Florida, by Captain Vaughn for three years. Company muster roll for September 12, 1863, report him absent on detached service with Ordnance Department by order of General Buckner. Dismounted for 121 days. Muster rolls continue to report him thus through June 30, 1864. Several muster rolls of detailed men in the C. S. Ordnance Department report him detailed by special order Number 105 on November 28, 1863. *

Ritchie, L. J., Pvt. Co. I.
Enlisted on March 20, 1863, at Conecuh County, Alabama, by Captain Amos for the war. Company muster rolls from September 12, 1863, through June 30, 1864, report him present. In September of 1863, he is shown on scout. Admitted to Ross Hospital, Mobile, Alabama, on January 17, 1865, with febris intermittens. Returned to duty on January 27, 1865.

Ricere, Talionis L. see Riviere, Talionis L.

Rivers, H.(Hincher) P., Pvt. Co. H.
Enlisted on September 4, 1862, at Mobile, Alabama, by Lt. Cooper for the war. Company muster roll for September/October 1863, report him absent without leave. November/December roll report him absent sick in Hospital. Muster roll for January through April 30, 1864, report him present. There is a roll for December 31, 1863, through June 30, 1864, which reports him absent with leave. Admitted to Ross Hospital, Mobile with pneumonia on December 13, 1863. Returned to duty on January 14, 1864. Drew clothing on September 10, 1864. Signed by his mark "X".

Rivers, William, Pvt. Co. H.
Enlisted on April 25, 1864, at Mobile, Alabama, by Lt. Cleveland for the war. Company muster rolls from December 30, 1863, through June 30, 1864, report him present. Admitted to Ross Hospital, Mobile, on August 1, 1864, with rubeola. Returned to duty on August 6,

1864. Drew clothing September 7, 1864. POW surrendered by Lt. General R. Taylor CSA to Major General E. R. S. Canby at Citronelle, Alabama, on May 4, 1865. Paroled at Gainesville, Alabama, on May 14, 1864. Residence show as Clarke County, Alabama.

Riviera, Talionis, L., Pvt. Co. B.
Enlisted on February 8, 1863, at Marianna, Florida, by Pvt. A. R. Godwin for the war. Company muster rolls from September 12, 1863, through June 30, 1864, report him present. Drew clothing on September 10, 1864. POW surrendered at Quincy, Florida, on May 11, 1865, by Major General Sam Jones CSA to Brigadier General E. M. McCook USV. Paroled at Quincy.

Robbs, William, H., Pvt. Co. H.
Enlisted on September 4, 1864, at Mobile, Alabama, by Lt. Cooper for the war. Company muster rolls from September 12, 1863, through June 30, 1864, report him present on extra duty as a teamster. Drew clothing on June 20, 1864, at Pollard, Alabama, and on September 7, 1864, location not given.

Roberson, Alexander, see Robinson, Alexander

Roberson, D. L., Pvt. Co. I.
Enlisted on October 4, 1862, at Conecuh County, Alabama. by Captain Amos. Note one data slip shows he enlisted on October 4, 1862, at Santa Rosa, Florida by Capt. Amos.

Muster rolls for September 1863, through December 1863, report him absent without leave since August 12. December muster roll reports him as deserted.

Roberson, G. F., Pvt. Co. I.
Enlisted on October 4, 1862, at Conecuh County, Alabama, by Captain Amos, for the war. Note one data slip shows he enlisted on October 4, 1862, at Santa Rosa, Florida, by Captain Amos. Company muster roll for September 12, 1863, reports him absent on detailed service since March 16, 1863, with Sub Department at Choctaw Bluff and General Buckner. In November he is shown as absent by order of General Buckner and on the muster roll of December 31, 1863, through April 30, 1864, he is reported as deserted. May/June 1864 muster roll reports absent, joined from desertion, absent sick.

Roberson, S. B., Pvt. Co. I.
Enlisted on October 4, 1862, at Conecuh County, Alabama, by Captain Amos for the war. Note one data slip shows he enlisted on October 4, 1862, at Santa Rosa, Florida by Captain Amos. Company muster roll for September 12, 1863, reports him absent without leave since August 1. November/December muster roll reports that he deserted. There is further information in his file on S. B. Roberson in the 2nd Army Corps as Assistant Surgeon. *

Roberts, Duncan, Pvt. Co. I.
POW surrendered at Citronelle, Alabama, on May 4, 1865. Paroled at Mobile, Alabama, on June 12, 1865. Residence-Monroe County, Alabama, age -17, eyes-dark, complexion-fair, hair-dark, 5 foot 4 inches.

Roberts, E. (Ervin), Pvt. Co. G.
Enlisted on May 16, 1863, at Camp Taylor by J. H. Marshall for July 30, 1864, or the war. He appears present on a Company muster roll for September 12, 1863. Transferred to Major Steede's Command by order of General Maury. He petitioned to remain in Co. B of Batt. of Ala. & Fla. Cav. See personal papers of **Lewis Roberts**.

15TH CONFEDERATE CAVALRY

Roberts, James, Pvt. Co. I.
Enlisted on June 14, 1864, at Santa Rosa, Florida, by W. B. Amos for the war. He appears present on a company muster roll for May/June 1864.

Roberts, James G., Pvt. Co. B.
Enlisted on March 11, 1862, at Marianna, Florida, by Colonel J. J. Finley for three years or the war. Company muster rolls from September 12, 1863, through June 30, 1864, report him present except when he was absent sick in October and November. Admitted to Ross Hospital, Mobile, Alabama, on November 29, 1863, with debility. Admitted to Ross Hospital again on January 14, 1864, with debility. Drew clothing on September 10, 1864. Admitted to Ross Hospital on July 21, 1864, with acuta dysenteria. Returned to duty on July 30, 1864. POW surrendered at Quincy, Florida, on May 11, 1865, by Major General Sam Jones CSA to Brigadier General E. M. McCook USV. Paroled at Quincy on May 22, 1865.

Roberts, Lewis, Pvt. Co. G.
Enlisted on May 16, 1863, at Camp Taylor by J. H. Marshall for the July 30, 1864, or the war. He appears present on a Company muster roll for September 12, 1863. Transferred to Major Steede's Command by order of General Maury. There is a petition in his file to remain in Co. B. It is approved by Major General Dabney Maury. The petition is dated September 13, 1863, and is signed by **Lewis Roberts, Erwin Roberts, W. G. Carter, T. M. Graham. G. W. Footte** and **Charles Havens**. *

Roberts, Samuel M., Pvt. Co. I.
Enlisted on June 24, 1863, at Conecuh County, Alabama by Captain W. B. Amos for the war. Company muster rolls from September 12, 1863, through June 30, 1864, report him present. POW surrendered at Citronelle, Alabama, on May 4, 1865. Paroled at Mobile, Alabama, on June 12, 1865. Age-20, eyes-brown, hair-dark, complexion-dark, 5 foot 7 inches, residence-Monroe County, Alabama.

Roberts, S. M. see Roberts, Samuel

Roberts, T. T., Pvt. Co. E.
Enlisted on April 9, 1864, at Brooklin, Alabama, by Captain Leigh for three years. Company muster rolls for March 1864, through June 1864, report him present. Drew clothing on September 2, 1864.

Roberts, Willis, Pvt. Co. B.
Enlisted on August 25, 1862, at Mobile, Alabama, by Captain Martin for three years or the war. Company muster rolls for September 12, 1863, through December 1863, report him present. Muster rolls for March through June 1864, report that he was absent on detached duty by order of General Maury. His name appears on a receipt roll for pay at $3 per day as a overseer for March and April 1864. His name appears on a roll of POW's on detached service commanded by Major G. B. Girard that were surrendered by Lt. General R. Taylor CSA to Major General E. R. S. Canby at Citronelle, Alabama, on May 4, 1865. Paroled at Meridian, Mississippi, on May 10, 1865. Residence shown as Mobile.

Robertson, H. (Herbert?) A., Pvt. Co. H.
Enlisted on September 8, 1862, at Mobile, Alabama, by Captain Murrell for the war. September 1863, muster rolls report him sick in quarters. Company muster roll for November/December reports him absent sick in hospital. No Horse from December 1, 1863. Admitted to Ross Hospital, Mobile, Alabama, with acute rheumatism on December 2, 1863. Returned to Duty on January 14, 1864. Muster rolls from December 31, 1863, through June

30, 1864, report him present in the company with no horse. Admitted to Yandell Hospital, Meridian, Mississippi, on April 12, 1865. His name appears on a roll of POW's of detailed men on ordnance duty commanded by Lt. Alec Mackay who were surrendered by Lt. General R. Taylor CSA to Major General E. R. S. Canby at Citronelle, Alabama, on May 4, 1865. Paroled at Columbus, Mississippi, on May 16, 1865. There is a data card in his file with some indication that he may have served in the 8th Alabama and 15th Confederate Cavalry. Residence shown as Mobile, Alabama.

Robins, T. A., Pvt. Co. E.
His name appears on a roll of POW's captured at Pine Barren, Escambia County, Florida, on November 17, 1864. Confined at New Orleans, Louisiana, on November 21, 1864. Transferred to Ship Island, Mississippi, December 10, 1864. Transferred from Ship Island to Vicksburg, Mississippi, on May 1, 1865.

Robinson, Alexander, Pvt. Co. D.
Enlisted on August 25, 1862, at Camp Tatnall, Florida, by Captain Vaughn for three years. Admitted to Ross Hospital, Mobile, Alabama, on September 17, 1863, with debility. Returned to duty on September 26, 1863. September company muster rolls report him on scout. November/December muster roll report him absent without leave and later rolls report that he deserted on December 19, 1863.

Robinson, D. L. see Robertson, D. L.

Robinson, G. F. see Roberson, G. F.

Robinson, S. B. see Robertson, S. B.

Robinson, William L., Pvt. Co. B.
Enlisted on March 14, 1862, at Marianna, Florida, by Colonel J. J. Finley for three years or the war. Company muster rolls for September 12, 1863, throught June 30, 1864, report him present. Drew clothing on September 10, 1864. POW surrendered at Quincy, Florida, on May 11, 1865, by Major General Sam Jones CSA to Brigadier General E. M. McCook USV. Paroled at Quincy on May 22, 1865.

Robrick, Andrew, J. see Roebuck, Andrew J.

Rodgers, J. F. see Rogers, J. F.

Rodgers, William, C., Pvt. Co. A.
Enlisted on February 2, 1864, at Tallahassee, Florida, by Lt. Fernandez for the war. He appears present on May/June 1864, company muster roll. Drew clothing on September 7, 1864. POW surrendered at Tallahassee, Florida, on May 10, 1865, by Major General Sam Jones CSA to Brigadier General E. M. McCook USV. Paroled Tallahassee, May 25, 1865.

Roebuck, Andrew, J., Pvt. Co. B.
Enlisted on May 5, 1862, at Marianna, Florida, by Captain Smith for three years or the war. He appears present on company muster rolls from September 12, 1863, through June 30, 1864, with one exception in September where he is shown as absent sick. Admitted to Ross Hospital, Mobile, Alabama, on October 31, 1863, with acute diarrhoea. Furloughed for 30 days on November 24, 1853. His name appears on a roll of POW's and deserters from the CSA entering the lines of the U.S. 16th Army Corps during April 1865. Captured at Greenville, Alabama, on April 20, 1865.

15TH CONFEDERATE CAVALRY

Rogers, J. D. see Rogers, W. D.

Rogers J. F.
Enlisted on September 17, 1861, at Milton, Florida, by Captain E. S. Amos for three years. Company muster roll for September/October 1863, report him present. On the November/December 1863 muster roll he appears as absent without leave. Muster rolls March through June 1864, report him present on special duty as courier for Lt. Colonel Meyers since March 1, 1864. Drew clothing on June 20, 1864, at Pollard, Alabama, and on September 2, 1864, with no location given. POW captured on November 17, 1864, at Pine Barren, Escambia, County, Florida. Confined at New Orleans, Louisiana, on November 21, 1864. Transferred to Ship Island, Mississippi, on December 10, 1864. Transferred from Ship Island to Vicksburg, Mississippi, on May 1, 1865.

Rogers, W. [William] D., Pvt. Co. E.
Enlisted on January 28, 1862, at Corinth, Mississippi, by Captain Dan Williams for two years or the war. Company muster rolls of November 1863, through April 1864, report that he was exchanged from Co. K, 1st Florida Infantry for **G. W. West** of Company Co. E, 15th Confederate Cavalry. Here he is shown as being absent sick at home. May/June muster roll reports him present. Drew clothing on June 20, 1864, at Pollard, Alabama. POW captured on November 17, 1864, at Pine Barren, Escambia, County, Florida. Confined at New Orleans, Louisiana, on November 21, 1864. Transferred to Ship Island, Mississippi, on December 10, 1864. Transferred from Ship Island to Vicksburg, Mississippi, on May 1, 1865. His name appears on a list of POW's that died at Ship Island. He died of dysentery on March 28, 1865. Buried in grave 143. Note: The graves at Ship Island, are no longer marked and many have washed away.

Rogers, William C. see Rodgers, William C.

Rooks, John J., Pvt. Co. B.
Enlisted on March 14, 1862, at Marianna, Florida, by Captain McVay for three years or the war. Admitted to Ross Hospital, Mobile, Alabama, on September 8, 1863, with gonorrhea. Returned to duty on October 8, 1863. Admitted to Ross Hospital, at Mobile on February 21,

1864, with remitten fever. Returned to duty on February 29, 1864. Company muster rolls for September 12, 1863, through June 30, 1864, report him present with the exception of January/February 1864, roll which shows him absent sick. POW surrendered by Lt. General R. Taylor CSA to Major General E. R. S. Canby at Citronelle, Alabama, on May 4, 1865. Paroled at Gainesville, Alabama, on May 14, 1865. Residence shown as Madison County, Alabama.

Rudd, J. R. see Rudd, J. R. R.

Rudd, J. R. R., Musician/Pvt. Co. A.
Enlisted on March 7,m 1862, at Station 3 of P. & G. RR by Captain Cross for three years. Promoted from Pvt. to Musician on August 1, 1863. September/October 1863, muster roll reports him absent on furlough. Company muster rolls from November 1863, through June 30, 1864, report him present. His name appears on a hospital muster roll at General Hospital, Marion, Alabama, for July and August 1864, as a patient. POW surrendered at Tallahassee, Florida, on May 10, 1865, by Major General Sam Jones CSA to Brigadier General E. M. McCook USV. Paroled at Tallahassee on May 14, 1865.

Rugeley, R. D., Pvt. Co. E. (Field and Staff)
Enlisted on September 17, 1861, at Milton, Florida, by Captain Amos for three years. Muster roll for September 12, 1864, reports him detached as Sergeant Major for 3rd Florida Battalion Cavalry. Company muster rolls for November 1863, through June 30, 1864, report him present. Drew clothing on June 20, 1864, at Pollard, Alabama, and September 10, 1864, with no location given. He signed a parole at 16th U.S. Army Headquarters in Montgomery, Alabama, on June 1, 1865. Eyes-blue, hair-dark, complexion-fair, 5 foot 8 1/2 inches. His parole is in his file. *

Rush, R. H., Pvt. Co. I. **(Bush, R. H.)**
He signed a parole at 16th U.S. Army Headquarters in Montgomery, Alabama, June 1, 1865. He is described as follows: Eyes-grey, hair-light, complexion-fair, 5 foot 9 inches. His parole is in his file. *

Russell, Frank, Pvt. Co. A.
Enlisted on April 21, 1862, at Monticello, Florida, by Captain Partridge for three years. Company muster roll from September 12, 1863, through June 30, 1864, report him absent as Ward Master at Greenville Hospital, Greenville, Alabama, since July 15, 1862, by order of Colonel Tattnall. He signed a parole at 16th U.S. Army Headquarters in Montgomery, Alabama, on June 1, 1865, and was paroled. Eyes-blue, hair-dark, complexion-dark, 5 foot 11 inches. His parole is in his file. *

Russell, George W., Pvt. Co. H.
Enlisted on September 4, 1862, at Mobile, Alabama, by Lt. Cooper for the war. Company muster rolls for September 1863, through June 30, 1864, report him present. Drew clothing on September 7, 1864. His name appears among a roll of POW of stragglers of various regiments CSA surrendered by Lt. General R. Taylor CSA to Major General E. R. S. Canby at Citronelle, Alabama, on May 4, 1865. Paroled at Mobile, Alabama, on May 21, 1865. Residence shown as Mobile, Alabama.

Russell, J. M., Pvt. Co. K.
Enlisted on March 17, 1862, at Washington County, Alabama, by Lt. Cooper for the war. Muster rolls from September 1863, through June 1864, report him either absent on detached service or absent sick. Admitted to Ross Hospital, Mobile, Alabama, August 9, 1864, with

15TH CONFEDERATE CAVALRY

febris intermittens. Returned to duty on August 15, 1864. POW surrendered by Lt. General R. Taylor CSA to Major General E. R. S. Canby at Citronelle, Alabama, May 4, 1865. Paroled at Gainesville, Ala., May 14, 1865. Residence is shown as Choctaw County, Ala.

Russell, John, Bugler/Chief Bugler Co. H/Field and Staff.
Enlisted September 4, 1862, at Mobile, Alabama, by Lt. Cooper for the war. Appointed Chief Bugler by Colonel Maury. Drew clothing June 10, 1864, at Pollard, Alabama. Admitted to Ross Hospital, Mobile, Alabama, June 30, 1864, with vulnus sclopeticum (gunshot wound). Sent to General Hospital, Selma, Alabama, August 4, 1864. Appears on a register of General Hospital (Soldiers Home Hospital) Shelby Springs, Alabama, from August 22, to October 6, 1864, with paraphlegia. Furloughed October 6, 1864. Admitted to 1st Mississippi CSA Hospital, Jackson, Mississippi, August 15, 1864, with paraphlegia. Furloughed October 7, 1864.

Rutherford, William, Pvt. Co. H.
Enlisted on April 22, 1864, at Mobile, Alabama, by Lt. Cleveland for the war. Company muster rolls from December 31, 1863, through June 30, 1864, report him present. Drew clothing on September 7, 1864.

Rutledge, I., Pvt. Co. F.
His name appears on a list of POW's that were surrendered by Lt. General R. Taylor CSA to Major General E. R. S. Canby at Citronelle, Alabama, on May 4, 1865. Paroled at Gainesville, Alabama, on May 14, 1865. Residence shown as Choctaw County, Alabama.

Rutledge, T. R., Pvt. Co. F.
Enlisted on April 8, 1863, at Camp Withers by Captain Arrington, for the war. Company muster rolls from September 12, 1863, through June 30, 1864, report him present. Drew clothing on August 29, 1864. His name appears on a list of POW's of Co. F commanded by Captain W. T. Holland that were surrendered by Lt. General R. Taylor CSA to Major General E. R. S. Canby at Citronelle, Alabama, on May 4, 1865. Paroled at Gainesville, Alabama, on May 14, 1865. Residence shown as Choctaw County, Alabama.

Rutledge, W. M., Pvt. Co. F.
Enlisted on April 8, 1863, at Camp Withers by Captain Arrington, for three years or the war. Company muster rolls from September 12, 1863, through June 30, 1864, report him present. Drew clothing on August 29, 1864. His name appears on a list of POW's of Co. F commanded by Captain W. T. Holland that were surrendered by Lt. General R. Taylor CSA to Major General E. R. S. Canby at Citronelle, Alabama, on May 4, 1865. Paroled at Gainesville, Alabama, on May 14, 1865. Residence shown as Choctaw County, Alabama.

Ruyiley, R. D. see Rugeley, R. D.

Ryan, A., Pvt. Co. G.
Enlisted on April 30, 1863, at Camp Taylor by J. M. Marshall for July 30, 1864, or the war. First muster roll on September 12, 1863, reports him absent on detached service. Muster rolls from September 1863, through April 30, 1864, report him present.

Ryland, Richard (Rich), Pvt. Co. I.
He signed a parole at 16th U.S. Army Headquarters in Montgomery, Alabama, on June 1, 1865, and was paroled at Montgomery. Eyes-blue, hair-dark, complexion-light 5 foot 9 inches. His parole is in his file.*

S

Salter, C., Pvt. Co. A.
Enlisted on June 24, 1864, at Pollard, Alabama, by Captain Ulmer for the war. Muster roll for May/June 1864, reports him present. Drew clothing on September 7, 1864.

Sanders, David, N., Pvt. Co. B.
Enlisted on January 26, 1864, at Marianna, Florida, by Colonel Murphy for the war. Company muster rolls for March/April 1864, report him absent on extra duty while muster roll for May/June 1864, reports him present. Drew clothing on September 10, 1864. POW captured at Mount Pleasant, Alabama, on April 11, 1865. Forwarded as prisoner from Mobile, Alabama, to Ship Island, Mississippi. There is a letter in his file written by Pvt. Sanders at Pollard, Alabama, on May 5, 1864, to President Jefferson Davis. He says he has fought with honor at Seven Pines, Battles in front of Richmond, Second Manassas, South Mountain, Sharpsburg, Fredricksbug and Chancellorsville and has remained a Private for three years. He states that he can not gain acceptance of his beloved's father as a private soldier and wishes a promotion as he feels qualified. Good letter with endorsement.*

Sanders, D. N. Jr. see Sanders D. N.

Sanders, W. H. see Saunders W. H.

Sanks, George, M., Pvt. Co. G.
Enlisted on October 4, 1862, at Conecuh County, Alabama, by Captain Amos for the war. Company muster rolls from September 12, 1863, through June 30, 1864, report him present. Later rolls show that he was enlisted at Santa Rosa, Florida, by Captain Amos.

Sanks, John W., Pvt. Co. I.
Enlisted on October 4, 1862, at Conecuh County, Alabama, by Captain Amos for the war. Company muster rolls from September 12, 1863, through June 30, 1864, report him present with one exception. September/October 1863, reports him absent on scout. Later rolls show that he enlisted at Santa Rosa, Florida, by Captain Amos.

Santos, F. see Santos T.

Santos, T., Pvt. Co. H.
Enlisted on June 7, 1863, at West Pascagoula, Mississippi, by Lt. Cleveland for the war. Company muster rolls from September 1863, through June 30, 1864, report him absent sick.

Sartor. W. C., Pvt. Co. E.
Enlisted on March 20, 1863, at Camp Lomax, Florida, by Captain Leigh for the war. Company muster rolls from September 12, 1863, through June 30, 1864, report him present but without a horse for a time. Drew clothing on September 2, 1864. Captured on November 17, 1864, at Pine Barren, Escambia County, Florida. POW transferred from New Orleans, Louisiana, to Ship Island, Mississippi, on December 10, 1864. Transferred from Ship Island to Vicksburg, Mississippi, on May 1, 1865.

Saunders, D. N. see Sanders David N.

Saunders, W. H., Pvt. Co. H.
Enlisted on June 6, 1864, at Mobile, Alabama, by Captain Bebe for the war. Muster roll for December 31, 1863, through June 30, 1864, report that he is absent detached by order of

General Maury. Commutation due for his horse from August 31, 1863. His name appears on a list, dated August 17, 1864, of persons employed by Major A. M. Paxton, Q. M. and Chief Inspector Field Transportation for District No. 3 as an agent. He was sent to the Army of The Trans Mississippi to procure horses and mules.*

Savage, Edward, E., Pvt. Co. B.
Enlisted on October 14, 1863, at Mobile, Alabama, by Captain R. S. Smith for the war. Company muster rolls report him present from September 1863, through June 30, 1864. Drew clothing on September 10, 1864. Admitted three times to Ross Hospital, Mobile, Alabama. Admitted on October 20, 1863, with debility. Returned to duty on October 20, 1863. Admitted on October 23, 1863, with gunshot wound. Returned to duty on December 1, 1863. Admitted March 7, 1864, with intermitten fever. Returned to duty on March 14, 1864. POW surrendered by Lt. General R. Taylor CSA to Major General E. R. S. Canby at Citronelle, Alabama, on May 4, 1865. Paroled at Gainesville, Alabama, in June 1865. Residence shown as Clarke County, Alabama.

Schwimley, H., Pvt. Co. F.
Enlisted on October 1, 1861, at Mobile, Alabama, by Major Hessie for three years or the war. Company muster rolls from September 12, 1863, through June 30, 1864, report him present. Drew clothing on August 29, 1864.

Scott, D. E., Pvt. Co. E.
Enlisted on September 10, 1862, at Camp Lomax, Florida, by Captain Leigh for three years. Admitted to Ross Hospital, Mobile, Alabama, with debility on October 19, 1863. Company muster roll for September 12, 1863, reports him present. Muster rolls for September through December 1863, report him absent sick in hospital in Mobile, Alabama. March through June 1864, he is shown as present. Drew clothing on September 2, 1864.

Scott, William, Pvt. Co. E.
POW surrendered by Lt. General R. Taylor CSA to Major General E. R. S. Canby at Citronelle, Alabama, on May 4, 1865. Paroled at Demopolis, Alabama, on June 23, 1865. Residence shown as Memphis, Tennessee.

Schruggs, Richard, Pvt. Co. A.
Enlisted on March 3, 1862, at Station No. 3 of P & G. RR. by Captain Cross for three years. Company muster roll for September 12, 1863, reports him present but dismounted from June 18, 1863. September/October 1863 muster roll reports him present and mounted since October 1, 1863. November/December 1863 muster roll reports him present on duty with Maury's horse artillery. Muster rolls for March through June 1864, report him present and dismounted from June 20, 1864. Drew clothing on September 10, 1864. Signed by his mark "X". POW surrendered at Tallahassee, Florida, on May 10, 1865, by Major General Sam Jones CSA to Brigadier General E. M. McCook USV. Paroled at Madison, Florida, on May 19, 1865.

Scurlock, Thomas, J., Pvt. Co. B.
Enlisted on February 14, 1863, at Marianna, Florida, by Lt. C. W. Davis for three years or the war. Muster rolls from September 12, 1863, through June 30, 1864, report him present but without horse for 48 days from October 3, 1863. Drew clothing on September 10, 1864. Officially surrendered at Tallahassee, Florida, on May 10, 1865, by Major General Sam Jones CSA to Brigadier General E. M. McCook USV. POW surrendered at Quincy, Florida, on May 11, 1865. Paroled at Qunicy, Florida, on May 22, 1865.

Scutt, L. E., Pvt. Co. B.
POW surrendered by Lt. General R. Taylor CSA to Major General E. R. S. Canby at Citronelle, Alabama, in May 1865. Paroled at Selma, Alabama, in May 28, 1865. Residence shown as Wilcox County, Alabama.

Seal, J. W., Pvt. Co. L.
POW captured at Mount Pleasant, Alabama, on April 11, 1865.

Sebley, W. F., Co. C.
Drew clothing on August 28, 1864. POW surrendered by Lt. General R. Taylor CSA to Major General E. R. S. Canby at Citronelle, Alabama, on May 4, 1865. Paroled at Gainesville, Alabama, in May 28, 1865. His residence is shown as Baldwin County, Alabama. A separate card in his file indicates that he was paroled in Selma, Alabama in May 1865.

Seele, R. F. see Steele, R. F.

Senterfeit, M. T., Pvt. Co. I.
Enlisted on October 4, 1862, at Santa Rosa, Florida, by Captain Amos for the war. Company muster roll for September/October 1863, reports him present. Future muster rolls through April 30, 1864, report home absent without leave or deserted.

Senterfeit, Robert, Pvt. Co. I.
Enlisted on November 12, 1862, at Santa Rosa, Florida, by Captain Amos for the war. Company muster rolls from September 12, 1863, report him absent without leave since July 3, or deserted.

Seymore, L., Pvt. Co. H.
Enlisted on June 17, 1863, at West Pascagoula, Mississippi, by Captain Murrell for the war. Muster rolls show that he mustered irregularly and was turned over to his proper command.

Shackelford, N. C., Pvt. Co. C.
Enlisted on May 12, 186?, at Stockton, Alabama, by Captain Barlow for three years or the war. Company muster rolls for September/October 1863, report him present. Admitted to Ross Hospital, Mobile, Alabama, on June 16, 1864, with gonorrhea. Sent to General Hospital at Spring Hill on June 20, 1864. Drew clothing on August 28, 1864. POW captured at Baldwin County, Alabama, on April 7, 1865. Confined at New Orleans, Louisiana, on April 13, 1865. Exchanged on May 11, 1865.

Shackleford, A. (Augustus) W., Pvt. Co. A.
Enlisted on September 12, 1863, at Camp Lomax, Florida, by Captain Partridge for three years. Muster rolls from September 1863, through June 1864, report him present. Mounted since October 15, 1863. Admitted to Ross Hospital, Mobile, Alabama, on January 14, 1864, with pneumonia. Furloughed for 30 days from February 2, 1864. Drew clothing on September 7, 1864.

Shackleford, John F., Pvt. Co. D.
Enlisted on November 10, 1862, at Camp Tatnall, Florida, by Captain McVay for three years. Muster roll reports him present on September 12, 1863. Admitted to Ross Hospital, Mobile, Alabama, on September 25, 1863, with debility. Furloughed on October 16, 1863, for 15 days. November/December muster roll reports that he died on December 15, 1863.

15TH CONFEDERATE CAVALRY

Shafer, A., Pvt. Co. F.
Enlisted on October 1, 1861, at Mobile, Alabama, by Major Hessie for three years or the war. September 12, 1863, reports him absent on detached service. Detached on December 2, 1862, at Commissary at Mobile by order of General Forney. From November 1863, through June 1864, he is show present on muster rolls. Admitted to Ross Hospital, Mobile, Alabama, on August 14, 1864, with syphilis primitive. Returned to duty on September 25, 1864. Drew clothing on August 29, 1864. POW surrendered by Lt. General R. Taylor CSA to Major General E. R. S. Canby at Citronelle, Alabama, on May 4, 1865. Paroled at Gainesville, Alabama, on May 14, 1865. Residence shown as Mobile, Mobile County, Alabama.

Shaw, J. Y., Pvt. Co. H.
Enlisted on September 4, 1862, at Mobile, Alabama, by Lt. Cooper for the war. Muster rolls report that he was transferred to Captain Winston's Battery by order of General Maury.

Shelton, James, Pvt. Co. F.
POW surrendered by Lt. General R. Taylor CSA to Major General E. R. S. Canby at Citronelle, Alabama, on May 4, 1865. Paroled at Gainesville, Alabama, on May 14, 1865. Residence shown as Mobile, Mobile County, Alabama.

Shelton, W. B., Pvt. Co. F.
POW surrendered by Lt. General R. Taylor CSA to Major General E. R. S. Canby at Citronelle, Alabama, on May 4, 1865. Paroled at Gainesville, Alabama, on May 14, 1865. Residence shown as Mobile, Mobile County, Alabama.

Shepard, Barry see Sheppard, Barry

Shepard, Daniel, Pvt. Co. A.
Enlisted on March 10, 1864, at Halls Mill, Alabama, by Captain Ulmer for the war. Company muster rolls from March 1864, through June 1864 report him present. Mounted as of June 27, 1864. Drew clothing on September 7, 1864. POW surrendered by Lt. General R. Taylor CSA to Major General E. R. S. Canby at Citronelle, Alabama, on May 4, 1865. Paroled at Gainesville, Alabama, on May 14, 1865. Residence shown as Jackson (?) County, Florida.

Sheppard, Berry, Pvt. Co. A.
Enlisted on March 7, 1862, at Station 3 of P & G RR by Captain Cross for three years. Muster rolls from September 12, 1863, through June 30, 1864, report him present. One exception was in March/April where he is shown as having been given a 40 days from April 23, 1864. Admitted to Ross Hospital, Mobile. Alabama, on October 15, 1863, with debility. Returned to duty on October 23, 1863. He was admitted again to Ross Hospital for intermitten fever on September 21, 1864, and returned to duty on September 24. Drew clothing on September 7, 1864. POW surrendered at Tallahassee, Florida, on May 10, 1865, by Major General Sam Jones CSA to Brigadier General E. M. McCook USV. Paroled at Tallahassee, Florida, on May 18, 1865.

Sheppard, William M., Pvt. Co. G.
Company muster roll for September 12, 1863, reports that he was discharged.

Sherrard, Joseph H., Pvt. Co. C.
Enlisted at Blakeley, Alabama, by Captain Barlow for three years or the war. September /October company muster rolls report him present. He was discharged on Surgeon's Certificate of Disability by order of General Maury. Paid $177.12 for service and use of his

horse from September 1 to December 5, 1863. Born-Coleraine (County Derry) Ireland, Occupation-carpenter, age-63, complexion-dark, eyes-hazel, hair-grey. 5 foot 8 3/4 inches. Discharged at Halls Mill, Alabama, on December 5, 1863, for general disability.

Shoemaker, John, Corporal Co. K.
Enlisted at Washington County, Alabama, by Lt. Cooper for the war. Muster rolls report him absent on detached service. January through April 1864, muster roll reports him absent sick in Choctaw County, Alabama. Admitted to Ross Hospital, Mobile, Alabama, March 24, 1864, with opthalmia. Returned to duty on April 14, 1864. Admitted again to Ross Hospital on October 15, 1864, with amamosis, sent to General Hospital Nidelet on November 30, 1864.

Shoemaker, L., Pvt. Co. K.
Enlisted at Washington County, Alabama, by Lt. Cooper for the war. Muster rolls report him absent on detached service. He appears on rolls as present from January 1864, through June 1864. POW surrendered by Lt. General R. Taylor CSA to Major General E. R. S. Canby at Citronelle, Alabama, on May 4, 1865. Paroled at Gainesville, Alabama, on May 14, 1865. Residence shown as Choctaw County, Alabama.

Sibley, A. O., Brevet 2nd Lt. Co. C.
Enlisted on April 18, 1862. He held commission as Jr. 2nd Lt. from April 18, 1862. Company muster rolls from September 12, 1864, through June 30, 1864, report him either present or as absent on detached service by order of Harry Maury. POW surrendered by Lt. General R. Taylor CSA to Major General E. R. S. Canby at Citronelle, Alabama, on May 4, 1865. Paroled at Gainesville, Alabama, on May 14, 1865. He signed a parole on May 14, 1865, at Gainesville, Alabama. The parole is in his file.*

Sibley, A. W., Pvt. Co. C.
Enlisted on November 10, 1863, at Halls Mill, Alabama, by Captain Barlow for the war. Muster roll for September/October 1863, report him present. Muster roll for January through June 1864, report him absent sick. Drew clothing on August 28, 1864. POW surrendered by Lt. General R. Taylor CSA to Major General E. R. S. Canby at Citronelle, Alabama, on May 4, 1865. Paroled at Gainesville, Alabama, on May 14, 1865. Residence shown as Baldwin County, Alabama.

Sibley, F. E., Pvt. Co. C.
Enlisted on May 12, 1863, at Stockton, Alabama, by Captain Barlow for the war. Muster rolls from September 1863, through June 1864, report him present. Drew clothing on August 28, 1864.

Sibley, O. Jr., 1st Lt. Co. C.
He appears on muster rolls and rosters from September 12, 1864, through July 1864, either as present or on detached service. Requisitioned for Co. C. on October 21, 1863, at Halls Mill, Alabama, 90 jackets, 95 pair pants, 174 shirts, 164 pair drawers, 84 caps. His name appears on a Inspection Report at Fort Morgan on June 14, 1864. POW surrendered by Lt. General R. Taylor CSA to Major General E. R. S. Canby at Citronelle, Alabama, on May 4, 1865. Paroled at Gainesville, Alabama, on May 14, 1865. He signed a parole on May 14, 1865, at Gainesville, Alabama. The parole is in his file with considerable paperwork.**

Sibley, W. H., Pvt. Co. C.
Enlisted on May 12, 1862, at Stockton, Alabama, by Captain Barlow for three years or the war. Muster roll from September 12, 1863, through June 30, 1864, report him present. Drew

15TH CONFEDERATE CAVALRY

clothing on August 28, 1864. Admitted to Ross Hospital, Mobile, Alabama, on March 24, 1865, with scabies. Returned to duty on March 27. POW surrendered by Lt. General R. Taylor CSA to Major General E. R. S. Canby at Citronelle, Alabama, on May 4, 1865. Paroled at Gainesville, Alabama, on May 14, 1865. Residence shown as Baldwin County, Alabama.

Silvester, James see Sylvester, J. H.

Simison, B. see Simonson, S. B.

Simmons, Ike, Pvt. Co. G.
Enlisted on October 10, 1861, at Dragoon Camp. by William Barnwell, for July 30, 1864, or the war. Initial muster roll for September 12, 1863, reports him absent on detached duty. Other rolls through April 30, 1864, show him present. Drew clothing on June 10, June 20 and September 10, 1864. Signed by "X" his mark.

Simmons, J. H., Pvt. Co. E.
Enlisted on December 5, 1862, at Camp Lomax, Florida, by Captain N. R. Leigh for the war. Muster rolls from September 12, 1863, through June 30, 1864, report him present. Drew clothing on September 2, 1864.

Simmons, Leroy, Pvt. Co. E.
Enlisted on September 4, 1861, at Milton, Florida, by Captain Amos for three years. September/October 1863, muster roll shows him present on detached duty as artilleryman. Muster roll November/December 1863, he is shown as present with no horse since November 1, 1863. March/April 1864, muster roll reports that he deserted from Halls Mill, Alabama, about January 15, 1864. "Has probably gone to the enemy at Pensacola, Navy Yard."

Simmons, L. L., Pvt. Co. H.
Enlisted on September 4, 1862, at Mobile, Alabama, by Lt. Cooper for the war. Muster rolls from September 12, 1863, through June 30, 1864, report him present. Admitted to Ross Hospital, Mobile on May 5, 1864, with febris remittens. Returned to duty on May 20, 1864. POW surrendered by Lt. General R. Taylor CSA to Major General E. R. S. Canby at Citronelle, Alabama, on May 4, 1865. Paroled at Gainesville, Alabama, on May 14, 1865. Residence shown as Marengo County, Alabama.

Simonson, (Simison) S. B., Pvt. Co. G.
Enlisted on March 22, 1862, at Dragoon Camp by William Boyles for July 30, 1864, or the war. Drew clothing on June 20, 1864. Admitted to Ross Hospital, Mobile, Alabama, on September 5, 1864, with febris, intermittens. Returned to duty on September 30, 1864. Muster rolls from September 12, 1863, through April 30, 1864, report him present with the exception of September/October 1863, when he was shown absent sick. POW surrendered by Lt. General R. Taylor CSA to Major General E. R. S. Canby at Citronelle, Alabama, on May 4, 1865. Paroled at Gainesville, Alabama, on May 14, 1865. Residence shown as Washington County, Alabama.

Simpson, B. F., Corporal, Co. K.
Enlisted on March 17, 1862, at Washington County, Alabama, by Lt. Cooper for the war. Muster rolls from September 1863, through April 1864, report him absent on detached service and absent on furlough. May/June 1864, muster roll reports him present. Drew clothing on August 28, 1864.

Simpson, Elisha, Pvt. Co. K.
Enlisted on March 17, 1862, at Washington County, Alabama, by Lt. Cooper for the war. Muster rolls from September 1863, through April 1864, report him absent on detached service and absent on furlough. May/June 1864, muster roll reports him present. Drew clothing on August 28, 1864. POW captured at Mount Pleasant, Alabama, on April 11, 1865. Forwarded from Mobile, Alabama, to Ship Island, Mississippi.*

Simpson, G. B., Pvt. Co. K.
Enlisted on February 20, 1863, at Halls Mill, Alabama, by Captain McKellar for the war. Muster rolls from September 1863, through April 1864, report him absent on detached service, absent on furlough or present. May/June 1864, muster roll reports him absent without leave. POW surrendered by Lt. General R. Taylor CSA to Major General E. R. S. Canby at Citronelle, Alabama, on May 4, 1865. Paroled at Gainesville, Alabama, on May 14, 1865. Residence shown as Washington County, Alabama.

Simpson, P. J., Pvt. Co. K.
Enlisted on March 17, 1862, at Washington County, Alabama, by Lt. Cooper for the war. Company muster rolls from September 1863, through December 1863, report him present. January 1864, through April 30, 1864, report him absent without leave. May/June muster roll reports him again present. Admitted to Ross Hospital Mobile, Alabama, on September 28, 1863, with gonorrhea. Returned to duty on October 24, 1863. Admitted to Ross Hospital again on November 18, 1863, with catarrh. Returned to duty on November 22, 1863.

Sirles, H. (Henry), Pvt. Co. C.
Enlisted on December 22, 1862, at Camp Powell, Alabama, by Captain Barlow for three years or the war. Company muster rolls from September 1863, through December 1863, report him present. January 1864, through June 30, 1864, he is reported absent sick. Admitted to Ross Hospital, Mobile, Alabama, on September 1, 1864, with febris intermittens. Returned to duty on September 14, 1864. POW surrendered by Lt. General R. Taylor CSA to Major General E. R. S. Canby at Citronelle, Alabama, in May 1865. Paroled at Mobile, Alabama, on May 19, 1865. Residence shown as State Line, Mississippi.

Sizemore, G. W., Pvt. Co. F.
Enlisted on April 15, 1862, at Stockton, Alabama, by Captain Barlow for three years or the war. Company muster rolls from September 1863, through June 1864, report him present. Admitted to Ross Hospital, Mobile, Alabama, on December 5, 1863, with intermitten fever. Returned to duty on December 8, 1863. Drew clothing on August 29, 1864.

Skillings, E., Pvt. Co. F.
Enlisted on June 14, 1864, at Camp Withers, by Captain Arrington, for three years or the war. Received pay as a farrier. Company muster rolls from September 1863, through June 30, 1864, report him present. Drew clothing on June 20, 1864, at Pollard, Alabama, and August 29, 1864, with location not stated.

Skinner, H. S., Sergeant Co. E.
Enlisted on September 17, 1861, at Milton, Florida, by Captain E. S. Amos for three years. Company muster roll for September 12, 1863, through June 30, 1864, report him present. Muster rolls show him on courier duty for Colonel Harry Maury from March 1, 1864. Drew clothing on June 10, 1864, at Pollard, Alabama, and again on September 10, 1864, with no location shown. He signed a parole at Headquarters of the 16th U.S. Army Corps in Montgomery, Alabama, on June 14, 1864. Eyes-blue, hair-light, complexion-fair, 5 foot 10 inches.

15TH CONFEDERATE CAVALRY

Slater, J. B., Pvt. Co. ?
POW surrendered at Tallahassee, Florida, on May 10, 1865, by Major General Sam Jones CSA to Brigadier General E. M. McCook USV. Paroled at Thomasville, Georgia, on May 15, 1865.

Slater, J. J., Pvt. Co. G.
Enlisted on July 30, 1861, at Mobile, Alabama, by B. C. Yancey for July 30, 1864, or the war. He appears present on muster rolls for September 1863, through December 1864. Muster rolls after December 31, 1863, report him as having been transferred to the Navy by order of Major General Maury.

Slauter, H. T., Pvt. Co. A.
Enlisted on March 7, 1862, at Station No. 3 of P. & G. RR by Captain Cross for three years. Company muster rolls from September 1863, through June 1864, report him present or absent sick. He was also reported to be dismounted from February 15, 1864. Drew clothing on September 10, 1864. Admitted to Ross Hospital, Mobile, Alabama, on September 16, 1864, with febris remittens. Returned to duty on September 17, 1864. POW surrendered at Tallahassee, Florida, on May 10, 1865, by Major General Sam Jones CSA to Brigadier General E. M. McCook USV. Paroled at Tallahassee, Florida, on May 15, 1865.

Slauter, J. H., Pvt. Co. A.
Enlisted on September 18, 1862, at Camp Tatnall (Lomax), Florida, by Captain Partridge for three years. He is also shown as having enlisted at Monticello, Florida. Company muster rolls from September 12, 1863, through June 1864, report him present. He is shown as dismounted after April 20, 1864. Drew clothing on September 7, 1864. Admitted to Ross Hospital, Mobile, Alabama, on September 11, 1864, with febris intermittens. Returned to duty on September 16, 1864. POW surrendered at Tallahassee, Florida, on May 10, 1865, by Major General Sam Jones CSA to Brigadier General E. M. McCook USV. Paroled at Madison, Florida, on May 18, 1865.

Sledge, J. N., Pvt. Co. G.
Enlisted on May 24, 1863, at Camp Taylor, by J. H. Marshall for July 30, 1864, or the war. Muster rolls show him absent without leave on September 12, 1863, and again on November/December rolls. Otherwise he is show present through April 30, 1864. Drew clothing on September 4, 1864. POW surrendered by Lt. General R. Taylor CSA to Major General E. R. S. Canby at Citronelle, Alabama, on May 4, 1865. Paroled at Gainesville, Alabama, on May 14, 1865. Residence shown as Greene County, Alabama.

Smee (Smea), George, Pvt. Co. G.
Enlisted on September 13, 1862, at Dragoon Camp by J. H. Marshall for July 30, 1864, or the war. Company muster rolls from September 12, 1863, through April 30, 1864, report him present. Drew clothing on June 20, and September 4, 1864. POW surrendered by Lt. General R. Taylor CSA to Major General E. R. S. Canby at Citronelle, Alabama, on May 4, 1865. Paroled at Gainesville, Alabama, on May 14, 1865. Residence shown as Mobile County, Alabama.

Smith, A. D., 1st Sergeant Co. K.
Enlisted on December 1, 1862, at Halls Mill, Alabama, by Captain White for the war. He is shown on furlough during September/October 1863, but muster rolls report him present through June 30, 1864. He was admitted to Ross Hospital, Mobile, Alabama, on July 23, 1864, with neuralgia. Returned to duty on August 1, 1864. POW surrendered by Lt. General R. Taylor CSA to Major General E. R. S. Canby at Citronelle, Alabama, on May 4, 1865.

Paroled at Gainesville, Alabama, on May 14, 1865. Residence shown as Choctaw County, Alabama.*

Smith, B. C., Pvt. Co. K.
Enlisted on May 1, 1864, at Halls Mill, Alabama, by Lt. R. A. Powe for three years. Company muster roll reports that his was absent on detached service by order of Major General Dabney Maury. POW surrendered by Lt. General R. Taylor CSA to Major General E. R. S. Canby at Citronelle, Alabama, on May 4, 1865. Paroled at Gainesville, Alabama, on May 14, 1865. Residence shown as Washington County, Alabama.*

Smith, B. K., Pvt. Co. K.
Enlisted on March 17, 1862, at Washington County, Alabama, by Lt. J. W. Cooper for three years. Company muster rolls report him on detached service until December 31, 1864, thereafter through June 30, 1864, he is shown as present. POW surrendered by Lt. General R. Taylor CSA to Major General E. R. S. Canby at Citronelle, Alabama, on May 4, 1865. Paroled at Gainesville, Alabama, on May 14, 1865. Residence shown as Choctaw County, Alabama.*

Smith, Ferdinand, Bugler, Co. F.
Enlisted on October 1, 1861, at Mobile, Alabama, by Major Hessie for three years or the war. September/October he is shown as absent sick in General Hospital in Mobile. Muster rolls November 1863, through June 1864, reports him present. Drew clothing on June 10, 1864, at Pollard, Alabama, and on August 29, 1864, with no location shown.

Smith, Horace, Pvt. Co. B.
Enlisted on January 26, 1864, at Greenville, Alabama, by Colonel Murphy for the war. Muster rolls report him present September 1863, through June 1864. Drew clothing on September 10, 1864. POW captured the night of April 8, 1865, at Blakeley, Alabama.

Smith, H. P., Pvt. Co. E.
Enlisted on June 1, 1863, at Camp Lomax, by Captain Leigh for three years. Reported to be without horse from June 1 to July 17, 1863. Company muster rolls report him present from September 1863, through June 1864. Drew clothing on September 2, 1864. POW captured at Mount Pleasant, Alabama, on April 11, 1865. His name appears on a list of POW's forwarded from Mobile, Alabama, to Ship Island, Mississippi.

Smith, Jacob, Pvt. Co. I.
Enlisted on March 5, 186?, at Conecuh County, Alabama, by Captain Amos for the war. Muster rolls for September/October 1863, report him absent without leave since August 25.

Smith, Joe, Pvt. Co. F.
Enlisted on April 16, 1863, at Camp Withers, by Captain Arrington for three years or the war. September 12, 1863, muster roll reports him absent on detached service. Muster rolls from September 1863, through June 1864, report him present. Drew clothing on August 29, 1864. POW surrendered by Lt. General R. Taylor CSA to Major General E. R. S. Canby at Citronelle, Alabama, on May 4, 1865. Paroled at Meridian, Mississippi, on May 17, 1865. Residence shown as Baldwin County, Alabama.

Smith, John, Pvt. Co. F.
Enlisted on October 1, 1861, at Mobile, Alabama, by Major Hessie for three years or the war. Company muster rolls for September 1863, through December 1863, report him detached as a teamster. In February he was transferred to CS. Navy.

Smith, Reuben, Pvt. Co. I.
Enlisted January 12, 1863, at Conecuh County, Alabama, by Captain Amos for the war. Muster roll for September 12, 1863, reports him absent without horse since September 25. September/ October 1863, muster rolls report him absent on detailed service with artillery from October 18, 1865. Muster rolls January 1864, through June 1864, report him present.

Smith, Richard L., Captain Co. B.
Enlisted on March 14, 1862, at Marianna, Florida, by Colonel J. J. Finley for three years or the war. Elected Captain on March 14, 1862. His name appears on a roster of the regiment at Pollard on March 14, 1862. Drew $140 per month pay as a Captain. He requisitioned one wagon body, forty feet of halter rope and four mule collars at Mobile, Alabama, on September 18, 1862. Drew for Co. B: 60 jackets, 113 pair pants, 79 shirts, 58 pair drawers, 61 caps, 30 blankets and one pair of shoes at Halls Mill, Alabama, on November 1, 1862. Requisitioned on July 21, 1863, at Mobile, Alabama, from ordnance department, 2 saddles, 2 blankets, 6 bridles, 200? Maynard Rifle Cylinders, 3700 musket caps, 4000 spoxting? caps, 10 pounds rifle powder, 40 pounds lead, 1 saddle, 1 bridle. There is a number of requisitions for a variety of items ie, Mule Collars (shuck and bark), 7 large wall tents, 6 axes, 1500 feet of lumber for flooring material, 2 gallons whiskey, 1 ounce Landinum, 1/2 pound saltpeter, 3 camp kettles, 7 mess pans, 3 bake ovens, 1 curry comb, 1 horse brush and etc. Company muster rolls for September 1863, through December 1863, report him present. Muster rolls from January 1864, through June 1864, report him on Extra Duty as a Field Officer by order of Colonel Maury. POW surrendered at Tallahassee, Florida, on May 10, 1865, by Major General Sam Jones CSA to Brigadier General E. M. McCook USV. Paroled at Quincy, Florida, May 11, 1865. There is considerable paperwork in his file.**

Smith, Robert, Pvt. Co. F.
Enlisted on April 16, 1863, at Camp Withers, by Captain Arrington, for three years or the war. First muster roll of September 12, 1864, shows him absent on detached service. Other company muster rolls from September 1863, through June 1864, report him present. Drew clothing on August 29, 1864. His name appears among a detail of men in Quarter Master Department CSA commanded by Major Thomas Peters captured in Mobile, Alabama. POW surrendered by Lt. General R. Taylor CSA to Major General E. R. S. Canby at Citronelle, Alabama, on May 4, 1865. Paroled at Mobile, Alabama, on May 14, 1865. Residence shown as Mount Vernon, Alabama.

Smith, T. M., Pvt. Co. K.
Enlisted on July 24, 1863, at Fairley's Ferry, Mississippi, by Captain McKellar for the war. His name appears on a descriptive roll for pay and clothing at Mobile, Alabama, on October 9, 1863. Age-18, eyes-dark, hair-dark, complexion-dark, 5 foot 10 inches, occupation-soldier, born in Wilcox County. He appears as absent on furlough on September/October 1863, company muster rolls. Again on December through April 1864, he is reported absent on furlough from April 11, 1864. May/June 1864, he is reported present. POW surrendered by Lt. General R. Taylor CSA to Major General E. R. S. Canby at Citronelle, Alabama, on May 4, 1865. Paroled at Gainesville, Alabama, on May 14, 1865. Residence shown as Pensacola, Florida.

Smith, T. R., Pvt. Co. E.
Enlisted on May 28, 1863, at Camp Lomax, Florida, by Captain Leigh for three years. Company muster roll for September/October 1863, report him absent on special duty as artilleryman or sick at hospital in Mobile, Alabama. Roll for November/December 1863, report him absent sick in hospital in Mobile. He is shown present on rolls March through June 1864. Drew clothing on September 2, 1864.

Snelling, G. W., Pvt. Co. A.
Enlisted on March 4, 1864, at Marianna, Florida, by Lt. Fernandez for the war. He appears present on a muster roll for May/June 1864, with pay due from enlistment.

Snelling, James, Pvt. Co. A.
Drew clothing on September 7, 1864. POW surrendered at Tallahassee, Florida, on May 10, 1865, by Major General Sam Jones CSA to Brigadier General E. M. McCook USV. Paroled at Quincy, Florida, on May 11, 1865.

Snowden, Caleb, Pvt. Co. I.
Enlisted on January 28, 1864, at Halls Mill, Alabama, by Captain W. B. Amos for the war. Company muster rolls from January through June 1864, report him present.

Snowden, H. A., Pvt. Co. I.
Enlisted on June 3, 1864, at Santa Rosa, Florida, by W. B. Amos for the war. He appears present on a muster roll for May/June 1864. POW paroled at Milton, Florida, on June 22, 1865.

Snowden, Henry, Pvt. Co. I.
Enlisted on January 12, 1863, at Conecuh County, Alabama, by Captain Amos for the war. September/October 1863, muster roll reports him absent on scout. November/December 1863, muster roll reports him present. He died on January 10, 1864.

Sohan, M. J., Pvt. Co. F.
Enlisted on October 1, 1861, at Mobile, Alabama, by Major Hessie for three years or the war. Muster rolls for 1863, report him detached at Government Fishery on September 1, 1863, by order of General Maury.

Solis, Richard, Pvt. Co. D.
Enlisted on November 2, 1862, at Camp Tatnall, (or Camp Lomax) by Captain Vaughn for three years. Muster rolls from September 1863, through April 1864, report him on detached service by order of General Clanton as a guide for Clanton's Brigade. May/June 1864, company muster roll reports him prisoner at Guard House at Mobile, Alabama (Pensacola?). Letter in his file with a date of August 19, 1884, indicates that he is sick in post hospital and directs the Captain [US] at Fort Barrancas to administer the Oath of Allegiance. There is paper work in his file.*

Soter, W. C. see Sartor, W. C.

Sartid, W. C. see Sartor, W. C.

Sowell, A. J., Blacksmith/Pvt. Co. E.
Enlisted on May 3, 1862, at Camp Perdido, by Captain Amos for three years. September/October 1863, company muster roll reports him present on special duty as a artilleryman. November/December 1863, muster roll reports him as blacksmith for the Regiment. Other muster rolls through June 1864, show him as artilleryman.

Spears, William J., Pvt. Co. B.
Enlisted on February 17, 1863, at Marianna, Florida, by Lt. C. W. Davis for the war. Company muster rolls from September 1863, through June 1864, report him present. Drew clothing on September 10, 1864. Admitted to Ross Hospital, Mobile, Alabama, on March 11, 1865, with acute diarrhoea. He was sent to General Hospital at Meridian, Mississippi,

15TH CONFEDERATE CAVALRY

on March 30, 1865. POW captured at Mount Pleasant, Alabama, on April 11, 1865. A note in his file indicates that his detail is to heard cattle on April 25, 1865. See personal papers of Major W. T. Edwards. POW surrendered by Lt. General R. Taylor CSA to Major General E. R. S. Canby at Citronelle, Alabama, on May 4, 1865. Paroled at Meridian, Mississippi, on May 10, 1865. Residence shown as Jackson, Florida.

Speer, W. J. see Spears, W. J.

Spein, W. F. see Spears, W. J.

Speir. W. T. see Spier, W. T.

Spier, W. T., Pvt. Co. E.
Enlisted on September 17, 1862, at Milton, Florida, by Captain Amos for three years. Company muster rolls from September 1863, through June 1864, report him present. Drew clothing on September 2, 1864. POW captured on November 17, 1864, at West Pensacola in Escambia County, Florida. His name appears on a register of POW's at New Orleans, Louisiana, that were transferred to Ship Island, Mississippi, on December 10, 1864. He was transferred to Vicksburg, Mississippi, on May 1, 1865.

Spin, W. F. see Spier, W. T.

Spivey, J. W., Pvt. Co. D.
Enlisted on April 24, 1862, at Pensacola, Florida, by Captain Vaughn, for three years. Company muster rolls from September 1863, through June 1864, report him present. One roll in September/December 1863, shows him on scout. Drew clothing on August 28, 1864. He signed by his mark.

Stabler, A. J., Pvt. Co. I.
POW surrendered at Citronelle, Alabama, on May 4, 1865. Paroled on June 16, 1865, at Mobile, Alabama. Residence shown as Monroe County, Alabama. Age-17, eyes-gray, complexion-sallow, 6 foot.

Stagner, D. H., Pvt. Co. I.
Enlisted on October 4, 1862, at Santa Rosa, Florida, by Captain Amos for the war. Muster rolls in 1863, show him absent without leave since July 3, (1863?) and deserted.

Stagner, John, Pvt. Co. I.
Enlisted on October 4, 1865, at Santa Rosa, Florida, by Captain Amos for the war. Muster rolls in 1863, show him absent without leave since July 3 or 5, (1863?) and deserted.

Staley, Albert M., Pvt. Co. B.
Enlisted on September 1, 1862, at Marianna, Florida, by Captain Smith for three years or the war. Company muster rolls from September 1863, through June 1864, report him present. At one point he is reported without horse for 20 days. Admitted to Ross Hospital, Mobile, Alabama, on March 11, 1864, with gonorrhea. Returned to duty on April 12, 1864. Drew clothing on September 10, 1864. POW surrendered at Tallahassee, Florida, on May 10, 1865, by Major General Sam Jones CSA to Brigadier General E. M. McCook USV. Paroled at Quincy, Florida, on May 22, 1865.

Staley, John F., Corporal/Sergeant Co. B.
Enlisted on March 14, 1862, at Marianna, Florida, by Colonel J. J. Finley for three years or

the war. Promoted from 1st Corporal to 5th Sergeant on November 1, 1863. Company muster roll for September/October 1863, report him present. November/December 1863, roll reports him absent on furlough for 15 days from December 16th, thereafter rolls through June 1864, report him present. Drew clothing on September 10, 1864. POW surrendered at Tallahassee, Florida, on May 10, 1865, by Major General Sam Jones CSA to Brigadier General E. M. McCook USV. Paroled at Quincy, Florida, on May 22, 1865.

Stapleton, C. A., Pvt. Co. C.
Enlisted on April 9, 1862, at Blakeley, Alabama, by Captain Barlow for three years or the war. Company muster rolls from September 12, 1863, through June 1864, report him present. Drew clothing on August 28, 1864. POW surrendered by Lt. General R. Taylor CSA to Major General E. R. S. Canby at Citronelle, Alabama, on May 4, 1865. Paroled at Gainesville, Alabama, on May 14, 1865. Residence shown as Baldwin County, Alabama.

Stapleton, E. O., Pvt. Co. C.
Enlisted on April 9, 1862, at Blakeley, Alabama, by Captain Barlow for three years or the war. Company muster rolls from September 12, 1863, through June 1864, report him present. Drew clothing on August 28, 1864. POW surrendered by Lt. General R. Taylor CSA to Major General E. R. S. Canby at Citronelle, Alabama, on May 4, 1865. Paroled at Gainesville, Alabama, on May 14, 1865. Residence shown as Baldwin County, Alabama.

Stapleton, J. B., Pvt. Co. C.
Enlisted on April 15, 1862, at Stockton, Alabama, by Captain Barlow for three years or the war. Company muster roll for September/October 1863, report him present. November/December 1863, roll reports him absent with leave, thereafter rolls through June 1864, report him absent sick. Drew clothing on August 28, 1864. POW surrendered by Lt. General R. Taylor CSA to Major General E. R. S. Canby at Citronelle, Alabama, on May 4, 1865. Paroled at Gainesville, Alabama, on May 14, 1865. Residence shown as Baldwin County, Alabama.

Stapleton, N. B., Pvt. Co. C.
Enlisted on January 12, 1862, at Camp Powell by Captain Barlow for three years or the war. Company muster rolls from September 1863, through June 1864, report him present. Drew clothing on August 28, 1864. POW surrendered by Lt. General R. Taylor CSA to Major General E. R. S. Canby at Citronelle, Alabama, on May 4, 1865. Paroled at Gainesville, Alabama, on May 14, 1865. Residence shown as Baldwin County, Alabama.

Stapleton, Reubin, Pvt. Co. C.
His name appears on a roll of POW's that were surrendered by Lt. General R. Taylor CSA to Major General E. R. S. Canby at Citronelle, Alabama, on May 4, 1865. Paroled at Gainesville, Alabama, on May 14, 1865. Residence shown as Baldwin County, Alabama.

Stapleton, W. F., Pvt. Co. C.
Enlisted on January 12, 1862, at Camp Powell by Captain Barlow for three years or the war. Company muster rolls from September 1863, through June 1864, report him present. Drew clothing on August 28, 1864. POW surrendered by Lt. General R. Taylor CSA to Major General E. R. S. Canby at Citronelle, Alabama, on May 4, 1865. Paroled at Gainesville, Alabama, on May 14, 1865. Residence shown as Baldwin County, Alabama.

Stapleton, W. L., Corporal Co. C.
Enlisted on April 9, 1862, at Blakeley, Alabama, by Barlow for three years or the war. Company muster rolls from September 1863, through June 1864, report him present. Drew

15TH CONFEDERATE CAVALRY

clothing on August 28, 1864. Drew clothing on August 28, 1864. POW surrendered by Lt. General R. Taylor CSA to Major General E. R. S. Canby at Citronelle, Alabama, on May 4, 1865. Paroled at Gainesville, Alabama, on May 14, 1865. Residence shown as Baldwin County, Alabama.

Starke, J. (James) C., Pvt. Co. G.
Enlisted on April 5, 1862, at Dragoon Camp by William Boyles for 30th of July 1864, or the war. Company muster roll for September/October 1863, report him absent sick. He was admitted to Ross Hospital, Mobile, Alabama, on September 26, 1863, with chronic bronchitis. Furloughed for 20 days on October 3. November/December 1863, roll reports him present. Company muster rolls from December 31, 1863, through April 30, 1864, report him absent on detached duty as courier for Major J. H. Cummins. Drew clothing on September 7, 1864. POW surrendered by Lt. General R. Taylor CSA to Major General E. R. S. Canby at Citronelle, Alabama, on May 4, 1865. Paroled at Gainesville, Alabama, on May 14, 1865. Residence shown as Monroe County, Alabama. There is paper work in his file.*

Starke, R. B., Sergeant Co. G.
Enlisted on February 22, 1862, at Dragoon Camp by William Boyles for July 30, 1864, or the war. Company muster rolls from September 1863, through June 1864, report him present. Drew clothing on June 20, 1864. He signed a Parole of Honor at Gainesville, Alabama, on May 14, 1865. His parole is in his file.*

Starke, W. H., Pvt. Co. C.
Enlisted on July 1, 1863, at Camp Powell by Captain Barlow for three years or the war. Company muster rolls from September 1863, through June 1864, report him present. Drew clothing on August 28, 1864.

Starke, W. H., Pvt. Co. K.
POW surrendered by Lt. General R. Taylor CSA to Major General E. R. S. Canby at Citronelle, Alabama, on May 4, 1865. Paroled at Gainesville, Alabama, on May 14, 1865. Residence shown as Baldwin County, Alabama.

Stayly, J. F. see Staley, John F.

Steadham, A. J., Corporal Co. C.
Enlisted on April 9, 1862, at Blakeley, Alabama, by Captain Barlow for three years or the war. Company muster rolls for September/October 1863, report him present. He is shown as absent with leave on November/December 1863, rolls. January through June 1864, he is reported present. Drew clothing on August 28, 1864.

Steadham, A. T. see Stedham, A. T.

Steadham, E. see Stedham, E.

Steadham. J. V. see Stedham, J. V.

Stedham, A. J. see Steadham. A. J.

Stedham. A. T., Pvt. Co. C.
Enlisted on November 10, 1863, at Halls Mill, Alabama, by Captain Barlow for three years or the war. Company muster rolls from November 1863, through June 1864, report him

present. Drew clothing on August 28, 1864. POW surrendered by Lt. General R. Taylor CSA to Major General E. R. S. Canby at Citronelle, Alabama, on May 4, 1865. Paroled at Gainesville, Alabama, on May 14, 1865. Residence shown as Baldwin County, Alabama.

Stedham, E., Pvt. Co. C.
Enlisted on November 26, 1862, at Camp Powell by Captain Barlow for three years or the war. Muster rolls for September/October 1863, report him absent sick and absent without leave. From November 1863, through June 1864, he is shown present. Drew clothing on August 1864. Admitted to Ross Hospital, Mobile, Alabama, on March 11, 1865, with scabies. Sent to General Hospital in Selma, Alabama, on March 16, 1865. POW surrendered by Lt. General R. Taylor CSA to Major General E. R. S. Canby at Citronelle, Alabama, on May 4, 1865. Paroled at Gainesville, Alabama, on May 14, 1865. Residence shown as Baldwin County, Alabama.

Stedham, John V. see Sedham, J. V.

Stedham, J. V., Pvt. Co. C.
Enlisted on October 26, 1862, at Camp Powell by Captain Barlow for three years or the war. Company muster rolls for September 12, 1863, reports him present. Muster rolls from September 1863, through December 31, 1863, reports him absent without leave. Muster rolls from January 1864, through June 1864, show him absent sick. Admitted to Ross Hospital, Mobile, Alabama, on September 18, 1863, with debility. Returned to duty on September 25, 1863. Admitted to Ross Hospital on October 16, 1863, with intermitten fever. Returned to Duty on October 17, 1863. Admitted to Ross Hospital on March 11, 1865, with rheumitismus. Sent to General Hospital in Selma, Alabama, on March 16, 1865. His file indicates that the was admitted again to Ross Hospital on March 23, 1865, with rheumatismus and this time he was sent to General Hospital in Meridian, Mississippi, on March 30, 1865. POW surrendered by Lt. General R. Taylor CSA to Major General E. R. S. Canby at Citronelle, Alabama, on May 4, 1865. Paroled at Gainesville, Alabama, on May 14, 1865. Residence shown as Baldwin County, Alabama.

Stedham, L. B., Pvt. Co. K.
POW surrendered by Lt. General R. Taylor CSA to Major General E. R. S. Canby at Citronelle, Alabama, on May 4, 1865. Paroled at Gainesville, Alabama, on May 14, 1865. Residence shown as Baldwin County, Alabama.

Steel, R. F., Pvt. Co. D.
Enlisted on April 3, 1863, at Pollard, Alabama, by Captain Gardner for three years. Company muster roll for September 12, 1863, reports him absent on extra duty at Pollard, by order or General Canty. Muster roll for September/October 1863, reports the same. November 1863, through February 1864, rolls shows him absent as cow driver at Pollard, Alabama. March/April 1864, muster rolls show him present on special duty near Bluff Springs, Florida. May/June 1864, muster he is shown as present. Drew clothing on August 28, 1864. Signed by his mark. There is some paper work in his file.*

Steele, R. H. see Steel, R. F.

Steele, W. C., Pvt. Co. F.
Enlisted on February 18, 1863, at Camp Withers by Captain Arrington, for three years or the war. Company muster roll for September 12, 1863, reports him absent on detached service. The next muster roll for September/October 1863, reports him deserted on September 1, 1863.

Steen, James see Stein, James

Stein, Albert, Jr., Pvt. Co. H.
    Enlisted on September 4, 1862, at Mobile, by Lt. Cooper for the war. Company muster roll for September 12, 1863, reports him on detached service as a courier to General Cummings. Company muster rolls from September 1863, through June 1864, report him present with the exception of November/ December roll which shows him absent sick in hospital. Drew clothing on September 7, 1864. He appears on a roll of POW's of Tobin's Light Battery, Semple's Battalion CSA commanded by Captain Thomas F. Tobin that were surrendered by Lt. General R. Taylor CSA to Major General E. R. S. Canby at Citronelle, Alabama, on May 4, 1865. Paroled at Meridian, Mississippi, on May 10, 1865. Residence shown as Mobile, Alabama. His name appears here under the heading: "The following men are doing duty in this battery by order of Lt. Gen. Taylor, not being able to reach their own commands." There is paperwork in his file.*

Stein, James, Pvt./2nd Lieutenant Co. I.
    Enlisted on September 24, 1863, at Halls Mill, Alabama, by Captain W. B. Amos for the war. Muster rolls for September/December 1863, reports him absent on scout. Subsequent rolls from November 1863, through June 1864, report him present. He was elected 2nd Lieutenant on October 24, 1864. He signed a Parole of Honor at Selma, Alabama, on June 14, 1865. His parole is in his file.*

Stephens, Burl see Stevens, Burrel

Stephens, Jacob, H., Pvt. Co. B.
    Enlisted on March 14, 1862, at Marianna, Florida, by Colonel J. J. Finley for three years or the war. Company muster rolls from September 1863, through June 1864, report him present. Drew clothing on September 10, 1864. POW surrendered at Tallahassee, Florida, on May 11, 1865, by Major General Sam Jones CSA to Brigadier General E. M. McCook USV. Paroled at Quincy, Florida, on May 22, 1865.

Stevens, Burrel, Pvt. Co. D.
    Enlisted on July 1, 1863, at Camp Lomax by Captain J. B. Vaughn for three years. Company muster roll for September/October 1863, reports him on scout a substitute for **M. H. Daily**. Muster rolls from November 1863, through June 1864, report him present with pay due. Drew clothing on August 28, 1864. POW captured at Mount Pleasant, Alabama, on April 11, 1865. His name appears on a list of POW's from Mobile, forwarded to Ship Island, Mississippi.

Stevens, Jacob see Stephens, Jacob H.

Stewart, John see Stewart J. W.

Stewart, John A., Pvt. Co. E.
    Enlisted on September 17, 1861, at Milton, Florida, by Captain E. S. Amos for three years. Company muster roll for September 12, 1863, reports him present. Muster roll for September/October 1863, reports him absent on furlough since November 29, 1863. November/December muster roll shows him absent without leave. Company muster roll from March 1864, through June 1864, shows him present. Drew clothing Sept. 2, 1864.

Stewart, J. W., Pvt. Co. F.
    Enlisted on February 18, 1863, at Camp Withers, by Captain Arrington for three years or the

war. Company muster rolls from September 1863, through June 1864, report him present with the exception of September/October 1863, roll which shows him absent on furlough. Drew clothing on August 29, 1864. POW surrendered by Lt. General R. Taylor CSA to Major General E. R. S. Canby at Citronelle, Alabama, on May 4, 1865. Paroled at Gainesville, Alabama, on May 14, 1865. Residence shown as Baldwin County, Alabama.

Stewart, R. W., Pvt. Co. E.
Enlisted on September 5, 1862, at Camp Lomax by Captain N. R. Leigh for three years. First Company muster roll for September 12, 1864, reports him present. Company muster rolls for September 1863, through June 1864, report him present on special duty as saddler for the regiment since November 26, 1863. Drew clothing on September 2, 1864. Drew clothing on June 18, 1864, at Pollard, Alabama and again on September 2, 1864, with no location given. He signed a Parole of Honor at Headquarters of the 16th U.S. Army Corps at Montgomery, Alabama, on May 30, 1865. Eyes-dark, hair-dark, complexion-dark, 6 foot 2 inches. His parole is in his file.*

Stewart, S. T., Pvt. Co. E.
Enlisted on September 12, 1861, at Milton, Florida, by Captain E. Amos for three years. Company muster roll for September 12, 1864, reports him present and without horse from June 1 to June 15, 1863. September/October 1863, muster roll shows him present. November/December 1863, muster roll reports him absent sick at home with no horse since November 1, 1863. March/April 1864, muster roll shows him present and without horse from November 1, 1863, to January 31, 1864. May/June 1864, he is shown present. Drew clothing on September 2, 1864. POW surrendered by Lt. General R. Taylor CSA to Major General E. R. S. Canby at Citronelle, Alabama, on May 4, 1865. Paroled at Gainesville, Alabama, on May 14, 1865. Residence shown as Santa Rosa County, Florida.

Stiggins, James, G., Pvt. Co. F.
Enlisted on April 15, 1862, at Stockton, Alabama, by Captain Barlow for three years or the war. Company muster rolls from September 1863, through June 1864, report him present. Drew clothing on August 29, 1864.

Still, Bartlett, Pvt. Co. E.
Enlisted on February 9, 1864, at Halls Mill, Alabama, by Captain N. R. Leigh for three years. Muster rolls from March 1864, through June 1864, report him present. Drew clothing on September 2, 1864.

Still, Richmond, Pvt. Co. I.
Enlisted on March 31, 1863, at Conecuh County, Alabama, by Captain W. B. Amos for the war. Company muster rolls from September 1863, through June 1864, reports him present. On September/October 1863, roll he is shown absent on scout.

Stilley, William, R., Pvt. Co. F.
Enlisted on January 8, 1863, at Camp Withers, by Captain Arrington for three years or the war. Company muster rolls from September 1863, through June 1864, report him present. Drew clothing on August 29, 1864. Card in his file with information on Special Order No. 189/47 which transferred him to Co. K, 3 Regiment N. C. Cav. on August 11, 1864.

Stilly, W. R. see Stilley, William R.

Stinson, Joseph, Pvt. Co. A.
Enlisted on May 20, 1863, Camp Lomax, by Captain Partridge, for the war. Company

muster roll for September 12, 1863, reports him absent on detached service as guide for General Clanton. Muster roll for September/October 1863, report him absent on furlough and dismounted October 20, 1863. November/December 1863, he is shown as absent without leave. Admitted to Ross Hospital, Mobile, Alabama, on October 19, 1863, with debility. Returned to duty on October 23, 1863. March/April 1864, muster roll shows him (deserted?) from Halls Mill, Ala. November 1, 1863.

Stinson, S. R., Pvt. Co. E.
Enlisted on April 17, 1861, at Milton, Florida, by Captain E. S. Amos for three years. Company muster roll for September 12, 1863, reports him absent on detached duty to work on gunboat at Montgomery, Alabama, since March 2, 1863, by order of General Buckner. He is shown thus from September through December 1863. Muster roll for March/April 1864, reports that he deserted from Mobile, Alabama, while on detached duty at ???chana's about January 15, 1864. "Has probably gone to the enemy at Pensacola Navy Yard."

Stokes, H., Pvt. Co. ?
His name appears on a list of POW's surrendered at Tallahassee, Florida, on May 10, 1865, by Major General Sam Jones CSA to Brigadier General E. M. McCook USV. Paroled at Quincy, Florida, on May 22, 1865.

Stokes, Peter, Pvt. Co. I.
Enlisted on June 1864, at Santa Rosa, Florida, by W. B. Amos for the war. His name appears on one muster roll for May/June 1864, where he is reported present.

Stokes, S. E., Corporal/Sergeant Co. G.
Enlisted on July 30, 1861, at Mobile, Alabama, by B. C. Yancey for July 30, 1864, or the war. First muster roll of September 12, 1863, he is reported absent on detached duty. On subsequent muster rolls from September 1863, through April 30, 1864, he is reported present. Drew clothing on June 30 and September 4, 1864. POW surrendered by Lt. General R. Taylor CSA to Major General E. R. S. Canby at Citronelle, Alabama, on May 4, 1865. Paroled at Gainesville, Alabama, on May 14, 1865. Here he is shown as 1st Sergeant. Residence shown as Mobile, Mobile County, Alabama.

Stokes, Thomas, N., Corporal/Sergeant Co. F.
Enlisted on August 29, 1862, at Camp Withers by Captain Arrington, for three years or the war. First muster roll of September 12, 1863, he is reported absent on detached duty. On subsequent muster rolls from September 1863, through June 1864, he is reported present. On later rolls he is shown as 4th Sergeant. Drew clothing on August 29, 1864. POW surrendered by Lt. General R. Taylor CSA to Major General E. R. S. Canby at Citronelle, Alabama, on May 4, 1865. Paroled at Gainesville, Alabama, on May 14, 1865. Residence shown as Monroe County, Alabama.

Stone, R. F., Pvt. Co. G.
Enlisted on September 15, 1861, at Dragoon Camp by B. C. Yancey for July 30, 1864, or the war. Muster rolls from September through December 1863, report him present. Company muster roll for December 31, 1863, through April 30, 1864, reports him absent with leave. Drew clothing on June 20, 1864. POW surrendered by Lt. General R. Taylor CSA to Major General E. R. S. Canby at Citronelle, Alabama, on May 4, 1865. He was paroled at Gainesville, Alabama, on May 14, 1865. His residence is shown as Mobile County, Alabama.

Strange, John, Pvt. Co. I.
Enlisted on June 22, 1864, at Santa Rosa, Florida, by W. B. Amos for the war. His name appears only on one muster roll for May/June 1864, and he is reported present.

Strange, W. M., Pvt. Co. I.
Enlisted on February 23, 1864, at Conecuh County, Alabama, by Captain Amos for the war. He was discharged on August 18, 1863, by order of General Clanton.

Strickland, J. F. see Strickland, J. S.

Strickland, J. H. see Strickland, J. S.

Strickland, J. S., Pvt. Co. A.
Enlisted on June 4, 1862, at Camp Lomax by Lt. Tucker for the war. Muster rolls from September 1863, through June 1864, report him present. On November/December 1863, roll he is shown as on daily duty as a courier. Drew clothing on September 7, 1864. POW captured at Mount Pleasant, Alabama, on April 11, 1865. His name appears on a list of POW's that were forwarded from Mobile, Alabama, to Ship Island, Mississippi.

Strickland, Robert, Pvt. Co. I.
Enlisted on April 20, 1864, at Santa Rosa, Florida, by W. B. Amos for the war. Muster rolls show him present through June 1864.

Stringer, J. B., Pvt. Co. D.
He signed a Parole of Honor at the 16th U.S. Army Corps Headquarters in Montgomery, Alabama, on June 19, 1865. Hair-light, eyes-gray, complexion-light, 5 foot 11 inches. His parole is in his file.*

Strong, G., Pvt. Co. K.
Drew clothing on August 28, 1864. POW surrendered by Lt. General R. Taylor CSA to Major General E. R. S. Canby at Citronelle, Alabama, on May 4, 1865. Paroled at Gainesville, Alabama, on May 14, 1865. Residence shown as Choctaw County, Alabama.

Strong, G. I. see Strong, G.

Stroud, J. S., Pvt. Co. H.
Transferred from Captain Rodes Company on July 8, 1863. Age-18, eyes-blue, hair-light, complexion-fair, 5 foot 8 inches, born-Russell County, Alabama, occupation-farmer. Enlisted on July 5, 1863, at Halls Mill, Alabama, by Captain J. W. Murrell for the war.

Stuart, John, A. see Stewart, John A.

Stuart, R. J., Pvt. Co. C.
Enlisted on December 28, 1863, at Halls Mill, Alabama, by Captain Gonzales for the war. He appears present on a muster roll from December 31, 1863, through June 30, 1864.

Stuart, R. W. see Stewart, R. W.

Stuart, S. T. see Stewart, S. T.

Stuckey, Augustus, Sergeant Co. I.
Enlisted on October 4, 1862, at Santa Rosa, Florida, by Captain Amos for the war. Company

15TH CONFEDERATE CAVALRY

muster rolls from September 1863, through June 1864, report him present. He is shown with the rank of 2nd Sergeant.

Stucky, Augustus see Stuckey, Augustus

Sturdevant. Mathew J., Pvt. Co. D.
Enlisted on May 19, 1862, at Pensacola, Florida, by Captain Vaughn for three years. Muster rolls from September 1863, through June 1864, report him present. His name appears on a roll of POW stragglers paroled at Selma, Alabama, during June 1865. Residence shown as Wilcox County, Alabama.

Sturdvant, P. see Sturdevant P.

Sturdevant, P., Pvt. Co. F.
Enlisted on September 16, 1862, at Camp Withers by Captain Arrington, for three years or the war. Company muster rolls from September 1863, through June 1864, report him present. Drew clothing on August 29, 1864.

Suares, A., Pvt. Co. C.
Enlisted on July 12, 1862, at Pensacola, Florida, by Captain Bright for three years. Drew clothing on August 28, 1864. POW surrendered by Lt. General R. Taylor CSA to Major General E. R. S. Canby at Citronelle, Alabama, on May 4, 1865. Paroled at Gainesville, Alabama, on May 14, 1865. Residence shown as Baldwin County, Alabama.

Suares, Aubrey see Auares A.

Suares, F., Pvt. Co. C.
Enlisted on July 1, 1862, at Camp Powell by Captain Barlow for three years or the war. Record also shows that he enlisted on July 1, 186?, at Camp Powell by Captain Barlow for three years or the war. Another card shows that he joined on April 25, 1862, at Camp Withers by Captain Cottrill for three years. First muster roll for September 12, 1863, reports that he is absent, detached as a guide on Pedido Bay. Company Muster rolls report him present from September 1863, through June 1864. Drew clothing on August 28, 1864. POW surrendered by Lt. General R. Taylor CSA to Major General E. R. S. Canby at Citronelle, Alabama, on May 4, 1865. Paroled at Gainesville, Alabama, on May 14, 1865. Residence shown as Baldwin County, Alabama.

Suares, Frank see Suares, F.

Suares, Thomas, see Suaress, Tom

Suaress, Tom, Pvt. Co. F.
Enlisted on January 1, 1862, at Camp Withers by Captain Arrington for three years or the war. Enlisted on January 2, 1862, at Camp Withers by Captain Arrington for three years or the war. Muster roll for September 12, 1863, reports him present. Company muster roll for September/October reports him absent sick in hospital in Mobile. Admitted to Ross Hospital, Mobile, on September 22, 1863, with intermitten fever. Furloughed on October 8, 1863, for 15 days (Name shown as Thos. Suas). Muster roll for March/April 1864, reports that he was transferred to C. S. Navy in February. Muster and pay roll of the C. S. Receiving Ship *Danube* from April 30, 1864, to June 30, 1864, shows **Thomas Suare**, Lands Master, pressed. On September 13, 1864, his name appears on a list of men transferred to the C. S. Navy at Naval Rendevous at Mobile, former Pvt. Co. F. 15th Confederate Cavalry.

Suerlock, T. I. See Scurlock, Thomas J.

Sullivian, Andrew, J., Pvt. Co. B.
    Enlisted on March 14, 1862, at Marianna, Florida, by Colonel J. J. Finley for three years or the war. Company muster rolls from September 1863, thorough June 1864, report him present on extra duty as a wagoner by order of Colonel Maury from August 5, 1862. Drew clothing on June 19, 1864, at Pollard, Alabama, and September 10, 1864, with no location given. POW surrendered by Lt. General R. Taylor CSA to Major General E. R. S. Canby at Citronelle, Alabama, on May 4, 1865. Paroled at Gainesville, Alabama, on May 14, 1865. Residence shown as Jackson County, Florida..

Sullivan, Putnam, Pvt. Co. B.
    Enlisted on February 1, 1863, at Marianna, Florida, by Lt. C. W. Davis for three years or the war. Company muster rolls from September 1863, through June 1864, report him present. Drew clothing on September 10, 1864. POW surrendered at Tallahassee, Florida, on May 11, 1865, by Major General Sam Jones CSA to Brigadier General E. M. McCook USV. Paroled at Quincy, Florida, on May 23, 1865.

Sumerall, W., Pvt. Co. H.
    His name appears on a roll of POW's surrendered by Lt. General R. Taylor CSA to Major General E. R. S. Canby at Citronelle, Alabama, on May 4, 1865. Paroled at Gainesville, Alabama, on May 14, 1865. Residence shown as Choctaw County, Alabama.

Summerall, James, Pvt. Co. H.
    Enlisted on June 5, 1863, at West Pascagoula, Jackson County, Mississippi, by Lt. Cleveland for the war. Muster rolls from September 1863, through December 30, 1863, report him absent sick in hospital. He appears on a descriptive roll for clothing at Halls Mill, on October 1, 1863. Here he is show to be 18 years old, eyes-dark, hair-dark, complexion-dark, 5 foot 4 inches, born in Clarke Mississippi, a farmer by occupation. He was admitted to General Hospital Ross, Mobile, Alabama on October 25, 1863, with debility. Furloughed on November 6, for 25 days. He was admitted again to Ross Hospital on December 2, 1863, with debility and returned to duty on January 14, 1864. On 1864 rolls he is shown as having been transferred to Tobins Battery on February 15, 1864, by order of General Maury.

Sumrall, James, see Summerall, James

Sunday, G. W. see Lundy W. G.

Sunday, J. G. see Sunday, John

Sunday, John, Pvt. Co. E.
    Enlisted on November 5, 1862, at Camp Powell by Captain E. S. Amos for three years. Company muster roll for September 12, 1863, reports him absent at home sick since August 20, 1863. Muster rolls for September through December 1863, report him present on special duty as a teamster. March 1864, through June 1864, he is shown on the rolls as present. Drew clothing on September 2, 1864.

Sunday, J. W., Pvt. Co. E.
    Enlisted on November 5, 1862, at Camp Powell by Captain E. S. Amos for three years. Company muster rolls for September 1863, through June 1864, report him present with one exception on November/December 1863, roll he is show absent without leave. POW captured at Pine Barren, Escambia County, Florida on November 17, 1864. His name

15TH CONFEDERATE CAVALRY

appears on a register of POW's at New Orleans, Louisiana, who were transferred to Ship Island, Mississippi, on December 10, 1864.

Sunday, W. G. see Lundy W. G

Surles, Calvin, Pvt. Co. A.
Enlisted on April 7, 1862, at Station 3 of P & G. RR by Captain Partridge for three years. His file also shows that he enlisted at Monticello, Florida. Company muster rolls from September 1863, through June 1864, report him present. Drew clothing on September 7, 1864. POW surrendered at Tallahassee, Florida, on May 10, 1865, by Major General Sam Jones CSA to Brigadier General E. M. McCook USV. Paroled at Tallahassee, Florida, on May 14, 1865.

Swann, Robert, Pvt. Co. K.
Enlisted on March 17, 1862, at Washington County, Alabama, by Lt. Cooper for the war. Company muster rolls from September 1863, through April 1864, report him present. On the May/June 1864, roll he is shown as being absent sick in Greenville Hospital. POW captured at Mount Pleasant, Alabama, on April 11, 1865.

Sylvester, J. H., Pvt. Co. F.
Enlisted on December 1, 1863, at Halls Mill, Alabama, by Captain Arrington for three years. Company muster rolls from September 1863, through June 1865, report him present. Drew clothing on August 29, 1864. POW surrendered by Lt. General R. Taylor CSA to Major General E. R. S. Canby at Citronelle, Alabama, on May 4, 1865. Paroled at Gainesville, Alabama, on May 14, 1865. Residence shown as Baldwin County, Alabama.

T

Tanner, C. L., Pvt. Co. B.
Drew clothing on September 10, 1864. POW captured at Mount Pleasant, Alabama, on April 11, 1865.

Tanner, Isaac, Pvt. Co. H.
Enlisted on July 21, 1863, at West Pascagoula, Mississippi, by Captain Murrell for the war. Muster roll for September/October 1864, shows that he was transferred to his proper command due to being irregularly mustered.

Tanner, Richard, Pvt. Co. H.
Enlisted on September 12, 1863, at Halls Mill, Alabama, by Captain Murrell for the war. On muster rolls for September through December 1864, he is shown absent sick in hospital. Muster rolls for January through June 1864, he is reported present. He appears on a descriptive list for pay and clothing on October 1, 1863. Age 37, eyes-grey, hair-dark, complexion-dark, 5 foot 8 inches, born Jackson County, Mississippi, a farmer by occupation. POW surrendered by Lt. General R. Taylor CSA to Major General E. R. S. Canby at Citronelle, Alabama, on May 4, 1865. Paroled at Gainesville, Alabama, on May 14, 1865. Residence shown as Jackson County, Mississippi. There is paperwork in his file.*

Tanskall, E. see Tunstall, E. S.

Taylor, A. T., Pvt. Co. A.
Enlisted on May 1, 1864, at Monticello, Florida, by Captain Ulmer for the war. May/June muster roll reports him present and dismounted since enlistment. Drew clothing on

September 7, 1964. POW surrendered at Tallahassee, Florida, on May 10, 1865, by Major General Sam Jones CSA to Brigadier General E. M. McCook USV. Paroled at Thomasville, Georgia, in May 1865. His parole is in his file.*

Taylor, Benjamin, Pvt. Co. K.
Enlisted on January 19, 1864, at Halls Mill, Alabama, by Lt. R.. A. Powe for the war. January through April 1864, reports that he is absent on furlough. May/June Muster roll shows him present. Drew clothing on August 28, 1864.

Taylor, B. F. see Taylor, Benjamin

Taylor, Daniel, Pvt. Co. K.
Enlisted February 20, 1863, at Halls Mill, Alabama, by Captain McKellar for the war. Company muster rolls from September 1863, through June 1864, report him present. Drew clothing on August 28, 1864. POW surrendered by Lt. General R. Taylor CSA to Major General E. R. S. Canby at Citronelle, Alabama, on May 4, 1865. Paroled at Gainesville, Alabama, on May 14, 1865. Residence shown as Wayne County, Mississippi. There is paperwork in his file. On a descriptive list for bounty he is shown as: age-31, eyes-hazel, hair-dark, complexion-dark, 5 foot 8 inches, born-Green County, Mississippi, a farmer by trade. Paid $50 bounty. See also listing for **Pvt. Robert L. Morre**, Co. K. *

Taylor, E. S., Pvt. Co. C.
Enlisted on May 20, 1862, at Mobile, Alabama, by Captain T. C. Barlow for three years. Company muster rolls from September 1863, through June 1864, report him present. Drew clothing on August 28, 1864. His name appears on a roll of POW stragglers surrendered at Meridian, Mississippi, by Lt. General R. Taylor CSA to Major General E. R. S. Canby, in May 1865. Paroled at Mobile, on May 19, 1865. Residence shown as Baldwin County, Alabama.

Taylor, F. B., Pvt./2nd Lt. Co. A.
Enlisted on March 7, 1862, at Station 3 of the P & G RR by Captain Cross for three years. Resigned from 1st Sergeant on February 3, 1863. Dismounted between February 3, 1863, and April 11, 1863. Promoted from Pvt. to Lt. on October 5, 1863. Company muster rolls from September 1863, through June 1864, report him present for duty. He appears on a roster as 2nd Lt. at Camp Cumming, on July 12, 1864. POW surrendered at Tallahassee, Florida, on May 10, 1865, by Major General Sam Jones CSA to Brigadier General E. M. McCook USV. Paroled at Tallahassee, Florida, on May 15, 1865. Hair-light, eyes-blue, complexion-fair, 5 foot 11 inches. His parole and considerable other paperwork is in his file.*

Taylor, John, Pvt. Co. E.
His name appears on a roll of POW's surrendered by Lt. General R. Taylor CSA to Major General E. R. S. Canby in May 1865. Paroled at Demopolis, Alabama, on June 23, 1865. Residence shown as Memphis, Tennessee.

Taylor, M. H., Pvt. Co. K.
Enlisted on March 17, 1862, at Washington County, Alabama, by Lt. Cooper for the war. All company muster rolls from September 1863, through June 1864, report him absent on detached service.

Taylor, Thomas, Pvt. Co. H.
Enlisted on September 4, 1862, at Mobile, Alabama, by Lt. Cooper for the war. Company muster rolls from September through December 1863, report him absent sick in hospital.

Admitted to Ross Hospital, Mobile, Alabama, on September 22, 1863, with chronic rheumatism. Returned to duty on January 14, 1864. On December 31, 1863, through June 1864, he is reported present. Drew clothing on September 7, 1864.

Taylor, W. B., see Taylor, W. R.

Taylor, William, see Taylor W. P.

Taylor, W. P., Pvt. Co. H.
Enlisted on June 17, 1863, at West Pascagoula, Mississippi, by Captain Murrell for the war. September/October muster roll shows him transferred as he was irregularly mustered. December 31, 1863, through June 1864, reports him present. Drew clothing on September 7, 1864. Admitted to Ross Hospital, Mobile, Alabama, on October 10, 1864, with febris intermittens and syphilis. Sent to General Hospital Nidelet on December 5, 1864. POW surrendered at Tallahassee, Florida, on May 10, 1865, by Major General Sam Jones CSA to Brigadier General E. M. McCook USV. Paroled at Tallahassee, Florida, on May 15, 1865. Hair-light, eyes-blue, complexion-dark, 5 foot 3 inches. His parole is in his file. *

Taylor, W. R., Pvt. Co. A.
Enlisted on April 18, 1862, at Station 3 of the P & G RR by Captain Partridge for three years. Muster rolls from September 1863, through June 1864, report him present with one exception. November/December roll shows him absent sick since December 24, 1863. Admitted to Ross Hospital, Mobile, Alabama, on December 24, 1863, with catarrh. Returned to duty on January 9, 1864. Drew clothing on September 7, 1864. POW captured at Mount Pleasant, Alabama, on April 11, 1865. He appears on a list of prisoners forwarded from Mobile, Alabama, to Ship Island, Mississippi.

Taylor, W. T., Pvt. Co. A.
Enlisted on March 17, 1862, at Station 3 of P & G RR by Captain Cross for three years. First company muster roll on September 12, 1863, reports him absent at General Hospital. Muster rolls from September through December 1863, report him present but dismounted from April 1, 1863, to November 24, 1863. March/April muster roll shows that he was detailed for twenty days from April 21, 1864, to go after a horse by order of General Maury. May/June roll he is shown present. Drew clothing on September 7, 1864.

Terrier, John, Pvt./Corp. Co. H.
Enlisted on September 4, 1862, at Mobile, Alabama, by Lt. Cooper for the war. First muster roll of September 12, 1863, shows him detached by order of General Maury. Thereafter he is shown as present on muster rolls from September 1863, through June 1864. Promoted to 4th Corporal from ranks on December 11, 1863. He is reported to have drawn clothing on September 7, 1864.

Terrin, D. J., see Turvin, D. J.

Tervin, D. J., see Turvin, D. J.

Terrvan, D. J., see Turvin, D. J.

Terivin, D. J., see Turvin, D. J.

Tevirn, David, J., see Turvin, D. J.

Thigpin, G., Pvt. Co. E.
He signed a parole at the Headquarters of the 16th U.S. Army Corps at Montgomery, Alabama, on June 9, 1865. Eyes-gray, hair-dark, complexion-light, 5 foot 9 inches. His parole is in his file.*

Thomas, John, Pvt. Co. K.
Enlisted on June 12, 1863, at Bayou La Batre by Captain McKellar for the war. Company muster roll for September/October 1863, reports him present but on rolls from November 1863, through April 30, 1864, he is shown absent without leave. May/June 1864, he appears as present on the roll. Drew clothing on August 21, 1864. On October 9, 1864, he appears on a descriptive roll for clothing and pay. He is described as; age-18, eyes-grey, hair-light, complexion-fair, 6 foot tall. He was born in Perry County, Alabama (?), a student by occupation.

Thomas, W. F., Pvt. Co. E.
Enlisted on September 6, 1863, at Camp Lomax, by Captain Leigh for three years. September 12, 1863, muster roll reports that he deserted the night of July 29, 1863, "whereabouts unknown".

Thomaston, John C., Pvt. Co. B.
Enlisted on March 14, 1862, at Marianna, Florida, by Colonel J. J. Finley for three years or the war. Company muster rolls from September 1863, through June 1864, report him present. On March 1, 1864, he was assigned special duty by Colonel Maury. Drew clothing on June 20, 1864, at Pollard, Alabama, and signed by his mark "X". Drew clothing again on September 10, 1864, with no location given.

Thompson, B., Pvt. Co. C.
Enlisted on April 15, 1862, at Stockton, Alabama, by Captain Barlow for three years. Company muster roll for September/October 1863, reports him present. In November 1863, through June 30, 1864, he is shown as absent without leave. Drew clothing on August 28, 1864. POW surrendered by Lt. General R. Taylor CSA to Major General E. R. S. Canby at Citronelle, Alabama, on May 4, 1865. Paroled at Gainesville, Alabama, on May 14, 1865. Residence shown as Baldwin County, Alabama.

Thompson, D. J., Pvt. Co. K.
Enlisted on March 17, 1862, at Washington County, Alabama, by Lt. Cooper for the war. Company muster rolls from September 1863, through June 1864, report him present. Drew, clothing on June 12, 1864, at Pollard, Alabama and again on August 28, 1864, with no location given. POW surrendered by Lt. General R. Taylor CSA to Major General E. R. S. Canby at Citronelle, Alabama, on May 4, 1865. Paroled at Gainesville, Alabama, on May 14, 1865. Residence shown as Choctaw County, Alabama.

Thompson, O., Pvt. Co. C.
Enlisted on April 9, 1862, at Blakeley, Alabama, by Captain T. C. Barlow for the war. All company muster rolls from September 1863, through June 1864, report him present except November/December 1863, roll where he is shown as absent without leave. Drew clothing on August 28, 1864.

Thompson, William, Pvt. Co. F.
Enlisted on February 5, 1863, at Camp Withers by Captain Arrington for the war. All company muster rolls from September 12, 1863, through June 1864, report him present except September/October 1863, where he is shown as sick in General Hospital. Admitted

to Ross Hospital, Mobile, Alabama, on October 13, 1863, with debility. Sent to General Hospital S. (Spring) Hill on October 14, 1863. His name appears among a roll of POW's who were stragglers that were paroled at Selma, Alabama, in June 1865. Residence shown is Butler County, Alabama.

Thrower, Henry, Pvt. Co. H.
POW surrendered by Lt. General R. Taylor CSA to Major General E. R. S. Canby at Citronelle, Alabama, on May 4, 1865. Paroled at Gainesville, Alabama, on May 14, 1865. Residence shown as Mobile County, Alabama.

Tillman, J. A., Assistant Surgeon, Field and Staff
His commission dates from April 16, 1862. Company muster rolls show him present from September 1863, through June 1864. He signed a requisition on August 12, 1864, at Pollard for six mess pans, three camp kettles and ten pcs. mosquito netting for the sick. There is considerable paper work in his file. The majority of the requisitions are for feed for the horses.**

Todd, J. M., Pvt. Co. F.
Enlisted on April 3, 1863, at Camp Withers by Captain Arrington for three years or the war. Admitted to Ross Hospital, Mobile, Alabama, on September 5, 1863. He is diagnosed with feigned rheumatism. On November 6, 1863, he is admitted again to Ross Hospital, Mobile, this time with acuta dysentary. Sent to General Hospital at Marrin, (Sp?) Mississippi, on November 17, 1863. Company muster rolls in September 1863, through December 1863, reflect these absences. From March through June 1864, he is reported present. Drew clothing on August 29, 1864. POW surrendered by Lt. General R. Taylor CSA to Major General E. R. S. Canby at Citronelle, Alabama, on May 4, 1865. He was paroled at Gainesville, Alabama, on May 14, 1865. His residence was reported to be Choctaw County, Alabama.

Todd, Joshua, Pvt. Co. F.
Enlisted on April 3, 1863, at Camp Withers by Captain Arrington, for three years or the war. All muster rolls from September 1863, through June 1864, report him absent sick, either at home or in Mobile. He appears on a register of Ross Hospital, Mobile, Alabama, on October 1, 1863, with chronic diarrhoea. Furloughed for 30 days on November 17, 1863. Drew clothing on August 29, 1864. POW surrendered by Lt. General R. Taylor CSA to Major General E. R. S. Canby at Citronelle, Alabama, on May 4, 1865. Paroled at Gainesville, Alabama, on May 14, 1865. Residence shown as Choctaw County, Alabama.

Tolar, William see Toolar, William

Tompkins, S. Y., Pvt. Co. C.
Enlisted on April 9, 1862, at Blakeley by Captain Barlow for three years or the war. Company muster rolls from September 1863, through June 1864, report him present. Drew clothing on August 28, 1864.

Tonart, (Tuart) William, Pvt. Co. D.
Enlisted on March 16, 1863, at Camp Tatnall, Pensacola, Florida, by Captain Vaughn for three years. Company muster roll for September 12, 1863, through February 29, 1864, report him present or on scout. Muster rolls from March 1864, through June 1864, report him present but absent without leave for 14 days since last paid. (Last paid December 31, 1863.) His name appears on a hospital muster roll dated March 1 to August 31, 1864, at General Hospital, Greenville, Alabama. POW captured at Mount Pleasant, Alabama, on April 11,

1865. His name appears on a list of prisoners forwarded from Mobile, Alabama, to Ship Island, Mississippi.

Toodle, George, Pvt. Co. G.
Enlisted on May 16, 1863, at Camp Taylor by J. H. Marshall for July 30, 1864, or the war. Company muster roll for September/October 1863, shows that he was transferred to Major Steeds Command by General Maury.

Toolar, William, Pvt. Co. A.
Enlisted on December 30, 1862, at Camp Lomax, by Captain Partridge for three years. Admitted to Ross Hospital, Mobile, Alabama, on September 25, 1863, with intermitten fever. Returned to duty on October 11, 1863. Admitted again to Ross Hospital on October 19, 1863, with debility. Returned to duty on October 23, 1863. Company muster roll for September 12, 1863, reports him present but dismounted form May 1, 1863. September/October 1863, muster roll reports him absent without leave and dismounted. November/December 1863, roll reports that he has deserted from Camp Halls Mill, Alabama, on October 30, 1863.

Tower, Charles, Pvt. Co. G.
Enlisted on June 20, 1863, at Camp Taylor, by J. H. Marshall for July 30, 1864, or the war. Company muster rolls for September/October 1863, report him absent sick. November/December 1863, muster roll reports that he was discharged by order or General Canty.

Townsend, William 3rd/2nd Lieutenant Co. E.
Enlisted on September 17, 1861, at Milton, Florida, by Captain E. S. Amos for three years. Company muster rolls from September 1863, through June 1864, report him present. His commission dates from May 7, 1862. POW captured on November 17, 1864, at Escambia County, Florida. He appears on a register of POW's at New Orleans, Louisiana, that were transferred to Ship Island, Mississippi, on December 17, 1864. He was transferred from Ship Island to New Orleans on April 28, 1865, to be confined on April 30, 1865. He was discharged on May 1, 1865. His file also shows that he was transferred from Ship Island to Vicksburg, Mississippi, on April 28, 1865. He signed a parole at Meridian, Mississippi, on May 13, 1865. His parole is in his file. There are several requisitions in his file.**

Traweek, L. W. see Trawek, L. M.

Trawek, L. M., Pvt. Co. I.
He appears on a register of paroled POW's for the month of June 1865. He signed a parole at the headquarters of the 16th U.S. Army Corps, in Montgomery, Alabama, on June 13, 1865. Eyes-hazel, hair-dark, complexion-fair, 6 foot.

Traywick, Robert, Pvt. Co. I.
Enlisted on October 4, 1862, at Conecuh County, Alabama, by Captain Amos for the war. Some file cards indicate that he joined at Santa Rosa, Florida. Company muster rolls from September 1863, through June 1864, report him present for the most part but sometimes absent on scout and on extra daily duty. POW captured at Mount Pleasant, Alabama, on April 11, 1865. His name appears on a list of prisoners forwarded from Mobile, Alabama, to Ship Island, Mississippi.

Trice, S. J., Pvt. Co. K.
Enlisted on March 17, 1862, at Washington County, Alabama, by Lt. Cooper for the war. Company muster rolls from September 1863, through June 1864, report him present except

he is shown as absent on detached service on November/December 1863, roll. Drew clothing on August 28, 1864. POW surrendered by Lt. General R. Taylor CSA to Major General E. R. S. Canby at Citronelle, Alabama, on May 4, 1865. Paroled at Gainesville, Alabama, on May 14, 1865. Residence shown as Choctaw County, Alabama.

Trice, T. E., Pvt. Co. K.
Enlisted on March 17, 1862, at Washington County, Alabama, by Lt. Cooper for the war. Company muster rolls from September 1863, through June 1864, report him present except he is show as absent on detached service on the November through April 30, 1864, roll. Drew clothing on August 28, 1864. POW surrendered by Lt. General R. Taylor CSA to Major General E. R. S. Canby at Citronelle, Alabama, on May 4, 1865. Paroled at Gainesville, Alabama, on May 14, 1865. Residence shown as Choctaw County, Alabama.

Triplett, T. H., 1st Lt. Co. A.
Enlisted on March 7, 1862, at Station 3 of the P & G RR by Captain Cross for three years. Muster roll for September 12, 1863, reports him absent on sick furlough. Elected 1st Lt. on March 7, 1862. Died on September 24, 1863.

Trull, D. C., Pvt. Co. I.
Enlisted on October 4, 1862, at Conecuh County, Alabama, by Captain Amos for the war. Company muster rolls from September 1863, through June 1864, report him present except on September/October 1863, roll where he is shown as absent on scout.

Tuart, William see Tanart, William

Tucker, G. H. see Tucker J. H.

Tucker, James R., Brevet 2nd Lt./1st Lt. Company A.
Enlisted on March 7, 1862, at Station 3 of P & G RR by Captain Cross for three years. Elected Jr. 2nd Lt. on March 7, 1862. Company muster roll for September/October 1863, reports him present. He was promoted to 1st Lt. on September 24, 1863. November/December 1863, muster roll shows him absent on detached service hunting up deserters by order of General Maury. March/April 1864, he is reported absent detailed as officer of Gun Boats ?? Pollard and Montgomery, Ala. by order of Colonel Maury as of April 29, 1864. Muster roll for May/June 1864, reports him absent on detached service. POW surrendered at Tallahassee, Florida, on May 10, 1865, by Major General Sam Jones CSA to Brigadier General E. M. McCook USV. Paroled at Tallahassee, Florida, on May 10, 1865. There is considerable pay vouchers and paper work in his file.**

Tucker, J. H., Pvt. Co. A.
Enlisted on April 7, 1862, at Monticello, Florida, by Captain Partridge for three years. First muster roll for September 12, 1863, reports him absent of sick furlough. Company muster roll for September/October 1863, reports him present but dismounted from October 10 to November 26, 1863. Thereafter through June 1864, he is shown as present but dismounted from time to time. He was admitted to Ross Hospital, Mobile, Alabama, on December 24, 1863, with catarrh. Returned to duty on December 25, 1863. Drew clothing on September 7, 1864. POW captured at Mount Pleasant, Alabama, on April 11, 1865. His name appears on a list of prisoners forwarded from Mobile, Alabama, to Ship Island, Mississippi.

Tucker, Joel,
His name only appears on a receipt roll for clothing on September 7, 1864.

Tunistall, P. R. see Tunstall, P. R.

Tunstall, E. S., Pvt. Co. F.
Enlisted on April 1, 1864, at Montgomery Hill, Alabama, by Captain Arrington for three years. Company muster rolls for March through June 1864, report him present. POW captured at Montgomery Hill, Alabama, on April 10, 1865.

Tunstall, P. R., Pvt. Co. F.
Enlisted on January 19, 1862, at Camp Withers by Captain Cottrill for three years or the war. Company muster rolls from September 1863, through June 1864, report him present. Drew clothing on August 29, 1864. POW surrendered by Lt. General R. Taylor CSA to Major General E. R. S. Canby at Citronelle, Alabama, on May 4, 1865. Paroled at Gainesville, Alabama, on May 14, 1865. Residence shown as Baldwin County, Alabama.

Tuner, Abel, Pvt. Co. G.
POW surrendered at Citronelle, Alabama, on May 4, 1865. Paroled June 3, 1865, at Mobile, Alabama. Residence-Mobile, Ala., eyes-gray, hair-light, complexion-fair, 5 foot 7 inches.

Turner, A. J., Pvt. Co. F.
Enlisted on October 9, 1863, at Halls Mill, Alabama, by Captain Arrington for three years or the war. Company muster rolls from September 1863, through June 1864, report him present. He was admitted to Ross Hospital, Mobile, Alabama, on February 29, 1864, with scabies. Returned to duty on March 25, 1864.

Turner, A. W., Pvt. Co. D.
Enlisted on December 1, 1863, at Camp Tatnall by Captain Vaughn for three years. Company muster rolls from September 1863, through June 1864, show him present on extra duty as a Forage Master and on extra duty with the Quarter Masters Department or on special duty.

Turner, Charles L., Pvt. Co. H.
Enlisted on September 4, 1862, at Mobile, Alabama, by Lt. Cooper for the war. Company muster rolls for September 1863, through June 1864, show him present as a teamster for the battery or absent detached by order of General Maury after February 11, 1864. He was admitted to Ross Hospital, Mobile, Alabama, on October 7, 1863, with acute dysentery. Returned to duty on December 1, 1863. He was admitted to Ross Hospital again on January 10, 1864, with chronic ulcer. Returned to duty on February 25, 1864. His name appears on a list of privates employed in the Medical Purveyors Department, Mobile, Alabama, as a laborer in the laboratory from February 11, 1864, through July 1864.

Turner, G. W., Pvt. Co. A.
Enlisted on March 7, 1862, at Station 3 of the P & G RR, Florida, by Captain Cross for three years. Company muster rolls from September 1863, through June 1864, report him present but dismounted from time to time. Drew clothing on September 7, 1864. Admitted to Ross Hospital, Mobile, Alabama, on May 18, 1864, with debilities. Returned to duty on June 8, 1864. There is a parole in his file signed at Thomasville, Ga. in May 1865.*

Turner, Noel, Pvt. Co. G.
Enlisted on May 25, 1863, at Camp Taylor, by J. H. Marshall for July 30, 1864, or the war. Company muster rolls for September 1863, through April 1864, report him present with one exception. November/December 1863, muster roll shows him absent with leave. Drew clothing on June 20, 1864.

15TH CONFEDERATE CAVALRY

Turner, R. H., Pvt./2nd Lt. Co. D.
Enlisted on October 17, 1862, at Camp Tatnall by Captain Vaughn for three years. September/October 1863, company muster roll show him absent sick at Greenville, Hospital. November/December 1863, roll reports him present. January/February 1864, roll reports him present and promoted to Jr. 2nd Lt. on January 10, 1864. He is reported present from that time through June 1864. There is paperwork in his file.**

Turner, William, Pvt. Co. I.
Enlisted on January 1, 1863, at Conecuh County, Alabama, by Captain Amos for the war. Records also show that he enlisted at Santa Rosa, Florida, by Captain Amos this same date. Company muster rolls for September 12, 1863, and the September/December roll reports that he is absent without leave since July 5. November/December muster roll reports that he deserted.

Turner, W. T., see Turner, William

Turvin D. J., Pvt. Co. E.
Enlisted May 1, 1861, at Camp Lomax, Florida, by Captain N. R. Leigh for three years. First muster roll on September 12, 1863, reports that he is a substitute for **B. N. Johnson** from May 1, 1863. September 1863, through December 1863, muster rolls report him absent sick on furlough. March/April 1864, muster roll reports him absent without leave and May /June muster roll shows him present. POW captured at Escambia County, Florida on November 17, 1864. There is a letter in his file written at New Orleans, Louisiana, on November 30, 1864; *"Captain Marston Dr. Sr. I would most respectfully ask permission to be allowed to take the Oath of Allegiance to the United States and be allowed to remain within the federal lines at the Navy Yard at Pensacola Florida and get employment in the quartermasters Department. I have served out my enlistment in the Confederate army and do not wish to be exchanged. i am 50 years old and do not want to serve any longer in the confederate Army yours respectfully yours David J. Tevirn of the 15th Confederate regt Cavalry."* His name appears on a register of POW's at New Orleans that were transferred to Ship Island, Mississippi, on December 10, 1864. He arrived at Ship Island on December 13, 1864, [this entry mistakenly states that he was captured at Pine Barren, Mississippi]. He made application at Ship Island to take the Oath of Allegiance and join the 1st Regiment U.S. Florida Cavalry. He was transferred from Ship Island to Vicksburg, Mississippi, on May 1, 1865. Admitted on May 6, 1865, to USA General Hospital No. 3, at Vicksburg from steamer with chronic bronchitis. Returned to duty on May 9, 1865. Here his age is shown as 51.

Turvin, Elija, Pvt. Co. I.
Enlisted on June 6, 1864, at Santa Rosa, Florida, by W. B. Amos for the war. His only record is a single muster roll for May/June 1864, where he is reported present.

U

Ullmer, A. J. see Ulmer, A. J.

Ulmer, A. J., Alex.?, Joseph A.?, Pvt./Sergeant Co. G.
Enlisted on July 6, 1863, at Camp Taylor by J. H.. Taylor for July 30, 1864, or the war. Company muster rolls for September 1863, through December 1863, report him present. Muster roll for January 1864, through April 1864, report him absent sick. Admitted to Ross Hospital, Mobile, Alabama, on March 26, 1864, with scabies. Returned to duty on March 30, 1864. His name appears on a roll of POW's (stragglers) which were paroled at Selma, Alabama, in June 1865. His residence is shown as Clarke County, Alabama. In a September

2, 1864, letter at camp near Mobile, **Joseph A. Ulmer** and Pvt. **J. D. Molett**, write to the Secretary of War CSA and apply to be named to the position of Cadet after having served as Privates for four years, as they desire to remain in the country's service after the war. The letter is in **J. D. Molett**'s service record file.

Ulmer, John, 2nd Lt./Captain Co. A.
Enlisted March 7, 1862, at Station 3 of P & G RR, Florida, by Captain Cross for three years. His commission was from March 7, 1862, with promotion to Captain on September 24, 1862. Company muster rolls for September/October 1863, report him present. November/December 1863, muster roll reports that he was absent on leave from December 20, 1863, until January 10, 1864, by order of General Maury. March/April muster roll shows that he was on leave of 30 days from April 23, 1864, then he is reported present through June. POW surrendered at Tallahassee, Florida, on May 10, 1865, by Major General Sam Jones CSA to Brigadier General E. M. McCook USV. Paroled at Tallahassee, Florida, on May 15, 1865. He is described as six foot tall, hair-dark, eyes-dark, complexion-dark. His parole is in his file with considerable other paper work. **

Underwood, M., Pvt. Co. C.
Enlisted on June 7, 1864, at Camp Powell by Captain Barlow for three years. There is but one company muster roll in his file, from December 31, 1863, through June 30, 1864, he is reported present and never having been paid.

Underwood, R. R., Pvt. Co. C.
Enlisted on October 25, 1862, at Camp Powell by Captain Barlow for three years. Company muster rolls from September 1863, through December 1863, report him absent detached by reason of Special Order No. 11, Med. Qtrs. Dept. Gulf, Mobile, August 24, 1863. Muster roll from January through June 1864, reports him absent without leave. Drew clothing on August 28, 1864.

V

Valverde, William, Pvt. Co. G.
Enlisted on May 12, 1863, at Dragoon Camp by William Boyles for July 30, 1864, or the war. Company muster roll for September 12, 1863, reports him absent on detached service. [in error?]. Muster rolls from September 1863, through December 1863, report him absent a POW in New Orleans. Finally a muster roll from December 31, 1863, through April 30, 1864, shows him absent on leave.

Van Epps, A. S., Pvt. Co. F.
Enlisted on November 26, 1862, at Camp Powell by Captain Arrington for three years or the war. Company muster rolls from September 1863, through June 1864, report him present. Drew clothing on August 29, 1864. He was admitted to Ross Hospital, Mobile, Alabama, on October 26, 1864, with febris intermittends. Returned to duty on November 12, 1864. He was admitted again to Ross Hospital on March 9, 1865, with febris intermittens. Returned to duty on March 23.

Van Horn, J. D., Pvt. Do. A.
Enlisted on November 8, 1862, at Camp Tatnall by Captain Partridge for three years. Company muster roll for September 12, 1864, reports him present and dismounted from June 30, 1863, until July 11, 1863. Muster roll for September/October 1863, reports him absent sick. November/December 1863, roll reports him absent without leave since December 20, 1863. March/April 1864, muster roll shows that he is present detailed in Quartermaster's

15TH CONFEDERATE CAVALRY

Department. May/June 1864, he is reported present. Drew clothing on September 7, 1864, and signed by his mark "X".

Vaughn, Langford, Pvt. Co. G.
His name appears on a report of prisoners and deserters forwarded to th Provost Marshal General, Mil. Div. West Miss. by the Provost Marshal, 3d Div. 13th Army Corps, McIntosh Bluff, Alabama, on May 5, 1865. "Taken prisoner by detail of the 35th Mis. Inf. while scouting." "Taken while at home in quest of a horse." His signed Parole of Honor is in his file dated May 2, 1865, at McIntosh Bluff, Alabama. *

Vaughn, B. F., Pvt. Co. D.
Enlisted on October 8, 1862, at Camp Tatnall, by Captain Vaughn for three years. Company muster rolls for September/October 1864, report him on extra duty with Clanton's Brigade since August 26. November/December 1864, roll shows him absent sick. Muster rolls for January 1864, through June 1864, reports him present. Drew clothing on August 28, 1864. His name appears on a roll of POW's among stragglers surrendered by Lt. General R. Taylor CSA to Major General E. R. S. Canby at Citronelle, Alabama, on May 4, 1865. Paroled at Mobile, Alabama, on May 19, 1865. Residence shown as Baldwin County, Alabama. His occupation is shown as verseer.

Vaughn, J. B., Captain Co. D.
Enlisted on April 24, 1862. Elected Captain on April 24, 1862. Company muster rolls for September 1864 through June 1865, report him absent on detached service by order of General Maury with Engineering Department in Mobile. POW surrendered by Lt. General R. Taylor CSA to Major General E. R. S. Canby at Citronelle, Alabama, on May 4, 1865. Paroled at Meridian, Mississippi, on May 11, 1865 . His parole is in his file. There is considerable other paper work in his file. **

Vesterling, A., Pvt. Co. H.
Enlisted on November 20, 1863, at Mobile, Alabama, by Captain Murrell for the war. Company muster rolls from September 1863, through April 1864, report him present. On a muster roll dated June 30, 1864, he is shown as absent sick. His name appears on a Hospital Muster Roll of General Hospital, Greenville, Alabama, for March 1, to August 31, 1864. He drew clothing on September 7, 1864. There is an entry that he drew clothing again on September 12, 1864, at General Hospital Greenville. His name appears on a roll of POW's among stragglers surrendered by Lt. General R. Taylor CSA to Major General E. R. S. Canby at Citronelle, Alabama, on May 4, 1865. Paroled at Mobile, Alabama, May 19, 1865. Residence shown as Mobile, Alabama.

Vesterling, Auguste, see Vesterling, A.

Vickery, J. W., Pvt. Co. D.
Enlisted on April 24, 1862, at Pensacola, Florida, by Captain Vaughn for three years. September/October 1863, muster roll shows him absent sick at home and having served extra duty for 60 days since last muster. November/December 1863, roll reports him absent without leave. On January through June 1864, muster rolls he is reported to have deserted on August 26, 1863. There is a pay voucher in his file in the amount of $145.60 for he and his horse for service May 1, 1863, through October 1863. [His horse drew slightly more at $73.60 versus $72.00.]*

Vickery, William, Pvt. Co. D.
Enlisted on January 16, 1863, at Camp Tatnall by Captain Vaughn for three years.

September/October 1863, reports him absent without leave since August 26, 1863. Muster rolls from November 1863, through June 1864, report him as deserted since August 26, 1863.

See **Vickery, J. W.** above.

Vickry, J. W. see Vickery, J. W.

Vickry, William, see Vickery, William

Videl, John, Pvt. Co. C.
Enlisted on April 9, 1862, at Blakeley, Alabama, by Captain T. C. Barlow for three years. Company muster rolls for September 1863, through June 1864, report him present. Drew clothing on August 28, 1864. POW surrendered by Lt. General R. Taylor CSA to Major General E. R. S. Canby at Citronelle, Alabama, on May 4, 1865. Paroled at Gainesville, Alabama, on May 14, 1865.

Videle, John see Videl, John

W

Waldrop, David, Pvt. Co. E.
Enlisted on May 18, 1862, at Gonzalia, Florida, by Captain N. R. Leigh for three years. Muster roll for September/October 1863, report him present. Muster roll for November /December1863, report him absent without leave. March/April 1864, muster roll shows him having deserted at Halls Mill, Alabama, about January 1, 1964, "has probably gone to the enemy at Pensacola, Navy Yard".

Walker. A. T., Pvt. Co. D.
Enlisted on May 1, 1863, at Camp Tatnall, Florida, by Captain Vaughn for three years. Several of his data cards indicate that he joined at Camp Lomax, on March 1, 1863. He appears present on company muster rolls from September 1863, through June 1864, with one exception in September/October 1863, roll he is reported absent with leave. Drew clothing on August 28, 1864. He signed a parole at the Headquarters of the 16th U.S. Army Corps in Montgomery, Alabama, on May 30, 1865. His description shows; hair-dark, eyes-blue, complexion-dark, 5 foot 5 inches. His parole is in his file.*

Walker, H., Pvt. Co. F.
His name appears on a roll of POW's surrendered by Lt. General R. Taylor CSA to Major General E. R. S. Canby at Citronelle, Alabama, on May 4, 1865. He was paroled at Gainesville, Alabama, on May 14, 1865. His residence is shown as Thomas County, Georgia.

Walker, Henry, Pvt. Co. A.
Enlisted on February 25, 1864, at Halls Mill, Alabama, by Captain Ulmer for three years. Company muster rolls for March through June 1864, report him present. May/June 1864, roll shows him dismounted since enlistment. He is reported to have drawn clothing on September 7, 1864.

Walker, H. H., Pvt. Co. K.
Enlisted on May 5, 1864, at Baldwin County, Alabama, by Lt. P. A. Poute for three years. He is shown present on one surviving muster roll for May/June 1864. POW surrendered by Lt. General R. Taylor CSA to Major General E. R. S. Canby at Citronelle, Alabama, on May

15TH CONFEDERATE CAVALRY

4, 1865. Paroled at Gainesville, Alabama, on May 14, 1865. Residence shown as Wayne County, Mississippi.

Walker, James, Sergeant Co. D.
Enlisted on September 22, 1862, at Camp Tatnall by Captain Vaughn for three years. Company muster roll for September/October 1863, reports him on scout. November 1863 through February 1864, he is shown absent sick. Admitted to Ross Hospital, Mobile, Alabama, on December 4, 1863, with acute diarrhoea. Returned to duty on December 21, 1863. Promoted from 5th Sergeant on January 1, 1864. March/April 1864, muster roll shows him present on special duty at Bluff Springs, Florida. May/June 1864, he is shown present. Drew clothing on August 28, 1864. POW surrendered by Lt. General R. Taylor CSA to Major General E. R. S. Canby at Citronelle, Alabama, on May 4, 1865. Paroled at Meridian, Mississippi, on May 11, 1865. Residence shown as Escambia County, Florida.

Walker, W. A., Pvt. Co. A.
Enlisted on April 18, 1862, at Monticello, Florida, by Captain Partridge for three years. Company muster rolls report him present from September 1863, through June 1864. At one point he is shown as serving on extra duty as a blacksmith. Drew clothing on September 7, 1864. POW surrendered at Tallahassee, Florida, on May 10, 1865, by Major General Sam Jones CSA to Brigadier General E. M. McCook USV. Paroled at Tallahassee, Florida, on May 18, 1865.

Walker, William A., see Walker, W. A.

Wallace, Robert, Pvt. Co. D.
Enlisted on October 26, 1862, at Camp Tatnall by Captain Vaughn for three years. Company muster rolls from September 12, 1863, through December 31, 1863, report him absent on detached service at Pollard, Alabama. Muster rolls from January through June 1864, report him present but dismounted for 60 days. Drew clothing on August 28, 1864. His name appears on a register of paroles given at Columbus, Georgia, May 30, 1865. There is a invoice bearing a date of 1864, submitted for a horse that was captured by the enemy and a horse that died at Camp Halls Mill. The amounts were $750 dollars and $500 dollars respectively. The invoice was approved by Lt. Colonel Myers. There is no indication in his file that the invoice was paid. There is paper work in his file.*

Walton, George, Pvt. Co. G.
Enlisted on February 10, 1862, at Dragoon Camp by William Boyles for July 30, 1864, or the war. Company muster rolls from September 1863, through April 1864, report him present and sometimes on detail as a teamster. He was reported to have drawn clothing on June 12, 1864, at Pollard, Alabama, and again on September 10, 1864, no location given. He signed by his mark "X'.

Walters, A. see Waters, Alexander

Waples, D. W. see Waples, W. D.
Captain and Adjutant Quarter Master, service records filed with Field and Staff.

Ward, A. J., Pvt. Co. F.
Enlisted on April 7, 1862, at Camp Withers by Captain Cottrell for three years or the war. Company muster rolls report him present from September 1864, through December 31, 1864. March/April 1864, muster roll reports that he deserted abut January 25, 1864. POW surrendered by Lt. General R. Taylor CSA to Major General E. R. S. Canby at Citronelle,

Alabama, on May 4, 1865. Paroled at Mobile, Alabama, on May 22, 1865. Residence shown as Jackson County, Mississippi.

Ward, Albert see Ward, A. J.

Ward, Celestina, Pvt. Co. I.
Enlisted on February 7, 1863, at Conecuh County, Alabama, by Captain Amos for the war. Company muster rolls from September 1863, report him absent without leave since June 10. November/December 1863, roll shows him as deserted.

Ware, Co. H.
Enlisted on September 1, 1863, at Halls Mill, Alabama, by Captain Murrell for the war. He appears present and no first name given on company muster roll September 12, 1863.

Ware, H. T., 2nd Lieutenant Co. K.
Enlisted on March 17, 1862, at Washington County, Alabama, by Lt. Cooper for the war. Elected 2nd Lt. on March 17, 1862. He was promoted to 2nd Lt. on December 27, 1862. Muster rolls from September 1863, through April 1864, report him absent on detached service. May /June 1864, roll reports him present. POW surrendered by Lt. General R. Taylor CSA to Major General E. R. S. Canby at Citronelle, Alabama, on May 4, 1865. Paroled at Gainesville, Alabama, on May 14, 1865. His parole is in his file.*

Ware, W. see Ware H. T.

Wask, J. J. Sergeant/Pvt. Co. E, see **Mask, J. J.**

Warters, Alexander see Waters, Alexander

Waters, Alexander, Pvt. Co. A.
Enlisted on March 7, 1862, at Station 3 of P & G RR by Captain Cross for three years. Company muster rolls from September 1863, through June 1864, report him present and sometimes on extra duty as a teamster. Drew clothing on September 7, 1864. POW surrendered at Tallahassee, Florida, on May 10, 1865, by Major General Sam Jones CSA to Brigadier General E. M. McCook USV. Paroled at Thomasville, Georgia, on May 20, 1865. He is described as; eyes-gray, hair-dark, complexion-dark, 5 foot 9 inches. His parole is in his file.*

Waters, I. P., Pvt. Co. ?
His name appears on a list of POW's surrendered at Tallahassee, Florida, on May 10, 1865, by Major General Sam Jones CSA to Brigadier General E. M. McCook USV. Paroled at Albany, Georgia, on May 6, 1865.

Waters, James, Pvt. Co. D.
Enlisted on June 18, 1863, at Camp Tatnall by Captain J. B. Vaughn for three years. Note: Some cards show he enlisted on June 18, 1863, at Camp Lomax. Company muster roll for September 12, 1863, reports him on extra duty by order of General Clanton. September /October 1863, muster roll reports him absent on extra duty for 60 days since last muster. November/December roll reports him absent without leave, thereafter through June 1864, he is show as having deserted on December 10, 1863.

Waters, J. L., Pvt. Co. D.
Enlisted on April 24, 1862, at Pensacola, Florida, by Captain Vaughn for three years. First

15TH CONFEDERATE CAVALRY

company muster roll for September 12, 1863, reports him present. September/October 1863, muster roll shows him on scout. On the November/December 1863, muster roll he is shown absent without leave and thereafter through June 1864, he is reported to have deserted on December 23, 1863.

Waters, Travis, Pvt. Co. D.
Enlisted on May 1, 1862, at Pensacola, Florida, by Captain Vaughn for three years. Company muster rolls for September/October 1863, report that he deserted on August 26, 1863.

Waters, W. H., Pvt. Co. D.
Enlisted on April 24, 1862, at Pensacola, Florida, by Captain Vaughn for three years. First company muster roll for September 12, 1863, reports him present. September/October 1863, muster roll shows him on scout. November/December 1863, he is show absent without leave and thereafter through June 1864, he is reported to have deserted December 23, 1863.

Watson, Henry, Pvt. Co. D.
Enlisted on May 1, 1862, at Pensacola, Florida, by Captain Vaughn for three years. First company muster roll for September 12, 1863, reports him on extra duty by order of General Clanton. September/October 1863, muster roll reports him on extra duty for 60 days since last muster. November/December muster roll shows him absent without leave and thereafter through June 1864, he is reported to have deserted on December 23, 1863.

Watson, K. see Watson, R.

Watson, R., Pvt. Co. A.
His name appears on a register of POW's paroled on June 19, 1865. He signed a parole at Headquarters of the 16th U.S. Army Corps at Montgomery, Alabama, on June 19, 1865. He was described as 5 foot 8 inches in height, hair-light, eyes-hazel, complexion-fair. His parole is in his file. There is a card probably filed in error for **R. Watson**, Pvt. Co. A. 1st Alabama Battery as having been listed on a register of General Hospital, Howard's Grove, Richmond, Virginia, on February 22, 1865. This man was transferred to Farmville on April 1, 1865.*

Watts, H. C. see Witt, H. C.

Watts, J. C., Pvt. Co. I.
Enlisted on February 22, 1864, at Halls Mills, Alabama, by Captain Amos for the war. He is shown present on two muster rolls for December 31, 1863, through June 1864.

Weatherford, C., Pvt./Corp. Co. F.
Enlisted on October 1, 1862, at Shell Banks, Alabama, by Captain Barlow for three years or the war. Company muster rolls from September 1863, through June 1864, report him present. Drew clothing on August 24, 1864. There is a letter in his file to be given to a soldier at the time of his discharge. The letter is dated 24th day of May 1862. He is shown as having enlisted as a private in Captain John H. Marshall's Independent Command of Alabama at Bayou La Batre, (Mobile Dragoons) on April 5, 1862, by Captain Boyles to serve one year. C. Weatherford is described as being a farmer born in Monroe County, 5 foot 2 inches tall, dark complexion, black hair, black eyes. He is entitled to a discharge due to pulmonary hemorrhage * [This man is related to **Red Eagle** aka **William Weatherford**]

Weaver, C. E., Pvt. Co. I.
Enlisted on April 5, 1863, at Conecuh County, Alabama, by Captain Amos for the war.

Company muster rolls or September/October 1863, report him absent without leave. November/December 1863, roll reports him as having deserted.

Weaver, G. L., Pvt. Co. I.
Enlisted on March 5, 1863, at Conecuh County, Alabama, by Captain Amos for the war. Company muster rolls for September/October 1863, report him sick at home. November/December 1864, roll reports him dead.

Weaver, J. C., Pvt. Co. K.
Enlisted March 17, 1862, at Washington County, Alabama, by Lt. Cooper for the war. Company muster rolls from September 1863, through June 1864, report him present and at times on extra duty, detached as a teamster. Drew clothing on June 10, 1864. POW surrendered by Lt. General R. Taylor CSA to Major General E. R. S. Canby at Citronelle, Alabama, on May 4, 1865. Paroled at Gainesville, Alabama, on May 14, 1865. His residence is shown as Lawrence County, Tennessee

Webb, Richmond, Pvt. Co. I.
Enlisted on February 11, 1863, at Conecuh County, Alabama, by Captain Amos for the war. Company muster roll for September 12, 1863, reports him sick in quarters. September/October 1863, roll reports him present. November/December 1863, he is shown absent with leave on 30 day furlough. From December 1863, through June 1864, rolls show him present. On June 3, 1865, he signs an Amnesty Oath declaring; "I am 44 years of age, my home is in Conecuh Co. Ala., I volunteered in Co. I 15th Confedt. Cav. Feby. 16, 1862, and served until Feby. 1, 1865, at which time I deserted. I have taken no further part in the existing rebellion." His declaration and his oath is in his file.*

Wedgin, G. see Widgeon, George

Weekley, C. see Weekly Charles

Weekley, J. B., Pvt.Co. C.
Enlisted on October 31, 186?, at Camp Powell by Captain Barlow for three years or the war. All muster rolls from September 12, 1863, through December 1863, report him absent without leave.

Weekley, Thomas, Pvt. Co. I.
Enlisted on October 4, 1862, at Santa Rosa, Florida, by Captain Amos for the war. Company muster roll for September/October 1863, report him without a horse and on extra duty as a teamster. November/December 1863, muster roll shows him dead.

Weekley, W. B., Pvt./Corp. Co. C.
Enlisted on April 15, 1862, at Stockton, Alabama, by Captain Barlow for three years. Company muster rolls from September 1863, through June 1864, report him present. Drew clothing on August 28, 1864. POW captured near Blakeley on April 7, 1865. His name appears on a roll of POW's forwarded from Fort Gaines, Alabama, to Ship Island, Mississippi, on April 11, 1865. His name appears on a register of POW's confined at New Orleans, Louisiana, on April 13, 1865. He was exchanged on May 11, 1865.

Weekley, W. E., Pvt. Co. C.
Enlisted on October 31, 186?, at CampPowell by Captain Barlow for three years or the war. Company muster rolls from September 12 to December 31, 1863, report him absent without

leave. His name appears on a register of Ross Hospital, Mobile, Alabama, admitted on June 19, 1864, with dysenteria. Died June 28, 1864. A prisoner of the Camp of Correction.

Weekly, Charles, Pvt. Co. C.
Enlisted on October 31, 1862, at Camp Powell by Captain Barlow for three years or the war. Company muster rolls from September 12, 1863, through June 1864, report him present. Drew clothing on August 28, 1864. Admitted to Ross Hospital, Mobile, Alabama, on October 19, 1863, with intermitten fever.

Weekly, J. B. see Weekley, J. B.

Weekly, Thomas see Weekley, Thomas

Weekly, W. B. see Weekley, W. B.

Weitzel, Charles see Wetzel, Charles

Wells, J. I., Pvt. Co. K.
Enlisted on September 5, 1862, at Camp Forney by Captain White for the war. On company muster rolls from September 1863, through June 1864, he is reported as present, absent, on furlough, absent, detached and finally shown present. POW surrendered by Lt. General R. Taylor CSA to Major General E. R. S. Canby at Citronelle, Alabama, on May 4, 1865. Paroled at Mobile, Alabama, on May 23, 1865. His residence is shown as Jackson County, Mississippi.

Wells, John I. see Wells, J. I.

Wentzel, Robert, Pvt. Co. G.
Enlisted on September 12, 1862, at Dragoon Camp by J. H. Marshall for July 30, 1864, or the war. Muster roll for September 12, 1863, reports him absent on detached service. Muster rolls from September 1863, through April 1864, report him present. Drew clothing on June 20, 1864. Signed by his mark. His name appears on a roll of privates on extra duty as a courier during August 1864.

West, G. W., Pvt. Co. E.
Enlisted on October 3, 1862, at Camp Lomax by Captain N. R. Leigh for three years. Company muster rolls for September/October 1863, report him present and without a horse since August 12, 1863. November/December 1863, muster roll reports that he was transferred and exchanged with Sergeant W. D. Rodgers of Co. F, 1st Florida Regiment Infantry. Admitted to Ross Hospital, Mobile, Alabama, on October 19, 1863, with debility. Returned to duty on October 20.

Westbrook, James, Pvt. Co. H.
Enlisted on September 4, 1862, at Mobile, Alabama, by Lt. Cooper for the war. Muster roll for September/October 1863, report him absent on furlough, thereafter from November 1863, through June 1864, he is reported present. Admitted to Ross Hospital, Mobile, Alabama, on January 9, 1864, with intermitten fever. Returned to duty on January 14, 1864. Admitted again to Ross Hospital on February 20, 1864, with remtten fever. Returned to duty on February 29, 1864. Once again he was admitted to Ross Hospital with hemorrhoids on July 17, 1864. Furloughed on July 29, 1864, for 15 days. Admitted to Ross Hospital on August 22, 1864, with enteritis. Returned to duty November 8, 1864. POW surrendered by Lt. General R. Taylor CSA to Major General E. R. S. Canby at Citronelle, Alabama, on May 4,

1865. Paroled at Meridian, Mississippi, May 14, 1865. His residence is shown as Marengo County, Alabama.

Wetzel, Charles, Pvt. Co. G.
Enlisted on April 12, 1862, at Dragoon Camp by J. H. Marshall for July 30, 1864, or the war. Company muster rolls from September 12, 1863, through April 1864, report him absent, detached to work on the gun boats.

Wheeler, J. H., Corp./Pvt. Co. C.
Enlisted on April 16, 1863, at Blakeley, Alabama, by Captain Barlow for three years or the war. Company muster rolls from September 1863, through June 1864, report him present. His name appears on a roll of deserters forwarded from Dauphin Island, Alabama to New Orleans, Louisiana on March 25, 1865. "The above named soldier deserted from the Confederate service, escaped from Mobile in an open boat, and gave himself up to Federal authorities at Dauphin Island, Ala." His name also appears on a list of POW's captured, deserted from the CSA that entered the Military lines of the 16th U.S. Army Corps during March 1865. "Captured at his own house near Danby's Mills, Alabama. Sent to Provost Marshal Army and Division West Miss., March 24, 1865." He was released at New Orleans upon taking the Oath on May 8, 1865. "Deserter, came into the lines at Fish River, Ala. March 21, 1865, Took the Oath of Allegiance on March 27, 1865." Residence- Morgan County, Alabama, eyes-blue, complexion-dark, hair-dark, 6 foot ½ inch.

Wheeler John H. see Wheeler J. H.

Whidden, W. B. see Whiddon, W. R.

Whiddon, William R. see Whiddon W. R.

Whiddon, W. R., Pvt. Co. A.
Enlisted on May 1, 1862, at Tallahassee, Florida, by Captain Partridge for three years. Company muster rolls from September 1863, through December 1863, report him present and present on extra duty as a teamster. March/April muster roll reports him absent on 60 days sick leave from March 15, 1864. Arm fractured on duty as a teamster. May/June 1864, muster he is shown present. His name appears on a list of POW's surrendered at Tallahassee, Florida, on May 10, 1865, by Major General Sam Jones CSA to Brigadier General E. M. McCook USV. Paroled at Madison, Florida, on May 19, 1865.

Whigham, T. G., Pvt. Co. K.
Enlisted on March 17, 1862, at Washington County, Alabama, by Lt. Cooper for the war. Company muster roll for September/October 1864, report him present. Thereafter he is shown on muster rolls through June 1864, sometimes present or sometimes absent but detached on extra duty as a teamster. Drew clothing on June 26, 1864, at Pollard and September 10, 1864, with no location given.

Whittey, John, Pvt. Co. F.
His name appears on a roll of POW's surrendered by Lt. General R. Taylor CSA to Major General E. R. S. Canby at Citronelle, Alabama, on May 4, 1865. He was paroled at Gainesville, Alabama, on May 14, 1865. His residence is shown as Mobile, Mobile County, Alabama.

Whitbe, T. W. see Whitbee, Thomas

15TH CONFEDERATE CAVALRY

Whitbee, Thomas, Pvt. Co. C.
Enlisted on April 15, 1862, at Stockton, Alabama, by Captain T. C. Barlow for three years. Company muster rolls for September 1864, through June 1864, report him absent on detached service as per Special Order No. 11, Headquarters Department of Gulf and Mobile, and Colonel H. Maury, August 24, 1863. Drew clothing on June 14, 1864, at Pollard, Alabama, and August 28, 1864, no location given. POW surrendered by Lt. General R. Taylor CSA to Major General E. R. S. Canby at Citronelle, Alabama, on May 4, 1865. Paroled at Gainesville, Alabama, on May 14, 1865. His residence is shown as Baldwin County, Alabama. There is some paperwork in his file.*

White, Alfred, Pvt. Co. K.
Enlisted on July 13, 1863, at Halls Mills, Alabama, by Captain McKellar for the war. Company muster roll for September/October 1863, reports him present. November/December muster 1864, reports him absent on detached service. January 1864, through April 1864, he is shown as present and the May/June 1864, muster roll reports him absent sick in General Hospital in Mobile, Alabama. He appears on a descriptive list for pay and clothing at Halls Mills on September 12, 1863. Age-19, eyes-blue, hair-light, complexion-dark, 5 foot 6 inches, born-Mobile, Alabama, a teamster by occupation. Admitted to Ross Hospital, Mobile, Alabama, with scabies on November 17, 1863, sent to General Hospital, Spring Hill, on December 3, 1863. Admitted again to Ross Hospital on June 28, 1864, with hypertrophy of the heart. Returned to duty on July 7. He was admitted once again to Ross Hospital on November 29, 1864, with febris remittens and sent to General Hospital Heustis on November 30. Drew clothing on August 28, 1864. POW surrendered by Lt. General R. Taylor CSA to Major General E. R. S. Canby at Citronelle, Alabama, on May 4, 1865. Paroled at Gainesville, Alabama, on May 14, 1865. His residence is shown as Baldwin County, Alabama.

White, Andrew, Pvt. Co. E.
Enlisted on November 5, 1861, at Camp Perdido, Florida by Captain Amos for three years. Company muster roll for September 12, 1863, reports him present. Roll for September/October 1863, reports him absent sick at Hospital in Mobile, Alabama. November/December 1864, reports him absent without leave. No roll on file for him from January 1864, through April 1864. Muster rolls from March through June 1864, report him present. Drew clothing on September 2, 1864.

White, Charles A., Pvt. Co. B.
Enlisted on February 13, 1863, at Marianna, Florida, by Lt C. W. Davis for three years or the war. Company muster roll for September 12, 1863, reports him present. September 1863, through December 1863, muster rolls reports him absent sick since September 16, 1863. Admitted to Ross Hospital, Mobile, Alabama, on September 22, 1863, with acute diarrhoea. Returned to duty on November 1, 1863. January/February 1864, muster roll does not state his presence of absence. March/April 1864, he is again absent sick. Admitted to Ross Hospital, Mobile on March 11, 1864, with gonorrhea. Returned to duty on March 18, 1864. Admitted again to Ross Hospital on March 30, 1864, with same complaint. Returned to duty May 3, 1864. May/June 1864, roll reports him present. His name appears on a list of POW's surrendered at Tallahassee, Florida, on May 10, 1865, by Major General Sam Jones CSA to Brigadier General E. M. McCook USV. He was paroled at Quincy, Florida, on May 22, 1865.

White, Drury, Pvt. Co. D.
Enlisted on October 5, 1862, at Camp Tatnall by Captain Vaughn for three years. Company muster rolls from September 1863, through June 1864, report him present, on scout, absent

without leave, absent without leave for 20 days, on special duty near Bluff Springs, and absent without leave for 35 days.

White, James, Captain Company K.
Enlisted on March 17, 1862. Elected Captain on March 17, 1862. Rate of pay was $160 per month. There are a number of requisitions in his file for a variety of items such as; horse shoes, nails, tents, rasp, sledge hammer, claw hammer, well bucket, 40 foot of rope, tent poles, cartridge boxes, cap pouches, haversacks, canteen straps, gun slings, packing boxes, 33 saddles, curry combs, bridles and halters, 24 saddle blankets. In December 1, 1862, he submitted a letter of resignation as commander or White's Cavalry a Independent Company attached temporarily to Major Boyles Battalion Partisan Rangers. He states that he is 49 years old and weighs 230 pounds and "not able to perform active service on horseback nor could I on foot. I have a large plantation & own forty slaves." The letter with endorsements is in his file.***

White, J. A., Pvt. Co. K.
Enlisted on November 17, 1862, at Halls, Mills, Alabama, by Captain White for the war. Company muster rolls for September/October 1863, report him present. November 1863, through April 30, 1864, he is shown absent sick. May/June muster roll reports him present. He was reported to have drawn clothing on August 28, 1864. POW surrendered by Lt. General R. Taylor CSA to Major General E. R. S. Canby at Citronelle, Alabama, on May 4, 1865. He was paroled at Gainesville, Alabama, on May 14, 1865. His residence is shown as Fayette County, Texas.

White, Joseph, Pvt. Co. D.
Enlisted on April 24, 1862, at Pensacola, Florida, by Captain Vaughn for three years. September 12, 1864, company muster roll reports him present. September/October 1864, the muster roll shows him absent sick at hospital. November/December roll shows him absent without leave. Muster rolls for January through June 1864, he is reported present, absent without leave for 16 days since last pay. Drew clothing on August 28, 1864. He signed by his mark.

White, Thomas, M., Pvt/Corp. Co. B.
Enlisted on March 14, 1862, at Marianna Florida, by Colonel J. J. Finley for three years or the war. Company muster rolls from September 1863, through June 1864, he is reported present. Promoted to 4th Corporal on November 1, 1863. Drew clothing on September 10, 1864. His name appears on a list of POW's surrendered at Tallahassee, Florida, on May 11, 1865, by Major General Sam Jones CSA to Brigadier General E. M. McCook USV. Paroled at Quincy, Florida, on May 22, 1865.

Whitey, William, Pvt. Co. D.
Drew clothing on August 22, 1864. He signed a Parole of Honor at the Headquarters of the 16th U.S. Army Corps. at Montgomery, Alabama, on June 1, 1865. He is described as 5 foot 10 inches, hair-dark, eyes-blue, complexion-fair. His parole is in his file.*

Whitley, W. B. see Whitey, William

Whitmire, William A., Pvt. Co. E.
Enlisted on September 17, 1861, at Milton, Florida, by Captain Amos for three years. Company muster roll for September 17, 1863, reports him present and without horse since August 1, 1863. September/October 1863, muster roll reports him sick at hospital in Mobile, Alabama. November/December he is shown present. Transferred to Captain Keyser's

15TH CONFEDERATE CAVALRY

Company I, 6th Alabama Regiment Cavalry on February 1, 1864, in exchange for **G. B. Hinote**. There is paper work in Pvt. Whitmire's file.*

Whittey. M. B. see Whitey, William

Widgeon, George, Pvt. Co. B.
Enlisted on March 14, 1862, at Marianna, Florida, by Colonel J. J. Finley for three years or the war. Company muster rolls from September 1863, through June 1864, report him present. Drew clothing on September 10, 1864. His name appears on a list of POW's surrendered at Tallahassee, Florida, on May 10, 1865, by Major General Sam Jones CSA to Brigadier General E. M. McCook USV. Paroled at Quincy, Florida, on May 22, 1865.

Wiggins, G. W., Pvt. Co. E.
Enlisted on September 17, 1861, at Milton, Florida, by Captain Amos for three years. Company muster rolls from September 1863, through June 1864, report him present. Drew clothing on September 2, 1864.

Wilkerson, Daniel see Wilkinson, Daniel

Wilkerson, Henry, Pvt. Co. I.
Enlisted on October 4, 1862, at Santa Rosa, Florida by Captain Amos for the war. Company muster roll from September 1863, through June 1864, report him present. On the fist muster he is shown present but sick in quarters.

Wilkins, C. E., Pvt. Co. C.
Enlisted on April 26, 1864, at Camp Powell by Captain Barlow for the war. Company muster roll for December 31, 1863, through June 1864, reports him present and had not been paid. Drew clothing on August 28, 1864. POW surrendered by Lt. General R. Taylor CSA to Major General E. R. S. Canby at Citronelle, Alabama, on May 4, 1865. He was paroled at Gainesville, Alabama, May 14, 1865. His residence shown as Baldwin County, Alabama.

Wilkins, C. F., Pvt. Co. C.
Enlisted on June 2, 1864, at Camp Powell by Captain Barlow for three years. Company muster roll for December 31, 1863, through June 1864, reports him present and had not been paid. Drew clothing on August 28, 1864. POW surrendered by Lt. General R. Taylor CSA to Major General E. R. S. Canby at Citronelle, Alabama, on May 4, 1865. Paroled at Gainesville, Alabama, on May 14, 1865. His residence shown as Mobile County, Alabama.

Wilkins, Charles see Wilkins, C. E.

Wilkins, Charles E. Pvt. Co. H.
Enlisted on September 4, 1862, at Mobile, Alabama, by Lt. Cooper for the war. Company muster rolls from September 1863, through June 1864, report him present. Drew clothing on September 7, 1864.

Wilkins, J. W., Pvt. Co. C.
Enlisted on April 12, 186?, at Stockton, Alabama by Captain Barlow for three years or the war. He is shown present on September 12, 1863, muster roll. Admitted to Ross Hospital, Mobile, Alabama, on October 15, 1863, with remitten fever and was furloughed for 20 days on October 20. It was reported that he died on November 5, 1863.

Wilkinson, David, Sergeant Co. D.
Enlisted on April 24, 1862, at Pensacola, Florida, by Captain Vaughn for three years. Muster rolls in September 1863, report him on extra duty since August 26, 1863, by order of General Clanton. November/December 1863, roll shows him absent without leave and thereafter he is reported as having deserted on December 20, 1863.

Wilkinson, Henry see Wilkerson, Henry

Williams, A. J., Pvt. Co. E.
His name appears on a receipt roll for clothing issued on September 2, 1864.

Williams, Albert, Pvt. Co. ?
His name appears on a register of POW's captured near Mobile, on December 18, 1864. Confined at New Orleans on December 25, 1864, transferred to Ship Island on January 22, 1865. He applied to take the Oath of Allegiance to the U.S. at Ship Island. Transferred to Vicksburg, Mississippi on May 1, 1865.

Williams, A. R., Pvt. Co. I.
Enlisted on January 22, 1864, at Halls Mills, Alabama, by W. B. Amos for the war. Company muster rolls for January through June 1864, report him present.

Williams, E. B., Pvt. Co. D.
Enlisted on June 3, 1864, at Milton, Florida, by Lt. Rice for three years. Company muster roll for May/June 1864, reports him present. He is shown as having drawn clothing on August 28, 1864.

Williams, J. B., Pvt. Co. I.
His name appears on a register of POW's surrendered at Citronelle, Alabama on May 4, 1865. Paroled at Mobile, Alabama, on June 16, 1865. Residence-Monroe County, Alabama, age-32, hair-dark, eyes-gray, complexion-dark, 6 foot 1 inch.

Williams, John, Pvt. Co. F.
Enlisted on January 17, 1862, at Camp Withers by Captain Cottrell for three years or the war. Muster rolls of September 12, 1863, initially show him present but he is reported to have been assigned to the Government Fishery on September 17, 1863, by order of General Maury. He was reported to have deserted on December 28, 1783. POW surrendered by Lt. General R. Taylor CSA to Major General E. R. S. Canby at Citronelle, Alabama, on May 4, 1865. Paroled at Gainesville, Alabama, on May 14, 1865. His residence is shown as Mobile, Mobile County, Alabama.

Williams, J. M., Sgt.
Replaced by substitute, see file of **Laurendine, J.** Pvt. Co. K.

Williams. J. W. see Williams Wilson

Williams, L. N., Pvt. Co. K.
Enlisted on April 10, 1862, at Mobile, by Lt. J. W. Cooper for the war. Company muster rolls from September through December 1863, report him absent detached. May/June 1864, muster roll shows him present. POW surrendered by Lt. General R. Taylor CSA to Major General E. R. S. Canby at Citronelle, Alabama, on May 4, 1865. Paroled at Gainesville, Alabama, on May 14, 1865. His residence is shown as Clarke County, Alabama. There is paper work in his file.*

Williams, Richard, Pvt. Co. G.
Enlisted on March 15, 1862, at Dragoon Camp by W. M. Boyles for July 30, 1864, or the war. Company muster rolls from September 12, 1863, through June 1864, report him present with one exception in September/October roll he is shown absent without leave. Drew clothing on June 20, 1864. POW surrendered by Lt. General R. Taylor CSA to Major General E. R. S. Canby at Citronelle, Alabama, on May 4, 1865. Paroled at Meridian, Mississippi, on May 11, 1865. His residence is shown as Oak Grove, Mississippi.

Williams, W.[William] L., Corporal Co. C.
Enlisted on May 12, 186?, at Stockton, Alabama, by Captain Barlow for three years or the war. Company muster roll for September 12, 1863, reports him present. Admitted to Ross Hospital, Mobile, Alabama, on October 16, 1863, with debility. Returned to duty on October 19, 1863. Muster rolls from September through December 1863, report him absent without leave.

Williams, James Wilson, Pvt. Co. D.
Enlisted on September 2, 1863, at Camp Ward by Captain Vaughn for three years. Muster roll for September 12, 1863, reports him present. September/October 1863, roll shows him absent sick in hospital at Mobile, Alabama. He was admitted to Ross Hospital, Mobile with debility on October 23, 1863. This roll shows that he enlisted on September 10, 1863, at Halls Mill, Alabama. November/December muster roll reports him present. He was discharged with a Surgical Certificate on January 23, 1863.

Williams, W. J. see Willliams Wilson

Williamson, A. C., Pvt./Sergeant Co. G.
Enlisted on July 30, 1861, at Mobile, by B. C. Yancey for July 30, 1864, or the war. Company muster rolls from September 1863, through April 1874, report him present or absent with leave. Drew clothing on June 20, and September 10, 1864. POW surrendered by Lt. General R. Taylor CSA to Major General E. R. S. Canby at Citronelle, Alabama, on May 4, 1865. Paroled at Gainesville, Alabama, on May 14, 1865. His residence is shown as Mobile, Mobile County, Alabama.

Williamson, Allen, Pvt. Co. E.
Enlisted on January 1, 1863, at Camp Lomax, Florida, by Captain N. R. Leigh for three years. Company muster rolls for September 1863, thorough June 1864, report him present, except the once he was absent sick at Spring Hill Hospital, Mobile, Alabama. POW captured at Escambia County, Florida, on November 17, 1864. His name appears on a register of POW's at New Orleans, Louisiana, confined on November 21, 1864, and transferred to Ship Island, Mississippi, on December 10, 1864. Transferred to Vicksburg, Mississippi, on May 1, 1865.

Williamson, F. A., Pvt. Co. G.
POW surrendered by Lt. General R. Taylor CSA to Major General E. R. S. Canby at Citronelle, Alabama, on May 4, 1865. Paroled at Gainesville, Alabama, on May 14, 1865. His residence is shown as Mobile, Mobile County, Alabama.

Williamson, G. W., Pvt. Co. K.
Enlisted on March 17, 1862, at Washington County, Alabama, by Lt. Cooper for the war. Company muster roll for September/October 1863, reports him present. On November/December 1863, muster roll he is shown absent sick. May/June 1864, he is shown absent without leave. POW surrendered by Lt. General R. Taylor CSA to Major General E. R. S.

Canby at Citronelle, Alabama, on May 4, 1865. Paroled at Gainesville, Alabama, on May 14, 1865. His residence is shown as Choctaw County, Alabama.

Williamson, Wiley R., Pvt. Co. E.
Enlisted on December 1, 1862, at Camp Lomax, Florida, by Captain N. R. Leigh for three years. Company muster rolls from September 12, 1863, report him present but September through December 1863, he is reported absent on sick furlough. March 1864, through June 1864, he is present on the roll. Drew clothing on September 2, 1864.

Willis, E., Blacksmith Co. C.
Enlisted on February 22, 1863, at Camp Powell by Captain T. C. Barlow for three years. He is reported present on all company muster rolls from September 1863, through June 1864.

Willis, Julius, Pvt. Co. G.
Enlisted on April 18, 1863, at Camp Taylor by J. H. Marshall for July 30, 1863, or the war. First muster roll on September 12, 1863, reports him absent on detached service. He is reported present on all other rolls through April 1864. Drew clothing on June 20 and September 20, 1864.

Wilson, A. H., Pvt. Co. I.
Enlisted on October 4, 1862, at Santa Rosa, Florida, by Captain Amos for the war. Company muster roll for September/October 1863, reports him present and having a horse since October 5. November/December 1863, he is shown absent with 40 day furlough. He is reported present on rolls from January to June 1864. He signed a parole at the Headquarters of the 16th U.S. Army Corps in Montgomery, Alabama, on June 20, 1864. He is described as 5 foot 11 inches tall, hair-dark, eyes-black, complexion-dark. His parole is in his file.*

Wilson, Albert F., Pvt. Co. H.
Enlisted on June 1, 1862, at Mobile, Alabama, by Captain McLomstry for the war. First company muster roll on September 12, 1863, reports him on detached service by order of General Maury since June 31, 1863. September/October 1863, muster roll indicated he was transferred to Captain Seldon's Battery by order of General Maury.

Wilson, H., Pvt. Co. E.
His name appears on a receipt roll for clothing on September 2, 1864.

Wilson, Isaac, Pvt. Co. I
Enlisted on October 4, 186?, at Santa Rosa, Florida, by Captain Amos for the war. He died at home in Pollard, Alabama, on August 22 of typhoid fever.

Wilson, John P., Pvt. Co. B.
Enlisted on March 14, 1862, at Marianna, Florida, by Colonel J. J. Finley for three years or the war. Company muster rolls from September 1863, through June 1864, report him present except March/April 1864, he was absent sick. Drew clothing on September 10, 1864.

Winningham, James H., Pvt. Co. H.
Enlisted on March 13, 1863, at Livingston, Alabama, by Colonel Coleman for the war. Company muster rolls from September 1863, through April 1864, report him present. He was admitted to Ross Hospital, Mobile, Alabama, on October 23, 1863, with onanism. Returned to duty on October 25. There is a duplicate muster roll for January through June 1864, which reports him absent, detached by order of General Maury. A information card in his file indicates that General Order No. 36 on June 15, 1864, ordered him to report to **W.**

15TH CONFEDERATE CAVALRY

H. Pritchard, Superintendent of the Alabama, and Mississippi Railroad. POW surrendered by Lt. General R. Taylor CSA to Major General E. R. S. Canby at Citronelle, Alabama, on May 4, 1865. Paroled at Mobile, Alabama, on May 23, 1865. His residence is shown as Autauga, County, Alabama.

Wise, Hezekiah, Pvt. Co. I.
Enlisted on October 4, 1862, at Santa Rosa, Florida, by Captain Amos, for the war. Company muster roll for September 12, 1863, reports him absent without leave since July 5. September/October 1863, muster roll shows him absent in arrest. November/December 1863, muster roll reports him absent without leave since December 29, 1863. From December 31, 1863, thorough June 1864, he is reported present but without a horse.

Witt, H. C., Pvt. Co. D & E.
Enlisted on November 10, 1862, at Camp Tatnall by Captain Vaughn for three years. Most muster rolls from September 1863, through June 1864, show him on scout, on detached service at Mobile, Alabama, on detached service with Engineering Dept., Mobile, or on special duty as a courier at Pollard towards Mobile. He was paid $3 per day extra as a overseer during December 1863 and January 1864. He signed by his mark. His name appears among a roll of POW stragglers surrendered by Lt. General R. Taylor CSA to Major General E. R. S. Canby at Citronelle, Alabama, on May 4, 1865. Paroled at Selma, Alabama, on May 28, 1865. His residence is shown as Butler County, Alabama.

Woodcock, T. S., Pvt. Co. G.
Enlisted on February 6, 1862, at Dragoon Camp by Willliam Boyles for July 30, 1864, or the war. Company muster roll of September 12, 1863, reports him present. September/October 1863, muster he is shown absent sick. Admitted to Ross Hospital, Mobile, Alabama, on November 23, 1863, with scabies. Returned to duty on December 14, 1863. From November 1863 through April 1864, muster he is reported absent without leave. Admitted to Ross Hospital in Mobile on June 2, 1864, with scabies. Sent to General Hospital Spring Hill on June 20, 1864. Drew clothing on September 4, 1864. POW captured at Little Escambia River, Florida, (near Pollard, Alabama) on December 17, 1864. His name appears on a register of POW's at New Orleans, Louisiana, confined on December 27, 1864. Transferred to Ship Island, Mississippi, on January 22, 1865. Transferred to Vicksburg, Mississippi, on May 1, 1865. Admitted to USA General Hospital No. 2, at Vicksburg on May 6, 1865, with acute diarrhoea. Admitted from steamer. Returned to duty [prison] on May 9, 1865. Age 23.

Wolker, A. H. see Walker, W. A.

Woods, M., Pvt. Co. C.
Enlisted on April 15, 1862, at Stockton, Alabama, by Captain T. C. Barlow for three years. Company muster rolls from September 1863, through June 1864, report him present except in November/December 1863, when he is shown absent without leave. John Woods, Pvt. Co. C was admitted to Ross Hospital in Mobile, Alabama, on September 4, 1864, with chronic rheumatism. Returned to duty on September 5, 1864. Drew clothing on August 28, 1864.

Wooley, James, Pvt. Co. G.
Enlisted on September 12, 1863, at Dragoon Camp by J. H. Marshall for July 30, 1864, or the war. Company muster rolls for September 1863, through April 1864, report him present and sometimes detailed as a ambulance driver. Drew clothing on June 20, 1864, at Pollard, Alabama. Signed by "x".

Wragg, John T., Pvt. Co. H.
Enlisted on September 2, 1862, at Mobile, Alabama. by Lt. Cooper for the war. Muster rolls for September/October 1864, report him absent detached by order of General Buckner on January 1863. November/December 1863, muster shows him detached by reason of physical disability by order of General Maury.

Wynn, C. B. see Wynns, Colbert

Wynns, Colbert, Pvt. Co. B.
Enlisted on September 12, 1862, at Marianna, Florida, by Colonel J. J. Finley for three years or the war. Company muster roll for September 12, 1863, reports him absent detached for Provost Duty by order of General Maury on June 17. Muster rolls from September 1863, through April 1864, report him present. On May/June 1864, roll he is shown absent on furlough. Drew clothing on September 12, 1864. His name appears on a list of POW's surrendered at Tallahassee, Florida, on May 11, 1865, by Major General Sam Jones CSA to Brigadier General E. M. McCook USV. Paroled at Quincy, Florida, on May 22, 1865.

Y

Yarborough, George S., Trumpeter/Pvt. Co. B.
Enlisted on March 14, 1862, at Marianna, Florida, by Colonel J. J. Finley for three years or the war. Company muster rolls from September 1863, through June 1864, report him present. Drew clothing on September 10, 1864. His name appears on a roll of POW's captured near Mount Pleasant, Alabama, on April 11, 1865.

Yarborough, Green, B., Pvt. Co. B.
Enlisted on August 16, 1862, at Marianna, Florida, by Captain Smith for three years or the war. Company muster rolls from September 1863, through June 1864, report him present. Drew clothing on September 10, 1864. His name appears on a roll of POW's captured at Clairborne, Alabama, on April 12, 1865.

Yarborough, John M., Pvt. Co. B.
Enlisted on May 3, 1862, at Marianna, Florida, by Captain McVoy. for three years or the war. Company muster rolls from September 1863, through June 1864, report him present, except December 1863, he is show absent sick since December 29, 1863. Drew clothing on September 10, 1864. His name appears on a roll of POW's surrendered at Tallahassee, Florida, on May 11, 1865, by Major General Sam Jones CSA to Brigadier General E. M. McCook USV. Paroled at Quincy, Florida, on May 22, 1865.

Yarborough, William H., Pvt. Co. B.
Enlisted on April 7, 1862, at Marianna, Florida, by Captain J. J. Fenley for three years or the war. Company muster rolls from September 1863, through June 1864, report him present. Drew clothing on September 10, 1864. His name appears on a roll of POW's surrendered at Tallahassee, Florida, on May 11, 1865, by Major General Sam Jones CSA to Brigadier General E. M. McCook USV. Paroled at Quincy, Florida, on May 22, 1865.

Yarbrough, George S. see Yarborough, George S.

Yarbrough, Green B. see Yarborough, Green B.

Yarbrough, John M. see Yarborough, John M.

15TH CONFEDERATE CAVALRY

Yarbrough, T. M. see Yarborough, John M.

Yarbrough, William H. see Yarborough William H.

Yeldell, John P., Pvt. Co. B.
Enlisted on March 10, 1864, at Greenville, Alabama, by Colonel Murphy for the war. Company muster rolls from March through June 1864, report him present. Drew clothing on September 10, 1864. His name appears among a roll of POW stragglers surrendered by Lt. General R. Taylor CSA to Major General E. R. S. Canby at Citronelle, Alabama, on May 4, 1865. Paroled at Selma, Alabama, on May 28, 1865. His residence is shown as Butler County, Alabama.

Yeldell, Robert A., Pvt. Co. B.
Enlisted on January 26, 1864, at Greenville, Alabama, by Colonel Murphy for the war. March/April 1864, muster roll shows him absent on extra duty. May/June 1864, muster reports him present.

Yeldell, William, A., Pvt. Co. B.
Enlisted on January 26, 1864, at Greenville, Alabama, by Colonel Murphy for the war. His name appears as present on a hospital muster roll at General Hospital, Greenville, Alabama, for March 1 to August 31, 1864. March/April 1864, company muster roll shows him absent sick. May/June 1864, muster reports him present. His name appears among a roll of POW stragglers surrendered by Lt. General R. Taylor CSA to Major General E. R. S. Canby at Citronelle, Alabama, on May 4, 1865. Paroled at Selma, Alabama, on May 28, 1865. His residence is shown as Butler County, Alabama.

Yeldell, W. R., Pvt. Co. B.
His name appears among a roll of POW stragglers surrendered by Lt. General R. Taylor CSA to Major General E. R. S. Canby at Citronelle, Alabama, on May 4, 1865. He was paroled at Selma, Alabama, on May 28, 1865. His residence is shown as Butler County, Alabama.

Yourbrough, W. H. see Yarborough, William H.

Z

Ziteron, A. M., Pvt. Co. K.
Enlisted on March 17, 1862, at Washington County, Alabama, by Lt. Cooper for the war. Company muster rolls from September 1863, through December 1863, report him absent sick. Muster rolls from January through June 1864, he is reported present. Drew clothing on August 28, 1864. POW surrendered by Lt. General R. Taylor CSA to Major General E. R. S. Canby at Citronelle, Alabama, on May 4, 1865. Paroled at Gainesville, Alabama, on May 14, 1865. His residence is shown as Choctaw County, Alabama.

Ziteron, G. W., Pvt. Co. K.
Enlisted on March 17, 1862, at Washington County, Alabama, by Lt. Cooper for the war. Company muster rolls from September 1863, through December 1863, report him absent on detached service. Admitted to Ross Hospital, Mobile, Alabama, on October 7, 1864, with acute diarrhoea. Furloughed on October 8, for 20 days. Muster rolls from January through April 1864, he is reported absent on furlough. May/June 1864, muster he is present. Drew clothing on August 28, 1864. POW surrendered by Lt. General R. Taylor CSA to Major General E. R. S. Canby at Citronelle, Alabama, on May 4, 1865. Paroled at Gainesville,

Alabama, on May 14, 1865. His residence is shown as Choctaw County, Alabama. There is some paper work in his file.*

Ziterow. G. W. see Ziteron, G. W.

Ziterrow, G. see Ziteron G. W.

Zitterrow. A. see Ziteron A. M.

15TH CONFEDERATE CAVALRY

APPENDIX

ORGANIZATION OF 15TH ALABAMA CAVALRY CSA
Data taken from National Archives and Records Administration 16mm microfilm, file 258 rolls 29, 30, 31, 32 and 33.

The Organization of 15th Confederate Cavalry (1st Regiment Alabama and Florida Cavalry) was completed in September 1863, by the consolidation of Murphy's Battalion Alabama Cavalry, the 3d Battalion Florida Cavalry, Captain Arrington's and Barlow's Companies Alabama Cavalry and Captain Smith's Company Florida Cavalry.

Field and Staff

Harry Maury, Colonel Commanding
Thomas J. Myers, Lt. Colonel

Company **A** 15th Confederate Cavalry (formerly Co. A 3rd Battalion Florida Cavalry.
Partridge Roth H.   Captain
Triplett Thomas H.   1st Lt.
Ulmer, John   2nd Lt.
Dawkins, James R.   2nd Lt.
Grantham, J. P.
Taylor, F. L.

Company **B**
Smith, Richard L.   Captain
Davis, John T.   2nd Lt.
Davis, Charles W.   2nd Lt.
Pittman, Robert J.   1st Lt.
Edwards, A.
Roulham, James B.   1st Lt.
Westman, James L.   C. Serg.

Company **C**
Barlow, T. C.   Captain
Sibley, Origan Jr.   1st Lt.
McDavid, R. M.   2nd Lt.
Sibley, A. O.   2nd Lt.

Company **D**
Vaughn, J. B.   Captain
German, John   1st Lt.
Rice, W. P.   2nd Lt.
Turner, R. H.
Morgan, W. A.   2nd Lt.

Company **E**
Leigh, N. R.   Captain
Feagin, A. P.   1st Lt.
Perrinot, George F.   2nd Lt.
Townsend, Wm.   2nd Lt.

Company **F**
Cottrill, Wm.	Captain
Elisworth, George	1st Lt.
Hall, Fred	2nd Lt.
Stone, John	2nd Lt.
Arrington, Edward T.	Captain
Hindman, Thomas	1st Lt.
Pierce, E. W.	2nd Lt.
Holland, Wm. T.	2nd Lt.
Grey, S. P.	

Company **G**
Hagan, James	Captain
Barnewell, Wm. Jr.	1st Lt.
Myera, Henry	2nd Lt.
Perryman, E. S.	2nd Lt.
Boyles, Wm.	Captain
Martin, Wm.	2nd Lt.
Billinglea, J. C.	1st Lt.
Hallett, L. J.	2nd, 1st Lt.
Hill, T. J.	2nd Lt.
Gaggam, George, G.	2nd Lt.
Harris, F. J.	

Company **I**
Amos, W. B.	Captain
Gates, E. S. L.	1st Lt.
Greene, W. W.	2nd Lt.
Gordon, F. M.	2nd Lt.
McCaskill, W. C.	
Stein, I.	

Company **K**
White, James	Captain
McWilliams, D.	Captain
Powers, R. A.	2nd Lt.
Worms, H. T.	2nd Lt.
Gray, Thomas, R.	2nd Lt.

ON THE FREE STATE OF JONES

Victoria E. Bynum in her book, *The Free State of Jones, Mississippi's Longsest Civil War* addresses the 15th Confederate Cavalry action of March 1864, as follows; [See page116 and Notes to Pages 116-118 on page 253-4.]

On February 7, 1864, Lieutenant General Polk advised Gen. Dabney H. Maury the "lawless banditti of Jones must "be dealt with in the most summary manner"and directed him to send the 15th Confederate Cavalry under the command of Colonel Harry Maury to attend to the problem. "Colonel Maury left Mobile for Jones County on March 2, 1864, and began his assault on deserters there three days later in a battle with the Knight Company at Big Creek Church." Colonel Maury commanded the Cavalry Regiment, a battalion of infantry and a section of artillery.

On March 17 Lieutenant General Polk reported to Gen. Samuel Cooper that Colonel Maury had succeeded in quashing the deserters of Jones County. Indeed, J. C. Andrews remembered a Saturday morning when he witnessed the execution of several deserters in Jones County. recalling several members of the Knight band "were all loaded on a wagon and driven to a large oak tree near Erratta [Errata] on the old St. Stephens Trade Road," he described how a detachment of Confederate cavalry tied the men to the tree limb, then ordered the wagon driven away, leaving the men's bodies swinging in the air. They hung there for days, said Andrews until their wives came and cut them down. Andrews identified the men as Mitchell, Blackledge and Smith. Other authors including Tom Knight, *The life and Activities of Captain Newton Knight and His Company and the "Free State of Jones."* and Ethel Knight *The echo of the black Horn* identify four men: Morge Mitchell, Jack Smith, Jesse Smith and Jack Arnal (Arnold).

See also OR, Vol. 32, pt II, pages 688-89, Vol. 32 pt I, page 499, Vol. 32 pt III, pages 711-12.

MOUNT PLEASANT

Mr. C. H. Dreisbach in his interview (see pages 13-14) with the *Mobile Register* gives a roster of English's Independent Cavalry Company as follows:
October 3, 1864. T. C. English, Captain- T. P. Atkinson, 1st Lt. - Jonathan English 2nd Lt.- Joseph Booth, 3rd Lt. - J. F. Boyles, 1st Sgt. - Joel Bullard, 2nd Sgt. - H. McKenzie, 3rd Sgt. - T. J. Booth, 4th Sgt. - John H. Fry, 5th Sgt. - James Earl, 1st Corp. - James Singleton - 2nd Corp. - Charles English - 3rd Corp. - T. R. Dean, 4th Corp.
Privates: W. W. Adams, M. Boyles, William Barr, W. J. Bayles, J. B. Belt, A. W. Bryant, John R. Coone. H. T. Crapps, T. J. Carter, H. Conway, Joseph Daniels, M. Deas, J. M. Dudley, W. M. Deas, J. Daily, C. H. Dreisbach, F. Earl, A. Feast, H. Fort. M. Ford, W. B. F. Green, W. Gibson, J. A. Griffin, John Greenwood Jr., J. Grissett, B. H. Harrison, C. H. Henderson, H. J. Hunt, John Hadley, B. F. Hardie, H. Jones, W. Kyle, T. H. Krouse, D. R. King, S. Lomax, J. J. Lock, Richard McGee, W. A. Matherson, S. Moniac, T. McCarthy, M. C. Middleton, R. H. Moon, E. T. Mosely, John A. Norwood, J. N. Powell, S. Rogers. R. J. Richardson, John W. Shomo, J. B. Steadham, S. H. Spencer, J. W. Stuggins, Joseph Stapleton, John Stapleton, R. Talbert, E. Thompson, C. Weatherford, A. McG. Weatherford, E. G. Wiggins, John L. White, John D. Weatherford, A. Boheman, O. P. Hall, Reuben Stapleton, Y. M. Dannelly.
Many of these men have names local to Baldwin County, Alabama and are included for that reason.

REFERENCES

Bergeron Jr., Arthur W. *Confederate Mobile,* University of Mississippi Press, Jackson, MS, 1991

Bynum, Victoria, E. *The Free State of Jones Mississippi's Longest Civil War*, The University of North Carolina Press, Chapel Hill, 2001.

Green, Arthur E. *Too Little Too Late - Compiled Service Records of the 63rd Alabama Infantry CSA*, Heritage Books Inc. Bowie, MD. 2001

Knight, Ethyl, *The Echo of the Black Horn*, The Maple-Vail Book Manufacturing Group, York, PA. 1951, reprint 2000.

Maury, Dabney Herndon, *The Recollections of a Virginian in the Mexican, Indian, and Civil Wars*: Electronic Edition http://docsouth.unc.edu/maury/maury.html

O. R. - *The War of the Rebellion a Compilation of the Official Reccords of the Union and Confederate Armies.* Government Printing Office 1880, Washington, DC.

Wheeler, Lt. Gen. Joseph, *Confederate Military Military History, Vol VIII, Alabama*, Confederate Publishing Company, 1899, reprint Broadfoot Publishing Co., Wilmington, NC, 1987.

Other books written by Arthur E. Green
Southerners at War - the 38th Alabama Infantry Volunteers. ISBN 1-57249-142 - 6
Gracie's Pride - the 43rd Alabama Infantry Volunteers. ISBN 1-57249-241- 4
Too Little Too Late - Compiled Military Service Records of the 63rd Alabama Infantry CSA with Rosters of Some Companies of the 89th, 94th and 95th Alabama Militia CSA. ISBN O-7884-1988-9

DOCUMENTS

No. 642

I, the undersigned, Prisoner of War, belonging to the Army of the Department of Alabama, Mississippi and East Louisiana, having been surrendered by Lieut. Gen. R. Taylor, C. S. A., Commanding said Department, to Maj. Gen. E. R. S. Canby, U. S. A., Commanding Army and Division of West Mississippi, do hereby give my solemn parole of honor, that I will not hereafter serve in the Armies of the Confederate States, or in any military capacity whatever, against the United States of America, or render aid to the enemies of the latter, until properly exchanged in such manner as shall be mutually approved by the respective authorities.

W. K. Cleveland
2d Lt Co H. 15th Confd Cav.

Done at Gainesville
this 14th day of May, 1865.

Approved   R. H. Jackson   Brig Genl C.S.A. (Commis'r)
           E. S. Dennis   Brig Genl U.S.A.

The above named officer will not be disturbed by United States authorities, as long as he observes his parole, and the laws in force where he resides.

E. S. Dennis
Brig. Gen. U. S. Vols.
and Prov. Mar. Gen.

[Form No. 5.]

The Confederate States,

To Pvt. R. Morris Ker, attached Discharged from Capt. Murrell's
Company 26 15th Regiment of Confederate Cavalry. DR.

	DOLLARS.	CTS.
Pay from 1st of May 1863 to 31st of October 1863 being 6 months, ... days, at Twelve dollars per month......	72	00
......pay as Com-g Horse 6 Mos at $12 p month	72	00
...... for traveling from ...... the place of my discharge		
to ...... the place of my enlistment, ... miles,		
at twenty miles per day, equal to ...... days, at ...... dollars per month.		
Subsistence for traveling as above ...... days, at ...... cents per ration or day..		
For Clothing not drawn		
Amount	144	00
...... for Army Asylum ...... $		
...... for Clothing overdrawn		
Balance Due	144	00

Received of Capt. A. McVay A.Q.M. Paymaster, Confederate States Army,
4th day of Nov 1863, One hundred & forty four dollars
...... cents, in full of the above account.

Pay 72.00

(Signed in Duplicate.)

Horse 72.00

Total ...... 144.00   R. Morris Ky

15TH CONFEDERATE CAVALRY

SPECIAL REQUISITION.—[No. 40]

1863
20th

For
- (102) One Hundred and two Jackets
- (104) One Hundred and four pairs Pants
- (110) One Hundred and ten Shirts
- (100) One Hundred pairs Drawers
- (100) One Hundred Caps
- (12) Twelve pairs Boots

I certify that the above requisition is correct, and that the articles specified are absolutely requisite for the public service, rendered so by the following circumstances: the clothing is much needed

W. B. Amos, Capt
Co. D

M. F. Gonzalez, Assistant Quartermaster C.S. Army, will issue the articles specified in the above requisition.

H. Maury, Col. Commanding

Received at Hall's Mills Ala. the 20th of Dec. 1863, of Capt. M. F. Gonzalez, A.Q.M.

C.S. Army 102 Jackets, 104 pairs pants, 110 Shirts, 100 pr Drawers, 100 Caps, 12 pr Boots. in full of the above requisition.

(Signed Duplicates)

W. B. Amos, Capt Co.
15 Confed Regiment

[No. 32.]

REQUISITION for Forage for Public Horses ______ in the service of Capt Amos Company I 15th Regiment Confed Cavalry C. S. Army, for thirty days, commencing the 1st of April 1864, and ending on the 30th of April 1864 at Pollard Ala.

Date of Requisition.	Number of Horses.	Number of Mules.	Number of Oxen.	Total No. of Animals.	Number of Days.	Number of Rations.	DAILY ALLOWANCE TO EACH ANIMAL. Pounds of Corn.	Pounds of Barley.	Pounds of Oats.	Pounds of Hay.	Pounds of Fodder.	TOTAL ALLOWANCE. Corn. Pounds of	Barley. Pounds of	Oats. Pounds of	Hay. Pounds of	Fodder. Pounds of	REMARKS.
April 1st 1864	101	—	—	101	30	3030	12	—	—	—	7	36360	—	—	—	21210	App'd. [illegible]
Required												36360	—	—	—	21210	
On hand to be deducted																	
To be supplied												36360	—	—	—	21210	

I CERTIFY, on honor, that the above Requisition is correct and just; and that I have now in service the number of Animals for which forage is required, and that forage has not been received for any part of the time specified.

W B Amos Capt Commanding Co I

Received at Pollard Ala the 1st of April 1864 of Capt W D Waples Quartermaster C. S. Army Thirty six thousand three hundred & sixty pounds of Corn, ______ pounds of Barley, ______ pounds of Oats, ______ pounds of Hay, and Twenty one thousand two hundred & ten pounds of Fodder, in full of the above Requisition.

(Signed in Duplicate)

W B Amos Capt Comdg
Co I 15th Confederate Regt Cavalry

ARMY OF THE CONFEDERATE STATES.

Certificate of Disability for Discharge.

Private _William Brunson_ of Captain _R L Smith_ Company _B_ of the _15 Confederate_ Regiment of Confederate States _Cavalry_ was enlisted by _Col J J Finley_ of the _6th Florida_ Regiment of _Ct Hunter_ at _Marianna Fla_ on the _14th_ day of _March_, 1862 to serve _Three_ years. He was born in _Edgefield_ in the State of _South Carolina_, is _Thirty (30)_ years of age, _Five_ feet _eleven_ inches high, _Dark_ complexion, _Hazel_ eyes, _Black_ hair, and by occupation when enlisted a _School teacher_. During the last two months said soldier has been unfit for duty _60_ days.

Genl Hosp Ross
STATION: Mobile Ala
DATE: February 1st 1864

J M Williams Surg in charge
(Commanding Company.)

We Certify, That we have carefully examined the said _William Brunson_ of Captain _R L Smith's_ Company, and find him incapable of performing the duties of a soldier, because of complete loss of vision of right eye and partial of left, the consequence of variolis one therefore respectfully recommend his final Discharge from service

J M Williams Surgeon P A C S

Board of Examiners _Graham_ H. Notts
Surg in Chge C S N P_C?_

Discharged this Feb'y 24 day of 1864, at Mobile

W R Gause Col Commanding the Post.

(DUPLICATE.)

SPECIAL REQUISITION.

6 — Six Mess Pans
6 " Six Camp Kettles
2 " Two Skillets & Lids (4 pcs)

July 22/64

I certify that the above requisition is correct, and that the articles specified are absolutely necessary for the public service, required so by the following circumstances That the Company are entirely destitute of such articles

W B Ames Capt Co. K, 15 Conf Cavalry

Capt W D Waples Quarter Master will issue the articles specified in the above requisition.

By order
Maj L H Partridge Commanding

Received at Camp Cumming Pittsylvania Co Va the 22 of July 1864
of Capt W D Waples, A.Q.M
"(6) Six Mess Pans "(6) Six Camp Kettles & (2) Two Skillets & Lids
in full of the above requisition.

W B Ames Capt Comdg Co. K
15 Conf Regt Cavalry

439

Headquarters 16th Army Corps,
OFFICE PROVOST MARSHAL,
Montgomery, Ala., June 9th, 1865.

I, the undersigned H. W. Bryant Private C, 15 C.S. Cav'l, **DO SOLEMNLY SWEAR** that I will not bear arms against the United States of America, or give any information, or do any military duty whatever, until regularly exchanged as a prisoner of war.

H. W. Bryant

DESCRIPTION:

Height, 5 feet, 10 inches.   Hair, Dark   Eyes, Gray
Complexion, Dark

I certify that the above parole was given by me on the date above given, and the above named Private will not be disturbed by United States authorities so long as he observes the conditions of his parole, and the laws and regulations in force where he resides.

BY ORDER OF MAJOR GENERAL A. J. SMITH.

Jos. Schlen
Capt. Ill. Inf., and Ass't Provost Marshal.

No. 1.

RECORD OF DEATH AND INTERMENT.

Name and number of person interred. **W. J. Cawthorn** No. 1916
Number and locality of the grave. **Elmira**
Hospital number of the deceased.
Regiment, rank, and company. **15th S.C. Cav. Priv. Co. I**
Residence before enlistment. **Washington Co. Fla.**
Conjugal condition, (and if married, the residence of the widow). **Married**
Cause of death. **Febris Typhoid**
Age of the deceased. **34 Years**
Nativity. **America**
References and remarks.
Date of death and burial. **Feby 26th**, 186**5**.—

Duplicates sent to the Adjutant General of the United States Army, and to the Sexton of the Cemetery.

Memoranda:

15TH CONFEDERATE CAVALRY

[Form No. 5.]

The Confederate States,

To....Private D C Clark................of....

Company....A....15th....Regiment of....Confed. Cavalry....DR.

	DOLLARS.	CTS.
For pay from 1st of Sept 1863 to 31 of October 1863, being 2 months, ...days, at Twelve dollars per month.	24	00
For retained pay due		
For pay for traveling from................the place of my discharge to................the place of my enlistment,....miles at twenty miles per day, equal to....days, at....dollars per month.		
For Subsistence for traveling as above....days, at....cents per ration or day.		
For Clothing not drawn Pay of Horse from 1 Sept to 31 Oct 1863 61 days @ 40¢ per day	24	40
Amount		
Deduct for Army Asylum....$		
Deduct for Clothing overdrawn		
Balance Due	**48**	**40**

Received of Capt Theod H Kimball A.Q.M. Paymaster Confederate States Army, at Meridian this....day of Nov 1863 Forty Eight dollars and Forty cents, in full of the above account.

Pay............24
Subsistence............
Pay of Horse............24.40
Dollars............48.40

Witness
John W Stacum

(Signed in Duplicate.)

D C Clark
Pvt. Co. A. 15th Conf Ca

The Confederate States,

To P. Hougonin detached from Capt Marshall's Co. Mobile Dragoons

For pay from 1st August 1862 to 31st Augt 1862
    being one month at twelve dolls p. month — 12.00
" retained pay — — — — — — — — —
" subsistence — — — — — — — — —
" Commutation of Horse 31 days at 40¢ p. day — 12.40
                                                                    24.40

Received at Mobile Ala this 6th day of Septr 1862 of Alex McVoy Capt & A.Q.M. twenty four 40/100 dolls in full of the above account

Pay — 12.00
Subsistence — —
Clothing & —
Comn Horse — 12.40
          24.40

P. Hugonin

(Duplicate)

ABOUT THE AUTHOR

ARTHUR E. GREEN is the grandson of a Confederate Veteran. He was born in 1937 near Selma, Alabama, and has lived with his wife, Karen, in Mobile, Alabama, for many years. He has three adult children. Art retired from the Alabama Port after thirty-two years as a deep-water ship unloading Plant Manager. He attended Auburn University and is active in local genealogical and historical societies. *Southern Boots and Saddles: The Fifteenth Confederate Cavalry* is his fourth book on Confederate regiments with Alabama ties.

www.ingramcontent.com/pod-product-compliance
Lightning Source LLC
Chambersburg PA
CBHW080732300426
44114CB00019B/2571